Lesbians and Lesbian Families

D1565939

Lesbians and Lesbian Families

Reflections on Theory and Practice

Edited by Joan Laird

Columbia University Press

NEW YORK

COLUMBIA UNIVERSITY PRESS
Publishers Since 1893
New York   Chichester, West Sussex
Copyright © 1999 Columbia University Press
All rights reserved
Chapter 3 is an expanded and altered version of an article in the *Journal of Marital and Family Therapy* (1998) , vol. 25.
Chapters 1, 5, 7, 8, 10, and 11 were originally published in *Smith College Studies in Social Work* (June 1993), vol. 63, no. 3.

Library of Congress Cataloging-in-Publication Data
Laird, Joan.
   Lesbians and lesbian families: reflections on theory and
practice/edited by Joan Laird.
      p.   cm.   Includes bibliographical references and index.
   ISBN 0-231-10252-6. — ISBN 0-231-10253-4 (pbk.)
   1. Lesbians–United States.   2. Lesbians–United States–Psychology.
   3. Lesbian couples–United States.   4. Lesbian mothers–United States.
   5. Family psychotherapy–United States.
   I. Title.
   HQ75.6.U5L25   1999
   305.48'9664'0973–dc21   98-36503

Casebound editions of Columbia University Press books are printed
on permanent and durable acid-free paper.
Printed in the United States of America
c 10 9 8 7 6 5 4 3 2 1
p 10 9 8 7 6 5 4 3 2 1

Sou
40399242
Souk
4/14/01

CONTENTS

ACKNOWLEDGMENTS

"Context is everything," I often tell my students and, oddly enough, it is my own social context that must be thanked for the production of this book. I could not have edited this volume ten years ago. In spite of the fact that at that time I had been a social work educator for over fifteen years, I had rarely read, seldom taught, and never written anything in the area of lesbian studies. Guilt by association, I must have thought. It wasn't until I moved to Northampton, Massachusetts, known as a lesbian-affirming environment, received some firm and persuasive nudges from my friends and colleagues, Sallyann Roth and Froma Walsh, to begin to speak and write in this area, and was pushed by my dean to do one of the famous Smith College School for Social Work Monday Night Lectures when the scheduled speaker (Thanks, Gary Sanders!) couldn't make it that my personal and professional selves began to merge in a new—and what has become a transformative—period in my life. So I want to thank that context, and several key figures in it.

Ann Hartman, the dean mentioned above and my life partner, must receive special mention here. Although she is always a part of every piece of work I produce, a source of steady and constant encouragement, always looking for strengths to surround her gentle suggestions and criticisms, my work in the area of lesbian studies profoundly affected her life as well. For most, to speak and write in lesbian studies is a public "coming out." It certainly was for me. And it almost always means outing one's life partner as well, in this case a well-known social worker who might make different public choices for herself. Thanks, Ann, for allowing me to choose my path even though you knew it would have implications for your own public persona. You are helping social work to more visibly claim its women-who-love-women leaders, past and present, and new social work students and practitioners their lesbian heroines.

Another part of my context must be thanked, the Smith College School for Social Work. The school offered support for this project in a number of ways. A grant from the Clinical Research Institute helped to fund invaluable technical support from Marti Lawrence Hawley, whose careful and patient assistance is much appreciated. A generous sabbatical leave policy helped me find the ever elusive time to complete this and other related projects, And finally, my editorship of the Smith College Studies in Social Work gave me a forum for producing a special issue titled *Lesbians and Lesbian Families: Multiple Reflections.* The six articles in that issue, which the school has generously allowed me to reproduce in this volume, provided the start-up culture for this larger project. Special thanks to the deans, Ann again, to Dean Anita Lightburn, and to Associate Dean Susan Donner who is represented herein.

When this project was in its infancy, the Council on Social Work Education revised its Curriculum Policy Statement to require that all bachelor's and master's social work programs include lesbian and gay content, thus providing another stimulus for further opening the profession's closet doors. Although the decision provoked some controversy, sexual orientation would now be added to the council's list of social categories to be addressed in all social work curricula. The triumvirate of "race, class, and gender" would be expanded to include sexual orientation. This, too, gave contextual permission to me and to many others to raise our voices in the field, as lesbian and gay mental health and social service professionals are doing in psychology and various counseling disciplines.

I would also like to thank my many good friends and colleagues, too many to name, those in the Happy Valley and those around the country and the world, who continue to share their ideas and their own work, to give me critical feedback on mine, and to provide an encouraging and loving context for going forth. But special mention must be made of Robert-Jay Green, my coeditor on another volume published during this period, who is always ready to discuss an idea and help solve a puzzle. I miss our nightly phone calls, but now at least we have an important coast-to-coast e-mail relationship! The dedicated and conscientious editors at Columbia

University Press have been most helpful and patient throughout this process. I am grateful to Gioia Stevens, now at Oxford University Press, who originally encouraged this project, to John Michel, executive editor, whose good humor and support have been much appreciated, and to Alex Thorpe, editorial assistant and Susan Pensak, senior manuscript editor, who have shepherded the manuscript through its final stages. It has been a pleasure to work with such a wise, kind, and professional staff.

Kudos to my eighty-one-year-old mother. We still struggle with language, but she has learned to open her boundaries in so many ways—and never dreamed of excluding my partner of thirty-three years from the family circle. And thanks to Duncan, Meg, and Hannah. My son Duncan has become a social worker himself, a gifted clinician and a supportive critic. He is always aware of context and trying to find new ways to deliver services. His wife Meg is a fine social worker, too. She and Duncan have generously shared their daughter Hannah with us. Hannah, now two, got herself born as this project was cooking along and managed to help hold its publication up a bit because those lovely hours in the life of an enchanting little child just couldn't be missed.

Lesbians and Lesbian Families

This book began its life as a special issue of the *Smith College Studies in Social Work* and has taken shape in an era when lesbians and gays, often called the last invisible minority, have become highly visible in national social and political discourse. In the last few years, many pro- and antigay initiatives have been launched, with some battles won and others lost on both sides. In 1992 Bill Clinton began his presidency with a commitment to eliminate the ban against gays in the military, a move that was quickly suppressed in favor of the discriminatory "Don't ask, don't tell" policy. Shortly thereafter the largest gay civil rights march in history took place in the nation's capital, its success minimized by official government counters. Antigay civil rights referenda were initiated across the country, but this effort foundered when the Supreme Court found Colorado's initiative unconstitutional. Many towns, corporations, and universities began to extend family benefits to same-sex couples, and advocates of the right to same-sex marriage began a long, courageous, and continuing effort in Hawaii to open up the option of legally sanctioned wedded bliss to gay men and lesbians. In some parts of the country, lesbian mothers continued to lose their children for no reason other than sexual orientation, at the same time that a rapidly increasing number of lesbians were choosing to bear or adopt children. And, at the same time that lesbians and gay men were achieving greater visibility and unprecedented gains in civil rights, they were also experiencing increased violence and renewed social and political oppression. There is a paradox here: "For gays to become politically active and to fight for their rights and protection, they must be safe enough to become visible: They are only safe to do so if those rights and protections are already in place" (Hartman 1993:245).

It is also paradoxical to realize that we live in a society that is willing to allow its gay men and lesbians to fight, indeed, to sacrifice their lives for their country, as long as they "pass" for heterosexual, that is, as long as they keep their sexual orientation secret, as long as they remain invisible.

These events and the discourses that explain them are part of the cultural and political context that surrounds all who are marginalized for their sexual orientation or gender-bending ways—gays, lesbians, bisexuals, transgendered, and transsexual people. Many sexual minorities are also multiply marginalized on the basis of color, gender, social class, religion, age, or other social categories. This process of social marginalization forms an ever present backdrop for understanding the lives of our lesbian, gay, bisexual, and transgendered clients, for constant critical reflection on the helping models we adopt, and for considering the issues both straight and gay practitioners encounter in their work with sexual minority clients.

Prior to Stonewall and to the 1973 American Psychiatric Association's decision to no longer assume that homosexuality was necessarily pathological, study of homosexuality was dominated by a search for etiology, for "cause," and treatment was often oriented to "cure." In the last twenty years, as studies have proliferated, this emphasis has shifted and a number of themes can be traced. First, the predominant effort has been one of exploring whether gay and lesbian individuals, couples, families, and children in gay- or lesbian-headed families are as mentally healthy and socially well-adapted as other populations. The convergent results overwhelmingly support the conclusion that, indeed, lesbians and gay men, as individuals, in couples, in families, and as parents are as mentally and socially healthy and, in some ways, perhaps more "functional" and "satisfied" than their heterosexual counterparts. Similarly, the children of lesbians also do as well as their peers along the many dimensions measured and, not surprisingly, tend to be more flexible and more tolerant of difference in others. The research has, of course, also emphasized the special problems lesbians and gays encounter, linking such problems to the impact of conducting their lives in environments that are disqualifying and hostile.

This research has been enormously valuable in undermining some of the prevailing mythologies about homosexuality, mythologies that have led to, for example, lesbian mothers losing custody of their children based solely on their sexual orientation or discrimination in housing or the workplace. It is, however, something of a "deficit" body of research in the sense that the unstated effort has been to "prove" that lesbians and gays are just as worthy as anyone else. It is not as proud a literature as it might be and few scholars have asked how it is that lesbians, gays, and their children do as well as others *in spite of* the fact they live and raise their children in an often destructive homophobic world. We know that homophobic oppression and social disqualification lead to individual despair and high rates of suicide among lesbian and gay adolescents, and that, in the past, silence and the need for secrecy contributed to the growth of a bar culture and continues to influence the rates of overdrinking among lesbians and gay men.

But do lesbian and gay identity and experience also lead to special strengths, special insights, special resiliencies? The clinical literature in particular tends to neglect this part of the story. A clear vision of the ways that sexism and heterosexism shape society's visions of lesbianism emerges from some of the work in this volume, thinking largely inspired by feminist theory. And, in the process, we begin to see some of the special strengths of the only minority group against which it is still legal to discriminate, strengths that, at least to some extent, come from standing at the margins and from having to be particularly alert to and critical of prevailing cultural and political discourses.

Furthermore, a psychological metaphor has dominated this field of study, as a generation of researchers has sought to capture the elements of gay and lesbian identity and the elusive "coming out" process. Coming out has been defined in developmental stage terms, analogous to the epigenetic quality of the life cycle process outlined by Erik Erikson. A "successful" coming out process seemed to mean a coming to full recognition and acceptance of a fundamental self, a self that was waiting all along to be discovered.

Postmodern and social constructionist thought is ushering in new ways to think about the self, about the making of an identity, any identity (see, e.g., Boxer and Cohler 1989; Gergen 1991). The self is seen as a narrative in the making, a narrative always being shaped in dialogue with others and, in the context of changing social conditions and changing social discourses, a narrative never finished. The past, our histories, our biographies, are continually recast to fit our present experiences as we edit and reedit our life stories. The postmodern revolution is beginning to shape the direction for a new gay and lesbian psychology, just as it is revolutionizing the arts, humanities, social sciences, and even the physical sciences.

All of these themes, and many others, are reflected upon in this volume, which focuses on theory, practice, and research in relation to lesbians, lesbian couples, and lesbian-headed families. The book is intended primarily for mental health practitioners, students, teachers, and researchers. Although much of what is written may also pertain to the experiences of gay men, bisexual men and women, or members of other sexual minorities, the choice made here was to focus on lesbians. Lesbian experience has been underrepresented in the research and clinical literature, as have been the experiences of women in general.

In part 1, "Lesbians and the Social Context," four authors examine the sociocultural surround in which lesbians learn how to think about themselves and are thought about by others. In chapter 1 Elaine Spaulding demonstrates how coming out cannot be understood simply as a stage process. In her view we must pay far more attention to the social contexts in which women and men come to experience themselves as lesbian or gay, a context permeated with sexism, heterosexism, and homophobia. Her work begins to get at what the anthropologist Gilbert Herdt (1992), who has been critical of the overemphasis on the inner experience of coming out, frames as the central questions for future research in this area:

1. What is it that lesbians/gays come out *to?*

2. What is it that lesbians/gays come out *as?*

In chapter 2 Susan Donner, in an unpacking of Goffman's notion of master status, examines the multiple ways that the ascription of a master status to lesbians on the basis of their sexual orientation or sexual object choice reduces them to a single dimension and obscures the complexity of lesbian identities and experiences. Furthermore, such ascriptions can attack and erode lesbian self-narratives, a theme she illustrates with two extended case examples that can be common in clinical practice.

Sexual orientation never stands alone; it is always raced, classed, and gendered, laced through with other cultural identities and cultural narratives. In chapter 3 I explore the intersections between gender and sexual orientation, examining larger cultural assumptions about lesbian gender identities and revisiting butch/femme mythology. What do lesbians themselves have to say about their gendered identities and how can their narratives inform our practice?

North Americans continue to battle over definitions and indeed ownership of the very notion of family. Lesbian and gay families are often portrayed as enemies to the entire notion of family, destroyers of family values, while lesbians and gays themselves are fighting for the right to have their families recognized and socially supported. In chapter 4 Ann Hartman explores current struggles over civil rights protections and entitlements for lesbians and gays. The multiple and complex aspects of this struggle, which became a major political issue around the "Don't ask, don't tell" policy for those who serve in the armed forces, is currently being dramatically exemplified in the effort to legalize same-sex marriage.

We have been taught that secrecy and silence, the inability to tell our lives, is debilitating, that if we cannot fully tell our stories we turn them inward, we internalize society's negative messages about us—as women, as people of color, as members of any oppressed groups. But we also use secrecy strategically and in strengthening ways (Laird 1993). Tara Healy, in the first chapter in part 2, "Lesbian Couples," in a fine example of research that privileges the voices of those studied rather than the preconceptions of the researcher, explores how lesbians themselves use the language of self-disclosure in varying contexts. She finds the women in her focus groups to be highly conscious of how and when they use particular kinds of self-defining language, of how they use "telling," silence, and secrecy strategically. One of the things that becomes evident from her work is that these women have developed considerable skills for evaluating their social contexts and for not internalizing the negative messages from their homophobic surrounds. This work is about strength and resilience in the face of marginalization.

Healy's chapter is followed by two works that explore particular clinical approaches in work with lesbian couples. In chapter 6 Kathryn Basham presents an extended case example of her work with a lesbian couple, guided on one level by a theoretical stance that integrates feminist, intergenerational, and social constructionist ideas and on another by an analysis of what she terms interactional and institutional "resistances." Resistances—defined as those thoughts, attitudes, feelings, patterns, and stories that interfere with the client's stated goals for change—are viewed as opportunities rather than obstacles and are used to explore the couple's inner and outer worlds. On yet another level Basham weaves in Hare-Mustin's (1989) conception of alpha and beta bias. Alpha bias is defined as exaggerating differences between groups—for example, between men and women—and beta bias as minimizing them. The careful scrutiny of alpha and beta bias is always a salient issue for therapists in examining their own assumptions as they try to enter the world of the lesbian or gay client.

In chapter 7 Carol Sussal argues that object relations theory, merged with a constant sensitivity to the sociocultural context, offers a particularly useful model for treatment of lesbian couples. This theory and its clinical derivatives, like any other, must be carefully screened for its use of language and for the potential heterocentrism that may be implicit in its basic concepts and tools. Some family therapy models, for example, assume the heterosexual family and privilege certain kinds of male/female role divisions and complementarities that are anathema to many lesbian couples, while developmental models may assume a heterosexual life path and fail to adequately account for constantly shifting social and historical contexts

In part 3, "Lesbians, Parenting, and Children," several authors probe various dimensions of the parent-child experience in lesbian-headed families. In chapter 8 Cheryl Muzio turns to the postmodern French feminist philosopher Luce Irigaray to explore the notion of lesbian invisibility and its meanings in the context of dominant sexist and heterosexist discourse. Muzio is particularly interested in the invisibility of the (for lack of another term) co-mother, the partner/lover of the mother who has brought children to the lesbian partnership from a former heterosexual relationship, carries and gives birth to the child within the context of the lesbian coupling, or is the partner who legally adopts. (In the field of adoption, as in the military, lesbians typically can adopt as long as they do not acknowledge their sexual orientation.)

In chapter 9 Betty Morningstar uses a developmental metaphor to highlight the various parts of the process of becoming a lesbian parent, which she views as a series of challenges and transitions rather than one of neat and tidy stages. There are many such challenges that are somewhat unique to lesbians, who, she notes, create a conundrum in a society in which women are to become mothers but lesbians are not to become mothers. Her work is enriched by a thorough consideration of a range of clinical issues that may arise in work with lesbians as they consider and choose parenting.

In chapters 10 and 11 in this section researchers go directly to lesbian mothers and to their children to learn more about lesbian-headed family life. Laura Lott-Whitehead and Carol Tully, using an ecological, multilevel approach, ask lesbian mothers what they view as the stresses on and strengths in their families of creation. In the process, we learn how these parents work to protect their children from social discrimination, again in part with the careful selection of language, and how they creatively draw on various networks of support. Ann O'Connell, too, takes an ethnographic-like approach in her exploration of how adolescents experience their mothers' coming out, listening directly to the voices of young people. As she rightly observes, the experiences of these youth are intimately intertwined with and complicated by their experiences as children of divorced parents, yet they too seem to develop creative strategies for coping and demonstrate how to use their experiences for personal strengthening.

There is much work to be done in the field of lesbian scholarship and so much to learn in the clinical arena. In part 4 we examine a few "Special Themes in Theory and Practice." One theme that has received only minimal attention in the clinical literature is that of the lesbian therapist–lesbian client relationship. Much has been written about the issue of boundaries, for example, in opposite-sex therapeutic relationships, but very little in terms of how this theme can play itself out in same-sex therapeutic relationships when both therapist and client are lesbian. For example, in many locations, lesbian communities can be very small, and one's social and professional lives are likely to intersect with those of clients. In chapter 12 Carolyn Dillon raises provocative questions as she uses a relational perspective to explore themes of mutuality and boundaries in these relationships.

In chapter 13 Sandra Anderson and Barbara Sussex research a question that has rarely been asked of lesbians: "What strategies do lesbians use to deal with trauma in childhood and what strategies do they use to cope with prejudice and discrimination as adults?" The strength and resilience displayed by so many lesbians in the face of histories of trauma and of living their lives in an atmosphere of oppression is nothing short of remarkable. Anderson and Sussex mine what can be learned from studies of resilience in children to search for the sources of lesbian strength. In the final chapter Jo Nol reviews the central tenets of control mastery theory, a theory that holds that people are motivated to adapt to reality, continually making and refining inferences about themselves and others. Some of these beliefs, however, may become "pathogenic," that is, they begin to operate in such a way as to restrict a person's abilities to pursue a fulfilling life. This conception reminds me of some of the work of postmodern therapist Michael White, who terms such negative and debilitating self-narratives "problem-saturated" and points out that they can cut off potential opportunities for a rewarding life. Nol applies control mastery ideas for their usefulness in clinical work with the lesbian client who, of course, is always challenged to construct a positive self-narrative in a context in which the available narratives from which to choose are largely negative.

All of the authors in this volume, in one way or another, have tried to contextualize lesbian experience, to connect private troubles with public issues, and to listen to the voices of lesbians themselves. I hope that their voices, singly and together, may offer the practitioner, whatever her or his discipline, some new ideas—ideas that will help to generate not prepackaged answers or prior assumptions to take into our offices and out into the field but some new and good questions that will help us allow lesbian clients and their children to tell their stories in ways that we can hear.

REFERENCES

Boxer, A., and B. Cohler. 1989. The life course of gay and lesbian youth: An immodest proposal for the study of lives. *Journal of Homosexuality* 17(3/4): 315–355.

Gergen, K. J. 1991. *The saturated self: Dilemmas of identity in contemporary life.* New York: Basic.

Hare-Mustin, R. 1987. The problem of gender in family therapy theory. *Family Process* 26:15–33.

Hartman, A. 1993. Editorial. *Social Work* 38:245–246, 360.

Herdt, G. 1992. *Gay culture in America: Essays from the field.* Boston: Beacon.

Laird, J. 1993. Women's secrets—Women's silences. In E. Imber-Black, ed., *Secrets in families and family therapy*, pp. 243–267. New York: Norton.

PART ONE

Lesbians and the Social Context

Unconsciousness-Raising: Hidden Dimensions of Heterosexism in Theory and Practice with Lesbians

Elaine C. Spaulding

SEX BETWEEN MEN historically has been a subject of professional interest, not so, sex between women. Until recently there has been no comparably extensive clinical or empirical reference to lesbian sexuality. Rather the
studies of homosexual men provided what little we know about lesbians. As
the women's movement matured and expanded in the 1980s, a proliferation
of studies emerged that focused on identifying and defining aspects of the
homosexual "coming out process" for women as well as men.[1]

This initial documentation of lesbian experience, however, tends to be
ahistorical, culturally vague, and makes little or no reference to the power and
responsibility of social institutions in the formation of self-perception and
ego identity. Gender, ethnicity, race, class, and other social positions have
tremendous influence on personal and social definitions of identity, differentially limiting or expanding individual and group freedoms and opportunities.

Our cultural lenses tend to shape the focus and scope of research, including that on lesbian development. In the last decade women's, feminist, and
gay studies curricula have developed in institutions of higher education.
However, in each of these areas lesbian studies remain peripheral, obscured
by the dominance of other related but different interests. Lesbians thus
have been empowered to speak but are unable to say.

In this chapter I define and discuss heterosexism, sexism, and homophobia from both a social point of view and at the level of individual experience. I then review major approaches to empirical research in the past decade on the lesbian coming out experience and make explicit the sociocultural context within which they are configured. The internalization processes of heterosexism are described through a review of clinical data. Examination of the data from these perspectives serves not only to enhance clinical sensitivity to the larger social context in which individuals experience themselves as gay but also to the hidden dimensions of heterosexism in theory. I end with an exploration of the implications of heterosexism for clinical practice with lesbians.

Heterosexism, Sexism, and Homophobia

Feminist scholars are studying individual and institutional forms and structures of oppression in order to examine built-in forms of sexism and racism. Many of the sociological and anthropological findings are applicable to lesbians as well, who do share the oppression of women. And some lesbians, of course, face triple oppressions, by virtue of their sexual orientation, sex, and skin color. In this essay the concept of patriarchy is used to describe social structures that are characterized by sexism, racism, and heterosexism. These terms denote differences within the experiences of the oppressed, but they are also interwoven within our culture.

Sexism may be defined as the economic exploitation and social domination of one sex by another, specifically of women by men (*Webster's* 1972). The study of sexism is intended to document how women are victimized by institutional and ordinary male behavior. *Heterosexism* is more than the belief that only heterosexual behavior and sexuality are of value; the term describes the significant and systematic social and cultural ethos that structures our social arrangements and shapes our views of lesbianism. Heterosexism permeates our cultural institutions and the belief systems that legitimate their structures. A social structure, once in place, takes on a life of its own. Therefore, the structured and systematic social processes of heterosexism that negatively affect lesbians require neither the presence of homophobic attitudes, opinions, or feelings, on the one hand, nor discriminatory acts or behaviors on the other.

Heterosexism is not simply a matter of the victimization of women; it has to do with the fact that women are defined in terms of men or not at all (Hoagland 1988). Additionally, the expectation of total sexual access to women not only legitimizes the male domination of women, it distinguishes heterosexism from sexism. Heterosexism can be viewed as a form of social control in which values, expectations, roles, and institutions normalize heterosexuality, which, in turn, is promoted and enforced formally and informally by structures in which men are dominant, that is, the patriarchy. Consequently, it is heterosexism more than sexism that defines adult competencies as the abilities to perform the culturally specific tasks of dating, partnering, marriage, and child rearing. Sexism implies that these adult competencies are distributed on the basis of gender and subsequently differentially valued (or devalued).

Although *homophobia*, defined as the irrational fear of homosexuality, is often blamed for creating the difficulties encountered by gays in the coming out process, the field of gay and lesbian studies has been dominated by a distinctly psychological approach (see, for example, Fein and Nuehring 1981; Gramick 1984; Hetrick and Martin 1988). The institutional nature of gay oppression has not been systematically analyzed. While the psychological frame of reference may be useful in understanding and treating those who suffer from homophobia, homophobia as a key concept does not illuminate the deeper, more pervasive cultural myopia that surrounds the topic of lesbianism.

Homophobia is a psychological event not analogous to sexism and racism, which are organized sociocultural phenomena. Homophobia can also be viewed as a psychological condition arising as the unanticipated result of an unconscious social process, namely, the prolonged, successful, and systematic effort to exclude homosexuals from access to scarce or valued economic and social resources, including that of self-esteem. Homophobia and heterosexism are thus intimately related phenomena, especially for heterosexual males who reportedly are more overtly and violently homophobic.

The Invisibility of Lesbianism Within Heterosexist Psychology

The dominance of heterosexism in a patriarchal social organization makes the lesbian experience unlike that of other minority groups. For example, unlike Jews, lesbians are not primarily targeted as scapegoats. They are not characterized as inferior or culturally backward, social descriptions that have been used to justify enslavement or economic exploitation, as in the case of Japanese and Chinese immigrants to this society. Their ancestral lands were not stolen and they were not rounded up and displaced on reservations as were Native Americans in the United States. They were not, like African Americans, defined as property and enslaved (Hoagland 1988).

Society does not even perceive lesbians per se, but rather continually rede-
fines lesbianism and lesbians in heterosexist terms.[2]

Because of the unexamined, hidden dimensions of heterosexist influence
and the inferior status of women, the professional literature has largely
ignored lesbians in the same ways that black women as a group have been
ignored. We consider black women as either "black (men)" or "women
(white)" but rarely as "black women." Similarly, we tend to consider lesbians
as either "women (heterosexual)" or "gay (men)" but not as "gay women."
Viewing lesbians through a heterosexist lens has resulted in the invisibility of
lesbian experience historically, culturally, economically, socially, and psychologically. The lesbian's identity is depicted as incomplete, since the lesbian is
not fulfilled through a relationship with a male, a serious threat to patriarchal
values.

Consider what the literature of psychoanalysis says from a heterosexist
perspective. The lesbian is often perceived as a (heterosexual) woman who
cannot get a man, who has not yet had the "right" (hetero)sexual experience,
or who has had the "wrong" (hetero)sexual experience with men. Some even
view the lesbian as a (heterosexual) man in a woman's body (Socarides
1978), clearly a "pathological" condition.

Some believe that a lesbian is a (heterosexual) woman who hates men, not
a woman who loves women. Psychodynamically, man hating is viewed as a
cause of lesbianism (Wolff 1971). The logic of traditional heterosexist values
asserts that a withdrawal of female sexuality from some men is an attack on
all men. Even though hostility toward men does not distinguish lesbians
from heterosexual women—or from men for that matter—only lesbians are
consistently and pejoratively described in this way. Heterosexual women
who are described as hostile to or envious toward men still retain their
positive status in relationship to men. It is "lesbian" that is devalued and
equated with man hating.

Lesbianism is frequently described in the literature as a phase of development in some (heterosexual) women's lives (see, for example, Blanck and
Blanck 1974:303). Implicit here is the idea that lesbianism is temporary,
a phase to be outgrown with maturity. Not only does this idea fail to
acknowledge the authenticity of lesbianism, but it avoids defining lesbianism at all, since this would require a definition apart from the centrality
of men. Similarly, lesbianism is frequently "explained" as a retreat from
oedipal anxieties. This heterosexist ideal recasts the lesbian as a psychological male or, possibly, a psychological bisexual if the lesbian is traditionally
"feminine" (Spaulding 1992).

Coming Out Research

The coming out process has been studied largely from an individual, psychological perspective and has focused on the experiences of the gay male (Chapman and Brannock 1987; Elliot 1985; Gramick 1984; Hess 1983; Hetrick and Martin 1987; Lewis 1984; Troiden 1989). When viewed from a heterosexist lens, the findings from the past ten years of research on lesbian identity development group themselves in predictable ways. The traditional model of full psychological development posits two complementary half-persons—the instrumental man and the expressive woman—becoming whole by joining with each other. This logic evokes two separate and mutually incompatible social and sexual perspectives, that of masculinity and that of femininity. It is not surprising, then, that lesbians have been regarded as either "butch" or "femme"—cultural representatives of or renegades from the institution of heterosexuality.

It is clear, in the coming out literature, that the experiences of gay men and women differ. Lesbians tend to be older than gay men when they recognize their same-sex feelings, older when they first engage in sex with women, and older when they come to define themselves as "gay." Lesbian instrumental behavior lags behind that of gay men, demonstrating the effects of heterosexist gender ideology on development.

Clearly, these findings are consistent with the sex-role socialization of our society in general. Male sexuality is seen as active, initiatory, demanding of immediate gratification, and divorced from emotional attachment; female sexuality emphasizes feelings and minimizes the importance of immediate sexual activity (de Monteflores and Schultz 1978:68).

Most studies also tend to define and characterize lesbian identity in evolutionary terms, describing stages, phases, and tasks in the coming out process (Coleman 1982) and positing various theoretical models of homosexual identity development (Cass 1979, 1984; Ponse 1978; Spaulding 1982) that accompany coming out. *Identity disclosure* and *coming out* are terms that came to denote a combination of psychological and social processes that take place on a number of levels.

Whatever the shortcomings of the coming out research, it represents an effort to move beyond the previous body of clinical and research literature. Earlier studies, carried out on samples of white male mental patients and prisoners, sought to discover the etiology of homosexuality, which was, of course, considered a pathological condition. Later studies were more sensitive to issues of same-sex desire and identity. Nonetheless, the focus remained on stigmatized homosexual secrets (Herdt 1992). The research, whether on the secret, private, or public nature of coming out, was organized by a single key structural principle, that of same-sex desire. The sexist and heterosexist cultural contexts surrounding coming out identity formation were not examined. Thus, coming out came to be understood on the basis of research on the decontextualized events of lone individuals, usually white, middle-class college students. Coming out was seen in terms of individual progression through various stages rather than as a complex, historically situated, social and cultural process (Herdt 1992).

Any description of lesbian identity that fails to take account of the cultural context has limited usefulness. Clearly, many variables influence the coming out process (Hanley-Hackenbruck 1988). Individual variables that account for immense differences include personality, family characteristics, religious upbringing, experience with sexuality, and the age of awareness of being different. These variables at least place a person in a family context. But many other forces influence the timing, sequence, and duration of experiences or stages in coming out. The coming out phenomenon must be studied in particular historical and social contexts in ways that attend to the influences of race, ethnicity, sex, age, geographic location, and other factors.

Of the early studies there are two that are particularly significant, those of Cass (1979) and Coleman (1982), which have been described as applicable to both lesbians and gay men. Each study provides only a superficial recognition of gender differences per se and does not acknowledge the gendered power base of the heterosexist social structure. The studies, taken together, highlight the thinking common to models of individual development. That is, both studies assume that identity acquisition is a linear developmental process and that the individual's interaction with an undefined and unexamined environment contributes to it.

The Cass (1979) stage model examined the development of the internal structures of homosexual identity formation that define the self. The stages include (1) identity confusion, (2) identity comparison, (3) identity tolerance, (4) identity acceptance, (5) identity pride, and (6) identity synthesis. In this view homosexual identity formation results from stage-related crisis resolution, a concept borrowed from Erik Erikson. At each stage the individual must evaluate and accept the stage-related characteristic perceptions and experiences of coming out. Resolutions of a stage-related crisis can take various forms, some leading to negative or destructive ends and characterized by the risk of identity foreclosure and the jettisoning of the remaining stages. Positive resolution of stage-related crisis overemphasizes a smooth transition from one stage to another, even though this is improbable and unsupported by empirical evidence. A second problem with a model of crisis resolution involves the definition of the concept of social. Unlike Erikson, Cass does not define social except to say that social forces shape the socialization of the individual. *Social* more accurately refers to the inter-personal realm of interactive experience. It is as though the social status and power of the individual is somehow separate from yet equal to that of the social order. This stage model does not even gender the individual. Since one's sense of opportunity, power, and safety directly derive from one's cultural status in the social order, this individualistic model of coming out exaggerates personal power and minimizes the many contextual forces that surround the coming out experience.

The Colemen (1982) stage model examines the internal development and outward expression of lesbian identity. The model is self-explanatory and includes five stages: (1) pre-coming out, (2) coming out, (3) exploration, (4) first relationships, and (5) integration. Coleman's study also describes stage-related developmental tasks in terms similar to those of Cass. The models differ, however, in the description of the internal processes used to protect the person from psychological distress. Coleman describes the use of ego defenses, behavioral problems, psychiatric symptoms, self-esteem, and intimacy needs. Much of the coming out process, described as an alternative psychological adolescence, is postulated as often transpiring later than chronological adolescence. The secret world of the gay bar and covert social networks are described as serving to make coming out an individual-ized puberty rite into an oppressed society (Herdt 1992). This model suggests that troubled homosexual adults should be resocialized by redevelop-ing a gay adolescence. The resocialization will lead to a sense of competency in gay adulthood. Again, the assumption is that adult competency is an outcome of earlier development instead of one determined by the nature of the culturally defined tasks themselves. As long as this reasoning prevails in formulations of identity development, the possibilities for redefining adult tasks will not occur; the question "What does one come out to be?" will never be asked.

Concepts of Lesbian Identity

Definitions of heterosexual identity have shaped studies and conceptions of homosexual identity. If heterosexuality is defined as the norm for individual identity, then homosexuality by default is an identity deviation. The

term *homosexual identity,* first used in the 1970s, still has no universally recognized conceptual, theoretical, or empirical definition. Dissimilar and
often contradictory meanings include (1) "defining" oneself as homosexual,
(2) a "sense" of oneself as homosexual, (3) an "image" of the self as homosexual, (4) the way a homosexual person "is," and (5) consistent "behavior"
in relation to homosexual-related activity (Cass 1984). Although some sociologists and psychologists have tried to transform negative cultural constructs into positive ones, the result has been the construction of homosexuality as a lifestyle and as a sexual preference, implying conscious choice
rather than identity development.

Most studies assume that the coming out process occurs in a context of
homophobia and thus explore the issues of stigma and its management.
However, stigma and stigma management are more than matters of individual awareness, experience, and strategy; cultural awareness and analysis are
necessary to assess the lethality of the individual's world. Studies of gay and
lesbian development uniformly fail, however, to place that development in a
social context where gender, race, and class are more significant than whether
one is "out" or "in" about homosexuality. The more ubiquitous and powerful
social structure of heterosexism does allow lesbians to manage stigma in ways
that gay men can not, since lesbians are not taken as seriously as gay men, just
as women are not, in general, taken as seriously as men. Heterosexual men,
moreover, may react more immediately and negatively to what they perceive
as the rejection of heterosexist privilege by gay men than they do to female
withdrawal of sexual interest. In addition, lesbians contend with less stigma,
since they may be seen as incomplete heterosexual women, more to be pitied
than censured. Violence toward lesbians, however, is greater than that
directed at heterosexual women (Herek 1989), although violence directed at
all women has increased. Unless our cultural standards become more flexible,
violence against lesbians is likely to escalate even further as women become
more independent of men.

Alternative Aspects of Development

To define lesbianism in nonheterosexist terms implies a recognition that
women can be defined apart from their relationships to men. The literature
on lesbians and lesbian relationships reflects the difficulty of adopting nonheterosexist terms and conditions. Several scholars have argued that lesbians
are not only ruled by patriarchal female socialization (Chodorow 1989) but,
because lesbian couples consist of two persons socialized to be women, these

relationships tend to be troubled by excesses of characteristics ascribed to women, such as emotional sensitivity and connectedness (Kaufman, Harrison, and Hyde 1984; Krestan and Bepko 1989; Roth 1989). Since women are said to be more concerned with connectedness than with separateness, and because lesbian couples may not be affirmed or their boundaries respected by the larger society, it is believed lesbian couples buffer the assaults to their integrity as a couple by turning inward. Thus more demands are made on the couple relationship for fulfilling all emotional needs and the relationship becomes "fused."

It is not clear, however, that lesbian relationships contain greater risk of fusion, merger, or symbiosis than those of other couples. Furthermore, even if lesbian relationships might be characterized as more fused than heterosexual relationships, it is not clear that these relationships are dissatisfying or dysfunctional for the couples themselves. In fact, argues Mencher (1990), the very characteristics often portrayed as troublesome in the clinical literature are cited by lesbians themselves as what is special and most satisfying about their relationships. All relationships include aspects of both attachment and separateness.

The attachment line (of development) considers the quality of the individual's relationships—the capacity to form and maintain stable relationships and the ability to integrate these into a sense of self in relation to another person. The separateness line considers the development of the individual as a self-contained and independent unit. Individuation, differentiation, and autonomy are developmental achievements that lead to a stable sense of self as separate, with a clear set of goals and values. The relationship between these two developmental lines is intimate and complex, with the individual's overall self-identity emerging as a product of "an ongoing dialectic between the self as separate and the self as experienced in its attachments to objects" (Blass and Blatt 1992).

Moreover, the theoretical construct of merger or symbiosis as a more primitive ego state belies the current complexity of theory. The early classic separateness theories evolved by Mahler and others describe separateness as hatching from early formative symbiotic relationships, founded on an immediate association of separateness and differentiation. These theories do not consider the predominance of attachment in distinguishing between separateness and differentiation. The attainment of separateness depends on a variety of relationships, which at different times in development vary in degree of differentiation of self and object (Blass and Blatt 1992). One needs to distinguish between pathological and normal aspects of undifferentiated adulthood and to examine forms of attachment before concluding that lesbian fusion represents a primitive ego state. This psychological conception of lesbians and lesbian relationships as fused or merged, interestingly, resembles various depictions of gender roles in which women are cast as dependent and childlike compared to males, who are seen as independent and differentiated.

Psychoanalytic models of individual development, whether based on classical analytic theory of drive development or on more contemporary psychoanalytic theories, claim universality. Such models purport to demonstrate normal (as opposed to pathological) psychological needs but rarely take into account varying cultural values and practices. By excluding cultural phenomena, developmental tasks such as walking cannot clearly be distinguished from those that are dependent on culture, such as the development of self-esteem. Freud's pleasure principle remains the conceptual regulator of the complex process of human development.

Psychoanalytic models of individual development are based on three major assumptions fundamental to sexism and heterosexism (Ogbu 1981). First, the origins of human competence are seen as rooted in early childhood experiences shaped primarily by infant-caretaker interactions and later extended to relationships with other family members and adults. In this assumptive view of the family the differential roles and responsibilities of women as child rearers are stressed. Second, it is believed that the nature of human competencies can be adequately studied at the microlevel of individual experience. Family and nonfamily institutions are excluded in microanalysis, thus reinforcing the importance of one woman in every person's development. The third and last assumption is that later educational, social, and vocational successes can be attributed to child-rearing practices.

These three assumptive bases strengthen the heterosexist view that only mothers form symbiotic relationships with their young, regardless of the influence of other family members or other persons or social institutions. The prevailing conventional norms for gender role functioning are taken as developmental necessities. Consequently, female ego development "allows" women to merge with their young and predisposes them to merge with other adults. The proposed developmental role for men is to provide "human support" for a child *against* symbiotic ties with the mother (Horner 1992:130–132). Men are hatched others for children. This view of human development is synchronic with the culturally prescribed institutionalized male roles of protector and representative of reality. Male cultural prerogatives, we have learned, define constructs of psychological independence (Chodorow 1989; Gilligan 1982), a process that is easily obscured by microanalytic methods. A nonsexist, nonheterosexist feminist analysis reveals the overriding influences of sexism and heterosexism in shaping prevailing theories of child development. Prescribed child-rearing patterns may be seen as culturally organized formulas for reproducing compulsory heterosexuality. Our cultural definitions of masculinity and femininity serve as standards of heterosexism that prescribe roles for human beings in such a way that men can act in the world and women can respond to it, thus limiting competencies by sex. In a feminist perspective women are not defined in terms of their connections to or sexual relationships with men or by their role in producing male soldiers, workers, and heirs.

A nonheterosexist model can reveal new domains of male and female cultural competence that recognizes the importance that both sexes have the capacity for attachment *and* autonomy, within themselves and in relationships to others. These adult competencies, however, must be understood in the context of the sociocultural surround. It is not sufficient to locate the origins of adult competency in individual experiences of the separation/individuation process. What is needed are ecological analyses of human development that eschew simple cause-effect developmental thinking and take into account the cultural contexts that influence the course of individual development.

A prolonged emphasis on the individual has overshadowed the importance of the impact of social, economic, and political systems on personality development. Moreover, the psychoanalytic literature has overemphasized the role of the individual caretaker (female) in child socialization. Primary caretaking is viewed as the "bridge" between the infant and reality, the "organizational matrix" of the developing child (Horner 1992). The interests of heterosexist society are not overtly considered in this model of development; it is assumed that heterosexuality is normal. The separation/individuation process does, however, document how poor progress during early subphase development is remarkably difficult to overcome in social arrangements that overvalue independence, individualism, and other white middle-class values based on secular Protestantism. This is not a portrait of universality in development, but a doctrine of cultural ideology. Child observation studies on "normal" heterosexual development, in circular fashion, contribute ever more detailed information on our cultural formulas for producing the variety of adult personalities that are valued within our dominant culture.

Implications for Clinical Practice

Clinical work with lesbians must include the exploration of both internalized heterosexism and sexism; the clinician, in fact, has an obligation to help individual lesbian clients become aware of the ways cultural myopia and cultural obliviousness can influence their lives and their self-concepts. A false sense of individual power or powerlessness may contribute to problems of self-esteem. Indeed, clients may not be aware that their self-concept reflects their own evaluation of the place of the lesbian self in the social order. Self-labeling does lead to instrumental behavior (Spaulding 1982), and unless heterosexist values and assumptions become matters for clinical attention lesbians are at risk for self-destructive behavior as well as violence directed at them. Many lesbians go to great lengths to avoid or deny their sexuality, including self-deception through heterosexual promiscuity or marriage (Falco 1991). In fact, most lesbians have had heterosexual experience, more than one-third have been married, and one-fifth have had children by men (Rothberg and Ubell 1985).

Lesbians are at risk during everyday personal, social, and work situations, and thus many choose to "pass." Various studies have identified behaviors that lesbians will use to avoid detection (Moses 1978) and those they will engage in to protect themselves (Ort 1987). The pervasiveness of these behaviors and situations provides important cultural information. Lesbians introduce lovers as "friends," do not talk about or lie about living situations, and use the pronoun *he* instead of *she* in referring to their lovers. Lesbians pretend to or actually do date men, pretend to or actually become engaged, pretend to or actually do marry. "Dates" are often gay men invited to social/work functions. Lesbians avoid gay friends when with heterosexual people and heterosexual friends when with gay people. Lesbians may uneasily participate in conversations of an explicit heterosexual nature. They experience and tolerate homophobic jokes from family, friends, or coworkers, or otherwise interact with people who are closed-minded and prejudiced. Lesbians worry about shame, ridicule, rejection, loss of respect, ostracism, sexual harassment, losing control of personal information through accidental means, gossip, cruelty, and physical violence. These behaviors are not simply signs of paranoia or personal idiosyncracies. The clinician should not see them as symptoms of illness or dysfunction but rather as internalizations of heterosexism and responses to a hostile environment.

While gay men also must be sensitive to the possibility of daily humiliation and physical harm, heterosexism grounds women in a different relation to heterosexuality than men. Women are subject to male observation in ways that men are not. Women are seen as objects that arouse and pre-cipitate men's sexual urges, which are assumed to be natural and compelling as well as powerful and uncontrollable. Lesbians, despite their potential dis-interest, are still subject to male sexual interest. Lesbians must constantly watch themselves in relation to men. They, like other women, learn how to watch men watching them, but they must take care not to appear too avail-able—or too unavailable. Male sexual harassment is an aspect of heterosex-ism that gay men do not experience in the numbers that lesbians do.

Permission for the phenomenon of sexual harassment is implicit in a het-erosexist culture in which male sexual access to women is assumed as a right. While this cultural assumption affects all women, lesbians are particularly vulnerable. Many lesbians report unwanted sexual comments and sexual advances from men who believe lesbians pose a special challenge for display-ing their prowess, a practice supported by heterosexist social structures. Even more insidious is the appropriation of lesbian sexuality for male heterosexual entertainment. It is not uncommon in lesbian experience that men want them to make love for them, with them, or with a wife or female partner. Sexual violence toward lesbians is another extension of heterosexist privileged access to women. Sexual taunting, battering, and rape are not confined to hetero-sexual women. The sexist illusion that women "ask for rape" would suggest that lesbians might be more protected from such violent practices, but, of course, they are not. Another heterosexual myth implies that women who are "too attractive" to men are the only ones raped. In fact, many lesbians who eschew heterosexist standards of "feminine" appearance and beauty are raped. In this sexist, heterosexist, and homophobic society gay men and women are threatened with physical violence, but gay women are also threatened with sexual violence.

The coming out literature, as I have indicated, presents lesbians (and gay men) as engaged in a process of individual transformation in which the per-son gradually feels more comfortable with a lesbian identity, psychologically safe, sound, and powerful. Certainly many lesbians do learn to tolerate and manage the negative opinions of significant and insignificant others. What some do not learn well, however, is to notice, appreciate, and understand the forces that shape the very environment within which their self-definitions take shape. Clinicians can help lesbian clients distinguish that part of real-ity they care about from the rest of reality that they may not care about. Not caring and not knowing have different consequences for lesbians. There are many and varied books and social and political events available to learn about lesbian and gay male experiences and culture. There are no longer any excuses for lack of information. Social workers must work with clients to put this information into an appropriate cultural context and to help their lesbian clients understand that there is no guaranteed psychological or physical safety available to them, that ordinary civility and respect are negotiated items.

Coming out is more than a process of individual psychological development in which a woman comes to accept her lesbian identity, and it is something more than recognizing and combating one's own internalized homophobia or that of others. Homophobia will continue to be pervasive until heterosexism itself is eradicated. Heterosexism implies an inherent conflict between attachment and autonomy, between separation and individuation, and a distribution of supposedly conflicting attributes by sex. Heterosexism not only subordinates women to men, but devalues female bonding. Adult competencies cannot be understood outside the cultural contexts in which they are shaped. A redefinition of female identity in general and lesbian identity in particular will not be possible until the assumptions and values of sexism and heterosexism no longer make sense, much less common sense.

NOTES

I would like to extend my appreciation to Betty Ann Sanders, whose feminist perspective helped shape some of the ideas in this chapter.

1. For purposes of the analysis in this paper, *coming out* is used as an umbrella term framing the psychological and social experience of assuming a lesbian identity.
2. This phenomenon will be highlighted by the use of parenthetical expressions in the text of this article.

REFERENCES

Blanck, G., and R. Blanck. 1974. *Ego psychology: Theory and practice.* New York: Columbia University Press.

Blass, R. B., and S. J. Blatt. 1992. Attachment and separateness. *Psychological Study of the Child* 47:189–203.

Cass, V. C. 1979. Homosexual identity formation: A theoretical model. *Journal of Homosexuality* 4(3):219–235.

— 1984. Homosexual identity: A concept in need of definition. *Journal of Homosexuality* 10:105–126.

Chapman, B. E., and J. C. Brannock. 1987. Proposed model of lesbian identity development: An empirical examination. *Journal of Homosexuality* 3/4:69–80.

Chodorow, N. J. 1989. *Feminism and psychoanalytic theory.* New Haven: Yale University Press.

Coleman, E. 1982. Developmental stages of the coming-out process. In W. Paul, J. D. Weinrich, J. C. Gonsiorek, and M. E. Hotvedt, eds., *Homosexuality: Social, psychological, and biological issues*, pp. 268–277. New York: William Morrow.

de Monteflores, C., and S. J. Schultz. 1978. Coming out: Similarities and differences for lesbians and gay men. *Journal of Social Issues* 34(3):59–72.

Elliott, P. E. 1985. Theory and research on lesbian identity formation. *International Journal of Women's Studies* 8(1):64–71.

Falco, K. 1991. *Psychotherapy with lesbian clients. Theory into practice*. New York: Brunner/Mazel.

Fein, S. B., and E. M. Nuehring. 1981. Intrapsychic effects of stigma: A process of break down and reconstruction of social reality. *Journal of Homosexuality* 7(1):3–13.

Gilligan, C. 1982. *In a different voice*. Cambridge: Harvard University Press.

Gramick, J. 1984. Developing a lesbian identity. In T. Darty and S. Potter, eds., *Women-identified women*, pp. 312–344. Palo Alto: Mayfield.

Hanley-Hackenbruck, P. 1988. "Coming out" and psychotherapy. *Psychiatric Annals* 18(1):29–32.

Herdt, G. 1992. *Gay culture in America: Essays from the field*. Boston: Beacon.

Herek, G. M. 1989. Hate crimes against lesbians and gay men: Issues for research and policy. *American Psychologist* 44(6):948–955.

Hess, E. P. 1983. Feminist and lesbian development: Parallels and divergencies. *Journal of Homosexuality* 23(1):67–78.

Hetrick, E. S., and A. D. Martin. 1987. Developmental issues and their resolution for gay and lesbian adolescents. *Journal of Homosexuality* 13(1):25–43.

— 1988. The stigmatization of the gay and lesbian adolescent. *Journal of Homosexuality* 14:163–183.

Hoagland, S. L. 1988. *Lesbian ethics: Toward new value*. Palo Alto: Institute of Lesbian Studies.

Horner, A. 1992. *Psychoanalytic object relations therapy*. New Jersey: Aronson.

Kaufman, P. A., E. Harrison, and M. L. Hyde. 1984. Distancing for intimacy in lesbian relationships. *American Journal of Psychiatry* 141(4):530–533.

Krestan, J., and C. S. Bepko. 1980. The problem of fusion in the lesbian relationship. *Family Process* 19:277–289.

Lewis, L. A. 1984. The coming out process for lesbians: Integrating a stable identity. *Social Work* (Sept.-Oct.): 464–469.

Mencher, J. 1990. Intimacy in lesbian relationships: A critical re-examination of fusion. Stone Center Works in Progress series, no. 42. Wellesley College.

Moses, A. E. 1978. *Identity management in lesbian women*. New York: Praeger.

Ponse, B. 1978. *Identities in the lesbian world: The social construction of self*. Westport, Conn.: Greenwood.

Ogbu, J. U. 1981. Origins of human competence: A cultural-ecological perspective. *Child Development* 52:413–429.

Ort, J. D. 1987. Enablers and inhibitors of lesbian dis-closure. Unpublished paper reported in *Psychotherapy with lesbian clients* by Kristine L. Falco. New York: Brunner/Mazel.

Roth, S. 1989. Psychotherapy with lesbian couples: Individual issues, female socialization, and the social context. In M. McGoldrick, C. Anderson, and F. Walsh, eds., *Women in families: A framework for family therapy.* New York: Norton.

Rothberg, B., and V. Ubell. 1985. The co-existence of system theory and feminism in working with heterosexual and lesbian couples. *Women and Therapy* 4(1):19–36.

Socarides, C. 1978. *Homosexuality.* New York: Aronson.

Spaulding, E. C. 1982. The formation of lesbian identity during the "coming out" process. Ph.D. diss., Smith College School for Social Work.

— 1992. The inner world of objects and lesbian development. *Journal of Analytic Social Work* 1(2).

Troiden, R. R. 1989. The formation of homosexual identities. *Journal of Homosexuality* 15:43–73.

Webster's new universal unabridged dictionary. 1972. 2d ed. New York: Simon and Schuster.

Wolff, C. 1971. *Love between women.* New York: St. Martin's.

CHAPTER TWO

Ascribing Master Status to Lesbians: Clinical Echoes of Identity Dilemmas

Susan Donner

Next time anybody calls me a lesbian writer I am going to knock their teeth in. I'm a woman and I'm from the South and I'm alive and that is that.

—*Rita Mae Brown*

THE INTENT OF THIS QUOTE and the identity of the woman together convey the complex and sometimes paradoxical nature of negotiating and living out aspects of a lesbian identity in our culture. Although Rita Mae Brown threatens to knock out the teeth of anyone who reduces her to the label of a lesbian writer, it is not because she is a closet lesbian. To the contrary. In many of her novels the main protagonists are often women whose lesbian identities are both public and comfortable. It is a piece of background information—important but not conclusively definitive. To label Rita Mae Brown a lesbian writer—to neatly wrap her up in that designation—is to commit a kind of psychological violence to an infinitely more complex reality.

In this chapter I will explore one very specific issue. That issue is the tension for many self-identified lesbians at being viewed by others almost exclusively in terms of being lesbian, at being ascribed a "master identity" rather than appreciated for the multidimensionality that characterizes all human beings. This chapter explores how that issue makes being a lesbian sometimes harder than it should have to be or what it is that might inspire the very successful Rita Mae Brown to threaten "to knock their teeth in." Implications for working clinically with lesbians for whom this is an active issue will also be discussed. The clinical considerations will deal more with attitude and understanding than specific therapeutic techniques. Attitude and understanding permeate, of course, all interventions of a technical nature because they shape how open one is to genuine listening. They provide a bedrock in terms of quality of attention and filter in or out what will be heard when in actuality the possibilities are always multiple.

Master Status Ascription

The message that I, at least, with the freedom of a postmodern reader, choose to see as embedded in the quote is as follows. Although categories are assigned by our society, and eventually by ourselves, in conceptualizing, organizing, privileging, and bounding aspects of what we constitute as self and identity, and although the categories are a powerful focus in our own experiences of self, the self can never be captured by a single category or an aggregate of categories. For a woman who is a lesbian there is the ever present danger of being seen and treated as LESBIAN, of being myopically viewed through a single lens that takes on the power of a "master status," a term coined by Hughes (1945) and elaborated upon by Goffman (1963) in his work on stigma. A master status subordinates and often submerges all other aspects of a person's ascribed identity. Once a woman carries the label *Lesbian*, a list of characteristics is implied that tends to overwhelm and submerge other previously held characteristics and even first-hand knowledge of the woman (Khayatt 1992). This occurs in spite of the fact that no personality trait or character configuration has ever been demonstrated to differentiate those who are homosexual and those who are heterosexual. Not infrequently even parents who have had a long and intimate relationship with an offspring may, when his or her homosexuality is disclosed, react as though their offspring has become a total stranger, a new and unknown person (Strommen 1993). Not only does this totalizing process distort the reality of an individual and render much of her humanity invisible, but it also suggests that the primary focus of a lesbian's life is her sexuality. Although sexuality is certainly not irrelevant, as Garnets and Kimmel (1993b) point out, sexuality, for many lesbians, may be secondary to affectional preferences or to other parts of identity or social role.

Issues of Sexuality

Master status attribution does not apply only to lesbians. Gay men and members of other socially marginalized groups may also be targeted. However, I am writing about lesbians in particular for many reasons. I can speak more directly from my own personal experience as a lesbian and I have considerable professional experience in working with lesbians. I also believe that a master status based on sexuality may cause more discomfort in gay women than attention to sexuality causes in gay men (Epstein 1987). Gay men are more apt to define their sexual identity in terms of sexual behavior than are gay women. Most societies are far more vigilant in controlling the sexuality of females than in controlling the sexuality of males. Politically, a lesbian sexual identity can be seen as a challenge to patriarchy, with its control of female sexuality (Epstein 1987). For some lesbians, however, having one's public identity labeled primarily in terms of one's sexuality can exacerbate the tension between how they experience themselves and how others see them.

Paradoxical Responses to Master Status

Before exploring further the implications of being assigned a master status, I would like to return to Rita Mae Brown's statement. This is not a statement made by a well-known writer struggling about whether to come out publicly as a lesbian. Nor, if one can make assumptions based on her writings and public persona, does she appear to be in the throes of ambivalence, fear, or guilt about her lesbian identity. To the contrary. In her novels many of her characters are "in-your-face" lesbians or certainly lesbians who aren't about to ask anyone to look the other way. They are lesbians who do not allow the other characters to define them as a problem. They are also willing to expend whatever energy is necessary to drop the problem back in the lap of whatever character is trying to unload it (Brown 1973). They go about living their lives unapologetically.

Without an understanding of the source of the quote, it might be read simply as a denial that being a lesbian has any meaning at all. Knowing anything about Rita Mae Brown's history of commitment to lesbian feminism is to know this can't be so. To resent and to oppose the psychological violence inherent in the imposition of a master status assignment implies neither that being a lesbian has little meaning to the self nor that all lesbians wish the issue of homosexuality to be without public meanings. The issue is much more who does the defining, what the definitions are, and how much room there is for complexity and difference within both public and private views (Epstein 1987). Being a lesbian is in fact a big deal. Concern with the restrictions of master identity, whether imposed from without or chosen from within as a response to environmental pressures, does not obviate the importance of negotiating one's lesbianism into one's overall identity. The issue of social identity offers an analogy. John Wideman in *Fatheralong* (1994) poignantly describes race as an all encompassing paradigm assiduously and systematically constructed around one's personhood that leaves one not knowing who one would be or could be without it. Although imperfect, a parallel can be made with the experience of a person who is identified or who identifies as a homosexual. Ideas about its meaning and the consequence of its existence may be so profound, destructive, and demeaning that one must vigorously reject those meanings that are falsely constructed, even if to do so in the midst of an environment saturated with irrelevant meanings can seem like a Herculean task. It is a small miracle that so many do it so well! Yet without active involvement in creating one's own set of meanings, one is at risk of becoming colonized by the negative meanings of others. Rejecting the ascription of a master identity is not, however, a denial of a piece of one's identity. A productive approach reflects more what bell hooks (1992) describes as she tries to sort out what of the many claims upon her identity (black, female, feminist, educator, Buddhist) nurtures the greatest reach in her development or what creates the widest circumference in the space of her personhood. As a woman who has spent much of her career working on issues of race, gender, and class, she refuses finally to be defined by them and their inherently limiting dualisms. These categories or multiple identities are never absent from her work, yet her work is not ultimately about them. She calls herself, when calling herself anything, "a seeker on the path" (16). A master identity allows for no seeking because it is a fixed and solid spot. Either one totally becomes that spot or one tries to break from that spot. Either way the spot defines the parameters.

Sorting Out Meanings

Part of the task for any lesbian is to discover for herself what being a lesbian means. This includes what it means in the world and as part of the self. She must also struggle with what she thinks it ought to mean and not mean in her internal and external worlds as well as with how much control she can and will exert over such meanings. She also needs to create space within her identity for integrating her sexual orientation as neither master status nor something incidental. The former implies a denial of the complexity of human experience and potential. The latter implies that sexuality and affectional preferences are unimportant and separable aspects of the self.

How one accomplishes such a daunting task in the face of a culture that either wishes to ignore homosexuality and to sweep it under the proverbial rug, as in "Don't ask, don't tell," or that punishes it by the denial of basic human rights is not a question for which time-honored answers are available. The struggles, however, of the last twenty-five years in the gay community and between the gay community and the rest of American society have offered up many more ideas than were ever before available in our culture (Epstein 1987; Garnets and Kimmel 1993a). The burgeoning of the gay rights movement following Stonewall and the proliferation of psychological, sociological, and political literature dealing with issues of coming out, alternative family forms, issues of gay and lesbian identity throughout the life cycle, political organizing locally and nationally, negotiation of relational issues in lesbian and gay couples, the deconstruction of pathologically oriented explanations, and descriptions of cultural aspects of the gay community and lifestyle have transformed what is now available to at least some lesbians as they venture toward establishing an affirmative lesbian identity.

Knowledge of recent intellectual, political, and cultural efforts within the lesbian and gay community may well support the task of identity consolidation and can offer considerable support to lesbians inside and outside of the clinical context. Negotiating the route to a secure and flexible sense of self that integrates sexual identity will occur within a broad spectrum of possibilities ranging from more private and selectively shared identities to very public and politically oriented stances. Any given individual may also approach her lesbian identity differently in different life stages and different life contexts. Within the clinical context working on what implications a lesbian sexual orientation has for one's life and sense of self is guided by the needs of the client. Choices belong to the client. Hopefully, the choices will be arrived at through a mutual understanding of the client's present situation, including relevant political circumstances, particular history, an appreciation of the environments in which she lives and functions, and some of the personality factors that already give life to her sense of self. Listening for echoes of master status issues may well become part of the clinical task.

Characteristics of Master Status

What are some of the characteristics of master status and the stigma carried with it? The issue of master status for gays and lesbians is a relatively recent phenomenon in history. It is important to understand that the currently prevalent idea about a homosexual as a *type* of person is a relatively recent one, novel to this century. In eighteenth- and nineteenth-century Western culture people were seen as engaging in sexual behaviors, not as possessing fundamental sexual identities. In the twentieth century, however, professionals from religion, medicine, and psychology began to label people who demonstrated any sign of homosexual preference as acting from some essential state of being, some inner core of the self (Richardson 1984). Although social constructionists, most importantly Foucault (1980), have been challenging this notion of an essential "self" linked to sexual behavior,[1] essentialist points of view dominate the tendency in Western culture to view the lesbian as a person with one overriding characteristic. Sexual orientation becomes synonymous with master status. Foucault put it rather bluntly when describing the historical shift in the discourse about homosexuality in general and male homosexuality in particular when he said, "The sodomite had been a temporary aberration: The homosexual was now a species" (1980:43).

Characteristics of a master status and the stigma that almost always accompanies it are as follows:

1. The characteristic is viewed as the most salient one an individual or a group possesses, a characteristic that obliterates or filters all others.

2. Persons possessing the defining characteristics are automatically placed in a group with all others possessing the characteristic and are then seen as exactly alike.

3. Persons with the characteristics are subject to a widely held set of interpretations and negative evaluations about both the characteristic and their personhood.

4. One characteristic of a person is generalized to other characteristics that are unrelated (Fein and Nuehring 1981; Goffman 1963; Hughes 1945).

The experience of becoming an object of such dehumanizing labeling can cause what Fein and Nuehring (1981) refer to as a reality shock—an assault to one's sense of self and one's sense of reality. It can initiate a destabilizing of one's self-conception as well as serious discrepancies between one's sense of self and what others reflect back about the self.[2] In the long run it may also provide an impetus to a positive reordering of one's sense of self. For some it may include a restructuring of one's social life within a community of others who carry the same master status and who may have a more balanced sense of what weight in the self sexual identity does or does not warrant. Perhaps most liberating of all, it can lead to a more compassionate and encompassing relationship with the wide and rich world of all human difference. It can lead to courage and a different way of being in the world that is very freeing (Laird 1994). Learning to value such difference in the self, and refusing to internalize any of the intended effects of master status assignment, brings an opportunity to learn to value the rich diversity in all of human experience (de Monteflores 1993).

No particular outcome is preordained in terms of one's response to a reality shock. Hopefully, one's response—in whatever form it assumes—builds on a more open, solid, and creative sense of self. The clinician needs to be attuned to this as a possibility, helping the client stay with whatever the nature of the struggle is in grappling with master status ascription. In all likelihood doing so will bring both pain and possibility.

Awareness of Oppression

To be attuned to master status issues for a lesbian client requires that a clinician be well informed and not in denial about the punitive stance much of society takes toward lesbians. In many instances oppression toward lesbians is not subtle and being known as a lesbian can carry penalties much more concrete than the psychological oppression of master status ascription.

Consider first that lesbians are subject to some or all of the following conditions (a few of which vary from state to state and institution to institution). In most states lesbians have none of the privileges or protections of marriage; they cannot adopt children or foster children; they may be denied rental property; they may be excluded from teaching school; they cannot join the military if they "tell"; they are increasingly victims of hate crimes; they are the only group for which jokes at their expense may not be publicly considered in poor taste; they have had state referenda denying them civil rights; they cannot hold particular positions in the hierarchy of many religious organizations; they are fair game for homophobic diatribes on increasingly influential talk shows; they may be shunned by both family and friends. This is by no means an exhaustive list of the kinds of oppressions a lesbian may encounter. Any woman who chooses the freedom that may follow from living openly or even semi-openly does so in the face of all of the restrictions above. Any clinician, gay or straight, must understand these restrictions and listen for the ways in which they are manifest. Sometimes the clinician must also assist the client in facing that these restrictions are indeed real. Furthermore, the client always has reason to be suspicious of the opinions and biases of the clinician.

Although the *Diagnostic and Statistical Manual of Mental Disorders* no longer equates homosexuality with pathology, many clinicians now more covertly hold that same view (Gould 1995). Part of being a lesbian is simply facing a reality most others do not face. Anger, sorrow, mourning, appreciating the ludicrous, losing courage, finding courage, doubt, and taking action will all be part of simply coming to grips with reality. The clinician must be open to multiple possibilities as well and have no investments in underhearing or overhearing what is there to be heard.

The Power to Define

Sorting out and warding off the self-diminishing effects of master status ascriptions is a demanding task. According one's lesbianism its due while not being trapped or trapping oneself into giving it more than its due is a delicate dance. The perfect balance of course exists only in myth. The degree to which it can even be approximated may become a somewhat idiosyncratic co-creation of the clinical relationship. For the alert clinician recognizing and actively reflecting on how pervasive the meaning of lesbianism may be in a client's life and sense of self—while being equally cognizant and reflective about those areas where it is totally irrelevant—frames much of the task. To accomplish this balance a clinician, regardless of theoretical orientation, must be educated about issues of homosexuality in the larger culture as well as in the more local context of the client's life, must be cognizant of her own potential homophobia, must have excellent listening skills, and above all must reserve for the client the power to self-define. Understanding the power dynamics inherent in acts of definition must become part of the clinical intervention.

The power to define and the powerlessness of being defined by others is a central concern of postmodern thought (Foucault 1980) and a theme in much of the literature dealing with internalization of oppression. To accept master status ascription is to allow oneself to be defined by others. Most people have some experience with negative externally imposed definitions of self, although to vastly varying degrees. When those definitions are forcefully and pervasively imposed, as is the case with gender, race, and sexual orientation, some internalization of those definitions is likely to occur. An appreciation of how a particular client has consciously opposed or unconsciously internalized the external definitions is part of the work in confronting and moving beyond master status. A deconstruction of the political and cultural processes involved in the imposition of master status may be an important liberating process when brought into the therapeutic work in a manner compatible with the individual's needs and clinical goals. Sometimes a question as simple as "Who says so?" "Where did they get the power to say so and have you believe them?" can catalyze the important therapeutic thread (White 1991).

Part of the clinical process will evoke reconstructions of past experiences of discordance between aspects of one's internal sense of self and external feedback. As Kohut (1984) discussed, all people have developed character- istic ways—some successful, some less so—of grappling with this discor- dance. It is a very common human theme and echoes of it will be manifest as a lesbian pushes beyond the confines of a master status identity. Because so many lesbians do not identify as such until adolescence or adulthood, the content of the early struggles with discordance may have nothing to do with sexual orientation or affectional preference. However, the emotions and thoughts that accompany earlier struggles in identifying as a lesbian may be similar, including fears of disapproval, a sense of isolation, shame in being different, a fear of punishment, a sense of loss (including loss of self- esteem), anxiety, anger, a wish to defy, and so forth. Some sense of fear and loss seems almost inevitable for people who are different in a culture that tolerates little difference (de Monteflores 1993). Although the intensity of these emotions will vary from person to person, tolerating them and giving them their due must occur. In time a sense of freedom and strength that gather in the process of bearing with and understanding (Beck 1989) may replace or at least diminish fear and sense of loss and allow the woman to more wholly embrace her homosexuality. Holding a belief in this possi- bility is in and of itself a therapeutic action.

Clinical Vignettes

The two following vignettes offer a glimpse into how issues of master status may arise in the clinical setting as well as thoughts about the role of the clinician. Each clinical example represents composite material from several different women.

The Case of Laura

Laura, an articulate white, professional, unpartnered woman in her late twenties, came seeking help around a fear that her important family con- nections were likely to fall apart. Her mother, to whom she had been very attached and whom she saw as the glue that held the rest of the family together, had recently died. Not only was her sense of herself in the world defined somewhat in terms of her relationship to her mother and many of their mutual caretaking functions, but she was unsure of her place in the family in the absence of her mother. Laura entered therapy somewhat depressed and anxious about her emotional future.

Although long dissatisfied with the lack of any lasting romantic relationship, nevertheless, until her mother's death, she had felt relatively satisfied with her adult life. Relieved that time had distanced her from her childhood, Laura had become used to being in control of her life and had successfully used her impressive will, intelligence, and considerable planning skills to shape a life compatible with many of her needs. She avoided situations that evoked her vulnerability and led an ordered life that centered around her professional work, friends, and her many family of origin connections and responsibilities. She had both humor and courage.

Then her mother died and what had seemed to her like firm ground began to shake. The loss of her mother, major in and of itself, presaged for her, she feared, other losses to come. She was unsure whether she and her siblings would regroup as a family or drift apart, leaving her feeling alone and emotionally adrift. Although she and her siblings had relationships with each other, early family dynamics bequeathed unresolved ambivalence and a history of silence about considerable family problems. She worried that maybe her mother's presence had kept them together. She also feared that she might have to carry responsibility alone for other family members of her mother's generation for whom she felt not love but a sense of duty.

As she spoke about her concerns for what would happen with her family, one of her fears began to center on uncertainty about what would remain of herself in the face of changes in her family constellation. Who would she be without her mother and who would she be without her ties to her siblings? With the loss of others came echoes of fears of loss of self, not in the sense of disintegration of self, but the loss of some sense of identity.

In addition to forming a lasting romantic relationship, Laura had several goals for herself. One was to reclaim a sense of hopefulness and belonging in the world in the face of the loss of her mother. Another was to work out aspects of her identity that were not tied to her mother or to her mother's view of her. Additionally, she hoped to be someone in her siblings' eyes other than the responsible one, to engage them in some necessary unresolved conflict, and to simultaneously build a new sense of family with them. The latter three goals she feared were inherently mutually exclusive.

Although she had friends of long duration and significant meaning and had lived a life of satisfaction in many areas, Laura did not have nor had not had romantic relations of any note. She felt this lack very deeply and the possible reasons for her aloneness were a source of puzzlement and frustration to her. Over time we came to appreciate together the powerful fears that accompanied the very real wish for a close relationship, including a feeling of betrayal to her mother. For a time she envisioned a husband and a family, and we talked in detail of what she imagined. Although Laura had been asked in a context that allowed for the possibility of a same-sex relationship, her first response was an emphatic no. The question was not pursued again until she began to talk about close women friends who would tease her about making life easy for herself by finding a woman partner. This opened the conversational space in a way that allowed us to explore the topic together (she knew I was a lesbian). The terrain into which this led had nothing to do with (until much later) what she saw as her preference, affectional or sexual, but everything to do with what she feared it would be like for people to see her as a lesbian. There were some fears about what it might mean professionally, but these seemed peripheral. The essence of her fear was expressed as, "Who will I be in the eyes of those I care about most?" Members of her family as well as old school friends played prominently in the scenarios we tried on together. Her answer to her own initial question was that she would be diminished and much altered in their eyes. She would be a Lesbian with a capital *L* and everything else about her would somehow shrink in comparison. She seemed to anticipate what Fein and Neuhring (1981) refer to as reality shock. Nothing would seem the same, particularly her relationships and her view of herself. Although no longer practicing any formal religion, traces of her religious upbringing caused her to worry about whether or not such a choice would be morally wrong, a scenario in which LESBIANISM would become an all encompassing identity. It would define conclusively and exclusively who she was.

Without making any assumptions about whether or not part of her reluctance to become more romantically active in her life had to do with fears of being a lesbian, we reimagined together all her own associations with what being a homosexual meant about a person. What followed in a much less distilled form than is presented here was a fair amount of surprise and embarrassment at the negative meanings she had internalized. Laura had to confront her learned homophobia and stereotypical assumptions of lesbians and gays. She was able to recognize the restrictiveness of the master status identity she assigned to lesbians and gays and her own fear that, if she assumed that status, everything else about her that was admirable would be stripped away in the eyes of others; she would lose her ability to define herself, surrendering it to others who would place her in a stereotyped and negative box. She had worked too hard and long in getting her life to be the way she wanted it to then hand it over to such a fate. Moreover, people would think of her more in terms of her sexuality, a part of herself she had downplayed. This became particularly problematic for her as she imagined family members having to confront the reality of her as a sexual being.

My aim during this process was primarily one of listening, helping her explain her thoughts and feelings, and assuring her that her thoughts and the conversations about them foreclosed nothing.

Every fear Laura experienced was explored. Every possible reaction a family member, friend, or professional associate might have was seriously considered in a context of understanding that sometimes a person's worst fears about becoming a lesbian could be realized. Laura certainly knew that lesbians can lose jobs, lose face, lose friends and family. Although knowing what I knew about the circumstances and relationships in Laura's life, it seemed improbable that the full catastrophe would occur, it was nevertheless important to explore her worst fears and consider them as part of the possibilities. More than losing her job or losing relationships was her concern with losing her sense of who she was if others saw her differently. The emotional tone of her fear as well as the language of it were most reminiscent of the fears she expressed in first seeking help. Although the impetus for her fear was now sexual identity, the themes were similar to those evoked by the death of her mother and her fear that her family would drift apart. The central question was one of identity, or, "Who will I be?" Laura recognized the theme and began to wonder where her sense of self came from. She began to question what she might have in herself that she could draw upon to disallow her sense of self to be so externally defined. Fears of differentness of any kind were always accompanied by her initiating an exploration of what gains such differentness might also allow.

Laura's remarkable strengths and her considerable determination always appeared in tandem with her often very poignant fear of vulnerability. Over time she could tolerate the vulnerability without having to fear it could take over. It never did. Every time she faced a fear she became a person who could face fear. She had developed a capacity that became part of her identity and that she knew was not externally imposed. The therapeutic work was to hold on to all the possibilities, help her bear her fear and sense of loss, and respect the integrity of any balance she established at any moment in time. I was also careful not to invest in any predetermined outcome. The complexity of the process and all she imagined, remembered, considered, and possessed as psychic resources gave the lie to her own worst fear that being a lesbian or carrying any other aspect of identity that was different would add up to the sum total of who and what she was. Anger that she might have to deal with master status issues replaced fear.

The subject of her sexual identity or of her romantic interests dropped from her work in therapy for a number of months. Several months later, however, she became involved with a woman and told me about it as though it was the most natural thing in the world for her to have done. She presented this new initially somewhat ambiguous relationship with little fanfare, even in light of her penchant for understatement. Although there was some reprise of the concerns and fears earlier discussed, they were brief and with little investment of energy. Loss this time was less around a sense of self and more focused on giving up previous ideas of what she thought her life would be like. Also, having involved herself in a real situation, she was able to confront that reality more directly. Although not spared incidents that confirmed some of her fears, for the most part reality was kinder than it sometimes is. Those people whose view of her mattered most mirrored back to her that although this was a major change and would take a little adjusting to, this hardly made her a new person to them. The people she cared about did not challenge the continuity of the person they knew her to be. If they had—and such is often the case—she probably would have had to process the challenge to her identity. Most of the adjustment came from the distance between her own conflictual views of what it meant to be a lesbian, the first being her own internalized and somewhat overloaded view, the second that which she actually experienced as she became a lesbian. Her transition into becoming a lesbian was remarkably smooth.

As she entered a lesbian relationship and gradually began to make that fact known in different parts of her life, and as she dealt with either the relief or disappointment in how others responded, concerns about master status issues receded. They did not disappear and probably never will entirely. Interactions in which a lesbian is seen through the myopia of a master status do not disappear from real life and so they are unlikely to disappear from one's psychic life. For Laura they have appeared mostly, however, in more superficial social interactions. Unlike the case for many lesbians, they did not disrupt her most significant relationships. The intensity of concern diminished mostly because the step she had taken was a satisfying one. Allowing herself to be different in a way she feared might be intolerable and sorting out for herself what the difference really meant to her and what it didn't mean to her and about her gave her more freedom to define herself from within. That had been part of her original goal when she came for help because of a changing family constellation. Paradoxically, the very thing she feared would restrict her sense of self the most assisted in an expansion of her sense of self.

The Case of Jillian

The second clinical example comes from the experiences of a white middle-aged woman, Jillian, who had been a lesbian for about ten years before coming into what would be her third round of therapeutic work. She came in not concerned with issues having to do with either her sexual orientation or relationships but because of her increasing anxiety about her career and the demanding responsibilities she had assumed on her job. Her new responsibilities put her in a position of some authority in a complex organization in which she previously had enjoyed her peer work relationships. She feared that with her new administrative responsibilities would come more opportunity for disagreement and conflict with her coworkers. Being liked by others and pleasing others had always been extremely important to her, and she feared that would now have to give way to other priorities. Although this issue was the focal point of the work, concerns related to being a lesbian also came to the fore as other events in her life unfolded.

As was the case with Laura, the experience of confronting the knowledge that others saw her in a very globalized and restricted way became an important theme in the therapeutic conversation. With Jillian it was a rude awakening and disturbed what she had assumed she had settled many years ago. Assuming a mostly open lesbian lifestyle had involved a struggle for her in that she was a woman who found some degree of conformity in life the most comfortable. Being fairly open about being a lesbian was uncomfortable. Nevertheless, over time she came to believe, and behaved accordingly, that not only was it important politically for lesbians to identify themselves as such but that ultimately for her own freedom and sense of self it was simply necessary. Various fears had returned from time to time, she reported, and at times her courage would fail her, but, for the most part, being a lesbian had become a welcomed and nonconflictual part of herself and her life. And then there came a dramatic reminder—at least dramatic for her—that being a lesbian was a problem in many people's eyes and that the word *lesbian* itself could exert an extremely negative power.

After several years in a relationship with Helen, a woman who was the mother of two children and who had not had a previous lesbian relationship, Jillian, who had no children, and Helen decided to combine households. This meant a move to another town and to a new school system for the children. For Jillian it also came on the heels of just beginning to deal with her altered relationship at work and a less secure sense of herself in that context.

Jillian and Helen discussed at length all the potential ramifications that the move, the lesbian relationship, and the combining of households might have on the children. Their view was that it offered the children some very real benefits but that for both of them socially it could make life more difficult and certainly more complex. Both agreed that the children should be in charge of what information they did or did not share with other children.

As Jillian talked in therapy about her new household, she at first seemed confident she would be able to manage their major changes, and the meanings for her as well as for Helen and the two children, quite successfully. Although she anticipated there would be stresses and problems, Jillian believed that she and Helen were equipped to handle whatever came their way. I tried to help her anticipate that the new venture might involve more upset and adjustment for all concerned than she expected. In fact, the new arrangement in the first few months posed a major challenge to everyone's equilibrium. To Jillian, in particular, seeing on a daily basis what it meant to a twelve-year-old boy that other children might discover that his mother was a lesbian became a brief but intense crisis.

Jamie, previously quite socially comfortable in his world and good at making friends, proceeded to bring no friends home for the first time in his life. Although Jillian and Helen talked with him many times about his worries over bringing friends home and tried to problem solve with him over the issue, he grew increasingly isolated from his peers. He said he couldn't stand the thought that other kids might call his mother a *lesie,* a popular junior high term, and was afraid he would get into fights if people started calling him a fag. It was more than he could handle, and his fear was so great that he could not consider that his peers did not have to know. Eventually he did begin to bring friends home and resumed an active social life. He started by bringing home friends whose parents his family already knew and whom he probably considered the safest bet.

For Jillian, however, this interlude provoked her own rage over feeling labeled and stigmatized. Through the experiences of her stepson she felt more dismissed and rejected because of her sexual orientation than she had ever felt before, although she was aware that the intensity of her feeling was also related to her feelings of rejection at work. Somehow, being a lesbian, as viewed, she imagined, through the eyes of these unknown twelve year olds, was what defined her utterly and completely. However, before Jillian could talk more openly about the impact this issue had upon her, she first needed to know that I did not believe that children were damaged by living in a lesbian household, something that could never be assumed given the myths in the larger cultural discussion. Jillian needed me to affirm to her that she was being a responsible stepparent to Jamie and that she was not destroying his life and his fragile developing identity.

With those issues addressed, Jillian would then use sessions as though they were an opportunity to convince the world that it was doing a grave injustice. She talked frequently of how disturbing it was that there were people who might not want to come to their house. "How," she would exclaim, "can a house be classified as a lesbian? It's just a house, and a damn nice one, and we are just people living in it!" When she began to hear herself talk about her house as if it too had a sexual orientation and was carrying a stigma, she then, with some assistance, could begin to consider why she was investing so much power in these children to label her, her family, and her house. "Playground politics" became her phrase for talking about what her stepson was going through and what she felt herself to be back in the middle of.

Playground politics was also what she felt vulnerable to at work. It was, in fact, a source of relief to realize that the focus of some of her concerns, both about being a lesbian and about being someone at work other than part of the gang, was in the heart of a twelve year old. The dismissive behavior of some twelve year olds took on an incredible defining power that she never would have accorded them in any other area. Though she had not seen herself as homosexual as a young adolescent girl, she did remember how much meaning the accusation of being "faggy" had among her own peers when she was that age and how much she had wanted to distance herself from such an unacceptable and totalizing label. She also began to see that this incident had remobilized her own homophobia and her earlier fears of being different or not belonging. She become aware that she was identifying with her stepson and that there was something about this age with which she was identifying that made the issue of her sexual orientation seem raw again.

As she talked repeatedly of all the things she was in addition to being a lesbian and how unfair it was that "people" were not seeing her for herself, she could see that she wanted to distance herself completely from being a lesbian at all. In her hurt and fear she was veering toward the stance that being a lesbian had little meaning at all. This was in contradiction to how she had been living as a lesbian and to the meanings that being a lesbian had for her. She saw the contradiction of her own vacillation between how humorous it seemed that junior high boys could precipitate such a crisis for her (she did not find it humorous on behalf of her stepson, however) and some rage at how unjust it seemed that she could be so labeled and written off at the same time.

The work in therapy around this issue, which, in fact, was tied in with many other issues related to her original concern about increased anxiety at work, was multifaceted. The rage, the fear, and the hurt over how she felt others were unfairly seeing her dominated the therapeutic conversation and simply needed to be accepted. Some of the shame she felt as she saw herself wanting to disown an important aspect of herself also needed to be accepted but was mitigated as she better understood her fears and as she could reconnect with how right and important it was for her to live as a lesbian. We also appreciated together the fact that everyone's sense of self is, to varying degrees, inextricably tied up with how others see one, particularly when Jillian began to talk about how powerful other people's views of her were as she remembered entering adolescence. That she felt now stigmatized and insulted made sense to her, but that was balanced by a realization that twelve-year-old minds—including the remnants of her own—were not the best authorities on what constitutes reality Nevertheless, for her the fact that twelve-year-old boys were doing the taunting and that the taunting was tied up with sexuality also necessitated a revisiting of how she had felt about becoming a sexual person of any kind at that age.

Furthermore, she needed to consider how it felt to her now that sexual aspects of herself were allegedly public. This opened up an avenue of exploration concerning her conflicts about female sexuality in general. Above all, that crisis fortuitously led to a reexamination of her powerful wish to conform and how powerful disapproval from others could be in threatening her sense of attachment and well-being. This became for her another opportunity to revisit these old issues and she began to better appreciate why she, in particular, was so vulnerable to master status assignment, an assignment twelve-year-old boys can make so well. In terms of reorganizing the role that assigning master status to homosexuals plays for those doing the assigning, the transparent psychological need in young adolescents to distance from any potential unwanted aspects of the self was of help to Jillian. It defused for her the impact of the labeling and helped her to let go of the problematizing way in which not just twelve year olds but society at large tends to deal with lesbians and gays.

To the extent that there was a resolution for Jillian, it came as she accepted, although with a sense of loss, that in the eyes of some others she always would be stigmatized. She came to appreciate, however, that the stigma did not have to be one that was so internally fueled. She certainly could tolerate that there would be differences in her internal sense of self and aspects of external feedback. Not only was she better able to own and recognize those internal voices that added to her sense of stigma but she was also better able to be selective about which external voices carried power and which could be background noise. Playground politics, for example, was best treated as background noise. Deconstructing the question of who had the power to define, and why, led into a labyrinth of intersecting questions and conversations that moved her to a better understanding of how some voices became empowered and others devalued. Over time the work led Jillian back into a commitment to a community and to a political view that makes sense of what uses in society stigma and master status serve. They don't serve truth.

Appreciating why Rita Mae Brown might want to knock the teeth in of anyone characterizing her as a lesbian writer will help the clinician appreciate the work imposed on lesbian clients struggling with master status issues. The struggle should not be confused with an unwillingness to become a lesbian or an inability to embrace that identity or lifestyle. It is, however, an invitation to listen for the myriad ways in which some lesbians reach for new self definition in the context of stigmatized, reductionistic, and straitjacketing reflections from without. This process is likely to be filtered through previously unresolved identity and self-development issues. Although the process for some may be very painful, it carries with it an opportunity for a more open, creative, and freer sense of one's self.

NOTES

1. A very provocative discussion about the ways in which the gay and lesbian community has responded to what are seen as the limitations and advantages of an essentialist position versus a constructionist position is available in Steven Epstein's article.

2. For some women becoming a lesbian presents no crisis at all and is experienced as an opportunity to pursue a strategy for dealing with gender power inequities in society (Faderman 1984).

3. For a discussion about using Kohut's theory in working with lesbians and gays, de Monteflores (1993) is a valuable resource.

REFERENCES

Beck, J. 1989. *Everyday Zen*. San Francisco: Harper.

Brown, R. M. 1973. *Rubyfruit jungle*. Plainfield, Vt.: Daughters.

de Monteflores, C. 1993. Notes on the management of difference. In L. D. Garnets and D. C. Kimmel, eds., *Psychological perspectives on lesbian and gay male experiences*, pp. 218–247. New York: Columbia University Press.

Epstein, S. 1987. Gay politics, ethnic identity: The limits of social constructionism. *Socialist Review* 93/94:9–54.

Faderman, L. 1984. The "new gay" lesbians. *Journal of Homosexuality* 10(3/4):85–95.

Fein, S., and E. Nuehring. 1981. Intrapsychic effects of stigma: A process of breakdown and reconstruction of social reality. *Journal of Homosexuality* 7(1):3–13.

Foucault, M. 1980. *The history of sexuality*. Vol. 1. New York: Vintage.

Garnets, L. D. , and D. C. Kimmel. 1993a. Lesbian and gay male dimensions in the psychological study of human diversity. In L. D. Garnets and D. C. Kimmel, eds., *Psychological perspectives on lesbian and gay male experiences*, pp. 1–51. New York: Columbia University Press.

Garnets, L. D., and D. C. Kimmel. 1993b. The meaning of sexual orientation. In L. D. Garnets and D. C. Kimmel, eds., *Psychological perspectives on lesbian and gay male experiences*, pp. 53–58. New York: Columbia University Press.

Goffman, E. 1963. *Stigma: Notes on the management of a spoiled identity*. Englewood Cliffs, N.J.: Prentice-Hall.

hooks, b. 1992. Tricycle. *Buddhist Review* (Fall), p. 40.

Hughes, E. C. 1945. Dilemmas and contradictions of status. *American Journal of Sociology* 50:353–359.

Khayatt, M. D. 1992. *Lesbian teachers: An invisible presence*. Albany: State University of New York Press.

Kohut, H. 1984. *How Does Analysis Cure?* Chicago: University of Chicago Press.

Laird, J. 1994. Lesbian families: A cultural perspective. *Smith College Studies in Social Work* 64(3):85–95.

Neves, P. 1994. Rite Mae Brown. In S. Bernstein, ed., *Uncommon heroes*. New York: Fletcher.

Richardson, D. 1984. The dilemma of essentiality in homosexual theory. *Journal of Homosexuality* 9(2/3):79–90.

Strommen, E. 1993. "You're a what?" Family members reactions to the disclosing of homosexuality. In L. D. Garnets and D. C. Kimmel, eds., *Psychological perspectives on lesbian and gay male experiences*, pp. 248–266. New York: Columbia University Press.

White, M. 1992. Deconstruction in therapy. In D. Epston and M. White, eds., *Experience, contradiction, narrative, and imagination*. Adelaide, S. Australia: Dulwich Centre.

Wideman, E. 1994. *Father along*, pp. ix–xxv. New York: Pantheon.

Gender and Sexuality in Lesbian Relationships: Feminist and Constructionist Perspectives

Joan Laird

IN THE 1980S two powerful bodies of scholarship resulted in two new metaperspectives that converged to begin a reshaping of the entire field of family theory and practice. The first was postmodernism, particularly social constructionist thought, which challenged essentialist notions about families and family processes as well as prevailing metaphors in family systems theory. The second was the feminist critique, which brought not only an intense examination of existing family theories for their failure to address gender as a powerful organizing variable in family life but also a revisioning of theory in a way that made gender awareness critical to family therapy practice. At times these metaperspectives traveled hand in hand. Feminist thinkers themselves were questioning prevailing essentialist assumptions about the meanings and practices of gender as well as of the family and its relationship to the larger society, making original and important contributions to postmodern theory. At other times they clashed, as some constructionist thinkers in the family field relegated feminist thought to the realm of the political, seeing it as inappropriate and impositional in constructionist approaches to practice. Other family therapists, on the other hand, worried that constructionist philosophy provided ways to absolve therapists from addressing the harsh realities and injustices in the larger society and in the family (Minuchin 1991).

One of the most influential and elegant contributions to the development of feminist family therapy theory was Virginia Goldner's 1988 article in *Family Process* titled "Generation and Gender: Normative and Covert Hierarchies." In a powerful challenge to prevailing ideas pioneered by Haley and Minuchin, which Goldner located in modernist cybernetic and structural thought, she argued that leading family theorists, with their family metaphors of hierarchy, organization, and organism, had left out one of the two major principles that organized family life, that is, sex or gender. Age and sex, she wrote, had been recognized in classic anthropological and sociological thought as fundamental kinship organizing principles the world over, yet only the concept of age, or generation, had been addressed in family therapy theory. Sex, or gender, had been ignored. Goldner wrote, "Gender and the gendering of power . . . *affect* family life; they *construct* family life in the deepest sense" (27–28).

Goldner did not differentiate between family forms and, thus, by implication, was writing about the more or less traditional family headed by a heterosexual couple. The assumption of heterosexuality has been common in almost all family theorizing until very recently, even in feminist family therapy theorizing. Goldner maintained that gender relationships organized not only the family but also "the politics of family therapy" (29). Gender relationships meant relationships between men and women, as the notion of gender was linked to the anatomical distinctions between the sexes. The (unstated) assumption seemed to be that there were two genders and two sexes and that we all knew what they were, a powerful dualism that has increasingly been challenged in feminist, lesbian, and queer studies as well as in anthropology, history, sexology, and other disciplines. Gender and generation organized all families everywhere. Gender was one of the two primary and "irreducible" variables in conceptualizing family and family relationships; race, class, and ethnicity (and, presumably, sexual orientation, although it is not mentioned) were secondary, consigned to a different level of analysis. Making a feminist and constructionist point, Goldner argued that gender dichotomies were not only constraining for women, they were constitutive, that is, they "determined what it was possible to know" (17).

In the last decade feminist writers including Goldner (1991) have questioned Western cultural assumptions about gender and sex, and the intersections between them, as well as heterocentric assumptions about the concept of family itself, in which traditional heterosexual family organization is usually implied and privileged while same-sex couples and other family forms are excluded. Recent feminist theorizing has also called into question the privileging of gender as an irreducible or even the primary variable in the organization of all family life. Certainly writers of Hispanic origin, African Americans, and other scholars of gender have argued that while gender may be the most salient issue for most white women it is often not the most life-organizing experience or aspect of identity for all women. Gender meanings and gender relations also vary across social class, inside and outside of family life. Goldner's earlier writing, by implication, would suggest that lesbian and gay couples, because they consist of two people who, because they are of the same sex and thus presumably of the same gender, would be free of gender politics.

Could Goldner, even though she clearly was describing heterosexual families and heterosexual politics (and taking into account variations by race, ethnicity, and social class), have been raising what might be one of the most relevant dimensions of lesbian (and gay male) couples as well? Is gender an irreducible and fundamental organizing principle for lesbian couples and lesbian-headed families? If so, how and in what ways? Is man, to paraphrase one of Goldner's questions, the measure of woman in lesbian relationships? To what extent does the dominant patriarchal discourse, with its cultural narratives about gender and sexual relations between men and women, also shape relations of gender and sexuality in lesbian relationships? How are such relationships constituted and narrated in lesbian couples?[1]

These questions and, in fact, any discussion of gay and lesbian families have largely been ignored both in family studies and in the marital and family literature. Allen and Demo (1995) reviewed nine leading journals in the family studies literature over a thirteen-year period and concluded that not only has little been published on lesbian and gay families but that the sexual orientation of family members is rarely included in any family research as well. Similarly, Clark and Serovich (1997), in a survey of the marriage and family literature from 1975 to 1995, found that gay, lesbian, and bisexual issues are for the most part ignored in the leading marriage and family therapy journals. In most writing and research in the lesbian and gay studies area, there has been some movement away from earlier problematic emphases on causation and pathology to more interest in identity issues and the dynamics of lesbian and gay relationships. However, the gender and sexuality dimensions of lesbian relationships are rarely addressed in the family field except as they enter discussions of couple satisfaction and cohesiveness or of what has been described as "fusion" in the lesbian relationship.

In this chapter, I explore some of the central narratives of lesbian gender, sex, and sexuality in terms of how they may or may not organize lesbian couple life.[2] I begin with a brief summary of some of the major contemporary feminist intellectual stances in unpacking the complex meanings and definitions of gender and gender relations in heterosexual relationships. I then contrast how gender and sexuality intersections in lesbian relationships are being theorized, considering how dominant cultural stories about lesbian gender and sexuality may or may not influence lesbian relationships. A proposal for practice that merges cultural, constructionist, narrative, and feminist ideas is outlined and illustrated with an extended case example. Although a practice example might focus on how gender and sexuality narratives influence any aspect of lesbian couple life, such as how couples handle money, the division of labor, or relationships with extended family and community, in this example I focus primarily on how such narratives can affect emotional and sexual connections.

The Many Meanings of Gender and Gender Relations

"Gender relations," writes Jane Flax (1990) in a statement that echoes Goldner, "enter into and are constituent elements in every aspect of human experience" (40). However, in Flax's view, gender never stands by itself. "The experience of gender relations for any person and the structure of gender as a social category are shaped by the interactions of gender relations and other social relations such as class and race. Gender relations thus have no fixed essence; they vary both within and over time" (40).

Deconstructing the meanings of gender and of gender relations is, indeed, the very business of feminist theory for, as Flax points out, there is no agreement on what gender is, how it is related to anatomical sex differences, how gender relations are constituted and change over time, or how gender relations intersect and interact with race, class, and other social relations. Furthermore, she asks:

> What are the relationships between heterosexuality, homosexuality, and gender relations? Are there only two genders? What are the relationships between forms of male dominance and gender relations? . . . Is there anything distinctively male or female in modes of thought and social relations? . . . Are gendered distinctions socially useful or necessary? (41)

Flax goes on to argue for what seems to be a circular process in that, although the meanings of being male or female vary across culture and time, gender relations create two types of persons—man or woman—and in turn are created by persons with anatomical differences—persons sexed male or female. In other words, Flax believes, sex and gender constitute each other. Gender attribution is, for the most part, genital attribution (Kessler and McKenna 1978). In addition, it is men everywhere who largely define and control gender relations, which are relations of domination and subordination.

Goldner (1991), in a later article, worked to unpack notions of gender development, challenging the either/or dualism that inhibits possibilities for males and females. She suggests that the development of a consistent and stable gender identity may not be possible or desirable. To do so,

> *requires* the activation of pathological processes, insofar as any gender-incongruent thought, act, impulse, mood, or trait would have to be disowned, displaced, (mis)placed . . . split off. . . . Since gender is a psychic and cultural configuration of the self that "cleanses" itself of opposing tendencies, it is, by definition, a universal, false-self system generated in compliance with the rule of the two gender system. (258–259)

How men and women differ has been a central quest in feminist theory. According to Rachel Hare-Mustin and Jeanne Marecek (1990), it is this issue of "difference" between men and women, males and females, that has preoccupied the search for the meanings of gender in psychology and in psychotherapy. They review what they see as two major lines of inquiry that have resulted in highly divergent and incompatible representations of gender. On the one hand, feminist researchers such as Hyde (1981), Maccoby and Jacklin (1975), and Eccles (Eccles 1989; Eccles and Jacobs 1986) have been attempting to differentiate genuine male-female differences from social stereotypes. In this body of research differences between males and females are seen as minimal; few are anatomically determined or biological and most are viewed as socially and culturally constituted and historically fluid (Hare-Mustin and Marecek 1990:22–23). Culture, then, inscribes nature, which is the weaker partner in the gender definitional controversy.

The second major line of inquiry, according to Hare-Mustin and Marecek, familiar to most psychotherapists, has grown primarily from the roots laid in the later 1970s by Jean Baker Miller in *Toward a New Psychology for Women* (1976) and Nancy Chodorow in *The Reproduction of Mothering* (1978), both leading edge works of their time. The search for difference was continued in Gilligan's (1982) work on the differences in moral reasoning between boys and girls and Belenky, Clinchy, Goldberger, and Tarule's (1986) research on women's ways of knowing. In the clinical realm the search for difference pioneered in these works is strongly identified with the working papers, published works, and ongoing research of the Stone Center at Wellesley College (see, e.g., Jordan 1986; Surrey 1985). Hare-Mustin and Marecek summarize this body of work as follows:

> Although these theories provide varying accounts of the origins of difference, they all emphasize deep-seated and enduring differences between women and men in what is referred to as core self-structure, identity, and relational capacities. . . . These theories represent differences between men and women as essential, universal (at least within contemporary Western culture), highly dichotomized, and enduring. (23)

Nicholson (1994) argues that these and other feminist theories building on the work of Chodorow, Gilligan, and Belenky and her colleagues, while they may seem nonessentialist, are actually examples of "biological foundationalism," that is, that they are rooted in the notion that gender, while it may differ across cultures or in how it is constructed in particular cultural contexts, is nevertheless based on distinctions of nature or anatomy. In this "coatrack" view of identity, she believes, "the body is viewed as a type of rack upon which differing cultural artifacts, specifically those of personality and behavior, are thrown or superimposed" (81). In her view the body is not essentially male or female, a constant, but rather is itself an important but variable element "in how the male/female distinctions gets played out in any specific society" (83).

It is highly debatable whether feminist thinkers such as Chodorow or Gilligan, who emphasize the power of male and female socialization rather than biological determinism, or their defenders, would agree that their work is essentializing of differences. Nevertheless, one can make the argument that the effects of this body of work seem to heighten the notion of "difference" in its valuing of women's supposedly unique capacities for mutuality and empathy. What Hare-Mustin and Marecek propose is shifting the terms of the debate itself away from "difference" and focusing on representations and meanings of gender, "including the political and social functions that the difference and no difference positions serve" (24). Similarly, Patricia Hill Collins (1997) argues that it is not the social construction of difference that is at issue, but the power relations that construct difference, that is, "the uses to which differences are put in defending unequal power arrangements" (75).

Feminist theorist Celia Kitzinger (1995) suggests that the essentialism-constructionist debate is growing stale and is impossible to resolve. She differentiates between what she terms "weak" and "strong" construction-ist positions. Weak constructionists tend to argue that such categories as maleness and femaleness, masculinity and femininity are social con-structions in the sense that they are historically and culturally variable, assuming different meanings in different contexts and different cultures. Weak social constructionists, in her view, endorse the idea that there are fundamental, anatomical, cross-cultural differences between the sexes. She says:

> The weak form of social constructionism is the familiar argument that socialization, conditioning, media, advertising, and social arrangements, which encourage heterosexuality and prohibit homo-sexuality, make it impossible to begin to understand lesbian or gay existence without reference to its social, historical, and political con-text. This argument is relatively unproblematic and is consistent with most psychological views that argue for, and document the role of, learning in human development. (142)

In contrast, however, the strong social constructionist, a stance Kitzinger herself embraces, extends this conception. At its most fundamental, it looks at the ways in which the taken-for-granted categories we use are themselves social constructions: the notions of heterosexual and sexual drive are seen as social categories or linguistic devices for ordering the world, which mod-ern Western culture reifies as "natural," "universal," and "the way things have to be" (342).

Strong social constructionists, perhaps best represented in French femi-nist writings, suggest that even such concepts as those of woman or race are not natural categories but categories that are constructed to mark "other-ness" and subordination.

Some historians, for example, Faderman (1991) and Jeffreys (1993), main-tain that the concept of lesbian and the stress on the lesbian's "difference" from other women was invented and began to spread in the late eighteenth and early nineteenth centuries in order to discredit and counter the threats to the patriarchal status quo posed by women who were becoming more educated, more independent of men, and demanding equal rights and social and family reform. Women's romantic friendships, once seen as an impor-tant training ground for heterosexual marriage, now became labeled as per-verted and pathological.

Women Marginalizing Women

In a related area of theorizing different positions on the centrality of gender in human relationships have at times divided feminists, as heterosexual women of color, white lesbians, and lesbians of color have been marginalized in the women's movement and in the marital and family therapy fields. The study of gender meanings and male-female relationships cross-culturally leads many contemporary theorists to conclude that gender and gender meanings are always raced and classed (see, e.g., Collins 1990; Spelman 1988).

Furthermore, gender, however constructed, may not always be the major organizing relational axis in white couples of Hispanic origin or in African American, Asian American, Native American, and other couples of color in North American society or, for that matter, in many other groups of white women.

Gender meanings and relations vary widely among cultural groups, influenced by such variables as migration experience, degree of acculturation, social class, geographical location, and a myriad of other factors. Cultural markers for masculinity and femininity, such as customs for dress, hair length and style, body shaving, the use of jewelry, and, indeed, for the very shape of bodies—female bodies in particular—vary widely from group to group and shift over time.

It wasn't so long ago that Katherine Hepburn shocked the nation by wearing slacks as she entered a hotel or that women in pants were routinely derided as butches or dykes; today blue jeans are standard dress for both sexes and across social classes and among many ethnic groups in this country and in many countries the world over. Men and women wear pony tails or get their hair bobbed, while both sexes may be found wearing earrings, gold neck chains, and bracelets. Few clues here about who's straight and who's gay, who's a nellie or who's a butch.

Lesbians of color have also challenged both heterosexual and lesbian feminist gender assumptions. Although all people, suggest postmodern thinkers such as Gergen (1991), carry multiple identities, for lesbians of color those multiple identities are not only painfully conscious but frequently at war with one another. Lesbians of color do not necessarily share the same priorities or privileges as white Anglo lesbians and are often isolated and marginalized in the lesbian community. And, for a range of powerful reasons, they may be rejected in their ethnic communities as well. They are, as Beverly Greene (1994) has phrased it, in triple jeopardy. Greene and Nancy Boyd-Franklin (1996) point out that African American partners in interracial lesbian relationships suffer potentially conflicting loyalties and may be at risk of oppression from several directions. Black lesbian feminist poet and essayist Audre Lorde (1984) wrote:

> Differences between ourselves as black women are also being mis-named and used to separate us from one another. As a black lesbian feminist comfortable with the many different ingredients of my iden-tity, and as a woman committed to racial and sexual freedom from oppression, I find I am constantly being encouraged to pluck out some one aspect of myself and present this as a meaningful whole, eclipsing or denying the other parts of self. But this is a destructive and fragmenting way to live. (63)

Pressures for gender and sexual conformity for lesbians of Latina origin may often be more extreme than it is for white Anglo women. Cherríe Moraga (1983), a Chicana lesbian, has been accused of aiding the genocide of the Chicana/o people. Gloria Anzaldúa (1987), Terri de la Peña (1994), and Olivia Espin (1992) are other lesbian scholars of Hispanic origin who have described both their connections to and their alienation from their heritages and their peoples, as they have resisted oppressive sexist and het-erosexist practices in their cultures, while Connie Chan (1989; Liu and Chan 1996) is representative of scholars who have described the intersec-tions of gender and sexual orientation in Asian American culture.

The Author's Narrative

At this point, before focusing on the intersections of gender and sexuality in lesbian relationships, it is important to locate my own current biases in the essentialist-constructionist debate. I take a "both-and" position in the sense that, although I would identity myself in many ways as a strong con-structionist, I agree with Kitzinger (1995), who concedes that empirically based, essentialist "knowledge" (or, in constructionist language, ideas) can be enormously useful politically in confronting stereotypes and in opening opportunities for liberation. One can point, for example, to Evelyn Hooker's (1957) groundbreaking research on gay men, which forced a new level of concern about the mental and social health of homosexuals, or Philip Blumstein's and Pepper Schwartz's (1983) comprehensive and com-plex comparison of heterosexual and homosexual couples, which pointed to the enormous strengths in gay and lesbian couples, or Charlotte Patterson's studies (1992, 1994, 1996) of children of lesbians, which strengthen the growing body of research documenting that such children do at least as well on measures of mental health and social adaptation as children raised in other family forms. Hopefully, these and other studies will have a positive effect on the discriminatory child custody decisions still made in many courts throughout the country.

Knowledge in postmodern thought is best thought of not as "truth" but as sets of ideas that have heuristic and generative value. Rather than taking a position on whether one can make fundamental causal assumptions about biological and/or anatomical distinctions concerning sex, gender, and sexuality, an essentialist position that is convincing to many and currently attracting considerable support among gay men and lesbians, I would argue that, whatever "natural" or inborn characteristics may exist, they are always greatly altered by and filtered through social, cultural, and political experience. Whatever kind of collective hunch reality is, it cannot be understood separately from the arbitrary and social conventions of language that not only shape our perceptions and our intersubjective responses but indeed may create what it is we expect to see.

I also endorse the social constructionist position taken by Hare-Mustin and Marecek that what is important, finally, are the ways in which gender (and other categories such as race and sexuality) are culturally storied, how they are represented over time and cross-culturally, how various individuals and couples rely on or do not rely on those stories as guideposts for their own lives, and how these stories are nested in and shaped by relations of power. Further, I tend to agree with Kitzinger (1995) that various labels and categories of gender and sexuality, or what Foucault (1979) called sexual scripts or discourses, are invented for purposes of dominance, regulation, and repression. However, as Kitzinger points out, "Social control of sexuality not only represses lesbian and gay identities, but also produces them" (141). It is a form of this latter issue that most interests me in this chapter. How do dominant discourses of gender and sexuality enter into and shape lesbian relationships? In what ways are lesbian gendering patterns and sexualities created by, imitative of, and constrained by social narratives birthed in the context of heterosexual politics?

There are risks in taking a strong and thus presumably an apolitical constructionist stance, as some feminist scholars, queer theorists, and some family therapy theorists have proposed. For instance, while it may be argued that dichotomous categories such as man-woman or lesbian-heterosexual woman have outlived their meaningfulness and their usefulness, to relinquish such categories may mean to cede the political edge that can emerge from taking charge of the label, from creating alternate and more empowering sets of meanings. The social category lesbian, although invented in a context of repression and used to designate the feared and hated other, can also offer a source of pride, a means to independence, and freedom from subordinating narratives. In other words, it can offer a banner, a site for cultural resistance and social innovation.

Lesbians and Gender: Dominant Cultural Narratives

What is the relationship between lesbians and gender? Are lesbians differently gendered than heterosexual women? Over the decades scholars, researchers, religious leaders, the general public, and lesbian and gay people themselves, in a tireless search for "cause," variously explained homosexuality in terms of sin and immorality, biological or genetic aberration, gender inversion, family pathology, or as some form of individual mental or psychological illness or disturbance. In the pages that follow I briefly review some of these "causal" arguments, focusing on issues of sex and gender.

The Biological Narrative

The search for the elusive gay gene continues as we near the end of the twentieth century. Biological theories are enjoying a revival and have attracted much interest and support from the gay community. Biological and genetic research tends to link opposite sex characteristics in children to propensities toward homosexuality, thus pointing to strong connections between gender identity and sexual orientation. Some studies suggest that the origins of homosexuality are neuroendocrine, that is, the brains of gay men share some characteristics with those of women and, similarly, the brains of lesbians share some characteristics with those of men. These conclusions are based on studies like those of Green (1987), who concluded that the majority of extremely gender atypical boys become gay or bisexual adults.

Using theories of genetics, a second set of researchers proceed from the hypothesis that homosexuality is heritable. Much of the evidence in support of such hypotheses comes from studies of identical (monogyzotic) and fraternal (dyzygotic) twins. If, for example, MZ twins reared together share a homosexual orientation in greater numbers than DZ twins, it suggests that shared genetic material is implicated.

There have been many criticisms of the twin studies, not the least of which is the fact that such studies assume "equal" environments for both MZ and DZ twins, an assumption many students of the family would find highly questionable. Further, samples tend to be small and studies go unreplicated.

Michael Bailey (1996; Bailey and Pillard 1997), a biological determinist himself, believes that biological studies hold great promise for shedding light on the origins of sexual orientation. Nevertheless, his enthusiasm is tempered with caution, as he points out that the state of research is one of "inconclusive complexity" (1996:129). Indeed, even most researchers who are engaged in, or otherwise sympathetic to, a biological research program "freely admit that neuroendocrine or genetic hypotheses about sexual orientation have not been supported to a degree of certainty that would justify their acceptance. Nor can critics . . . reasonably claim that they have been adequately falsified" (1996:126).

If some studies have offered some evidence supporting biological explanations for male homosexuality, the evidence for locating the origins of lesbianism in genetic or neuroendocrine studies seems extremely weak. Few studies have been conducted using lesbian samples and most that have been completed offer little support for such explanations. Nevertheless, biological ideas appeal to large numbers of lesbians and gay men who themselves report powerful early memories of being "different" or gender nonconforming, which they tend to link with their later coming out as lesbian or gay. There are, of course, certain political advantages to claiming that sexual orientation is biological in origin and not a "choice." If this is the case, presumably gay men and lesbians cannot be faulted for choosing homosexuality and can make a case for making sexual orientation, like race, a "suspect class" (see Hartman, this volume).

Kitzinger and Wilkinson (1997) caution that biological models conflict with radical feminist analyses of heterosexuality that argue against defining lesbianism as not "natural" or "normal." Heterosexuality and homosexuality, they believe, are constituted only in relation to each other. Further, they believe that biological essentialist arguments fail to explain the experiences of many, many women for whom sexuality and sexual identity are fluctuating, fluid, and dynamic.

Psychodynamic and Psychoanalytic Narratives

Other scholars, identified with ideas originating in psychology and psychoanalytic theory, for decades explained homosexuality in terms of psychosexual perversion. Some argued that homosexuality was a matter of inadequate developmental resolution. In Freudian theory lesbianism was attributed to the failure to resolve the Oedipus complex, resulting in the female identifying with the father, desiring to possess the mother sexually but, at the same time, faulting the mother's lack of a penis (Brown 1995). Others argued that it resulted from inappropriate patterns of gender functioning on the part of parents, while still others have linked homosexuality with personality characteristics, favoring diagnoses of narcissistic or sociopathic personality disorder. Both psychoanalytically oriented clinicians, as well as those few marital and family theorists who addressed the issue at all, also implicated what they saw as dysfunctional parent-child relationships or poor and disordered role modeling on the part of parents. The search for causes began to wane, however, after the upsurge of the gay liberation movement following the 1969 Stonewall rebellion and the subsequent 1973 decision by the American Psychiatric Association to remove homosexuality from the mental disease category. I am aware of only one article in the family therapy literature before 1980, a 1972 case study in *Family Process* offensively titled "My Stepfather Is a She." In this case the "solution" was to find another home for an acting out teenage son of a lesbian and her partner, a solution rarely favored in other family literature of the time.

Burch (1995), writing from a psychoanalytic perspective, points out that psychoanalytic theorists have historically linked lesbian development with conceptions of disordered gender. Lesbianism was (and, presumably, still is by many) seen as a disturbance in gender identity. "From this perspective," she suggests, "lesbianism does not signify a female-to-female connection at all but instead a male-identified woman who seeks a woman for herself" (288). If that were the case, presumably both partners in a lesbian couple would be male-identified, unless one is a misguided heterosexual woman who is a victim of seduction or other circumstances. The lesbian-as-masculine conception, of course, leaves unexplained the feminine lesbian. The feminine lesbian is troublesome for such theorizing since she is less visible or detectable, either by other lesbians or by heterosexuals. She is more difficult to differentiate from heterosexual women, an enigma to those who would argue that homosexuality is a matter of gender inversion. Furthermore, she is, like the bisexual woman, often suspect in the world of lesbian politics (Ault 1994; Rust 1995). Both bisexual women and femmes are seen in some lesbian circles as women who can "pass" as heterosexual, who can take advantage of heterosexual privilege when they so choose, and who may leave a lesbian partner for a man.

Other Explanations

Another theory suggests that most lesbians are plain, even ugly, and thus unable to attract men, a notion that does not explain the fact that many self-identified lesbians have been married or have had brief or more enduring intimate and sexual relationships with men. It rests on the assumption that all women desperately wish to be with men and to have a man, an assumption that preserves heterocentric and patriarchal culture. Such a notion makes it difficult to explain the many women renowned for their great physical beauty who have been known or rumored to be lesbians, or the fact that some make their livings in occupations that demand glamour or exploit female beauty and sexuality. It ignores the fact that many lesbians complain about being frequently flirted with and "hit on" by men, who are not respectful of their choices and who believe in their own power to seduce. This phenomenon is related to another narrative that suggests that all a lesbian needs is "one good fuck" from a man and she will be forever cured.

Another heterosexist cultural explanation suggests that lesbians are embittered man-haters. Their numbers are said to be swelled by women who have suffered horrible injustices like incest, rape, or battering at the hands of men. Yet there is no convincing evidence that lesbians experience rates of incest, rape, or battering any different from those of heterosexual women. What is the case is that since lesbian couples consist of two females, and females are far more likely to have had an experience of incest, rape, or battering than men, the rates in lesbian couples will be much higher than in heterosexual couples.

Gender Prescriptions and the Butch-Femme Narrative

Given the various explanations for what causes lesbianism, with their attendant gender and other stereotypes, how are these cultural narratives applied to the understanding of lesbian relationships? Several of the narratives mentioned above have had and continue to have destructive effects on lesbian identity and self-esteem, that is, on the ways lesbians construct their self-narratives, while some of the more negative explanatory stories have gone out of fashion or can be easily dismissed out of hand by most lesbians. However, the seemingly heterocentric butch-femme narrative, with its imitative implications, is a cultural story that has had a powerful impact within the lesbian subculture and deserves more discussion. It is, in fact, the most common cultural narrative for the gendered nature of lesbian relationships.

How else, the mythology suggests, would lesbians be able to organize their lives, divide tasks and responsibilities, or have sex together?

Some lesbian writers (see, e.g., Slater 1995) imply that the heterosexual world has little to offer lesbians in their coupling and family-making efforts, that lesbians have little to learn from heterosexual models. Lesbians, they insist, have no relational scripts, no parental or family role models and, in a sense, must invent themselves and their family cultures anew. This assumption, it seems to me, suggests that there is very little we lesbians can learn from heterosexual couples, from our families, from our heterosexual friends and peers. It is an assumption that seems to imply that all heterosexual relationships are about are differences in gender and sex, and thus about inequality. Are they not also about humanity? About loving and hating? About caring and violence? About teaching and learning? About negotiation and problem solving, inside and outside of the relationship? About establishing boundaries? Lesbians, I would argue, learn how to be human beings, lovers, parents, and so on, that is, they construct their identities in the same myriad of families and larger cultural contexts as heterosexual women.

Further, given that heterosexuality is compulsory in this society and for so long was the only visible or positive source of models and images for coupling and parenting, it is understandable that lesbians look to those familiar cultural narratives for ideas about how to constitute their self stories and their relationships.

"Butch" and "femme" are metaphors in lesbian language and culture, used by many lesbians themselves to describe and characterize how gender definitions shape their identities and relationships as well as those of other lesbians they know. However, butch-femme is a metaphor for the lesbian relationship that is far more complex than a simple imitation-of-heterosexual-gender-roles explanation suggests. It is a metaphor that, among lesbians, is constantly changing in its meanings. These meanings shift over time and must be referenced to their historical and cultural contexts. Like many stereotyping cultural narratives, the butch-femme narrative can be creative, adaptive, and even liberating for lesbians searching for ways to successfully couple, and it can also unnecessarily constrain relational practices and possibilities.

The butch-femme metaphor has been used in social discourse in a way that conflates the lesbian's gender identity and her sexual orientation, representing these categories as essential, enduring, and, as Burch (1995) points out, universal, that is, holding true across class and racial groups and historical times. Chodorow (1992) too suggests that the link between gender and sexual orientation in theories of development is so strong that "developing homosexual boys are 'feminized,' as if it is only by being feminine that a male could desire another male, and developing lesbians are 'masculinized,' described as tomboys—a homosexual woman must be masculine . . . to desire women" (293).

As I mentioned earlier, psychoanalysts, psychologists, sexologists, geneticists, and others have conducted exhaustive searches for gendered causes and explanations of homosexuality, while heterosexuality, the unmarked social category, is assumed and has required no explanation. In recent years, several feminist thinkers have turned a critical eye on this conundrum. Chodorow (1992), for example, points out that homosexuals have development stories while heterosexuals do not. Furthermore, she believes these stories cannot be linked to sexual dimorphism; rather, sexual orientation can only be explained in terms of a particular individual's life history and cultural location. There may be, she suggests, many differing homosexualities and heterosexualities.

Golden (1987) distinguishes between two types of lesbians, primary and elective. We can think about this categorization as an explanatory narrative. Primary lesbians are those who, for as long as they can remember, have had a sense of difference from other girls. Many of these women construct an I-was-born-a-lesbian self-story. Golden herself, however, does not argue for a biological explanation. She describes the elective lesbian as a woman who may come out in adulthood and may choose lesbianism for many reasons, some of which may have to do with wanting to transcend the politics of patriarchy. These women explain their choices in a variety of ways.

Certainly people define themselves as lesbian in many ways and for many reasons. Some women who have never had sex with women choose to identify as lesbian for personal, political, or communal reasons, while other women who may conform to stereotyping cultural images of lesbians live their entire lives in heterosexual relationships. Sexual orientation and sexual identity, as Brown (1996) points out, are not always congruent.

Lesbians—so-called primary or elective and everything in between—feel some pressure to explain their identities and their sexual attractions to women in ways that women attracted to men, heterosexual women, rarely question. In spite of the fact that there is next to no evidence to date that would support the biological explanation for those who have experienced themselves as different all their lives, many lesbians can only explain their early sense of "difference" within the context of this narrative.

The postmodern theorist, however, would argue that the power of the biological identity narrative can be attributed in turn to the fact that the biological story is a very powerful and privileged one in the larger culture. The workings of this and other dominant narratives illustrate the power of social discourse to shape the very content of our selective memory-making processes. As Levi-Strauss (1963) pointed out some time ago and many others have since, we make ourselves up as we go along from remembered fragments or what he termed *bricolage*. Identity making, or what I would call the construction of a self story, is always a retrospective process, a restorying, reconstructing, reweaving of experiences as they have been assigned language in the larger cultural discourse and by us.

This process may be seen most clearly in women who come out, to themselves and others, in early or later adulthood and are faced with reconstructing their identities, their narratives of self, to fit their changing lives. Many of these women accept the notion that they now have discovered their "true" selves, as if somehow the true self has always lurked underneath, hidden from view or unconscious until discovered, an idea fostered and promoted in much of psychoanalytic theory. Influenced and constrained by the repertoire of stereotyping cultural stories for explaining lesbian gender, sexuality, and the relationships between them, such women must find a self narrative that will somehow fit privileged cultural meanings of lesbianism, which, as I said, conflate gender and sexuality.

One of the problems with research in this area, which may be used to support the hypothesis that gayness or lesbianism is biological, is that it is often late adolescents or adults who are explaining their sexual orientation from a retrospective position. Kitzinger and Wilkinson (1997) point out that "this focus on adolescence is a consequence of an essentialism that assumes a dormant, true lesbian self waiting to be discovered or revealed at puberty or shortly thereafter" (190). It does little to explain the experiences of women who may change their self-identity from heterosexual to lesbian in early, mid, or even late adulthood. From their research with women who made transitions from heterosexuality to lesbianism (1997) they concluded that

adult women who make such transitions are no more driven by biology or subconscious urges than they are when, for instance, they change jobs; such choices could be viewed as influenced by a mixture of personal reevaluation, practical necessity, political values, chance, and opportunity. (189)

As Boxer and Cohler (1989) point out, we are always reshaping our life narratives to fit new evidence, reconstructing history to help make sense of the current situation. Lesbians, in reconstructing their self-stories and identities retrospectively, seize upon early experiences that may explain this more recent turn of events—often the familiar tomboy or crush-on-a-woman-teacher story (Laird 1989, 1993). Heterosexual women who were tomboys or who had crushes on their teachers or best girlfriends do not later sexualize these stories and do not draw upon them to explain their heterosexuality. As anthropologist Kath Weston (1996) suggests, when adults look for signs of homosexuality in their childhoods, they tend to reach for gender rather than sexuality stories, finding signs of male characteristics and activities. Reminiscences such as "I liked to fix things with my dad's tools," "I was the best shortstop on the boy's team," "I've always been aggressive," "I was the son my father never had," "I loved cowboy hats and guns," "When I was a baby they couldn't get me into a dress," "I wanted high-top sneakers," "I begged my parents to let me cut my hair short like my brother's" confirm that the newly emerged lesbian must have always had tendencies in that direction. Says Weston:

> You might think that lesbians would want to dismiss the tomboy-grows-into-a-dyke narrative for the stereotype that it is. But drawing upon the inversion model, a woman can use gender to argue for the "realness" of her gay identity. How? She slips continuity into her descriptions of the ways she has gendered herself over the years. She reminds you that her first words were, "Play ball," but forgets to tell you about the time she tried out for cheerleading or homecoming queen. (44)

Weston, in her ethnographic analysis of the gendering in lesbian narratives, which she suggests is "designed to complicate contemporary discussions of gender," says that her informants taught her that one cannot focus exclusively on gender, that such an endeavor "obscures the very aspects of race, class, and nation that give gender shape" (1). Exploring life at the margins illuminates the center. She says:

> Placing same-sex relationships at the center of an attempt to rethink gender makes the modes of gendering more obvious. There's less temptation to believe that bodies tell you all you need to know about the meanings of words such as "masculinity" and "femininity." Or that biology supplies the fixed template upon which culture works its

variations. Or that gendered differences are always male-female differences. (3)

Weston's work suggests that gender dichotomies in lesbian life are enormously complex.

I said earlier that the butch-femme metaphor as applied to lesbian couples can have many meanings and shifts in various historical and cultural contexts. For example, Kennedy and Davis (1993), in their historical-cultural study of working-class lesbians in Buffalo from the mid-1930s to the early 1960s, concluded that butch-femme relations were not so much imitative of heterosexual culture but a means to liberation for lesbians, a way to gain prerogatives generally available only for men. In an analysis of the butch-femme process in the 1980s, the lesbian historian Sheila Jeffreys (1993), who believes it is crucial that lesbian gender and sexuality be performed consciously as part of a lesbian politics and a lesbian ethics, suggests that there has been a backlash within the lesbian subculture similar to the backlash against feminism described by Susan Faludi (1991). She suggests that the political conservatism of the 1980s, helped by AIDS hysteria, had a particularly damaging effect on the lives of lesbians and gay men.

> An upsurge in anti-gay feeling precipitated changes in the lesbian community, more acceptance of gay male politics and priorities, and, interestingly, a return to the sexological model by some lesbian theorists. There was a new politics of outlawry, of sexual deviance which depended upon the constructions of sexology . . . in direct contradiction to lesbian feminist philosophy. (xi)

Jeffreys sees the advocacy of pornography, sadomasochism, and the move to rigid butch-femme role-playing in lesbian relationships by many lesbians as a movement within the lesbian subculture of the eighties that was and is undermining of and indeed hostile to the lesbian feminist consensus developed in the seventies.

Gendered divisions located in the butch-femme metaphor cannot be easily measured or compared with gendered divisions of masculinity and femininity in heterosexual couples and do not hold constant in defining relational domains in such issues as the handling of roles, money, or sex. Domains such as work, appearance, and sex *do* organize lesbian relationships, but in lesbian couples, identifying more with one gendering style than another (i.e., more masculine or more feminine, more butch or femme) does not guarantee privilege or power. Not only do gendered behavior and identity seem to have different sets of meanings for each partner in every relationship, but the nuances of how those relations are played out in everyday life are enormously variable and complex and the role divisioning far more flexible than in most heterosexual couples. Many lesbians use the butch-femme metaphor as a template for relationships consciously, creatively, and playfully, performing gender and sexuality in ways that are not rigid or constraining but that may be freeing in terms of mastering new learning ("Let me be the butch today, OK? I'll load the car up and you do the dishes." "You look like you've had a a bitch of a day. You play the tired husband while I get you a beer and finish up dinner") or may add spice and innovation to sexual expression. Weston finds that consistent divisions of power and control, usually identified with the butch or more masculine role, do not seem to hold up over time in lesbian couples. Some couples more or less successfully try to share power in every domain, while in other couples each partner may be more powerful in one domain and less in another. Furthermore, one woman's butch is another woman's femme, as gender is always mediated by race, social class, local context, historical time, and so on. What counts for butch in one context may be femme in another, as "who's on top" changes literally and metaphorically. For Weston the question becomes less "Who's got the power?" and more "What makes for equality in a relationship?" "Forget about getting rid of power differences by tossing out gendered differences. Think instead about how to do gender in ways that keep you and your lover on a par" (195). That seems to be what lesbian couples do.

In a sort of cultural paradox, while some narratives emphasize the "masculinity" of lesbians, others imply that lesbian relationships are troubled because both partners have been socialized to be "feminine" and thus at risk of fusion. Weston's ethnographic findings, at least in terms of what she found to be enormous flexibility in lesbian couples, support the quantitative research of Green, Bettinger, and Zacks (1996). These researchers, among other things, revisited the common assumption that, as a consequence of female gender-role socialization, lesbian couples have a tendency to move toward merger or fusion. This assumption has dominated psychoanalytically oriented clinical literature on lesbians (see, for example, Burch 1982, 1986; Elise 1986; Lindenbaum 1984) and also formed the central thesis of Krestan and Bepko's (1980) pioneering article on lesbian relationships in the family therapy literature. Presumably, because lesbian couples consist of two people socialized to be women (caring, nurturing, emotionally expressive, sensitive, empathic, connected, and so on), the tendency is for lesbian couples, when they face stress or conflict, to become emotionally reactive and mutually overdependent. Further, because lesbians constitute their relationships in an atmosphere that is heterosexist and homophobic, and may be cut off from supports, resources, and even their own families, Krestan and Bepko argued that there is a tendency for couples to turn inward, adopting a two-against-the-world posture. This stance, in turn, adds pressure to the relationship to meet all of each partner's emotional needs, forcing the couple inward.

In their review of research on lesbian and gay male couples, and in their own research, Green and his colleagues found that, compared to heterosexual married couples, same-sex couples are more cohesive, much more flexible, and report greater satisfaction with their relationships. They coin the term *gender straightjacketing* to describe a set of assumptions under which heterosexist male-female couple stereotypes are wrongly superimposed on the experiences of lesbians and gay men in couples. These assumptions do "not leave space for that alternative possibility that homosexual behavior may reflect being differently gendered than heterosexual males or females" (208). If this is so, there is less reason to think that lesbian couples enact in rigid ways what are seen by some theorists as feminine attributes that put couples at risk of fusion or merger.

Mencher (1990), also revisiting the notion of fusion, suggests that the very processes that in lesbian couples have been termed fusion, such as the capacity for mutual empathy and connectedness, are in fact what lesbians themselves cite as special about their relationships and the levels of intimacy achieved.

Burch (1995), writing from a psychoanalytic perspective, suggests that

> between lesbians, gender exchanges may serve to expand the woman's sense of gender, not to confirm it. Lesbians may not be escaping from the constraints of femininity into masculinity . . . although that is how many express it. Instead they may be striving for an escape from the limitations of gender categories altogether, into something more variable and fluid, a transcendance of gender roles. These different expressions of gender require us to rethink rigid notions of gender identities as being fixed at an early age or as being unitary and one-dimensional. (304)

To summarize, historical, popular, and professional discourses provide conflicting and constraining prescriptions about the meaning of gender and how gender is and should be enacted in lesbian life. These narratives, heavily influenced by heterosexist and patriarchal worldviews, shape lesbians' self stories and images of gender. They may also be challenged and creatively rewritten to make possible new options and new meanings in the enactment of gender.

Narratives of Sex and Sexuality

If heterocentric and heterosexist gender narratives have dominated myth-making about lesbians and, at times, lesbian narratives about themselves, cultural narratives of lesbian sex and sexuality have been equally dominated by dichotomous heterosexist assumptions. Sex, referring to biological anatomy, except for the rare aberration, has been a variable usually taken for granted and quite separate from cultural process in both research and in everyday discourse. There are no gradations in this binary opposition fundamental to Western culture. One is either male or female. Not only do we, in this society, call upon surgical intervention to correct the infant who does not correspond to cultural ideas for sexual anatomy, but, linking gender development closely to anatomical sex, we assiduously watch for and correct, in the development of children, what might be perceived as gender aberrations, as Goldner (1991) suggests, by default creating "false selves."

The postmodern era has ushered in, however, new questioning concerning the relationships between gender and biological sex as well as the meanings of sex and sex differences. In the last decade, particularly in feminist and queer theorizing, in medical science, and even in popular culture, previously unquestioned assumptions about biological sex and about the relationship between sex and gender are being challenged.

Gender bending and blending—in cross-dressing, female and male impersonation, and in the transgender/transsexual movement—is becoming a more visible phenomenon, exemplified in popular culture by the attention it has received on talk shows for at least a decade, by such cultural icons as Madonna and Dennis Rodman, and in such films as *La Cage Aux Folles, Victor/Victoria, Tootsie, The Crying Game,* and *Priscilla, Queen of the Desert.* Our stereotypical assumptions about gender and sex are played with, turned topsy-turvy, in film and fiction in a way, interestingly, that shocks less and provokes far less public controversy than, for example, does the simultaneous "coming out" of Ellen Morgan on television and Ellen DeGeneres in real life. Creative manipulation of cultural gender and sex assumptions is more or less acceptable, in film, on Halloween, at Mardi Gras festivals, and at costume parties, as we learn we cannot always believe what we see. Real-life "trans" behavior of all kinds, however, is seen to undermine the social order.

Feminist theorists such as Judith Butler (1990, 1993), Susan Bordo (1997), and Ann Bolin (1994) have challenged dualistic notions of body and gender. As Bolin, in a study of transsexual and transgender phenomena, writes:

> Despite the power of genitals in assigning sex, late-twentieth-century medicine has produced increasingly sophisticated methods for determining biological sex and identifying "invisible" physiological components such as chromosomes, hormones, internal gonads and reproductive structures. It is ironic that, the more scientific and complex the determinants of biological sex become, the less they can be relied upon to indicate gender. (453)

Cultural studies of berdache traditions, of people who occupy a position in various American Indian and other societies of a third gender, pose "serious challenges to scientific paradigms that conflate sex and gender" (447). In white North American society the transgenderist "unsettles the boundaries of polarity and opposition in the gender schema by suggesting a continuum of masculinity and femininity, renouncing gender as aligned with genitals, body, social status and/or role" (447).

Bisexuality and transgenderism are often linked with homosexuality as sexual perversions or at least as sharing sexual minority status. This is a highly politicized issue for lesbians, many of whom see transsexuals and bisexuals as traitors, captured by patriarchal discourse and perpetuating the "myth" of gender identity as a primary way in which heterosexuality is normalized and privileged. Paula Rust (1995), among others, has described the complex and often negative ways that lesbians think about and define bisexuality, while Clare Hemmings (1997) suggests that both bisexuality and transsexuality seem to serve as tropes in feminist and queer studies for reexamining the relationships between gendered and sexed subjectivity and between our gendered selves and our sexed bodies. There is a moving and painful scene in transgenderist Leslie Feinberg's novel, *Stone Butch Blues* (1993), when the central character, the S/HE, Jess, contemplates beginning the process of transforming her alien-feeling female body into a male body. She believes hormonal change, becoming male, might open up the world for her in new ways. Her lover, Theresa, however, finds her own identity as woman/femme in relation to Jess as woman/butch and sees promise of the expansion of her own world in the just beginning women's movement.

As their sexed and gendered subjectivities collide, Theresa tells Jess she must leave. To stay with Jess would mean a betrayal of both her lesbianism and her feminism.

The larger cultural discourse on lesbian sexuality may be even more destructive for lesbians than cultural discourses of gender. Lesbians, in their understandings of and narratives about their own sexuality in a culture dominated by male norms for sexual behavior, may be even more vulnerable than heterosexual women to tales of deficiency. The entire topic of lesbian sex has been largely invisible and buried in silence; thus deficit narratives are less available for challenge and change.

Paradoxically, although "sex" and sexuality permeate our consciousness daily, and we are inundated with virtually no holds barred images in the media, sexuality—and particularly women's sexuality—is a topic generally ignored in the counseling literature outside of sexology and sex therapy. It has been largely ignored in the family therapy field in relation to all couples and has been virtually invisible in relation to lesbian couples (Baber and Allen 1992). Not surprisingly, although lesbians report that they greatly value the emotional and intellectual connections and intimacy possible in lesbian relationships, many harbor feelings of sexual inadequacy. It is difficult to hold fast to a positive self narrative in the context of a larger social discourse that either renders one invisible or defines one as defective.

For both heterosexual and lesbian women scientific and cultural constructions of women's sexuality take shape in a context in which ideas about and norms for male sexuality are privileged. In our society conceptions of sexuality have also been dominated by biological and medical metaphors. Advocating for a social constructionist approach to conceptualizing sexuality, Tiefer (1995) describes the constructionist goal as one of defining, locating, and understanding sexuality in personal, relational, and cultural—rather than physical—terms. Sexuality has assumed increased social importance, she believes, in an era in which youth and health are glorified and death denied. Furthermore, "in a world where gender remains very important while the proofs of gender adequacy become more elusive, sexual knowledge and performance, for both men and women, need to serve the function of proving gender adequacy, too" (25).

There are several dominant narratives about lesbian sexuality that focus on deficits, serve as cultural constraints, and can operate in lesbian relationships as "problem-saturated stories" (White and Epston 1990). These narratives, which contain grains of "truth," include:

1. Lesbians are skilled at sharing, intimacy, and emotional closeness, but are inhibited sexually.

2. Lesbians, in relationships in which both partners have been socialized as women to be passive, dependent, and nurturing, have difficulty initiating sexuality, in taking an active, assertive role in encouraging sex. Nichols (1987) suggests that "two women together, each primed to respond sexually only to a request from another, may rarely even experience desire, much less engage in sexual activity" (103). As Baber and Allen (1992) express it, "Our society suppresses a discourse of female desire" (61).

3. Socialized to deny their own sexuality, many women know little about their own bodies and their own sexual arousal potential. (A counternarrative argues that women know more about what women like and therefore are able to pleasure other women more skillfully than men).

4. Lesbians join together too quickly and intensely, in a relationship of often deeply gratifying but short-lived passion that quickly dissipates, leading to the common problem of "lesbian bed death" early in the relationship (Nichols 1987).

5. Unlike most men, lesbians conflate sex and love to the point where the sexual relationship is extremely vulnerable to other turbulences in the relationship. Women, fused together or too emotionally close, cannot put aside their irritations, angers, and hurts to enjoy sex in the same way that, for example, gay men do. This problem is enhanced if one member of the couple has a brief outside sexual liaison, which may be quickly defined as "love," needlessly and prematurely undoing the couple's relationship. Many gay men, on the other hand, are able to separate love and sex in a way that allows them to enjoy a variety of sexual partners without impinging on their primary committed relationship (Blumstein and Schwartz 1983).

6. Women who have been in heterosexual relationships where they may have experienced sexual pressures, exploitation, and even violence, or where sex became a powerful bargaining chip in the relationship, may have learned sexual strategies that do not work well in lesbian relationships.

7. Women simply are not as sexual as men, they do not "need" sex in the same way and their sexual repertoires are severely limited.

8. Sexuality demands the excitement, thrills, and tension provided by the male and by sex-gender difference. Exciting sex requires power

differentials, an adversarial relationship. Opposites attract; sameness and familiarity, on the other hand, breed laziness if not contempt.

These are just some of the common stories of lesbian sexuality, stories that may more or less fit lived experience and that find some support in empirical research. Blumstein and Schwartz (1983), for example, found that of the four types of couples studied (heterosexual marrieds, heterosexual living together partners, gay men, and lesbians), lesbians reported both the lowest frequency of genital sex and the greatest rate of ebbing of genital contact after two years. "Lesbian bed death," that is, the diminishing of genital sexual activity, is frequently reported in clinical case studies (see, e.g., Goodrich, Rampage, Ellman, and Halstead 1988; Iasenza 1996), as lesbians, in what seem to be substantial numbers, seek therapeutic help for issues of sex and intimacy. But often what is at stake is a discrepancy between their experiences of intimacy and sexuality and the narratives available to them for understanding and evaluating their own sexuality. For example, sexual satisfaction in this society is highly linked to heteronormative images of penetration and orgasm. Lesbians may include many diverse kinds of sexual and affectionate expression in their intimate relationships—hugging, stroking, kissing, fondling—actions that are not defined as the "real" thing in social discourse and hence may be undervalued by lesbians themselves. Further, heterosexist and homophobic cultural narratives can trigger guilt and shame on the part of the lesbian, resulting in inhibitions or constraints on free sexual expression.

What also seems clear is that sexual expression changes over time in all long-term committed relationships. The frequency of sexual intercourse declines in heterosexual relationships just as genital activity appears to in many lesbian relationships but, as Baber and Allen (1992) point out, " a broader definition of intimacy would acknowledge the expanded repertoire of behaviors that couples construct over time" (78).

Lesbians also must guard their sexual expression from public view. There are very few contexts available in which lesbians can freely express affection in the ways that heterosexual couples take for granted—the extended hugs and kisses in airports or hospital rooms, holding hands, sitting with one's arm around one's lover in her parent's living room. These kinds of prohibitions lead to rituals of interaction that are safe and adaptive in public spaces but constraining when they carry over to the lesbian couple's private life.

Implications for Practice

What does all this have to do with practice with lesbian couples? First, it should be remembered that lesbian couples come to therapy with any of the issues for which any couple comes for help—the loss of a partner or job, help in negotiating conflicts in parenting or work sharing, or relationships with their families of origin. Like other couples, they may struggle with conflict over household and parenting issues, with emotional distance, with substance abuse, or even interpersonal violence. What is unique, of course, is the fact that the couple consists of two people sexed and, to varying extents, gendered in the ways that this society sexes and genders females and viewed as either masculine or feminine women by others and by themselves, but nevertheless women—and thus in a different relationship to patriarchy. Lesbian couples are couples that forge their relationships in social contexts likely to be sexist, heterosexist, oppressive, and potentially dangerous.

If therapists, whatever their own sexual persuasion, are knowledgeable about lesbian life in context, critically aware of the potential for sexist, heterosexist, and homophobic biases in the theories and models they use, and working to come to terms with their own sexism, heterosexism, racism, and classism, it is likely that whatever models of marital and family therapy have proved useful in work with heterosexual couples will prove helpful in work with lesbian couples. Crawford (1987), Falco (1991), Iasenza (1995), Roth (1989), and Slater (1995) are among those who have offered thoughtful approaches to therapy with lesbians and lesbian couples that are sensitive to the cultural contexts in which lesbians forge their lives.

In general, however, psychoanalytic, psychodynamic, and family systems theories have been highly criticized for their sexist and heterosexist biases, as well as their ethnocentrism, as the experiences of women, particularly women marginalized in the larger society, have been ignored and/or pathologized. Marriage and family theory has always privileged heterosexual coupling. In this section I describe what I believe are fundamental principles for an approach to practice in general and lesbian couples in particular that offer potential for being sensitive to lesbian experiences and lesbian meanings and avoid prepackaged or normative assumptions about gender, gender relations, or sexuality in lesbian couples.

First, however, a word about the gender and sexual orientation of the therapist. I do not believe that "matching" the gender and/or sexual orientation of therapist and client is necessary. What is important, in the approach that follows, is one's critical stance toward one's own cultural and normative assumptions about gender and sexuality and one's willingness to question them. What is important is the therapist's awareness of and willingness to examine the social and cultural narratives that support and constrain the lesbian's experience and the ability to explore how those narratives enter the life of the lesbian.

CULTURE AS THE CENTRAL METAPHOR FOR THERAPY   I have suggested elsewhere (Laird 1994, 1998) that culture should not be thought of as an abstract or relatively fixed set of attributions, shared traditions, country of origin, or even shared agreement about norms for living, common beliefs, and so on. Culture is fluid and emergent, always moving and changing, as people constantly recreate themselves, their narratives, and their contexts and, in turn, are themselves changed. It is always a matter of intersections—intersections of class, race, ethnicity, gender, age, and experiences, which themselves are diverse and changing. Culture is performative and improvisational. That is, we situate and communicate our cultural meanings as we move through time and space, improvising as we go along. We make ourselves up, forcing our experiences to fit into particular sets of meaning. Culture is also political, allowing room for what some have called a moral or just therapy (Waldegrave 1990).

Using culture as our central metaphor for practice avoids the machinelike corporate metaphors of family systems theories and the pathologizing medical metaphors dominant in psychodynamic and psychoanalytic theories. It provides a way for therapists to stay close to the ground of everyday life experience. Thus the therapist working with lesbian couples on one level can draw upon the same categories that students of culture use to understand human experience and that people themselves use in describing and understanding themselves and others. They are experience-near categories such as language, discourse, performance, story, myth, ritual, meanings, and beliefs. On another level, the therapist needs to become an "informed not-knower" (see below), an explorer of lesbian culture and history in relation to the larger cultural context.

TAKING AN ETHNOGRAPHIC STANCE   The cultural metaphor then implies an ethnographic stance on the part of the therapist (Falicov 1995; Laird 1989, 1994, 1998). Whether we call this stance "not knowing" (Anderson and Goolishian, 1992), "cultural naiveté" or "respectful curiosity" (Dyche and Zayas 1995), or, my preference, "informed not knowing"

(Shapiro 1996), what the ethnographer-therapist does is to try to meet culture on its own terms, as much as possible leaving behind her own cultural biases and preunderstandings, to enter the experience of the other as unfettered with prior assumptions as possible. But the ethnographer is not without knowledge, experience, theory. She uses her long period of professional study and life experience not to predict answers or to surface some pattern, structure, or organization of experience she is sure exists but to ask the best questions possible, the questions that will surface her cultural informant's narrative.

In preparing for work with lesbian couples, then, one should be as "knowledgeable" as possible but bereft of assumptions, to be prepared for the fact that this couple's experience may mirror the experiences of others and it may be quite unique. Learning about the history, culture, and everyday life experiences of lesbians can alert us to the "good question" to ask. It cannot give us prepackaged answers.

In the issues explored in this chapter—gender, sex, and gender-sex relations—it means entering the therapeutic conversation with no previous assumptions about this couple's gendered identities, roles, relations, or sexual behavior, but rather with many ideas that may stimulate good and fruitful questions.

ASSUMING A NARRATIVE STANCE   A narrative stance for therapy, pioneered by Andersen (1987, 1991), Anderson and Goolishian (1992), and White and Epston (1990), among others, merges with an ethnographic stance that is highly respectful, collaborative, and nonhierarchical. It assumes that all experience is constituted and reflected in language (and in silence, in the unsaid). It is one in which the expression of multiple ideas and possibilities is encouraged, a stance in which the therapist searches for strengths, for prior successes, for new and unique outcomes (White 1992). Further, it is a therapy that fosters *transparency* on the part of the therapist, that is, a situating of the therapist's ideas in her own knowledge and experience that may be relevant and useful but are not privileged in the conversation.

Lesbians have rarely had the opportunity to fully tell their own stories unburdened with the listener's prior understandings, which are likely to contain very strong notions about gender and gender relations, sex and sexuality. One of the most powerful advantages of the ethnographic/narrative stance is that it provides a context in which the teller is also telling her own story to herself, listening to her own story in a new way, and finding new opportunities, new possibilities in the therapeutic conversation. Listening here, as Weingarten (1995) expresses it, means listening in a way that is authenticating, respectful, and welcoming.

DECONSTRUCTING CULTURAL SELF NARRATIVES   The art of "listening," of course, is central to most therapies. But listening almost always means listening for material that will fit the therapist's well-schooled prior knowledge about how to understand the self narrative. Deconstruction has many possible meanings. I use it here rather loosely to suggest a process of examining—indeed interrogating—the implicit meanings, privileges, oppositions, paradoxes, constraints, and silences in personal narratives and larger social discourses. It also means listening in a way that Hare-Mustin (1994) has called bringing the social discourse into the mirrored room, that is, in a way that locates client narratives in family and social prescriptions and proscriptions that may unduly influence the client's self narrative. Weingarten (1995) has described this process as "cultural resistance," while I (1989) have argued that women in particular need to deconstruct larger cultural narratives and genres of speaking and storying that privilege male narratives and male ways of storying. White and Epston (1990) suggest therapists need to help clients examine the fit between the stories that have shaped their self ideas and behaviors but that do not fit their "lived experience."

For the lesbian couple, one dimension likely to be crucial lies in the connections between the couple's troubles and social narratives that are disqualifying, marginalizing, delegitimizing, trivializing, and demeaning—narratives that render them invisible

Such narratives are often double-binding, as in the case of lesbian mother social narratives. Lesbians by definition are not mothers—therefore, they are not real women. Lesbian mothers are not fit mothers; therefore, they have no right to be mothers. Helping clients deconstruct the meanings and sources of often paradoxical social and personal narratives that negatively define their shared enterprise, their sexuality, and their choices can be enormously freeing and strengthening.

RESISTING CULTURE   The deconstruction process suggests a further step, one not only of interrogating narratives that may be subjugating but of undermining them, resisting them. This step suggests a merger of feminist, lesbian feminist, and other antioppression theories as well as ethnographic/narrative ideas, particularly as we suspect that the client's more destructive self narratives have their origins in social and familial experiences that privilege the stories of others and subjugate her own. The pursuit of truth is abandoned in postmodern therapy; therapy becomes for many an enterprise that is clearly value driven (Laird 1995). Although some therapists have challenged the idea of bringing culture into the therapy room (for example, Hoffman 1992) others, such as Goldner (1988), suggest there is a difference between the therapist's being moral and moralistic, and, I would add, there is a difference between being essentialist and being political. White (1994) argues that, like it or not, every therapeutic act is a political one, while McGoldrick, Anderson, and Walsh (1989) suggest that a therapy that is not feminist is doomed to replicate dominant patriarchal cultural imperatives.

In work with lesbian couples, resisting culture often becomes a matter of replacing social narratives that do not offer affirmation of the relationship or open up opportunity with narratives that appreciate and celebrate what may be unique, strong, and adaptive about their lives.

BEYOND THE MIRRORED ROOM TOWARD A JUST PRACTICE   Finally, I believe therapists, like ethnographers, are in a unique position to bring the stories of what seem the exotic—the other, in this case the lesbian couple— into the dominant discourse, into professional literature, into the community, into the legislatures and courts of the land. Cultural discourses are not only shaped by relations of knowledge and power but also by ignorance. The telling of the lesbian couple and family story in ways that can be heard not only hold the prospect for teaching the world about lesbian experience, but they can teach all of us, regardless of our sexualities, something about ourselves. Just as African Americans and others can teach us about the strengths in collectivism, for example, so lesbians can model for us ways to do gender and sex in couple relations that promote the vision quests for both partners.

Therapists can also be instrumental in assessing available resources in the community for lesbian couples and families, identifying gaps and needs, and working to make the community and its institutions more welcoming and responsive to lesbian families.

Pam and Katie: A Case Illustration

Pam and Katie, a white, professional couple ages fifty-four and forty-nine, respectively, who had been together in a committed life partnership for twenty-five years, had been in therapy a few years earlier. As Katie's two daughters from a former marriage had approached adolescence, Katie had finished college and gone on to graduate education in hospital administration. She had become increasingly focused on her career but felt it was extremely difficult to change the role-sharing balance that had evolved during the early years she and Pam had been together. Katie had taken more responsibility for the home and parenting, while Pam had become a very successful and hardworking journalist with a demanding speaking and travel schedule. Both were stuck in what Katie described as a heterosexual-like marriage, without the social privilege that comes with it, and both had difficulty changing their priorities. At the time, they saw a structural family therapist who helped them consider what changes they wished to make. In a series of ten sessions that included the successful completion of several "homework" assignments, they concluded that they had made significant progress. Pam had trimmed her travel schedule and had taken more household responsibility, while Katie had become more flexible about her household standards and had advanced in her field.

Although some of these gains had not held up well over time because, they felt, those patterns were very difficult to break, they were returning to therapy now with a differently defined problem, one both were very concerned about. Their sexual relationship had virtually come to a halt over the last few years, primarily because Katie was no longer interested in either sex or physical affection. Pam was accepting of the situation, but often felt isolated and rejected, while Katie thought something was wrong with her and couldn't understand why her interest in sex with Pam seemed to have, as she phrased it, "died." Committed to monogamy and to a future together, Pam still hoped for a renewal of their sexual relationship, while Katie said that she believed their relationship had evolved to a "companion" stage that had its disappointments but was "enough for her."

In exploring their couple and sexual "herstory" together, I learned that the early years of their relationship had been characterized by a lively, loving, and extremely passionate and mutually gratifying sexual relationship. They described times, especially when their daughters were away visiting their father, when they spent the entire day in bed together, frequently making love. With some gentle probing from me, they described a relationship in which Pam generally was the initiator and the more experienced, skilled lesbian lover of women, while Katie was the joyfully receptive "lovee." Early in the relationship Katie, who had only had sexual experience with male partners, made some efforts to make love to Pam, who would become rigidly self-protective. Pam acknowledged that it had always been very difficult for her to allow herself to be touched but maintained that her gratification came from mutual affection and fondling and pleasuring Katie.[3] The pattern for the sexual relationship was established as Katie gave up trying to reciprocate. Although some of the fiery initial passion dissipated over time, they both felt that their sexual life together had been highly successful for many, many years.

A Gendered Couple

One of the many things I wondered about, in the course of our conversations together, was what each thought about sex and sexuality in general, lesbian sex in particular, and where they thought these ideas had come from. Even though this couple was part of an extended lesbian family-friendship network, neither woman had ever talked with other lesbians about their sexual relationships and both rather sheepishly admitted that they had never read any of the lesbian literature on this topic. Psychologically minded, each had at times looked to their family patterns for understanding. Pam, for example, whose parents had been divorced when she was a very young toddler, had always felt rejected by her father, a situation she felt had led to her feeling sexually unattractive and undesired by men. Her solution, she said, was one that satisfied both her parents. In many ways she imitated her father, becoming the lost "man of the house," repairing the loss by becoming a highly competent and loving daughter to her mother and admired role model for her younger sister. Tall, attractive, and highly comfortable in the world of male-dominated journalism, Pam had always known she was "different" and in adolescence had self-identified as a "butch," although she had always been closeted except with a few lesbian friends. She felt that one reason she had chosen Katie was that she was so "feminine." Katie also had children, two daughters, which Pam felt was an important part of the initial attraction, for she had always wanted children but had thought it was an impossibility in her life. She had, she said, in a sense recreated her family of women. While Pam had valued her abilities and her success as a lover of women, she also felt that she herself was sexually defective and unattractive, suspecting that Katie had really never wanted to make love to her. "She never really tried very hard," she said.

Katie's sexual herstory was quite different. An early maturer, with a father who was highly seductive with her, she had experimented with sexual intercourse as a young teenager and had had one highly passionate four-year relationship with a boy during high school and college. She found oral sex in this relationship even more exciting than intercourse but said the sexual relationship in her six-year marriage to a different man had been disappointing. Her husband had been an indifferent and unskilled lover, interested only in hasty intercourse and his own satisfaction and disinterested in affection, foreplay, or oral sex. She saw herself as a "second-shift wife" and had emerged from her seven-year marriage tired and resentful. As a teenager, she had seen herself as promiscuous and "bad," and she sometimes wondered whether it was only secret and illicit sex that turned her on. In the early years of her relationship with Pam she felt that their role sharing was much more mutual and satisfying than in her heterosexual marriage, even though she was still very much the housewife, and that sex with Pam was "naughty" and thus more exciting than conventional sex.

Pam and Katie, who for most of their years together had led an extremely closeted life, had also been closeted about sex, even in their own home. Katie, particularly, in the earlier years had lived in terror that she would lose custody of her daughters, so would allow no expression of affection except under the most protected of circumstances—when her daughters were asleep or away. To this day, she said, she still jumped and would become irritated if Pam tried to give her a hug or hold her hand in the daytime or when the drapes were open.

Katie also acknowledged, even though she felt their role balance had shifted and Pam was making efforts to share more of the unpaid work in their lives, that she had built up a high level of resentment and anger over the years. Like many women, she mused, she probably had learned to gain some power in the relationship by withholding sex, but, she thought, maybe it had become a habit and had backfired on her. Katie reported, too, that she had had a hysterectomy three years earlier but didn't think it was relevant to her sexuality, since she was taking hormones. She had not experienced any emotional upheaval at the time and, in fact, enjoyed not having to deal with menstruation. As the therapist asked more about that, Katie began to wonder whether indeed her sexual arousal potential hadn't significantly diminished after the surgery.

As their stories unfolded, the therapist occasionally asked questions that might help clarify how each woman, separately and together, made sense of their experiences. She frequently explored where they thought their ideas had come from, and whose views they expressed, checking to see if what she heard was indeed what they wanted to say and trying to understand not only the "culture" they had mutually created in their own family but how their family culture was embedded in larger cultural contexts of meaning. What effects had these various ideas had on their relationship? She offered no interpretations or advice but worked to continue to "thicken" their narratives (Laird 1994). As is often the situation, as clients listen to themselves (and in this case, to their partners as well), in an atmosphere where the therapist is welcoming, curious, and "not-knowing" in the sense of not prematurely intruding her own "knowledges" or too quickly interpreting the meanings of their utterances, they begin to hear their own stories differently and to locate in them possibilities for change.

For example, at one point Pam said, "You know, I just assumed that Katie no longer really loved me or was attracted to me, but I have to say I have no idea if what we've been going through is typical for lesbian couples. I am a very private person and I really have never talked to anyone else about sex." A question from the therapist prompted Katie to say, "God, I never even asked the doctor if my hysterectomy might have any effects on my sexual responsiveness and he never volunteered any information." Both connected their "ignorance" on these matters to a lingering sense that sex in general and lesbian sex in particular was not something one talked about with others and to their reluctance to "come out" to doctors or other such people in their lives.

Katie also confessed that she would very much like to be free to be more affectionate with Pam, but she found it difficult to become sexually aroused and felt that if she was affectionate she would be expected to have genital sex, which had become increasingly uncomfortable and unsatisfying for her. In fact, she found it difficult to think about sexually pleasurable activity not connected to the "orgasm goal." "If I become excited," she said to Pam, "you'll get the message I want to have oral sex when I don't, and then I'm in the position of rejecting you and you get hurt. But not having sex doesn't mean I don't love you. I wish you could understand that." Pam said that what she wanted was to be close and affectionate, that that was what was very important to her, that it wasn't genital sex that made her feel loved.

The therapist, in deconstructing their narratives, helped them explore how they had developed their ideas about what "good sex" and the relationship between sex and love "ought" to be. What picture of what a sex life ought to be like do you have in your heads? How is it, she mused at one point, that you are defining nongenital sex and affection as negative? How is it that you somehow feel that other kinds of sex are bad or deficient? What keeps you from being more unique and innovative in your sex life, from doing more of what you both have said you want very much and enjoy a great deal?

Pam and Katie agreed with each other that many of their ideas about sex seemed to come from patriarchal heterosexist ideas about sex. Somehow sex wasn't sex if it didn't end in orgasm; Katie wouldn't be satisfied and Pam wouldn't have been a successful lover. They were surprised when the therapist told them she knew many lesbian couples who had fully enjoyable sex lives and had never or rarely had genital sex. Leaning on the cultural idea of ritual, the therapist also talked about how practices (in this case, the rituals of sex and affection) that had worked well and were adaptive during one period of their lives might no longer be so useful. Cultural performances invested with the power of ritual are difficult to discard. Katie, for example, terrified of losing custody of her children, had hidden her lesbian identity from her family and even from her children for many years. Although she had been out to her family and children for some time now, she began to talk about how all of the ways she had acted to protect the secret still constrained her spontaneity and her ability to be affectionate. Even though her daughters were now living away from home, the private space of her own home still felt public to her. Both women commented on the fact that one of the few times they could still be really sexual with one another was on vacations away from their own home. The therapist wondered what they might want to try to disrupt this ritual and, interestingly, the couple developed an assignment familiar to therapists: they decided to spend some time each night simply holding and caressing one another to see how it would go. After a period of time, they reported that sometimes they went on to have very slow and gentle genital sex that didn't necessarily end in orgasm for Katie but was, nevertheless, highly pleasurable.

When they came for help, Katie and Pam were both trapped in heterosexist and male-normative prescriptions for what a sexual life was supposed to be like. They both felt so inadequate and defective that they hadn't felt free even in the spaces of their own territory to explore and innovate, to find affectional/sexual experiences that would be mutually gratifying. As these prescriptions were deconstructed the couple began to resist them as normative for their lives, disrupting older rituals of sex and building new ones. The continuing therapeutic conversation also led to a reexamination of some of the other assumptions they felt were impinging on their relationship. Although it was clear to them, for example, that Pam was the butch and Katie the femme, and both liked it that way, there were times when Katie wished Pam would take on more of what they defined as femme roles and she could allow herself to be more butch.

To cite just one example, Pam did almost all of the driving, but Katie argued that Pam was an absent-minded and sometimes careless driver, while she would become "nervous and critical," an "awful back-seat driver." Often they would end up in heated arguments about what Katie described as "near misses." Pam loved to drive, however, and didn't want to leave the driver's seat, a metaphor for her pride in her butch role. As they talked about it, Katie proposed that she do the local driving and Pam, who never seemed to tire, do more of the long distance driving. Pam was agreeable to this arrangement, which seemed to work quite well. Gradually, they began to consider other ways their rather stereotypical notions of butch and femme had locked them into some couple interactions that were less than optimal in their current life.

In this chapter I have explored some of the current debates in feminist and lesbian theorizing about gender, sex, and sexuality, exploring how major cultural narratives may or may not organize lesbian couple life, ending with suggestions for practice that lean on cultural, constructionist, narrative, and feminist metaphors. The discussion ends with an extended case example. I pay special attention to the complexity of the butch-femme narrative, one prominent both in lesbian culture and in the larger social discourse. In seems clear, to return to one of Goldner's initial questions, that while gender, sex, and sexuality (always intersecting with race, class, and other social narratives) *do* organize lesbian couple relationships, they do so in different ways than they do in heterosexual couples. Man, it appears, is and is not the measure of woman in lesbian relationships. He can be, to the extent that cultural narratives rooted in patriarchy dominate the couple's self narratives; he is not, to the extent that lesbians in many ways are generally freer than heterosexually coupled women to innovate ways of doing gender and sex and to resist patriarchal and constraining prescriptions for loving and living.

NOTES

1. This is not to agree that gender is the only or even always the primary or most important organizing variable in heterosexual or lesbian couples cross-culturally. But, as Goldner maintains, it is certainly a crucial theme in the everyday and intergenerational politics of most couples.

2. The question of how generation, in terms of family of origin relationships, is also important in exploring lesbian couple and family relationships will not be addressed here.

3. This is not an unusual phenomenon. In fact, it was a sort of badge of honor for the "stone butch" and is described in Leslie Feinberg's *Stone Butch Blues* (1993).

REFERENCES

Allen, K. R., and D. H. Demo. 1995. The families of lesbians and gay men: A new frontier in family research. *Journal of Marriage and the Family* 57:1–17.

Andersen, T. 1987. The reflecting team: Dialogue and meta-dialogue in clinical work. *Family Process* 26:415–428.

Andersen, T. 1991. *The reflecting team: Dialogues and dialogues about the dialogues.* New York: Norton.

Anderson, H. J., and H. Goolishian. 1992. The client is the expert: A not-knowing approach to therapy. In S. McNamee and K. J. Gergen, eds., *Therapy as social construction*, pp. 25–39. Newbury Park, Cal.: Sage.

Anzaldúa, G. 1987. *Borderlands/La Frontera: The new Mestiza.* San Francisco: Spinsters/Aunt Lute.

Ault, A. 1994. Hegemonic discourse in an oppositional community: Lesbian feminists and bisexuality. *Critical Sociology* 20(3):107–122.

Baber, K. M., and K. R. Allen. 1992. Women's sexualities. In K. M. Baber and K. R. Allen, eds., *Women and families: Feminist reconstructions*, pp. 64–101. New York: Guilford.

Belenky, M. F., B. M. Clinchy, N. R. Goldberger, and J. M. Tarule. 1986. *Women's ways of knowing: Development of self, voice, and mind.* New York: Basic.

Blumstein, P., and P. Schwartz. 1983. *American couples: Money, work, sex.* New York: Morrow.

Bolin, A. 1994. Transcending and transgendering: Male-to-female transsexuals, dichotomy and diversity. In G. Herdt, ed., *Third sex, third gender: Beyond sexual dimorphism in culture and history*, pp. 447–486. New York: Zone.

Bordo, S. 1997. Anorexia nervosa: Psychopathology as the crystallization of culture. In M. M. Gergen and S. N. Davis, eds., *Toward a new psychology of gender*, pp. 423–453. New York: Routledge.

Boxer, A., and B. J. Cohler. 1989. The life course of gay and lesbian youth: An immodest proposal for the study of lives. *Journal of Homosexuality* 17(3/4):315–355.

Brown, L. 1995. Lesbian identities: Concepts and issues. In A. R. D'Augelli and C. J. Patterson, eds., *Lesbian, gay, and bisexual identities over the lifespan: Psychological perspectives*, pp. 3–23. New York: Oxford University Press.

Burch, B. 1982. Psychological merger in lesbian couples: A joint ecological and systems approach. *Family Therapy* 9:201–208.

Burch, B. 1986. Psychotherapy and the dynamics of merger in lesbian couples. In T. S. Stein and C. J. Cohen, eds., *Contemporary perspectives on psychotherapy with lesbians and gay men*, pp. 57–71. New York: Plenum.

Burch, B. 1995. Gender identities, lesbianism, and potential space. In J. Glassgold and S. Iasenza, eds., *Lesbians and psychoanalysis: Revolutions in theory and practice*, pp. 287–307. New York: Free.

Butler, J. 1990. *Gender trouble.* New York: Routledge.

— 1993. *Bodies that matter*. New York: Routledge.

Chan, C. S. 1989. Issues of identity development among Asian-American lesbians and gay men. *Journal of Counseling and Development* 68:16–20.

Chodorow, N. 1978. *The reproduction of mothering*. Berkeley: University of California Press.

— 1992. Heterosexuality as a compromise formation: Reflections on the psychoanalytic theory of sexual development. *Psychoanalysis and Contemporary Thought* 15(3):267–302.

Clark, W. M., and J. M. Serovich. 1997. Twenty years and still in the dark? Content analysis of articles pertaining to gay, lesbian, and bisexual issues in marriage and family therapy journals. *Journal of Marital and Family Therapy* 23:239–253.

Collins, P. H. 1990. *Black feminist thought: Knowledge, consciousness, and the politics of empowerment*. New York: Routledge.

Collins, P. H. 1997. On West and Fenstermaker's "Doing difference." In M. R. Walsh, ed., *Women, men, and gender: Ongoing debates*, pp. 73–75. New Haven: Yale University Press.

Crawford, S. 1988. Lesbian families: Psychosocial stress and the family-building process. In Boston Lesbian Psychologies Collective, eds., *Lesbian psychologies: Explorations and challenges*, pp. 195–214. Urbana: University of Illinois Press.

de la Peña, T. 1994. Chicana, working class and proud: The case of the lopsided tortillas. In J. Penelope, ed., *Out of the class closet: Lesbians speak*, pp. 195–206. Freedom, Cal.: Crossing.

Dyche, L., and L. H. Zayas. 1995. The value of curiosity and naïveté for the cross cultural therapist. *Family Process* 34:389–399.

Eccles, J.S. 1989. Bringing young women to math and science. In M. Crawford and M. Gentry, eds., *Gender and thought*, pp. 36–58. New York: Springer-Verlag.

Eccles, J., and J. Jacobs. 1986. Social forces shape math participation. *Signs: Journal of Women in Culture and Society* 11:368–380.

Elise, D. 1986. Lesbian couples; the implication of sex differences in separation-individuation. *Psychotherapy* 23:305–310.

Espin, O. 1992. Cultural and historical influences on sexuality in Hispanic/Latin women: Implications for psychotherapy. In M. L. Anderson and P. H. Collins, eds., *Race, class, and gender: An anthology*, pp. 141–146. Belmont, Cal.: Wadsworth.

Faderman, L. 1991. *Odd girls and twilight lovers: A history of lesbian life in twentieth-century America*. New York: Columbia University Press.

Falco, K. L. 1991. *Psychotherapy with lesbian clients: Theory into practice*. New York: Brunner/Mazel.

Falicov, C. 1995. Training to think culturally: A multidimensional framework. *Family Process* 34:373–388.

Faludi, S. 1991. *Backlash: The undeclared war against American women*. New York: Crown.

Feinberg, L. 1993. *Stone butch blues*. Ithaca: Firebrand.

Flax, J. 1990. Postmodernism and gender relations in feminist theory. In L. J. Nicholson, ed., *Feminism/Postmodernism*, pp. 39–62. New York: Routledge.

Foucault, M. 1979. *The history of sexuality*. London: Allen Lane.

Gergen, K.J. 1991. *The saturated self: Dilemmas of identity in contemporary life*. New York: Basic.

Gilligan, C. 1982. *In a different voice: Psychological theory and women's development*. Cambridge: Harvard University Press.

Golden, C. 1987. Diversity and variability in women's sexual identities. In Boston Lesbian Psychologies Collective, eds., *Lesbian psychologies: Explorations and challenges*, pp. 19–34. Urbana: University of Illinois Press.

Goldner, V. 1988. Generation and gender: Normative and covert hierarchies. *Family Process* 27:17–31.

— 1991. Toward a critical relational theory of gender. *Psychoanalytic Dialogues* 1(3):249–272.

Goodrich, T. J., C. Rampage, B. Ellman, and K. Halstead. 1988. *Feminist family therapy: A casebook*. New York: Norton.

Green, R. 1987. *The "sissy boy syndrome" and the development of homosexuality*. New Haven: Yale University Press.

Green, R., J. B. Mandel, M. E. Hotvedt, J. Gray, and L. Smith. 1986. Lesbian mothers and their children: A comparison with solo heterosexual mothers and their children. *Archives of Sexual Behavior* 7:175–181.

Green, R-J., M. Bettinger, and E. Zacks. 1996. Are lesbian couples fused and gay male couples disengaged? Questioning gender straightjackets. In J. Laird and R-J. Green, eds., *Lesbians and gays in couples and families: A handbook for therapy*, pp. 185–230. San Francisco: Jossey-Bass.

Greene, B. 1994. Lesbian women of color: Triple jeopardy. In L. Comas-Diaz and B. Greene, eds., *Women of color: Integrating ethnic and gender identities in psychotherapy*, pp. 389–427. New York: Guilford.

Greene, B, and N. Boyd-Franklin. 1996. In J. Laird and R-J. Green, eds., *Lesbians and gays in couples and families: A handbook for therapy*, pp. 251–271. San Francisco: Jossey-Bass.

Hare-Mustin, R. 1994. Discourses in the mirrored room: A postmodern analysis of therapy. *Family Process* 33:19–35.

Hare-Mustin, R.T., and J. Marecek. 1990. Gender and the meaning of difference. In R. T. Mustin and J. Marecek, eds., *Making a difference: Psychology and the construction of gender*, pp. 22–64. New Haven: Yale University Press.

Hemmings, C. 1997. *Reading bodies: Transsexual and bisexual photographic representations*. Paper presented at the Stonewall Center Lunch Series, University of Massachusetts, January.

Hoffman, L. 1992. A reflexive stance for family therapy. In S. McNamee and K. J. Gergen, eds., *Therapy as social construction*, pp. 2–24. Newbury Park, Cal.: Sage.

Hooker, E. A. 1957. The adjustment of the overt male homosexual. *Journal of Projective Techniques* 21:17–31.

Hyde, J. S. 1981. How large are cognitive gender differences? *American Psychologist* 36:892–901.

Iasenza, S. 1995. Platonic pleasures and dangerous desires. In J. Glassgold and S. Iasenza, eds., *Lesbians and psychoanalysis: Revolutions in theory and practice*, pp. 345–373. New York: Free.

Jeffreys, S. 1993. *The lesbian heresy: A feminist perspective on the lesbian sexual revolution*. North Melbourne, Australia: Spinifex.

Jordan, J. 1986. *The meaning of mutuality*. Work in Progress no. 23. Wellesley, Mass.: Stone Center Working Paper Series.

Kennedy, E. L., and M. D. Davis. 1993. *Boots of leather, slippers of gold: The history of a lesbian community*. New York: Routledge.

Kessler, S. J., and W. McKenna. 1978. *Gender: An ethnomethodological approach*. Chicago: University of Chicago Press.

Kitzinger, C. 1995. Social constructionism: Implications for lesbian and gay psychology. In A. R. D'Augelli and C. J. Patterson, eds., *Lesbian, gay, and bisexual identities over the lifespan: Psychological perspectives*, pp. 136–161. New York: Oxford University Press.

Kitzinger, C., and S. Wilkinson. 1997. Transitions from heterosexuality to lesbianism: The discursive production of lesbian identities. In M. R. Walsh, ed., *Women, men, and gender: Ongoing debates*, pp. 188–203. New Haven: Yale University Press.

Kitzinger, C., S. Wilkinson, and R. Perkins. 1992. Theorizing heterosexuality. *Feminism and Psychology* 2(3):293–324.

Krestan, J.A., and C. S. Bepko. 1980. The problem of fusion in the lesbian relationship. *Family Process* 19:277–289.

Kurdek, L. 1995. Lesbian and gay couples. In A. R. D'Augelli and C. J. Patterson, eds., *Lesbian, gay, and bisexual identities over the lifespan*, pp. 243–261. New York: Oxford University Press.

Laird, J. 1989. Women and stories; Restorying women's self-constructions. In M. McGoldrick, C. Anderson, and F. Walsh, eds., *Women in families: A framework for family therapy*, pp. 427–450. New York: Norton.

— 1993. Lesbian and gay couples and families. In F. Walsh, ed., *Normal family processes*, pp. 282–328. 2d ed. New York: Guilford.

— 1994. Family therapist as anthropologist-constructivist. In E. Sherman and W. Reid, eds., *Qualitative research in social work*. New York: Columbia University Press.

— 1995. Family-centered practice in the postmodern era. *Families in Society: The Journal of Contemporary Human Services* 76(3):150–162.

— 1998. Theorizing culture: Narrative ideas and practice principles. In M. McGoldrick, ed., *Revisioning family therapy: Race, class, and gender in clinical practice*, pp. 20–36. New York: Guilford.

Levi-Strauss, C. 1963. *Structural anthropology*. New York: Basic.

Lindenbaum, J. P. 1984. The shattering of an illusion: The problem of competition in lesbian relationships. *Feminist Studies* 11(1):85–103.

Liu, P., and C. S. Chan. 1996. Lesbian, gay, and bisexual Asian Americans and their families. In J. Laird and R-J. Green, eds., *Lesbians and gays in couples and families: A handbook for therapists*, pp. 137–152. San Francisco: Jossey-Bass.

Lorde, A. 1984. Our difference is our strength. In A. Lorde, *Sister outsider*. Freedom, Cal.: Crossing.

Maccoby, E. E., and C. N. Jacklin. 1975. *The psychology of sex differences*. Stanford: Stanford University Press.

McGoldrick, M., C. M. Anderson, and F. Walsh, eds. 1989. *Women in families: A framework for family therapy*. New York: Norton.

Mencher, J. 1990. *Intimacy in lesbian relationships: A critical re-examination of fusion*. Working Paper Series no. 42. Wellesley, Mass.: Stone Center for Women's Development.

Miller, J. B. 1976. *Toward a new psychology of women*. Boston: Beacon.

Minuchin, S. 1991. The seductions of constructivism. *Family Therapy Networker* 15(5):47–50.

Moraga, C. 1983. *Loving in the war years*. Boston: South End.

Nichols, M. 1987. Lesbian sexuality: Issues and developing theory. In Boston Lesbian Psychologies Collective, eds., *Lesbian psychologies: Explorations and challenges*, pp. 97–125. Urbana: University of Illinois Press.

Nicholson, L. 1994. Interpreting gender. *Signs: Journal of Women in Culture and Society* 20:79–105.

Osman, S. 1972. My stepfather is a she. *Family Process* 11:209–218.

Patterson, C. J. 1992. Children of lesbian and gay parents. *Child Development* 63:1025–1043.

Patterson, C. J. 1994. Children of the lesbian baby boom: Behavioral adjustment, self-concepts, and sex role identity. In B. Greene and G. M. Herek, eds., *Lesbian and gay psychology: Theory, research, and clinical applications*, pp. 156–175. Newbury Park, Cal.: Sage.

Patterson, C. J. 1996. Lesbian mothers and their children: Findings from the Bay Area Families Study. In J. Laird and R-J. Green, eds., *Lesbians and gays in couples and families: A handbook for therapists*, pp. 420–437. San Francisco: Jossey-Bass.

Roth, S. 1989. Psychotherapy with lesbian couples; Individual issues, female socialization, and the social context. In M. McGoldrick, C. Anderson, and F. Walsh, eds., *Women in families: A framework for family therapy*, pp. 286–307. New York: Norton.

Rust, P. C. 1995. *Bisexuality and the challenge to lesbian politics: Sex, loyalty, and revolution*. New York: New York University Press.

Shapiro, V. 1996. Subjugated knowledge and the working alliance: The narratives of Russian Jewish immigrants. *In Session: Psychotherapy in Practice* 1(4):9–22.

Slater, S. 1995. *The lesbian family life cycle.* New York: Free.

Spelman, E. V. 1988. *Inessential woman: Problems of exclusion in feminist thought.* Boston: Beacon.

Surrey, J. 1985. *Self-in-relation: A theory of women's development.* Work in Progress no. 13. Wellesley, Mass.: Stone Center Working Papers Series.

Tiefer, L. 1995. *Sex is not a natural act and other essays.* Boulder: Westview.

Waldegrave, C. 1990. Social justice and family therapy. *Dulwich Centre Newsletter,* pp. 5–47.

Weingarten, K. 1995. Radical listening: Challenging cultural beliefs for and about mothers. *Journal of Feminist Family Therapy* 7(1/2):7–22.

Weston, K. 1996). *Render me, gender me: Lesbians talk sex, class, color, nations, studmuffins,* pp. 45–86. New York: Columbia University Press.

White, M. 1989. Deconstruction and therapy. In D. Epston and M. White, *Experience, contradiction, narrative and imagination: Selected papers of David Epston and Michael White, 1989–1991,* pp. 109–151. Adelaide, S. Australia: Dulwich Centre.

White, M. 1994. *The politics of therapy: Putting to rest the illusion of neutrality.* Mimeo. Adelaide, South Australia: Dulwich Family Centre.

White, M., and Epston, D. 1990. *Narrative means to therapeutic ends.* New York: Norton.

CHAPTER FOUR

The Long Road to Equality:
Lesbians and Social Policy

Ann Hartman

In 1992 in Houston, I talked about the cultural war going on for the soul of America. And that war is still going on. We can not worship the false God of gay rights.

—Pat Buchanan

THUS SPOKE PAT BUCHANAN, with some accuracy. There is a cultural war going on in America, a war that deeply divides our nation on issues that have fundamental moral meanings and implications. This cultural war is being fought in the courts, polling booths, press, state and federal legislatures, and, tragically, in violent confrontations in the streets. Many issues are at stake in this cultural war: gun control, the distribution of resources, and the survival of the welfare state. But perhaps the issues that generate the most passion—the most conflict—are those that concern the family and who will have control over its definition. Controversies over reproductive rights and homosexual marriage and parenting lie at the heart of what has come to be called the "family values" debate.

Lesbians and gay men are currently very much in the center of this cultural war as their rights, their entitlements, and even their bodily protection are hotly debated in the enactment of procedures, laws, policies and in public discussion. For the dominant moral and cultural views of the nation are not limited to opinion and discussion but are translated into social policies and procedures that define the relationship between the state and the individual as well as between people and their social and economic worlds. These policies shape people's lives in hundreds of ways. They determine, to a large extent, the nature of the political, social, and economic context of daily life. It is, thus, essential for clinicians to be knowledgeable about this context and to be sensitive to the meanings of these policies and procedures in the lives of their clients.

What is social policy and where does it reside? Social policy is a part of what one might broadly term public policy. Public policy consists of that body of laws, regulations, statutes, executive orders, and programs that emanate from the various branches and levels of government. It includes economic, military, social, and myriad other areas of policy about which the government takes collective action. The sources of public policy are many and include the Constitution, the Supreme Court, as well as the other federal, state, and local courts, the various lawmaking bodies on every level, and the executive and administrative offices of federal, state, and local governments. Public policy intentions and values are not only expressed in legislative enactments but also through the extent to and manner in which laws and regulations are actually implemented.

Social policies, which are a part of public policies, are those that pertain to the ordering of social relations, including the protection of civil rights, the distribution of social benefits, and the meeting of social need. Clearly, all areas of governmental action have some direct or indirect impact on social well-being, social structures, and the quality of life, but some are more specifically focused on social issues.

Social policy also goes beyond enactments at the various levels of government to include procedures and policies established in the private sector by businesses, educational institutions, and other private associations, policies that have crucial implications and may or may not be monitored and shaped by governmental force. The government's role vis-à-vis the private sector is to prohibit discriminatory actions and to protect the constitutional rights of individuals and groups. For example, civil rights, affirmative action, fair employment legislation, as well as antidiscrimination legislation establish how nongovernmental organizations may operate in some social realms and give those who have experienced injustice recourse through the courts.

Social polices reflect the dominant values and preferred "truths" of a society, particularly of those in power. The enactment of law and policy, however, may also change such truths and eventually alter values. For example, in the 1954 landmark *Brown v. the Board of Education* case, the Supreme Court repudiated the notion that "separate" could be "equal." This defining decision not only began to change behavior, it also came to establish new truths and eventually to alter many people's fundamental values. Thus such enactments not only reflect but also create dominant and preferred truths.

Social policies, laws, and procedures can also be defining of individual and group identity. As powerful statements about individuals or groups, they mirror society's attitudes—whether members of the group are valued or devalued, elevated or oppressed, supported or marginalized. These attitudes, so powerfully translated into our society's structure, shape people's sense of themselves.

Currently, when gay men and lesbians look into the mirror of public policy they see an enormously confusing and contradictory picture. This nation is going through a period of rapid social change, even a social revolution, in terms of attitudes about and policies directed at gay men and lesbians, with the result that gay people occupy what might be called a liminal position, betwixt and between acceptance and continued rejection. Twenty-five years ago heterosexism and homophobia were so rampant and so consistent that, as difficult as the situation was, gay men and lesbians knew where they stood, could not miss the messages, and conducted themselves accordingly. Today, lesbians and gay men are no longer so widely and totally silenced, despised, or as likely to be diagnosed as mentally ill, but, nevertheless, widespread acceptance, protection, and equality are yet to be attained. Private attitudes change more slowly and thus it is difficult to take an accurate reading of the situation. This leaves gay men and lesbians without clear guidelines concerning their social and legal position and often uncertain in terms of what they may do or say without reprisal. It is often not clear whether they will be protected or suddenly face discrimination or even punitive action.

In this chapter the current status of the social policy context as it relates to lesbians will be explored. This exploration, however, will be difficult, quickly outdated, and incomplete, as such a task is rather like attempting to take aim at a rapidly moving target. For example, twenty-five years ago the notion that the partners of gay and lesbian employees should be eligible for benefits would have been unthinkable. As of today, following the lead of such pioneers as Levi Strauss and Stanford University, over five hundred major businesses, universities, and governmental agencies are offering domestic partner benefits, and new firms are constantly being added to that roster, a recent notable addition being IBM.

The struggle for the soul of America and for the conscience of the nation has put civil rights and protections and even recognition and equal treatment of gays and lesbians in the center of public attention. What are the implications of this struggle? First, I look briefly at the major areas where social policy and the lives of lesbians intersect and attempt a status report on these central areas. It must be remembered that many of these policies and enactments concerning the rights, protections, and entitlements of gays and lesbians exist on state and local levels and there is enormous variation in terms of what policies exist and how they are implemented. Therapists working with lesbian clients must not only be able to identify these intersections but must also be aware of the situation in their particular state and locality.

I then examine some of the major precedent-setting cases that have begun the process of reshaping social policy on the long and obstacle-laden path toward equality for gays and lesbians. I also explore some of the small but telling local actions that communicate community attitudes and how precarious the position of a lesbian may be. The persistence and courage of the complainants who go through years of litigation as stand-ins for their fellows are both astounding and admirable.

I then examine in some detail the current issue that is capturing national attention, namely, same-sex marriage. Unthinkable twenty years ago and now on the verge of becoming a reality in one of our fifty states, this possibility is creating panic and backlash in many quarters, an anticipatory legislative response on the federal level and in many states, and ambivalence in the lesbian and gay community. This examination will exemplify the policy issues and the cultural struggle, demonstrating the complex and interminable legal struggles, the expression and shaping of public attitudes, and the ever present danger of intensified backlash.

Civil Rights: Sparkling Moments and Dark Days

The Equal Protection Clause of the Fourteenth Amendment of the U.S. Constitution requires that states afford equal protection of the laws to all residents. Also, the Supreme Court interprets the Due Process Clause of the Fifth Amendment to impose the same requirement on the federal government. But what does this mean? Like all provisions of the Constitution, this commitment acquires meaning through cases decided by the courts. Thus, to discover what equal protection under the law actually means to lesbians and gays, we must turn to court cases explicitly addressing this theme.

On May 20, 1996, the Supreme Court struck down Proposition 2, the amendment to the Colorado state constitution that had been passed in that state by a 53 percent to 47 percent margin. This amendment had nullified existing civil rights protections for homosexuals and also forbade the passage of any new antidiscrimination laws. By a six to three majority vote, the forceful opinion stated that "a state cannot deem a class of persons as strangers to its laws" (Excerpts 1996). The opinion of the court was that this amendment so singled out one group in violation of the Constitution's guarantee of equal protection under the law and was so foreign to American traditions that it was only explicable on the basis of animus.

This momentous decision, this sparkling judicial moment, effectively ended what had become a nationwide effort on the part of the political right to establish similar legislative constraints in other states and municipalities. The Court's decision and the minority opinion are instructive in understanding the civil rights struggle. Judge Scalia, writing for the minority, accused his colleagues of taking sides in "the cultural wars" and of making a political—not a judicial—decision. Referring to *Bowers v. Hardwick* (1986), he wrote, "If it is constitutionally permissible for a state to make homosexual conduct criminal, surely it is constitutionally permissible for a state to pass other laws merely disfavoring homosexual conduct." Referring to the fact that Colorado was one of the first states to repeal its sodomy laws, he continued, "But a society that eliminates criminal punishment for homosexual acts does not necessarily abandon the view that homosexuality is morally wrong and socially harmful" (Greenhouse 1966).

Finally, he argued that the Colorado constitutional amendment had been put in place by the most democratic of procedures. Justice Scalia seems to have forgotten that it is the responsibility of the Court and the spirit of the Constitution to protect people, when necessary, from the will of the majority if that will violates the rights of some portion of that population. In this democracy, in the final analysis, such tyranny by the majority is limited by the Constitution and particularly by the Bill of Rights. It is the courts and ultimately the Supreme Court to which oppressed minorities must turn for protection from such tyranny. Sometimes the Court stands against the majority, moving beyond the constraints of assumed truths and dominant notions, and creates major change in our society as it did in the case of *Brown v. the Board of Education*. At other times the courts protect the status quo, responding to the dominant discourse, and interpret the Constitution in such a way that the minority is not protected, as, for example, with the stunning defeat for gay rights of the famous 1986 *Bowers v. Hardwick* case, in which the criminalization of sodomy was upheld. The Court determined that the right to privacy that had been vigorously protected by the Court in other cases did not extend to individuals in same-sex sexual relationships.

To return to the Colorado case, as momentous as this decision was, it is important to stress that it does not protect gays and lesbians from discrimination. It is still legal in forty states to discriminate on the basis of sexual orientation. It simply made it clear *that it is unconstitutional to pass a law or ordinance forbidding the passage of laws that protect homosexuals from discrimination* .

The key issue in antidiscrimination judgments is whether or not a population has been determined to be a "suspect class." When an identified group is a suspect class, any action that might be considered to discriminate against or limit the rights of that group is subject to *heightened scrutiny*. In other words, in such a situation discrimination is *suspected*, and *important and compelling* governmental interests must be identified or the enactment or law will be found to be in violation of the Constitution, particularly in violation of the principle of equal treatment under the law. A suspect class must meet three criteria: subjection to a long history of persecution for irrational reasons, inability to obtain redress from nonjudicial branches of government, and immutability of the trait that characterizes that class, making it impossible or highly unlikely for members to escape from the class. Race, for example, is a suspect classification, and thus any action that uses race as a basis for treating members of a particular racial group differently than others is presumed to be invidious and constitutionally prohibited. Several efforts to establish sexual orientation as a suspect classification have not been successful on the basis of failure to meet the third requirement: immutability. Obviously the support in some quarters of the view that homosexuality is biologically or genetically determined has important political implications in considering the suspect class issue.

In regard to judicial opinion in this area, another sparkling judicial moment occurred when Judge Spiegel, in finding the Cincinnati, Ohio, version of Colorado Proposition 2 unconstitutional long before the Supreme Court acted, handled the suspect class issue by stating that homosexuals were a "quasi-suspect class" (Logue 1994). Avoiding the issue around biological determinism, he held that "sexual orientation is set in place at a very early age and is involuntary and unamenable to change. It is a deeply rooted complex of factors including predisposition toward affiliation or bonding with the opposite and/or same sex. It is distinct from conduct" (29). On the basis of having determined sexual orientation to be a quasi-suspect classification, Judge Spiegel held that sexual orientation is rarely an appropriate basis for unequal legal treatment. Spiegel concluded that the Cincinnati proposition "does not demonstrate a devotion to democracy . . . but rather makes a mockery of it" (29).

The long road to the affirmation of the civil rights of lesbians and gays for the most part lies ahead, although some progress has been made. Sanctioned by the *Bowers v. Hardwick* decision, twenty states continue to have antisodomy statutes in place, and, as long as the cultural climate in a state supports the criminalization of homosexuality, it is unlikely that such states will move to protect the civil rights of a "criminal" population. But there was another very brief sparkling moment, as when, on May 16, 1997, in a moving ceremony complete with tears of joy and carnations, Maine's governor, Angus King, signed a bill that inserted only two words—sexual orientation—into the state's antidiscrimination law, thus making Maine the tenth state to enact such legislation. Said King, "We're talking about your friends and your relatives—whether you know it or not. People who want to live and work, love and play just like everyone else" (Perry 1997). A small group of legislators and advocates had been working to achieve the inclusion of lesbians and gays in the antidiscrimination law since 1976 when the bill was first introduced and defeated 85 to 54 in the house and 21 to 10 in the Senate. In this long effort the bill was finally passed in 1993, only to be vetoed by then Governor McKernan. The measure, which prohibits discrimination in employment, housing, loans, and public accommodation, however, was still in jeopardy as the cultural war continued. Two Maine groups, the Christian Civic League and the Christian Coalition of Maine, brought the issue before the voters in a referendum in 1997 and won repeal of the enactment. After twenty years, it still "ain't over 'till its over!" One can easily see how difficult it is to end discrimination on a state-by-state basis. However, efforts to include sexual orientation in federal civil rights legislation have consistently failed. Because the inclusion of sexual orientation in broader civil rights legislation on a federal level appeared to be impossible, strategists narrowed the focus to discrimination against gays and lesbians in employment but even that has gone down to defeat.

The World of Work

The changing and uncertain position of gays and lesbians in our society is also exemplified in the world of work. There is no place where a person is more vulnerable than on the job and, despite gains, that vulnerability is still very present for many gays and lesbians.

On the positive side, the move to offer domestic partner benefits, a radical experiment a short time ago, is now widespread and rapidly growing. Currently, as mentioned earlier, approximately five hundred companies have begun to offer domestic partner employee benefits, in addition to many colleges, universities, states, and municipalities. The decision by the Episcopalian General Convention to offer benefits to domestic partners of clergy and other employees provides a recent example (Episcopalians 1997).

The fight for domestic benefits has represented a social policy victory for gay activists, but very few employees have been taking advantage of these programs. Although it was anticipated that 3 to 4 percent of the workforce would make use of this option, less than 1 percent have actually participated in those institutions offering benefits. For example, at Xerox only two hundred out of forty-seven thousand employees have elected to do so.

In some cases, of course, both partners are covered through their employment and they are unneeded. There are, however, other deterrents. One is cost. Not only are some plans very costly to the employee but also the benefits received by an unmarried partner are considered a taxable compensation by the IRS, and the employed partner must pay taxes on those benefits, which raises the cost considerably. Married heterosexual couples do not endure this tax burden.

Finally, many gays and lesbians do not claim domestic partner benefits because of fear of discrimination should their sexual orientation become known. Not only is there a fear of subtle discrimination but, in forty states, an employee can be fired in the private sector simply on the basis of sexual orientation. For many gay and lesbian employees the availability of domestic partner benefits, although rarely used, does provide a safety net should a partner become unemployed, and many say that although they are not currently using the option its existence would be an important consideration in seeking or accepting a new job.

Domestic partner benefits, although an important step in the long struggle for fair treatment in the workplace—in this case, equal pay for equal work—will not be widely used until lesbians and gays are protected from job discrimination. At this point only ten states have passed legislation banning employment discrimination on the basis of sexual orientation. Interestingly, these laws are rarely called into action. Again, observers speculate that coming out publicly to pursue a discrimination case is too dangerous or threatening a prospect. Nonetheless, it is likely that the existence of the laws in the ten states, the publicity surrounding the enactment, and the calls for voluntary compliance have deterred employers from acting on the basis of discrimination. Not surprisingly, the states that have enacted antidiscrimination legislation are those that in general have a progressive record in this area. They include all of the New England states except New

Hampshire, the progressive north midwest states of Wisconsin and Minnesota, and the western states of California and Hawaii.

Again, although a step in the right direction, progress in fighting discrimination in the workplace has been characterized by halting steps forward accompanied by half-steps backward. In some states complaints are heard by a separate commission, not one dealing with other discrimination cases. Lack of understanding or conviction on the part of those reviewing the cases undermines the usefulness of the law, and training for those investigating the complaints is minimal. Also, few states keep statistics that show outcome. In Vermont, which does keep such figures, of the seventeen cases filed, nine were dismissed or closed, seven remain open, and only one situation resulted in payment to the complainant.

Of all the initiatives on the lesbian and gay rights agenda, perhaps the most crucial is job protection. Efforts are ongoing to extend national antidiscrimination laws to include sexual orientation. In September 1996 the Senate, to everyone's surprise, came within one vote of approving the Employment Non-discrimination Act (Schmitt 1996). Gay activists had backed off from any more general and broad-based civil rights legislation, as they were sure such legislation was doomed to defeat. The more limited focus on the right to work, they felt, held more promise of success. The timing for the vote was a brilliant strategy; it was taken on the same day that the Senate overwhelmingly passed the Defense of Marriage Act (which will be discussed later). Many who had voted for this antigay measure wanted to assure their constituencies that they were fair-minded and took the opposite position on discrimination against gays and lesbians in the workplace.

The Employment Non-discrimination Act is being reintroduced in the House and the Senate although gay advocates and political observers agree that chances for passage are fairly slim. Interestingly, most polls show that a majority of the American public think that gays and lesbians' right to work should be protected. It seems that, on balance, the American work ethic outweighs homophobia. Public support, however, weakens when the jobs under consideration demand close human contact, as in the case of school teachers, demonstrating the public's complex attitudes. The credo seems to be, "Homosexuals ought to be allowed to work, but not around children." This abiding suspicion and distrust allows conservative lawmakers to use the threat of gays and lesbians in the most sensitive jobs to defeat any effort to protect gay men and lesbians from employment discrimination.

Although laws against discrimination in the workplace on the basis of sexual orientation have been defeated on the federal level and exist in only ten states, in some situations and in a somewhat limited way gays and lesbians hired by governmental bodies have some protection, at least from being fired without cause.

As early as 1968 a federal court held, in *Norton v. Macy*, that due process requires, before the Civil Service fires or refuses to hire on the grounds of sexual orientation, an employer to establish a rational relationship between the person's sexual orientation and the efficacy of government operation. Norton won his case on the basis that no rational relationship existed, because "he did not flaunt or carelessly display his unorthodox sexuality in public." This decision, of course, holds open the possibility that if a person "flaunts" or "carelessly displays," he or she may be dismissed. The roots of "Don't ask, don't tell" can be found in this decision. In a subsequent case (*Singer v. U.S. Civil Service Commission* 1977) the court seized on the distinction between private homosexual activity and public homosexual expression. The Court found against Singer because he openly and publicly "flaunted" his activities while identifying himself as a member of a federal agency, thus bringing discredit upon the government and impeding the efficiency of service. In yet another case (*U.S. Customs Service v. National Treasury Union* 1982) a customs official was reinstated because his homosexuality "did not manifest itself in any way . . . that would reflect unfavorably on Customs." By 1977 "Don't ask, don't tell" had become firmly established in governmental policy.

The situation of gays and lesbians in the military demonstrates most dramatically the ambivalence, inconsistency, and homophobia that exists, perhaps less obviously, in most workplaces. The "Don't ask don't tell" policy established in the military early in the Clinton administration takes the position that authorities must not inquire about or otherwise investigate the sexual orientation of a member of the armed forces and that a member may not in any way identify himself or herself as a homosexual. That policy is a metaphor for the confusion, inconsistency, and punitiveness of American public policy toward gays and lesbians. It also legislates what has long been an onerous burden of gays and lesbians: secrecy, pretense, and silence. First, the policy may well express what many Americans feel: "I can tolerate homosexuality as long as I don't see it, have direct experience of it, or know about it." This oppressive policy makes secretiveness and dishonesty a necessity for gays and lesbians in the military, makes them invisible, and communicates to them their unacceptability. The irrational nature of the policy is also obvious, as defenders say that it would make personnel uncomfortable living in such close quarters with *known* homosexuals. Does it make people more comfortable to *not know* which of the comrades they are showering with is gay? A magical and childlike but also highly discriminatory notion is built into the "Don't ask, don't tell" policy.

As limited as the policy is, after three years in place it is clearly violated with frequency, as the number of gays and lesbians forced out of the military is rising. In 1996, according to the annual report of the Service Members Legal Defense Network, 850 people were discharged, the largest number and the highest rate of discharge since 1986. Further, although women make up only 13.1 percent of the armed forces, they account for 29 percent of those discharged for homosexuality or for violating the "Don't ask, don't tell" rule. Reports of investigations, threats, and interrogations continue to surface and the situation is getting worse. The SLDN has documented 443 specific violations of the military's policy in 1996, 80 more than in 1995 (Moss 1997). Perhaps the most outrageous violation has been the pursuit and identification of highly regarded career navy man Timothy McVeigh through his personal e-mail correspondence. The courts have reinstated McVeigh, but this does not undo what must have been for him a heart-wrenching and life-altering experience.

The continued pain and threat for homosexuals in the armed forces and the cost of homophobia to individuals and to our nation was brought home most tragically in the recent suicide of a Navy pilot who was facing an investigation concerning homosexual behavior and flew his plane into a Colorado mountainside.

Educational and Religious Institutions

The policies established by the major institutions in our society play a central role in constructing and expressing the moral positions and values that in turn have a powerful effect on society as a whole and upon those who are a part of or are subject to the policies of those institutions. One of the most important and formative of social institutions is the schools.

The positions taken and the value climate of the schools are crucially important in shaping the attitudes and beliefs of the young. This climate, be it supportive, tolerant, or hostile to homosexuality, has an enormous impact on gay and lesbian youth, who must spend a good part of each day in the school situation. Gay and lesbian students report high rates of harassment, rejection, even violence, and drop out rates are high; A recent study found that 97 percent of the gay youth interviewed experienced negative attitudes from classmates and over half feared harassment (Sears 1991).

A widely publicized recent case has already begun to make a difference as school administrators have been served notice that they can be held liable if they do not offer the same protection to abused and harassed gay and lesbian youth that they do to others. Jamie Nabozny suffered violence, harassment, and vicious abuse throughout his high school career in Ashland, Wisconsin. On one occasion he was beaten so severely that he had to be hospitalized. He and his parents approached school administrators asking for help on many occasions, but their pleas were ignored and they were even met with antigay comments. Finally, Jamie and his family, with great courage, sued for damages on the basis that the school leadership had not offered the same protection to Jamie as they would in other situations of harassment and abuse. Typical of the long and torturous road such cases tend to travel, the Federal Court first responded by throwing the case out. On appeal, however, a precedent-setting appellate court spelled out the constitutional obligation of schools as public institutions to treat the abuse of gay and lesbian students as seriously as they would the abuse of any student. The appellate court returned the case to the Federal Court for trial, where a jury unanimously found in favor of Jamie and a settlement was reached of close to $1,000,000 (Logue 1997; Logue and Buckel 1996).

This has been a particularly important case in terms of the issue of protection for gay and lesbian youth. The fact that it was the first such case to come to trial and the size of the settlement meant that the case was widely publicized. Publicity for such cases is obviously vital to change efforts, as groundbreaking legal decisions can begin to alter behavior and even attitudes. Across the nation school administrators got the message that the abuse and harassment of gay and lesbian students can be costly indeed to them personally and to their institutions. Gay advocacy groups are being deluged by requests from school personnel for information and help in dealing with situations of harassment. In fact LAMBDA, who tried the case, has prepared a follow-up publication offering guidance and information to schools and parents (*Stopping* 1996).

Violence and harassment are among the many issues that schools must face. Supreme Court decisions have emphasized two roles for the educational system. First, the schools must provide a forum for free speech by teachers and students. Some years ago the Court took the position that "it can hardly be argued that either students or teachers shed their constitutional rights to freedom of speech or expression at the schoolhouse gate" (*Tinker v. Des Moines Independent School District* 1969).

Second, the court has found the school to be a tool for the inculcation of the norms and duties imposed by society (*Ambach v. Norwick* 1979). Clearly, these two goals are often in conflict; one of the primary purposes of the protection of free speech is to make it possible for dissenters to speak against commonly held norms and beliefs. Public schools must weigh these two conflicting interests, as must the courts when these conflicts come to adjudication. The second goal, the inculcation of societal norms, creates in the schools a unique setting in which greater restriction of First Amendment rights is permissible than in other public institutions. The key issue, of course, is the determination of what those societal norms are and who defines them. The decades since the Stonewall uprising have witnessed some groundbreaking cases in which the societal norms and the protection of First Amendment rights have met head to head.

In the seventies college campuses became a major arena for the struggle over the rights of gay and lesbian students to express themselves, to assemble, and, finally, to gain financial support from their parent institutions commensurate with that received by other student groups. An early dramatic and precedent setting case, *Gay Students Organization of the University of New Hampshire v. Bonner* (1974) established that gay student organizations may not be denied resources or treated in any way differently from other organizations. Gay students at the University of New Hampshire organized in 1973 and shortly thereafter held a dance that took place without incident, but was immediately followed by an objection from the then governor, who complained to the university about the propriety of "allowing such a spectacle."

The GSO then produced a play and published a newsletter, "The Fag Rag," which was distributed at the performance. Following the play, the governor, who seems to have forgotten New Hampshire's famous state motto, "Live free or die," wrote the university trustees and then president Bonner threatening to cut off all funds unless they took positive action to rid the campus of "indecency and moral filth" and "socially abhorrent behavior." Bonner acted in accordance with the governor's instructions and was promptly sued by the GSO.

The students were victorious and the court stated that "the University, acting here as the instrumentality of the state, may not restrict speech or association simply because it finds the views expressed by any group abhorrent" (*Gay Students v. Bonner* 1974). Subsequent cases have leaned on this precedent.

The courts in general have been supportive of the rights of college students, and gay and lesbian student organizations have flourished on campuses across the country. However, they have rather consistently used an interesting and limited justification for their protective stance, that is, in each case, the student's expression or association has been defined as having a political function or purpose. The courts have failed to acknowledge that nonpolitical private speech and association must be protected under the First Amendment. This crucial issue speaks to continued reliance on "Don't ask, don't tell" in all of its forms.

Even in the famous early case of *Frick v. Lynch* (1980), when Frick won the right to take another male student as his date to a high school prom, the justification for the decision rested on the view that because Frick had a history of being politically active, taking a same-sex date to the prom was a political and not simply a private act, that is, an act expressing a political position.

In maintaining a balance between the protection of First Amendment rights and the inculcation of community norms, the courts have tended to be more willing to limit freedom of expression in secondary and primary schools. The courts have taken the position, one that lies deep in American tradition, that it is the right and the responsibility of local school boards and school administrators to determine the content of curriculum. Recently the notion of "curriculum" has been extended to mean anything sponsored by the schools (*Hazelwood School District v. Kuhlmeier* 1988), which vastly broadens the control of school boards and administrators. Further, whereas the school's ability to censor was once based on a demonstration that student expression would disrupt the learning process (*Tinker v. DeMoines Independent Community School District* 1969), seventeen years later the court redefined the justification for limiting students' expression to "inappropriateness," leaving school authorities able to define any references to sexual orientation "inappropriate."

The control of school curricula is obviously central in the socialization of young people. The Rainbow Curriculum, a brave effort by Queens, New York schools to present a picture of diverse families, including gay and lesbian families, went down to defeat. Recently, an interesting situation in Amherst, Massachusetts, illustrated this struggle. Local artists prepared for exhibit a collection of photographs of gay and lesbian families, entitled "Love Makes a Family." The elementary schools in Amherst planned to hang the exhibit, which served to be a challenge in the conflict between free speech and the inculcation of societal norms. A small group of Amherst parents brought suit against the schools to force them to cancel the exhibit. There followed a communitywide controversy around giving children an opportunity to see the pictures. Ultimately, the court decided, in this progressive college town, that the photographic exhibit could be shown, which may have been an accurate representation of the norms and values of Amherst. A court attending to community norms in another community could well have made make a different decision. In another stuggle in the cultural wars, the school board in Merrimack, New Hampshire, passed a policy prohibiting any positive, or even neutral, discussion of gay or lesbian issues in school, even in private sessions between counselors and students (GLAD fights censorship 1996). Gay advocates, the ACLU, and the National Education Association joined forces against the school district and won. This victory not only removed the policy but contributed to the election of a new school board.

As heartening as such progress is, the power implicit in the control of the schools has not been lost on the radical right. Following the Supreme Court's declaration that Colorado's Proposition 2 was unconstitutional, many of the rightist groups have shifted their agenda to gaining control of local school boards and committees with considerable success. With lack of interest and low turnout in school elections, a small well-organized group can easily gain control of school policy and shape curricula. A major agenda item is the exclusion and repudiation of any material that acknowledges or expresses acceptance or toleration of homosexuality and the espousal of family values, as defined by this group.

The courts have been less ready to support the First Amendment rights of teachers than students in the school system. This, of course, has relevance for lesbians' experience in the workforce but also for the educational climate established in the schools. Teachers have been dismissed for making "unauthorized comments" in the classroom and for the private declaration of homosexual orientation. The role of the teacher in primary and secondary schools in promoting societal norms has placed considerable restraint on their First Amendment rights. The vulnerability of teachers, even in a progressive community in a state that has enacted legislation to protect gays and lesbians from discrimination, was demonstrated recently when a "star" teacher in the Brookline, Massachusetts, schools came out to her ninth-grade social studies class and was immediately threatened with a lawsuit from a student's family on the student's behalf, claiming severe emotional distress and seeking over $300,000 in damages.

In *Gaylord v. Tacoma School District* (1988) the State of Washington Supreme Court upheld the dismissal of a teacher "for immorality based on his status as a known homosexual." The court emphasized the importance of teachers as role models and stated that the presence of gay or lesbian teachers might be interpreted as expressing approval or encouraging imitation. Of course, it doesn't occur to the court that gay and lesbian young people also require role models and that perhaps all children could benefit from the modeling of diversity and respect for difference. If the radical right's school control campaign is successful, we will see an even more hostile environment for gay and lesbian teachers and students and more support for vicious heterosexism, so destructive for gay and lesbian youth.

Therapists working with lesbian young people must be aware of the climate within which they must survive as well as of school governing policies, policies that reflect and re-create the dominant discourse. These are policies that often offer youth few options and reinforce negative images of themselves.

Another institution that touches the lives of people in crucial ways is organized religion. Perhaps no institution has struggled more or been more divided on the subject of homosexuality. While some religious groups have led the fight to continue the oppression of gays and lesbians, other religious groups have taken leadership in the struggle for liberation. As value-based cultural institutions, the churches and synagogues are in the center of the battle for the soul of Americans. Lesbians and gay men for whom connection with religion has important meaning are drawn into this struggle and may be either supported or condemned by their own religious group.

Some religious institutions are very clear on their total condemnation of homosexuality and the justification of sanctions and punitive responses. Others, attempting to draw a fine line, take the position that homosexuals should not be denied civil rights at the same time they maintain a view that homosexuality is a "disordered condition." Still others are struggling with how far the door should be open to active participation and leadership by gays and lesbians, even to the ordination of ministers and rabbis, a controversial issue demanding considerable attention from Protestant and Jewish groups across the country. Religious organizations are coming down on both sides of the question. The Evangelical Lutheran Church of America recently expelled two small churches in San Francisco that had hired homosexual pastors. In April 1996 the United Methodist Church's legislative body voted to retain the position that homosexual practice is incompatible with Christian teaching.

In May 1966 the Episcopal Church took a different position, in a widely publicized decision. The Episcopal Church Court met to rule on two charges brought against Bishop Righter: heresy for having signed a statement that he approved the ordination of noncelibate homosexual priests and violation of his ordination vows for having ordained a homosexual deacon. Seven of the eight bishops serving on the court ruled that the bishop did not violate the Church's core doctrines. Although not specifically announcing an overarching policy on the matter, this decision left the way open for bishops to ordain gay men and lesbians should they wish to do so (Niebuhr 1996). It is felt that this groundbreaking decision will have major repercussions throughout Protestant churches.

Although attracting little publicity and less well known, many Christian and Jewish clergy are reaching out to gay and lesbian parishioners, not only attempting to meet their spiritual needs but joining with them in advocacy efforts. Clergy quietly officiate at commitment ceremonies and other important rituals and invite gays and lesbians to actively participate in services, recognizing and validating them before the entire congregation. In some major urban areas there are churches and synagogues primarily led by and focused on the spiritual needs of gays and lesbians. These activities are not without risk. For example, the Congregational Church of Patchogue, New York, dismissed their minister, Rev. Renwick Jackson, for performing a commitment ceremony for a lesbian couple in a church in another community (McQuiston 1995).

In the past decade there has been a growing effort on the part of some therapists to be more aware of and sensitive to the spiritual lives of clients. Yet many therapists still tend to avoid the topic of religion and spirituality with clients in general. But with so much conflict and confusion on the part of churches over the subject of homosexuality, and with the common assumption that religion is generally antihomosexual, therapists are probably even more likely to avoid this topic with gay and lesbian clients. To do so, however, is to ignore an important dimension in many clients' lives, one that need not always be a source of pain and rejection but that has the potential for offering support, validation, and important spiritual, social, and cultural resources.

Lesbian Families

Perhaps no area of social policy affects people more deeply and sometimes more painfully than policies governing intimate relations. This is the area in which the state more intrusively enters the personal lives of the citizenry. Social policies define the family and determine family rights, responsibilities, and entitlements. Policies determine parental rights, settle custody disputes, property rights, and even follow couples to the grave, determining whether people can be buried together. I have dealt in more depth elsewhere with social policy as it affects gay and lesbian families (Hartman 1996) but will summarize some of the major issues here.

As in every other area, policies concerning the family are rapidly changing, fought out on a case-by-case basis across the country with varied outcomes. Location, as with most issues in this cultural war, makes an enormous difference. With our federal system, policies and the outcome of cases in New York, Massachusetts, Minnesota, or Hawaii will be quite different than in some of the other states. Only when the federal government intervenes, through legislation or Supreme Court action, is a national standard established.

The definition of family occupies the center of the social policy debate and is imbedded in much of the legal framework of this society. The term appears 2,086 times in the United States Code, 2,140 times in New York laws, and 4,149 in California enactments (Robson 1994). If an intimate human group is not defined as family, it is excluded from the rights, benefits, protections, and entitlements encoded in these enactments.

Lesbians and gay men have advocated for the inclusion of same-sex couples in the definition of the family. There has been some progress in using this strategy, beginning with the 1989 precedent-setting *Braschi v. Stahl* case, in which the judge presiding over New York State's highest court stated that the government's proper definition of "family" should not "rest on fictitious legal distinctions or genetic history, but instead should find its foundation in the reality of family life." The opinion in this case set forth the following criteria for determining family status: 1. The degree of emotional commitment and interdependence (this includes such evidence as interwoven social life, holding oneself as a couple/family, visiting each other's families of origin), 2. financial interdependence, 3. cohabitation, 4. longevity, and 5. exclusivity. Although this victory was greeted with enthusiasm by many, it must be noted that the requirements for a lesbian or gay couple to qualify as a family are considerably more demanding than for a heterosexual couple, who need only a civil marriage. I will return to this issue later. Other courts, following this precedent, have begun to make similar decisions. The current drive to legalize same-sex marriage, which will be discussed in some detail, is another strategy for tackling the family definition issue.

A second crucial, complex, and highly sensitive issue involves child custody. In some state courts lesbian and gay parental rights are being protected, whereas, in many areas, a lesbian can lose custody solely because she is a lesbian and therefore considered damaging to a child. In *In re: Ward*, an outrageous case in Florida, the judge removed a girl from her mother because the mother was a lesbian, awarding custody to the father, with whom the child had had very little contact. The father had been convicted of the murder of his previous wife. Troubled by the fact that the mother's adult daughter was a lesbian, the judge ordered the change of custody "to give the child a chance." Shortly after the decision came down, the mother died of a heart attack, obviating appeal efforts that were in process (Custody and visitation 1997).

One of the most highly publicized situations has been the Virginia case of Sharon Bottoms. In September 1993 Judge Buford Parsons, Jr. awarded custody of Sharon's son Tyler to her mother, Kay Bottoms, on the grounds that Sharon had violated the state's sodomy law. That ruling was overturned by the court of appeals in June 1994, and Tyler went home to his mother. This decision was then reversed in a sharply divided 4–3 decision by the State Supreme Court, and Tyler again went to his grandmother. What is of particular significance in this case is the justification presented in the majority opinion. They wrote, "We have previously stated that living daily under the conditions stemming from active lesbianism practiced in the home may impose a burden on the child by reason of the social condemnation attached to such an arrangement, which will inevitably affect the child's relationship with its peers and with the community" (Bull 1995:33).

The position is thus taken that parents should be deprived of their child because the world is discriminatory and homophobic. This is in direct conflict with a principle established in *Palmore v. Sudoti* (1984), the custody case involving a white child whose divorced mother married an African American man. The biological father claimed that it was not in the best interests of the child to grow up in a racially mixed marriage because of prejudice and stigmatization. The case was finally heard by the U.S. Supreme Court, which ruled for the mother on the grounds that she should not be deprived of the custody of her child because of the racist views of the community. Justice Berger wrote:

> The question is whether the reality of the private biases and the injury they might inflict are permissible considerations for the removal of an infant child from the custody of its natural mother. We have little difficulty concluding that they are not. The Constitution cannot control such prejudices but neither can it tolerate them. Private biases may be outside the reach of the law, but the law cannot, directly or indirectly, give them effect. (433)

Other courts have found *Palmore* relevant in gay and lesbian child custody suits (*R.L.B.* 1985; *M.P. v. S.P.* 1979).

Not only are biological mothers vulnerable, the co-parent who may plan for, nurture from birth, and support a child is even more vulnerable. Most courts have ruled that she has no rights following the breakup of her relationship with or the death of the biological mother. It is interesting that the same court that heard the *Braschi* case decided in *Matter of Alison D. v. Virginia M.* (1991), a case in which a couple planned together and gave birth to a child through artificial insemination, that the lesbian nonbiological mother was not within the definition of parent and could not bring a petition for visitation against the child's biological mother.

In another case, after the death of her biological mother, the custody of Kristen, the five-year-old daughter two women had jointly planned for and raised, was awarded to the biological mother's parents. The grandparents adopted the child and forbade any contact with Janine, the co-parent. Janine fought in court for five years for custody and finally, when the child was ten, and old enough to tell the court her wish, which was and always had been to be with Janine, the custody order was reversed and Kristen went home (Benkov 1994).

Recently, a Pennsylvania court, in a position much more congruent with the *Braschi* decision, "found that the non-biological mother and child were members of a family and that there was sufficient evidence that the non-biological mother had a parental relationship to the child and therefore has standing to seek parental custody" (Custody and visitation 1997).

In an attempt to legitimate the rights of the co-parent, efforts have been made to make it possible for the co-parent to adopt a child in situations where the biological mother has sole permanent custody, such as when the father is dead, has relinquished parental rights, or when the child was conceived through artificial insemination to an unmarried women. This effort has been successful in New York, California, Oregon, Massachusetts, Washington, Alaska, Vermont, and the District of Columbia.

For many years lesbian couples have fostered and adopted children in need of homes, but not without difficulty. Although only two states prohibit adoption by same sex couples (Florida and New Hampshire), and only one prohibits fostering (New Hampshire, that "Live free or die" state again!), the road to fostering and particularly to adoption is fraught with obstacles, since agency policy may well dictate the rules. Some agencies or sympathetic adoption workers look the other way while the lesbian adopts as a single parent and agency, worker, and applicant play the "Don't ask, don't tell" game. This is not, of course, the most comfortable or secure situation for anyone involved.

The growing lesbian "baby boom," in which one member of a couple gives birth to a child though artificial insemination, gives rise to a whole new series of social policy concerns that remain, for the most part, unresolved. These concerns include control of sperm banks, the need for standards around how many times a donor may be used, requirements about information that must be made available, the right to be artificially inseminated and the right of doctors to refuse to do this, and the responsibilities and rights of the donor in a known donor insemination situation. All these issues are in need of thoughtful review and policies or guidelines should be developed that will protect and respect everyone in the situation: the child, the biological and nonbiological mothers, and the donor.

These social policy issues have enormous impact on the emotional life of the lesbian family. The fear of discovery and possible rejection when adopting as a "single" parent, the insecurity faced when parental rights are not protected, the problem for the couple's relationship and for the parent-child relationships when one of the parents is not legally validated, the uncertainty and unknowns of artificial insemination in situations where there are no guidelines in terms of ethical practice and adequate information, the various threats and confusions that can surface when a couple, for many good reasons, decides to use a known donor are a few of the issues that can emerge. Therapists working with lesbian parents must be aware of all these issues and should encourage couples to get as much information as they can about the laws, policies, and practices in their locality. Many couples may want to use joint counseling sessions to explore their concerns and plan together how they want to proceed. Others may seek help because of the tension, stress, and uncertainty growing out of these complex family matters.

To Wed or Not to Wed

Same-sex marriage has suddenly taken the spotlight, becoming the lightning rod for the fierce emotions produced in the cultural wars. This was neither planned nor anticipated by gay strategists but was precipitated by a small but determined band of activists in Hawaii. In fact, neither gay/lesbian advocacy groups nor the ACLU were originally willing to take the Hawaii case of the three couples who decided to test the possibility of same sex-marriage in their very open and progressive state.

The surprising success of the Hawaii effort, the enormous public interest, and the powerful backlash as the radical right has taken on same-sex marriage as a convenient centerpiece of their antigay campaign have brought the issue front and center.

There are many reasons gay/lesbian organizations were reluctant to pursue same-sex marriage at this time. In the first place, gays and lesbians themselves are divided concerning whether this is a prize they want to win. Many feel that marriage is a troubled institution and that lesbians and gays would be in danger of assuming these difficulties should they take on marriage. Many feel that gays and lesbians should continue to develop their own culture, their own forms of association, that imitating heterosexual marriage would constrain and destroy this creative and liberating effort. As comedian Kate Clinton quipped, "The freedom not to marry is one of the things I enjoyed about being gay" (quoted in Dunlop 1996b).

In a fascinating analysis appearing in *Signs*, Ruthann Robson has taken a strong position not only against marriage but against the major effort central to the lesbian/gay political agenda of broadening the definition of the family to include lesbian and gay families. She writes:

> I propose that lesbian resistance to the family should become more elemental: resistance to being either included or excluded, resistance to the power of the category of family within legal theory and legal practice to define, redefine, sanction, and appropriate lesbian existence. This proposition is normative, political, and perhaps even ethical and aspirational. (1994:976)

Critiquing the *Braschi v. Stahl Associates* (1989) decision that has been heralded as a major step in achieving equity for gay and lesbian couples, she points out the powerful social control and exclusionary elements in the court's definition of the family.

> As expressed in *Braschi*, the requisite familial functions mimic the most traditional of marriages, including its economic practices within a capitalistic culture. *Braschi's* factor of "financial commitment" as well as the court's use of economic facts prove the elusive requirements of "dedication, caring, and self-sacrifice." (985)

She points out that "the not so implicit message is that lesbian and gay relationships will be accorded the status of family only to the extent that they replicate the traditional husband-wife couple" (987). In other words, lesbians and gays would have access to the benefits, entitlements, and privileges attached to "family status" only if they behaved in the very prescribed manner described in *Braschi*. It is interesting to note that a heterosexual couple, no matter what their behavior or the nature of their commitment or relationship, is legally and in social policy defined as a family as long as they are married.

Robson concludes that lesbians, rather than requesting inclusion in the privileged legal category of "family," should advocate for the abolition of benefits based on "family" status. Interestingly, this is the policy position taken by social worker Fred Barbaro eighteen years ago. In the midst of the Carter-inspired 1970s enthusiasm about developing family policy, Barbaro warned of the social control and exclusionary implications of this approach (Barbaro 1978).

That the push to legalize same-sex marriage is ultimately conservative is evidenced by some of the support it has received, despite panic on the part of Congress and the far right. For example, the most eloquent gay supporters of same-sex marriage have been gay conservatives who argue that marriage promotes mainstream ideals—"social cohesion, economic security, and economic prudence"—in the words of Andrew Sullivan, editor of the now conservative *New Republic*. Rich Tafel, head of the Log Cabin Republicans, argues with his right-wing fellow Republicans: "You can't have it both ways—accusing gays of being promiscuous and then denying us the right to incorporate into monogamous legally recognized relationships" (both quoted by Rich 1996:A19). As Ellen Goodman (1996) writes, "Putting marriage, a profoundly conservative institution, at the center of gay rights upends the stereotypes. It presents an image of stable couples in search of lifetime commitments" (4). A recent book by Georgetown University law professor William Eskridge, Jr. (1996) expresses this view in his title, *The Case for Same-Sex Marriage: From Sexual Liberty to Civilized Commitment*. It is his thesis that if society gives its blessing to same-sex marriages gay couples would behave increasingly like straight couples. That is exactly what concerns many gays and lesbians.

Other gay advocates, although perhaps supportive of same-sex marriage as a long-term goal, feel strongly that other essential and more attainable goals should be achieved first and express concern about the energy and resources now drawn into the marriage battle. First, they feel, should come the repeal of sodomy laws, still on the books in twenty states, the end of discrimination in employment and housing, and forceful action in the face of continued violence against and vicious harassment of gays and lesbians.

Finally, many feel that hitching the lesbian and gay agenda to the same-sex marriage star is political suicide. They are certain that the country is not ready for this change. Further, because so many Americans are bitterly opposed to same-sex marriage, they fear the drive for it could fuel a backlash that could threaten some of the hard-won gains already in place.

On the other side, however, those supporting the same-sex marriage campaign point out that this major change obviates many of the struggles that are now taking place on a piecemeal basis to gain the privileges and protections for gay and lesbian couples and families that are attached to heterosexual marriage. The conviction that our legal system should not be based on the family is perhaps a laudable one but hardly pragmatic. How long would it take to change the thousands of times the term *family* is used in the national code and in the laws of the fifty states?

Others argue that even if this battle is lost the discussion itself has altered public discourse. Domestic partner rights and privileges that were seen as radical a decade ago now emerge as a middle-of-the-road option when compared with the marriage demand. When a new political position develops that pushes the boundaries out to either the right or the left, the "center" tends to shift in that direction, as was dramatically demonstrated when candidate for president Michael Dukakis, in the context of the shift to the right in the Reagan campaign, felt he had to repudiate the American Civil Liberties Union, the function of which is to defend the first ten amendments to the Constitution.

On the other hand, sometimes when an extreme position is taken on one issue, strategy dictates that the position be softened by taking the opposite side on the next issue. This was demonstrated by the remarkable showing made by the bill prohibiting discrimination against homosexuals in the workplace, which lost by only one vote in the Senate. It came to the floor immediately after the overwhelming approval of the Defense of Marriage Act, and many senators voted for both as the second position softened the first. In any event, the same-sex marriage issue is upon us, as is the predicted backlash. Where it will all end is beyond prediction.

The story of this struggle is both moving and instructive, reflecting the courage and tenacity of the group that has sought to bring about this revolution, the generosity and commitment of the attorney who took on the case that no one wanted and who has almost entirely devoted his practice to the cause, the responses on the mainland to the Hawaii effort, which say so much about the diversity of opinion in this diverse nation, and the frightening intensity of the backlash (Gallagher 1997).

In 1990 one gay and two lesbian couples applied for marriage licenses to test whether the Hawaiian constitution, which is explicit about discrimination on the basis of sex and guarantees equal protection under the law, would protect same-sex marriage. The couples and their small group of advocates sought ACLU representation, but, after months of consideration, they were turned down. Gay advocacy groups took the same position. Dan Foley, former ACLU attorney, agreed to take the case, and in May 1991 the suit against the state was launched, citing violation of both equal protection and the right to privacy. In September of that year Hawaiian circuit court judge Robert Klein threw the case out, stating that same-sex couples are not protected by state laws concerning the right to marry and that restricting marriage to a man and a woman is a "rational legislative effort to advance the general welfare of the community" (Landmarks 1997:24).

Foley and the couples began the long appeal process, and in May 1993 the Hawaiian State Supreme Court overruled the lower court, saying that same-sex couples do have a right to marry, unless the State can provide a compelling reason why it should ban such unions. The case was returned to the lower court for trial but the hearing was delayed for years while conservative groups attempted unsuccessfully to intervene.

It was three years before the case was finally heard by Judge Kevin Chang. In the meantime, in response to the positive ruling by the Supreme Court and the very real possibility that same-sex marriages could come to pass in Hawaii, gay organizations and advocates such as LAMBDA joined the shoestring operation that had been supporting the effort, and antigay forces on the mainland organized the "defense of marriage" campaign. The case was finally heard in September 1996, with state lawyers trying to provide as the required "compelling reason" the principle that disallowing same-sex marriage benefits children. This was the old argument used against previous attempts to institute same sex-marriage, as in *Singer v. Hara* (1974), when the court found that "marriage is related to the public interest in affording a favorable environment for the growth of children." This, of course, ignores the point that many heterosexual couples are unable or choose not to have children, while many lesbian and gay couples do afford favorable environments for the growth of children.

The lawyers for the plaintiffs were able to produce evidence not only of the number of children growing up in such families but, even more important, could produce extensive research demonstrating that children raised in gay and lesbian families are as well adjusted as children in heterosexual families, research that was unavailable in 1974 (Patterson 1992, 1994, 1996).

On December 3 Judge Chang, in a groundbreaking forty-six-page opinion, ruled that the State failed to make a rational or compelling argument and that the refusal to allow same-sex couples to marry violated the state constitution. Judge Chang further acknowledged the fitness of lesbian and gay parents, the well-being of their children, and the value of diverse families. Far from being an attack on marriage, Judge Chang concluded that allowing gay people the freedom to marry would strengthen that institution and benefit families (Wolfson 1997).

The following day he granted an appeal to return the case to the State Supreme Court before licenses are actually granted, but most observers think that the higher court will uphold Judge Chang. Of course, it still isn't over. Anti-same-sex-marriage forces in Hawaii are working toward calling a constitutional convention to alter the constitution and make it possible to exclude same-sex marriage, but the earliest that could happen would be the year 2000. By then the State may have had experience with same-sex marriage and would have to consider annulling the thousands of marriages that may already have taken place.

Response on the mainland has been mixed, intense, and swift. Many of the major columnists examined the issue, taking positions that could have been predicted. Rather surprising and warming was the lead editorial from the venerable *New York Times*. Wrote the editor:

> Opponents of same-sex marriage invoke religious traditions and family values. Allowing same-sex couples to marry, they assert, would somehow diminish the meaning of marriage for heterosexuals. These arguments, uncomfortably similar to those raised in resistance to repealing miscegenation laws a few decades ago, cannot obscure the entrenched anti-gay bigotry underlying much of the public dialogue, nor can it disguise the fundamental unfairness of the government of denying a whole class of citizens the benefits that flow from civil marriage. (Editorial 1996:10)

The predictions of backlash if anything underestimated the intense reaction that the possibility of same-sex marriage would raise. Most dramatic and far-reaching was the passage, in the House of Representatives by a 342 to 67 margin and in the Senate by an 85 to 14 margin, and the signing by President Clinton of the Defense of Marriage Act. This highly political piece of legislation, anticipating the affirmation of same-sex marriages in Hawaii, appeared just at the end of the presidential campaign and was sponsored in the Senate by the Republican presidential candidate. It not only denies to same-sex couples all federal benefits such as Social Security and Veterans Benefits but also permits states to ignore same-sex marriages performed in other states. This is in direct contradiction to Article 4 of the Constitution, which requires that full faith and credit be given in each state to the public acts, records, and judicial proceedings in every other state.

Many observers have no question that the act, clearly a political ploy, is in serious violation of the Constitution, but the process to put that to the test will take years. First, the Hawaii Supreme Court must review and approve Chang's ruling, marriage licenses will have to be issued, and a same-sex couple from the mainland will have to marry, return to home, apply for state benefits based on marital status and be refused, bring suit against the state, and begin the long, slow, and torturous road through the legal system to the Supreme Court. This not only requires time, enormous resources, and dedication but also a pioneering effort, much like the efforts of the Hawaii couples, James Nabozny, and the many others who with great courage have put themselves on the line at great personal cost.

Not only was the Defense of Marriage bill passed but since the first Hawaii decision conservative legislators have been proposing laws in their state legislatures to ban same-sex marriage and prevent recognition of such marriages performed in other states. To date, sixteen states have passed such legislation, and many are in the process of considering this option (Dunlop 1996b).

It is difficult to predict the overall outcome of this most contentious battle of the cultural war. It is possible that same-sex marriage will take place in Hawaii and be accepted in some states. It is likely that the Defense of Marriage Act and the acts in states that prohibit the recognition of marriages performed in other states will be found unconstitutional on the basis of their violation of the "full faith and credit" requirement of Article 4.

The Future

The last twenty-five years has been a time of enormous change in public attitudes toward lesbians and gay men and in popular culture. Some of these changes are perhaps most dramatically witnessed in the media, where, for example, not only did Ellen de Generes, a popular television situation comedy star, come out both on the program and in her personal life, but the vice president of the United States applauded her and her contribution. Perhaps the most important change is that homosexuality is no longer invisible, no longer silenced.

The changes are also apparent in the day-to-day lives of lesbians, although this period of transition can result in uncertainty and confusion.

There are many situations that are difficult for lesbians and gays to assess and it is easy to make a wrong step with very painful or difficult consequences. To some extent, although sharply divided, the majority of Americans are ahead of slow moving federal and state legislators. For example, most Americans believe that homosexuals should have the right to work, but this right continues to be unprotected by the federal government and in forty states.

Certainly, some important steps have been taken toward equality for and the protection of gays and lesbians, but it is obvious there is still a long way to go. Most striking is that not only are gay and lesbian families excluded from the rights, responsibilities, and privileges attached to heterosexual marriage, but it is also legal to discriminate against them in employment as well as in housing, loans, educational, and other facilities in forty of the fifty states, simply on the basis of sexual orientation. The intensity of the cultural war around family values, so ably described by Judith Stacey (1996), demonstrates how far the country is from granting true equality. This cultural war shows no signs of abating. In fact, small successes in the gay rights struggle have served as convenient rallying points for the radical right in their efforts to gain control of "the soul of America."

It is impossible to predict where the long road will end and how far we will be able to travel. Change is slow, but once people gain a sense that they are entitled to equal treatment it is hard to turn them back. Perhaps one can join with the optimism of the *New York Times* editors who began their editorial on the freedom to marry with, "Chances are that Americans will look back thirty years from now and wonder what all the fuss was about" (Editorial 1996:10).

NOTE

Stopping the anti-gay abuse of students in public high schools is available from Lambda Publications, 666 Broadway, Suite 1200, New York, NY, 10012.

REFERENCES

Ambach v. Norwick, 441 U.S. 68 75–80. 1979.
Barbaro, F. 1979. The case against family policy. *Social Work* 24:455–457.
Benkov, L. 1994. *Reinventing the family*. New York: Crown.
Bowers v. Hardwick, 478 U.S. 186 (1986).
Braschi v. Stahl Associates, 74 NY 2d 201, 543 N.E. 49, 544 N.Y.S. 2d 784 (1989).
Bull, C. 1995. Losing the war: The courts disregard evidence in denying lesbian mother custody of her son. *Advocate*, May 30, p. 33.
Custody and visitation. 1997. *LAMBDA Update* (Winter), 14(1):15.

Dunlop, D. W. 1966a. Fearing a toehold for gay marriages, conservatives rush to bar the door. *New York Times*, March 6, p. A13.

— 1996b. Some gay rights advocates question efforts to defend same-sex marriage. *New York Times*, June 7, p. A12.

Editorial. 1996. The freedom to marry. *New York Times*, April 7, p. 10.

Episcopalians vote not to bless same-sex unions. 1997. *Boston Globe*, July 21, p. A4.

Eskridge, W. 1996. *The case for same-sex marriage: From sexual liberty to civilized commitment.* New York: Simon and Schuster.

Excerpts from court's decision on Colorado's provision for homosexuals. 1996. *New York Times*, May 21, p. A20.

Frick v. Lynch, 4 91 F Sup 381 D.R.I. 1980.

Gallagher, J. 1997. Marriage, Hawaiian style. *Advocate*, February 4, pp. 22–28.

Gay Students Organization of the University of New Hampshire v. Bonner, 367 F Supp 1088. 1974.

Gaylord v. Tacoma School District. 88WASH 2nd 286P 2d 1340, 434 U.S. 879. 1997.

GLAD fights censorship. 1996. *GLAD Spring Briefs* May, p. 2.

Goodman, E. 1986. What'll happen with gay marriage? *Hampshire Gazette*, December 9, p. 4.

Greenhouse, L. 1996. Gay rights can't be banned, high court rules. *New York Times*, May 21, pp. A1, A20.

Hartman, A. 1996. Social policy as a context for lesbian and gay families: The political is personal. In J. Laird and R-J. Green, eds., *Lesbians and gays in couples and families: A handbook for therapists*, pp. 69–85. San Francisco: Jossey-Bass.

Hazelwood School District v. Kuhlmeier, 108 S.Ct 562. 1988.

Landmarks on the road to legal gay marriage. 1997. *Advocate*, February 4, 24–25.

Logue, P. 1994. Cincinnati: The anatomy of a victory. *LAMBDA Update* (Fall), 11(3):1, 29–30.

— 1997. Near $1 million settlement raises standard for protection of gay youth. *LAMBDA Update* (Winter), 14(1):1, 8.

Logue, P., and D. Buckel. 1996. LAMBDA success in Jamie Nabozny's case is victory against anti-gay violence. *LAMBDA Update* (Fall), 13(3):1, 6.

Matter of *Alison D. v. Virginia M.*, 77 N.Y. 2d651, 572 N.E. 2d 27, 569 N.Y.S. 2d 586. 1991.

Matter of *Alison D.*, Court of Appeals, New York State, May 2. 1991.

McQuiston, J. T. 1995. Lesbian bans divide church, and a minister loses his job. *New York Times*, August 4, p. B4.

Moss, J. 1997. Losing the war. *Advocate*, April 15, pp. 27–30.

M.P. v. S.P., 169 NJ Super.425, 438–439, 404 A 2d 1256, 1263. 1979.

Niebuhr, G. 1996. Episcopal bishop absolved in gay ordination. *New York Times*, May 16, pp. 7, 18.

Norton v. Macy, 417 F. 2d at 1167. 1968.

Palmore v. Sidoti, 104 SCt. P1879. 1984.

Patterson, C. J. 1992. Children of lesbian and gay parents. *Child Development* 63:1025–1042.

Patterson, C. J. 1994. Children of the lesbian baby boom: Behavioral adjustment, self-concepts, and sex role identity. In B. Greene and G. M. Herek, eds., *Lesbian and gay psychology: Theory, research, and clinical application*, pp. 156–175. Newbury Park, Cal.: Sage.

Patterson, C. J. 1996. Lesbian mothers and their children: Findings from the Bay Area families study. In J. Laird and R-J. Green, eds., *Lesbians and gays in couples and families: A handbook for therapists*, pp. 420–437. San Francisco: Jossey-Bass.

Perry, N. 1997. Governor signs gay rights bill into Maine law. *Portland Press Herald*, May 17, pp. 1a, 8a.

Rich, F. 1996. Beyond the Birdcage. *New York Times*, March 13, p. A 19.

R. L. B., Alaska Sup Ct. 1985.

Robson, R. 1994. Resisting the family: Repositioning lesbians in legal theory. *Signs: Journal of Women in Culture and Society* 19:975–996.

Schmitt, E. 1996. Senators reject gay marriage bill and job bias ban. *New York Times*, September 11, pp. A1, A16.

Sears, J. T. 1991. *Growing up in the South: Race, gender, and journeys of the spirit*. New York: Harrington Park.

Singer v. Hara, 11 Wash, App. 247, 522 P. 2d 1187. 1974.

Singer v. U.S. Civil Service Commission, 429 US 1034. 1977.

Stacey, J. 1996. *In the name of the family*. Boston: Beacon.

State of New York Court of Appeals. 1989. July 5, no. 108.

Stopping the anti-gay abuse of students in public high schools. 1996. New York: Lambda.

Tinker v. Des Moines Independent Community School District, 393 U.S. 503, 506. 1969.

U.S. Customs Service v. National Treasury Union, Chapter 142, 77, LAB. ARB (BNA) 113, 117. 1982.

Wolfson, E. 1997. Hawaii marriage breakthrough: Only the beginning. *LAMBDA Update* (Winter) 14(1):1, 6.

PART TWO

Lesbian Couples

CHAPTER FIVE

A Struggle for Language:
Patterns of Self-Disclosure in Lesbian Couples

Tara Healy

IS ADVERSITY THE MOTHER OF INVENTION? Getting through an ordinary day requires lesbians to become creative managers of public and private interactions. Every day we make conscious and unconscious decisions about how to present or conceal our identities and our intimate relationships. Special events such as holidays, weddings, reunions, and work functions stretch our capacities for creativity. The language of self-disclosure reflects this ingenuity.

Since homosexuality has been designated a "sin," a "crime," and an "illness" at various times in history, it has long been considered a stigma-carrying status (Conrad and Schneider 1980; Goffman 1963). The historical developments of various modes of social control over "deviant" populations, including homosexuals, has been explored by Conrad and Schneider. Although "deviant" groups have unique characteristics, consideration of shared dynamics has added to our understanding of the psychological and social challenges faced by persons devalued by society.

Sociologists have extensively explored the relationship between the formation and management of identity and the social context, especially for those groups labeled deviant. Many populations contend with the challenge of managing the difficult interactions associated with deviance. Goffman specifically explores the implications of stigma-carrying status for identity formation, group alignment, and information control. His concept of passing is frequently used in relation to ostensibly concealed lesbian identity.

The examination of social interaction in a specific stigmatized group can have implications for other devalued populations. For example, Davis (1961) explored the strained social interaction between "normals" and those considered deviant by virtue of their "visible disability." In this study, Davis highlights normalizing behavior important to both normals and stigmatized persons. Davis's concept of deviance disavowal applies to groups whose stigmatized status becomes visible when the stigmatized characteristic is disclosed. Decisions about disclosure are faced by many groups, such as those who have an invisible illness (e.g., multiple sclerosis), a limitation (e.g., inability to read), or a characteristic (e.g., homosexuality). Glaser and Strauss (1981) present a paradigm of "awareness context," which refers to the combination of what each person in a given situation knows about the identity of the other and about how one's own identity is viewed by the other (54). Their description focuses on people who are dying, but can be applied to a number of contexts and populations, including homosexuals. The language of self-disclosure used by lesbians may be considered applicable to a variety of populations facing a devalued classification in society.

Erving Goffman's analysis of the management of stigma (1963) informs more recent considerations of gay and lesbian identity management. For example, Berger (1990) notes: "The predominant situation for most gay men and lesbians is one in which they pass; that is [their] homosexuality is not known to others" (328). Moses (1978) found that fewer than one quarter of the lesbians studied "can be said to have 'come out' to most of the people they know" (62). Twelve years later Eldridge and Gilbert (1990) found comparable percentages: three quarters of their sample had not disclosed their lesbian identity to the world at large (57). Potter and Darty (1981) describe lesbians as an "almost invisible segment of American society" (187), while Ponse (1976) notes that "heterosexual assumption" is an important feature of social interaction: "[It] means simply that parties to any interaction are presumed to be heterosexual unless demonstrated to be otherwise" (317). This feature both facilitates passing and creates barriers to self-disclosure.

Lesbian and gay identity formation has typically been described in terms of stages (Berger 1983; Cass 1979; Coleman 1982; de Monteflores and Schultz 1978; Minton and McDonald 1984). While all these theories are presented with sensitivity to the power of antihomosexual attitudes in the dominant culture, all focus on the importance of self-disclosure in the process. Self-disclosure is commonly referred to as coming out, both in the literature and in the subculture. de Monteflores and Schultz (1978) stress the tension between the individual and society in a coming out process: "We prefer to conceptualize coming out as a feedback loop regulating the relationship between the gay person and society . . . belying a linear progression model" (62). Minton and McDonald (1984) emphasize the "life spanning process" of identity development leading to "personal acceptance of a positive gay self-image and a coherent personal identity" (91). While self-disclosure is seen as an important aspect of developing a positive view of oneself as a lesbian, the difficulties in accomplishing this are not at all simplified by any of these authors.

Some recent literature emphasizes internalized homophobia as the major impediment to gay and lesbian mental health. For example, Sophie (1987) defines internalized homophobia as "an internalization of negative attitudes and assumptions concerning lesbianism" (53). She goes on to posit: "The opposite of self-disclosure, keeping information entirely to oneself, is an affirmation of internalized homophobia" (70). Here secrecy is associated with a lesbian holding negative attitudes about herself. Internalized homophobia appears as a key concept in much practice and research literature (see, e.g., Browning 1988; Decker 1984; Falco 1991; Kahn 1991).

Even though lesbians and gay men remain an essentially hidden population, many studies of gay and lesbian life still herald self-disclosure as a sign of mental health, whereas secrecy is often viewed as a central problem for gays and lesbians. However, Eldridge and Gilbert (1990) find indications of high self-esteem and overall life satisfaction in their "hidden" sample of lesbian couples. In addition, they note, "Nondisclosure is apparently as adaptive for some . . . as high levels of disclosure is for others" (57–58). Cain (1991) challenges the assumption that secrecy is a problem in his study of gay men:

> Disclosure of homosexuality is now generally viewed in the professional literature as more desirable than secrecy; disclosure is often seen as evidence of a healthy gay identity, whereas secrecy has come to be viewed as socially and psychologically problematic. . . . This article shows that decisions concerning disclosure and secrecy are related to a variety of situational and relational factors that are largely distinct from gay identity development. (67)

What can we learn about the process of coming out by examination of the language of self-disclosure? What does being "out" mean to lesbians? To what extent should degree of self-disclosure serve as definition of mental health for lesbians? Are social workers participating in pathologizing the adaptive strategies lesbians use to manage their identities in an often unaccepting and sometimes hostile world? These are some of the questions that this exploratory study hopes to address.

Method and Sample

Qualitative methodology was chosen because the purpose of the research was to expand our understanding of the strengths and creativity used by lesbians in their language choices. Quantitative methodology would require lesbians to fit their language choices into the categories set forth by the researcher, thereby limiting the richness of the data. My personal history of having participated in a quantitative study of lesbian couples contributed to my decision to use qualitative methodology. I remember being asked, on a questionnaire, when I had "come out." The question left me stymied and I wanted to tell the researcher, "It's not that simple!" In this research I wanted to capture a level of complexity in lesbian responses not allowed by such limiting questions.

A sample of eight lesbian couples participated in two separate focus groups (Morgan 1988). The most accessible informants were part of my own lesbian community. I began by contacting lesbian couples in my community, two of whom then actively sought out others to participate in the research. One subgroup of couples arranged to be in the same discussion group together. My partner and I were both active participants in the two focus groups. All were informed before attending that the discussion would focus on how we handle events such as holidays and children's weddings. This topic was provided as a stimulus for discussion of information control and coming out issues in various contexts. A discussion about handling holidays and other events was expected to address ways we interact with the heterosexual world in our families of origin, with our children, with colleagues, and in other contexts. Language choice would be illustrated by descriptions of interactions.

In forming the focus groups I chose lesbians who were in later stages of lesbian identity formation (according to any of the stage theories already mentioned). All the women were part of an active lesbian community and had been living together in committed couple relationships for some time. I assumed that lesbians face different and more complex issues with regard to interfacing with the heterosexual world once they form a couple. For example, a single lesbian does not have to decide whether or not to bring her partner with her to a family reunion.

The lesbians in this sample were all middle-class homeowners. Fifteen women were white and one was black. They ranged in age from the late twenties to the mid-fifties. Most of the couples had been together for at least five years, although time together ranged from five to twenty years.

Before beginning each discussion, focus group procedures were briefly described and written informed consent for participating in this research was obtained. Participants were later contacted to make sure they did not want to withdraw their permission. This article, the results of the research, was then given to each member to review prior to publication. All who participated continued to enthusiastically support the research, including my intention to publish an analysis of our discussions. All appreciated receiving a copy of the paper and no one had second thoughts about being included.

The central question put to each group as a stimulus for discussion was, How do we handle holidays, our adult children's weddings, or other events? This was a reiteration of the question provided ahead of time. Each discussion group lasted approximately two hours. Both discussion groups were tape recorded and transcribed. Content analysis was done using the constant comparative method of grounded theory (Chenitz and Swanson 1986; Glaser and Strauss 1967).

I used the classical coding methods developed and described by Corbin and Strauss (1990) and Strauss (1987). I began with open coding of potentially significant phrases by underlining with various colors. These were then converted to notes in wide margins for initial coding of specific interactions. Specific words such as *lover* and *companion* and actions such as "going together to an event" were highlighted. Specific uses of language were later coded as public or private language, direct or indirect language. Decisions to include or exclude one's partner originally were designated as indirect actions. I chose to focus on the categories of public and private language, context, and affective response. In the next stage axial coding was used to explore relationships between type of language choice, context, and feelings. For example, comfort and discomfort were associated with acknowledgment and rejection. During the period of selective coding, core categories were chosen. Themes such as repetitions in coming out were coded in relation to the frequency of occurrence. Relationships among the categories were developed in theoretical memos, and the transcripts were again analyzed for consistency with the memos. When associations between categories did not withstand this scrutiny they were either revised or dropped. The major themes remained consistent throughout this later phase of analysis. The core categories chosen were saturated through constant comparative methods. These are the categories that will be presented in this chapter.

Affirming Language

Language that was affirming of lesbian identity was expressed and received in both verbal and behavioral forms. When affirming language was received, lesbians felt validated, acknowledged, and accepted. When acting or speaking in self-affirmative ways lesbians felt authentic, proud, and strong. Explicit verbal language was chosen carefully by lesbians and reflected respect for personal relationships and contexts. Explicit verbal acceptance by others was rare. Much more common was the language of behavior.

The Spoken Word

The choice to be very direct with language, such as using the word *lover*, was usually reserved for private conversations with someone of emotional importance to the lesbian. After Ann and Kristy became a couple, Ann's choice to take her son aside to say, "You realize, don't you, that Kristy is my lover?" was motivated by the importance of her children in her life and her desire to have no ambiguity with them. Her son's response, although on another level of directness, was also affirming: "Of course, I'm glad you have a companion."

Molly also felt it important to be very clear with her daughter: "I remember coming out to my daughter. It was very, just emotional . . . . I cried and told her I was a lesbian. She was wonderful. She said, 'Awesome.' " Both expressions were direct and affirmative. Women who came out at younger ages often described having used such direct language with parents as opposed to children.

Language choice often reflected respect for persons and contexts while remaining affirmative. Leanne cited respect for her godmother and for her age (eighty), as well as her positive relationship with her, as factors influencing her language choice:

> I made the conscious decision to say "my companion" . . . and not say "lover." . . . For someone her age . . . it just wouldn't be appropriate. I felt really good about it—I felt good about myself that I felt confident enough to be able to do that.

Leanne's choice affirmed her identity as a lesbian and her relationship with her lover while considering her godmother's feelings.

Can Behavior Speak Louder Than Words?

Behavioral language refers to actions that either validate or conceal lesbian identity. A lesbian's choice to include or exclude her partner at an event is a form of behavioral language. Examples included bringing one's partner to a high school or family reunion or leaving one's partner at home when visiting family. When a lesbian acts in a manner that she feels either expresses or conceals her identity as a lesbian, she is using behavioral language.

Consistently, throughout these discussions, lesbians did not claim being "out" in their families without direct verbal disclosure, no matter how overt their behavioral language. Ann stated that she is not out to her mother, never having "discussed it" with her. Nonetheless her behavioral language is very overt and self-affirming: she brings her lover on family visits, sleeping with her lover in her mother's house and in her own home when her mother visits; Ann has even danced with her lover in her mother's presence at her son's wedding. Her mother responds in behavioral language as well by sending cards to her lover, asking about her lover, and generally assuming her lover is part of her life. Although the fact that the nature of the relationship is not verbally articulated allows for a level of ambiguity not acceptable in her relationship with her son, her out behavior with her family of origin reaffirms the meaning and importance in her life of her committed couple relationship.

Septima describes similar choices for using behavioral language in her family of origin, stating that her use/nonuse of verbal language is related to respect for the family culture: "We haven't actually come out formally but it is very clear to everyone [in the family] that we really love each other, and that's the important thing." Septima and her partner also spoke of their longevity as a couple as making a behavioral statement. They have been together for twenty years.

For these two women, both of whom feel they are not concealing their lesbian relationship in the family even though they are not "officially coming out," family affirmation is received and appreciated through the behavioral language of acknowledgment. The language choice is felt to be sensitive to the relationship and context rather than negating to the lesbian.

It is interesting to contrast the statements of Ann and Septima that they are not "out" to their families with Dawn's statement:

> I am totally out at work and I never announced it either . . . . When I started working, I just talked about Nanette . . . We're doing this . . . we're doing that. After about a month at work . . . one young woman asked me and I said "Yes."

Although someone in her workplace did ask about her relationship with verbal explicitness, it appeared that Dawn made a decision to be out with behavioral language, treating her life as open and natural. Several other women used the same workplace tactic.

Gail stated:

> Well . . . the thing is that individually the people I work with know that I am a lesbian and know that my lover's name is Molly because I talk about her and I, you know, in a relationship sense, and in "your husband's name is . . . . 'I and Molly' . . . " and that's the way we talk about our relationships.

Mary also speaks of behavioral language in the workplace:

> At work I have never actually announced that I am a lesbian, but everybody I work with absolutely knows it. . . . I remember each year there was a little progression.

The decision to talk about one's partner as significant in one's life, although not explicitly referring to lesbianism, was felt to be affirmative and was described as coming out in the workplace. In contrast, the same type of behavioral language in families was not claimed to be coming out.

Buying a house was also viewed as self-affirming behavioral language by this group of lesbians. In response to Virginia's struggle about coming out to her family, Karen told her, "They will probably know when we buy a house together." Pat [Septima's partner] noted, "Actually I think it was when we bought the house together that it was something more. I mean we started getting Christmas cards addressed to both of us." While some couples received increased acknowledgment from families upon buying a house, others experienced increased negation. For Diane and Melissa, buying a house together resulted in increased problems with family. Diane's mother became openly hostile to Melissa, stopped asking about her, and was cold whenever in Melissa's presence. These were all received as strongly negating behaviors in reaction to the self-affirming act of buying a house. Both positive and negative responses indicated that the self-affirming behavioral language of buying a house was "heard."

Negating Language

The previous example illustrates how self-affirming behavior sometimes triggers a negative reaction. For lesbians there are many contexts in which self-affirmation precipitates negating responses. Negation involves denial or rejection of lesbian identity. In addition, negation of lesbian identity may be generated by the lesbian herself. Self-censoring occurs when a lesbian constrains her behavior out of concern that she might otherwise face rejection or other negative responses. Negation is consistently associated with uncomfortable feelings.

Received Negation

Lesbian couples face negation of their identity and their status as a couple in many ways and in much of the environment. The negation discussed by these lesbians, however, was heavily focused on immediate family, whether parents, siblings, or children. This was evidence of the importance of these relationships and the intensity of pain associated with negation in the family.

Directly spoken denunciation was very rare, but when it occurred it was powerful:

> KAREN: *My mother threatened to kill me . . . . We don't communicate in my family, so when something does [get said] . . . it [is] . . . to the other extreme. And that's what we all fear—we really do. I mean, I actually had forgotten how they reacted.*

Karen's parents still don't visit, although several years have passed. In the face of even this extremely negating response, Karen believes that coming out to family is an important self-affirmative act: "You are not really complete until you do."

The power of silence is a far more common language of negation directed toward these women. Melissa responded strongly to Karen's story about her mother: "This is what we all fear . . . being cut off . . . they'll be angry." Melissa goes on to describe how anger is expressed in her family by prolonged, disconnecting silence. She faced this silence following the Christmas she chose to spend with gay friends. Diane also described silence as the punishment for objectionable behavior in her family. Virginia provided the following description of a period of silence in her family:

> My sister said: "I don't like the way you live your life." Then I said something like, "That really hurts." We didn't talk for a very long time. Two months or so went by. My birthday came and went and she

didn't . . . I was really depressed, but not enough to call. I didn't call. Then we talked once when she was at my parent's house. And then she sent an Easter card and wrote, "I didn't like you for awhile but now I like you again."

Silence and not sending cards were received as negating language and the breaking of the silence with sending cards and the positive statement of "liking you" were received as affirming, although neither woman directly refers to Virginia's lesbian identity.

Self-Censoring

The pain of constriction was illustrated by descriptions of self-censoring behaviors. Most of these lesbians experienced not bringing their lover to family, work, or social occasions as self-negating behavioral language. Virginia has a close and loving family. Before she and Karen became a couple, spending the holidays with her family was a joyous occasion. Now she feels sad when she returns "home" because she leaves her lover behind. The pain of this self-censoring behavior is steadily increasing her discomfort with concealing her lesbian identity from her family.

Even for women who have either verbally or behaviorally revealed their lesbian identity in many contexts, and with many persons, struggles with self-censoring persist. Some lesbians noted that the struggle is at times an internal one.

> MELISSA: *My friends know to invite you [her lover]. . . . We don't go. It's uncomfortable for us; they don't care. They really don't care. [later]It's a struggle. . . . It's part of me, and—and a lot of it was how I was raised. I keep making these rules for myself. I don't make any lies about who I am.*

Sometimes self-censoring is strongly related to context rather than to an internal limitation. Self-censoring can also be associated with an exclusion from affirmation, as Molly's description illustrates:

When your [her lover's] brother and sister-in-law were holding hands in the front seat and your mother said, "Oh, they are so much in love; it is so sweet," I felt hurt . . . I knew I couldn't do that with you, that it would not be O.K. I knew it wouldn't be O.K. with you [her lover]. I did feel sad. I felt like, "Well, we're in love too. I want you to know that too." And they did say they liked me, they let me know that—so it wasn't that they didn't acknowledge me.

Even though Molly's lover, Gail, is verbally explicit with her family concerning her lesbian identity, self-constraint is exercised with regard to affectionate touching.

A degree of self-censoring in some contexts was pervasive whether or not a lesbian was generally out in her life. These lesbians exhibited a wide range of complexity in relation to degrees of self-censoring. Choices about verbal disclosure, behavioral disclosure, and self-censoring behavior appeared to be highly context sensitive. Verbal self-disclosure (even in many contexts) was rarely accompanied by a total lack of self-censoring behavior.

Parallel Process

The concept of parallel process is used here to refer to the emotional, cognitive, and behavioral responses of persons who receive information about the lesbian or gay identity of someone they know. They, too, as they incorporate this knowledge, go through a process that reflects the coming out process of an individual lesbian. Both can be painful in a culture that stigmatizes homosexuality. Through this parallel process, family, friends, colleagues, and others who become aware of someone's lesbian identity must decide not only how to respond to the designated individual but also how to manage this information in a variety of social contexts.

Parallel process appeared to be a useful lens through which to view the difficulty many families experience when they become aware of having a lesbian member. For some participants the concept of parallel process stimulated empathy for those to whom they had come out and appeared to soften the blow of negation received from significant others in response to disclosure of their lesbian identity. In a sense, they must come out too.

Ann notes that loved ones go through a parallel process of coping with the information that there is a lesbian family member:

> I think sometimes family members . . . we go through our own process of coming out to ourselves, and, you know, it takes a certain amount of time to come out to yourself and deal with it. And then sometimes we then give it to our families, and say this is it. They have to look at their own prejudices, their own stereotypes of what it means, loss if it means, you know, grandchildren . . . so I think it takes time to do it

too, and we forget that we have done it. I remember putting a toe in the water and then running back.

Mothers in the group described how their children had to deal with anti-homosexual attitudes and behaviors in the world, another aspect of the parallel process phenomenon. Molly, for example, noted that the children have to decide whether they are going to keep coming out about their mother's lesbian identity "if they choose to let people know what's going on in their lives." Nanette described observing her children's pain:

> It was very painful to me to see the pain that brought about with my children. One time, one of my son's friends wasn't allowed to come to the house. The mother wrote me a note thanking me for inviting her daughter, but because of some "lifestyle," or, you know, some phraseology like that . . .

She went on to remember her daughter struggling with how to respond to homophobic jokes at school. This group was keenly aware that their loved ones shared the negation of public disapproval of lesbians.

The Unending Process

The unending process of coming out refers to the ongoing need to make decisions about self-disclosure. All the informants in this study had stories about coming out over and over and over again. Coming out, clearly, is not something a lesbian does once and for all at a given point in time. Sometimes the repeated self-disclosure was with the same person, particularly a family member, and sometimes in a similar context, such as the workplace. It is clear from these discussions that issues of self-disclosure span a lesbian's full lifetime and do not cease when a certain level of identity formation is reached.

When lesbians first come out in their families, even if they are verbally explicit, their disclosure is usually met with some level of initial denial. Kristy used direct verbal disclosure when she first informed her family about her sexual orientation. She was single at the time. A few years later when Kristy brought a lover into the family to spend Christmas, her sister responded as if her lesbian identity was new information. This news had a powerful impact on Kristy's sister, who dramatically informed Kristy that she could no longer be considered a suitable guardian for her nephews; Kristy's sister said she would have to change her will accordingly. This was received as strong symbolic negation. Years later, when Kristy was going through a separation, her sister entrusted her children to Kristy's care for one of their school vacations. This, on the other hand, seemed a strong symbolic act of validation.

Gail described a similar experience of going through layers of discomfort within herself as she repeated the process of coming out in her family:

> I told my family . . . my brothers, my parents, and said I was a lesbian, but at the time I was by myself. Then we went to my brother's wedding. . . . I mean we talked as an association, you know . . . we never came out and said, "Well you know we're a lesbian couple." . . . It felt good to be out. . . . My brother was all right.

Gail contrasted this good feeling to imagining that it would have felt "excruciating" to be there if she were not out.

She also reported that when visiting her mother with her lover she had to repeatedly insist that she and her lover sleep together even though she had come out directly years before. Dawn also reiterated her coming out when she brought Nanette home with her. Nanette felt validated by Dawn's insistence that they be recognized as a couple:

> I've always been very appreciative of Dawn because she brought me to her family, and they wanted me to be assimilated in a certain way— her friend or whatever—and she insisted that I be known as her lover and that we sleep together—not do any of the little charades.

Although both Gail and Dawn had been explicitly out in their families as single women, becoming part of a couple and introducing their lovers to their families raised the level of awareness of lesbian identity. There followed either new levels of acceptance or rejection. Repetition of coming out over time can mean working through layers of discomfort with one's lesbian identity for both the individual lesbian and her family. Gail's statements indicate that the process can enhance a sense of well-being and self-esteem.

The Paradox of Self-Preservation

Decisions about disclosure often entail paradox. In order to preserve her physical, economic, or emotional safety, a lesbian may believe that concealing her lesbian identity is necessary. At other times nondisclosure may so jeopardize her sense of well-being that she will risk her safety in the service of her sense of personal integrity. Coming out at work, for example, may be perceived as a potential risk to economic well-being. Not coming out at work when one's partner faces a life-threatening illness may be perceived as too severe a limit on one's emotional well-being. By protecting one aspect of her being, a lesbian might jeopardize the safety of another.

Self-preservation was understood to warrant whatever level of behavior was needed to secure safety, even if it entailed a direct lie. These women would not readily choose to lie even when feeling insecure. Although many were behaviorally "out" in the workplace, most alluded to some work experience in which it was not safe to be out. Although lying was understandable and respected in this community, lying was also strongly connected to the power of antihomosexual attitudes. Mary's story highlights an awareness of danger.

> Do you remember when the four of us were in Argentina and we were in the back seat and the guy asked us, asked me, because I was the interpreter, if we all had husbands? Now these three women do not understand Spanish but they understood that man when he said that and I could *feel* all three of those people: "Tell him yes! Tell him we all have husbands" And I said "YES, we all have husbands," and I could hear the sigh of relief. And he calmed right down. You know, I had to think, like, "Do I tell? We're all lesbians here!" I knew that would not be wise. I lied. We all have men at home; we're here having a good time. Now what does that mean? Really, what does that mean?

Mary's question reveals the paradox of the struggle to be self-affirming in a context of assumed strong antihomosexual attitudes. That which secures safety in the perception of a lesbian may, in fact, entail the explicit self-negation implied in a lie about oneself. These women noted that a single heterosexual women might have lied too, because single women can be thought of as available for heterosexual attention. The lie, however, is quite different for a lesbian in this context because it denies her identity—an identity formed within a world that degrades it. A heterosexual woman may simply be denying a status that may be temporary. The difference in culture accentuates the ambiguity of language even when spoken.

Struggle for Language

A struggle for language was the primary theme I noted in both discussion groups. Leanne and Jan noted the following about a visit from five-year-old twin grandchildren:

LEANNE: *They asked what Jan was, was she my husband? Is that how they put it?*

JAN: *Yes, they want some language, yes.*

ANN: *We do too.*

DIANE: *Your [her lover's] sister's kids call me "Aunt Diane" and your brother's children call me "Aunt Diane and Uncle Melissa"... "Aunt Melissa"... your nephew at some point turned to me and said: "You're family."*

One of Leanne's grandchildren expressed the dilemma in the unabashed language of childhood. Woven through this struggle for language were themes of affirmation, negation, process, and paradox.

The struggle for language reflected an unending process of coming out. Patterns of language choice reflect not only a pattern of self-disclosure but also a sensitivity to context and relationship. The most important aspect of language choice was whether it was affirming or negating.

Occasions such as weddings and holidays were pivotal events that provided an arena for new levels of identity affirmation or negation. Self-affirming behavior did not require an affirming response to be a positive experience. Choosing not to go to events, choosing to go without one's lover, separating for holidays, and self-censoring behaviors were generally experienced as self-negating. Attending events together, dancing together at weddings, talking about one's partner as naturally included in one's life all represent self-affirming behaviors. Such inclusive behavior normalized lesbian relationships. More often than not lesbians who behaved in self-affirming ways received affirming responses.

An important finding was that behavioral language could be self-affirming even in the absence of direct verbal self-disclosure. This affirmation was experienced even in the context of the family where women did not claim to be out unless they had been verbally explicit about their lesbian identity. Being "behaviorally out" in the workplace was felt to be strongly self-affirmative. In contrast to the family, explicit verbal disclosure was not required in the workplace to claim being out.

Everyone participating in this study readily recognized the unending process of coming out. It was a common occurrence that a direct verbal or behavioral disclosure met with increases in either affirmation or negation. In families there was usually a recognizable parallel process of coping with the awareness of a lesbian member. For some there was also a parallel process concerning disclosure to others, especially children and their friends and spouses. Many repetitions were often required before negation through denial lessened in families. Many appeared to work through layers of their own discomfort as they repeatedly insisted on some recognition, especially in their families.

Although the paradox of self-preservation appears prominently in Mary's story about lying, there was general respect for the need to secure safety in a variety of contexts. Safety might refer to physical safety, as in South America, economic safety, as in the workplace, or emotional safety, as inside the family. Although the price of safety may entail a degree of self-negation, protecting the self also was strongly self-affirming.

Over the past several months, since the focus groups were held, many participants have expressed the hope that I do more research because they found the discussion group so valuable. Some women have spoken to me about not separating for the holidays for the first time. Others have sought support during social gatherings of the lesbian and gay community concerning holiday stress. Some said they found my literature review interesting and others found particular parts of my analysis personally helpful or validating.

These findings are in agreement with Cain's study of gay men (1991) in that they suggest that clinicians evaluate ways to depathologize secrecy and consider more closely the contradictory demands faced by lesbians and gay men in society. The findings are also consistent with Eldridge and Gilbert's (1990) conclusion that nondisclosure is as adaptive for some lesbians as disclosure is for others. The diversity of languaging was apparent even in this small and highly homogeneous sample. Lesbians in general are a much more diverse group.

The types of language choices that emerged in this study are consistent with those Ponse (1976) describes. Is a lesbian visible only if she speaks in the language of direct verbal disclosure? The conclusion that lesbians are generally hidden may not reflect the prevalence and importance of behavioral language to lesbians.

Applying these findings in practice may require shifting our focus. Most striking is the importance of whether a given language choice is felt to be self-affirming or self-negating to a lesbian. Behavioral language may not be immediately evident to the clinician as having self-affirming value for a lesbian. A lesbian chooses her language of self-disclosure or concealment within the many contexts in which she lives, works, and plays; these contexts have histories and cultures to which lesbians respond with creative energy. As clinicians, whether gay, lesbian, or heterosexual, we must listen more carefully and be open to hearing all forms of language. For example, a lesbian may be struggling with a family that overtly accepts her explicit self-disclosure but, at the same time, reacts with negating behavioral language. A clinician open to the complexity of languaging for lesbians may help a lesbian make sense out of such a highly complex situation, one in which she may feel threatened or uncomfortable. Placing the discomfort in the situational or relational context can facilitate both understanding and change. A social worker's view of mental health is powerful. These findings suggest that social workers consider closely how we define mental health for lesbians. If internalized homophobia is overemphasized, there is a risk that consideration of negative social forces will be neglected. If self-disclosure is overemphasized by a clinician, she may inadvertently imply that lesbians who choose some degree of secrecy are responsible for their own problems.

The equation of lesbian mental health with disclosure has the potential of being damaging for the lesbian who lives and works in contexts that carry the possibility of severe negative consequences for self-disclosure. The ramifications of antihomosexual attitudes in some families, distinct cultures, and in different classes may well be powerful forces in the lives of lesbians, which should not be discounted by clinicians. As we hope to facilitate the capacity for self-affirmation, we must not minimize risk. For many lesbians, choices entail paradox. To affirm one aspect of their being may be to jeopardize the safety of another. Let us take care to listen to all aspects of our lesbian clients' stories, even the parts not spoken aloud.

The concept of parallel process can help clinicians normalize the difficulty families have integrating information about a lesbian member. Most important, the concept can help lesbians bear the brunt of forceful negation by family members, recognizing that such responses are part of a process rather than an end point.

Recognition that coming out is an unending process can be helpful to a clinician responding to lesbian clients stressed by a variety of life events. Lesbians seek the services of social workers for the same kinds of problems as everyone else. New problems, such as a medical diagnosis, a loss, or a child's school problems, may give rise to decisions concerning disclosure in new contexts for lesbians. Evaluation of the costs and benefits of disclosure can be enriched by considering the meaning of language choice in the social contexts associated with stressful events or circumstances. Just as the special events discussed by these lesbians gave rise to the possibility of affirmation or negation, so do the stressful life events that bring lesbians to social workers.

The voices of these lesbians illustrate that adversity can be the mother of invention. Social workers can validate and facilitate an expanded repertoire and increased flexibility in the ongoing struggle for language faced by lesbians.

REFERENCES

Berger, R. M. 1983. What is a homosexual? A definitional model. *Social Work* 28(2):132–141.

Berger, R. M. 1990. Passing: Impact on the quality of same-sex couple relationships. *Social Work* 35(4):328–332.

Browning, C. 1988. Therapeutic issues and intervention strategies with young adult lesbian clients: A developmental approach. In E. Coleman, ed., *Integrated identity for gay men and lesbians: Psychotherapeutic approaches for emotional well being*, pp. 45–52. New York: Harrington Park.

Cain, R. 1991. Stigma management and gay identity development. *Social Work* 36(1):67–73.

Cass, V. C. 1979. Homosexual identity formation: A theoretical model. *Journal of Homosexuality*, 4(3):219–235.

Chenitz, W. C., and J. M. Swanson. 1986. *From practice to grounded theory*. Menlo Park, Cal.: Addison-Wesley.

Coleman, E. 1982. Developmental stages of the coming-out process. *American Behavioral Scientist* 25(4):469–482.

Conrad, P., and J. W. Schneider. 1980. *Deviance and medicalization, from badness to sickness*. St. Louis: Mosby.

Corbin, J., and A. Strauss. 1990. Grounded theory research: Procedures, canons, and evaluative criteria. *Qualitative Sociology* 13(1):3–21.

Davis, F. 1961. Deviance disavowal: The management of strained interaction by the visibly handicapped. *Social Problems* 9:120–133.

de Monteflores, C., and S. J. Schultz. 1978. Coming out: Similarities and differences for lesbians and gay men. *Journal of Social Issues* 34(3):59–72.

Eldridge, N. S., and L. A. Gilbert. 1990. Correlates of relationship satisfaction in lesbian couples. *Psychology of Women Quarterly* 14(1):43–62.

Falco, K. L. 1991. *Psychotherapy with lesbian clients*. New York: Bruner/Mazel.

Glaser, B. G., and A. L. Strauss. 1967. *The discovery of grounded theory: Strategies for qualitative research*. New York: De Gruyter.

— 1981. Awareness contexts and social interaction. In G. Stone and H. Farberman, eds., *Social psychology through symbolic interaction*. New York: Wiley.

Goffman, E. 1963. *Stigma*. Englewood Cliffs, N.J.: Prentice-Hall.

Kahn, M. L. 1991. Factors affecting the coming out process for lesbians. *Journal of Homosexuality* 21(3):47–70.

Minton, H. L., and G. J. McDonald. 1984. Homosexual identity formation as a developmental process. *Journal of Homosexuality* 9(1):91–104.

Morgan, D. L. 1988. *Focus groups as qualitative research*. Newbury Park, Cal.: Sage.

Moses, A. E. 1978. *Identity management in lesbian women*. New York: Praeger.

Ponse, B. 1976. Secrecy in the lesbian world. *Urban Life* 5(3):313–336.

Potter, S. J., and T. E. Darty. 1981. Social work and the invisible minority: An exploration of lesbianism. *Social Work* 26(3):187–197.

Sophie, J. 1987. Internalized homophobia and lesbian identity. *Journal of Homosexuality* 14(1/2):53–65.

Strauss, A. L. 1987. *Qualitative analysis for social scientists*. New York: Cambridge University Press.

CHAPTER SIX

Therapy with a Lesbian Couple:
The Art of Balancing Lenses

Kathryn Karusaitis Basham

COUPLE THERAPY TYPICALLY CHALLENGES a clinician to balance
alliances and to avoid coalitions with each partner in order to ensure fair-
ness and empathic attunement. Since the training of most therapists has
assumed heterosexuality, when therapists work with lesbian couples they
have the additional challenge of trying to understand the ways in which
these couples may be uniquely different from heterosexual couples as well
as the ways they may be quite similar. Maintaining a delicate balance of
awareness of both similarity and difference becomes an ephemeral ideal or
an attainable goal depending on the therapist's awareness of the powerful
attitudes and biases that may, in spite of the best intentions, haunt the
therapeutic relationship.

Rachel Hare-Mustin's (1989) discussion of the problem of alpha and beta
bias in deconstructing gender is also especially relevant to the exploration
of various impasses that can emerge in the course of therapy with lesbian
couples. In this situation alpha bias is defined as the exaggeration of differences and beta bias as the minimizing of such differences. Each clinician
should walk very carefully along the path of respectful acceptance of diversity without exaggerating differences (where the risk is polarization and
bigotry) or ignoring important differences (where the risk is the illusion of

homogeneity and the disqualifying of unique experience). In this chapter I aim to explore the balancing of these potential biases as a way to negotiate the contextual impasses that can occur in couple therapy. I hope to provide both beginning and more seasoned clinicians with a range of perspectives in therapeutic work with a lesbian couple.

Resistance and Couple Therapy

In a recent paper (Basham 1992) I offer a multilevel review of feminist, intergenerational, and object relations theoretical perspectives on resistance, in addition to a framework for identifying and managing resistance in couple therapy, that guides the investigation of individual differences as well as interactional and societal factors. A new assessment tool yields a complex synthesis of institutional, interactional, and intrapersonal resistances. However, here I focus specifically on institutional and interactional resistances, grounding my analysis in feminist, social constructionist, and intergenerational family theories. A thorough analysis of intrapersonal resistances will be explored in another article.

Although the phenomenon of resistance is widely accepted throughout the world of therapy, differences in theoretical orientation influence the ways in which it is defined. Resisting is defined here generically as all those thoughts, beliefs, attitudes, feelings, patterns, and stories that interfere with the client's goals for change. These resulting impasses are considered the inevitable cornerstones of therapy and contain rich symbolic meaning for the couple even though they also thwart change. Rather than viewing these obstacles or impasses as obstructionistic and potentially annoying, I view them as opportunities to explore both the client's internal and outer worlds in order to facilitate a smoother journey. In this vein, approaching resistance positively as evidence of the client's strengths and adaptability will be a primary theme throughout this chapter.

With careful attention to the maintenance of balance between the recognition of similarities and differences, I present an examination of and strategies for overcoming resistances that disrupt therapy, obstruct change, and create therapeutic impasses in work with lesbian couples. Since definitions of resistance in couple therapy vary according to theoretical perspective, a review of common conceptions of the classical concept in psychoanalytic, systems, feminist, and social constructionist frameworks may be helpful. Several questions that reflect different theoretical positions inevitably arise in this investigation.

Classical Psychoanalytic Theory

In psychoanalytic theory resistance is seen as an unconscious process of conflictual drives that must be worked through. Certainly early analytic thinking supported the view that resistance relates to repression and the dissociation from consciousness of conflictual thoughts and then later to the "repetition compulsion" (Freud 1900, 1914). Developments in theory led Freud, in the *The Ego and the Id* (1923), to replace the repression view of resistance with one in which resistance surfaces in the interplay between defense mechanisms and the emerging libidinal and aggressive drives. A thorough summation of Freud's views on resistance can be found in his book *Inhibitions, Symptoms, and Anxiety* (1926), in which he categorizes resistances according to their source in the id, ego, or super-ego. Later, still retaining an emphasis upon intrapsychic phenomena, ego psychologists such as Anna Freud shifted the focus from resistance as a defense against libidinal and aggressive impulses to an elaboration of ego and superego functions. In her landmark book, *Ego and the Mechanisms of Defense* (1936), Anna Freud promoted the idea that ego defenses are transformed into transference resistances that interfere with the course of therapy.

In current-day practice psychodynamically oriented clinicians focus on resisting as an active process rather than a static entity. For example, Schafer (1983) offers a compelling critique of the reification of resistance as a fixed construct in language, encouraging clinicians to identify and actively grapple with this dynamic process.

Object Relations Theory

In an object relations theoretical perspective the following question is raised: Is resistance a reenactment of internalized object relations? Such a line of questioning is grounded in the belief that adults who have suffered deprivation, insensitivity, or abuse during childhood have developed internalized object relations that encapsulate the fears, earlier pains, and defenses constructed to protect against such emotional insults (Grotstein 1967; Kernberg 1975, Teitelbaum 1991; Winnicott 1958). In summary, in object relations theory resistance is seen as the by-product of layers of defenses that have developed to protect an individual from reexperiencing unresolved developmental ruptures. Resisting may then occur because of unrealistic desires or attempts at object replication in adult life.

Family Theory

Some family therapists, particularly those who hold to a psychodynamic/ object relations perspective, strongly endorse the construct of intrapsychically based resistance as a cornerstone of therapy. Structural and intergenerational family theorists, on the other hand, view resistance as important, yet place far less emphasis on its role in therapy. For example, intergenerational family theorists describe repetitive patterns of interaction as heritages from one's family of origin that serve to regulate the degree of "stuck-togetherness" that inhibits self-differentiation within the family (Bowen 1978; Kerr and Bowen 1988; Lerner 1989). These patterns of distancing, conflict, underfunction/overfunction, and triangulation serve to maintain a balance of self-differentiation and connection within the family, yet they also sustain maladaptive relationship patterns that paradoxically reduce anxiety but thwart change. Therapy becomes a matter of differentiating from these relationship patterns in the family.

Family theorists who draw upon social constructionist ideas view resistance somewhat differently. Social constructionist or narrative family therapists such as Harlene Anderson, Tom Andersen, the late Harry Goolishian, Michael White, and David Epston (Andersen 1987; Anderson and Goolishian 1992; White and Epston 1990) are interested in multiple ideas and perspectives on the nature of a problem. They view problems as socially constructed and always filtered through our "languages" for perceiving and experiencing them. Resistance, in this light, is understood as the client's pursuit of her own ideas and goals as she sees them and is redefined in terms such as Hoffman's (1981) idea of resistance as persistence or De Shazer's (1982) view of resistance as "a unique way of cooperating." If an impasse is observed, the clinical dialogue should be directed toward an expression of perceptions, meanings, and narratives that may be subjugated (Doherty 1991; Efran, Luken, and Lukens 1990) or that might shed clarity on a mismatch of goals. If the resistance or persistence is too tightly held, then perhaps a couple may restrict itself to stereotypical and rigid functioning; if too loosely held, then the couple struggles with chaos.

Feminist Theory

Any discussion of resistance in couple therapy requires attention to institutional and societal factors as well as interactional and intrapersonal factors. Patriarchy is said to be the pervasive and influential context in which both men and women are psychologically constructed (Carter 1992; Goldner 1991; Hoffman 1990), leading to omnipresent patterns of inequality among both lesbian and heterosexual couples. A couple that challenges the basic inequality in power relationships and "resists" the status quo assumes an activist position (Gilligan 1991). Consequently, resisting in this feminist framework takes on a different cast, one of facilitating rather than thwarting change. More recently a number of contemporary authors have been interested in exploring the interface between postmodernism, feminism, and psychoanalysis (Flax 1990; Hoffman 1992; Saari 1991). Major contributions from this perspective include challenging alpha-biased assumptions that tend to posit a universal position for all women and to exaggerate gender differences, questioning of gender orthodoxy, and retaining vigilance about the daunting and pernicious effects of patriarchy.

Now that various key definitions of resistance have been briefly summarized, I explore ways in which the sociopolitical and family of origin contexts interface with couple therapy, specifically paying attention to institutional and interactional resistances. Again, resistance will be generically defined as all those thoughts, beliefs, attitudes, feelings, patterns, and stories that interfere with stated goals for change. The feminist notion of resisting as a constructive challenge to a stultifying status quo also will be stressed.

The terms *resistance* and *resisting* will be used interchangeably to capture the active dynamic involved in the process. Institutional resistances will primarily be defined according to feminist and social constructionist theories, while interactional resistances will be understood in terms of a feminist intergenerational theory perspective.

I begin with a discussion of institutional and interactional resistance in therapy. Following this, I present a clinical illustration of therapy with a lesbian couple to demonstrate the challenges in maintaining a balanced view that guards against alpha bias (exaggerating differences) and beta bias (minimizing differences) while negotiating the various contextual impasses that emerge.

Institutional Resistances

Systems, social constructionist, and feminist theories are especially useful in identifying and understanding institutional resistances. Institutional resistances may be quite pronounced, especially during the early phases of couple therapy. These resistances include all those contextual influences that serve to obstruct the flow of progress toward goals mutually agreed upon by client and clinician. The therapist should be alert to listening for client narratives of socioeconomic class, religion, race, gender, sexual orientation, age, ableism, and other locations of diversity and to understanding how these sociocultural narratives are entering the therapeutic conversation. Institutional resistances in work with lesbian couples typically include (at least) the following factors: 1. sociocultural influences, 2. embedded unequal power relationships, 3. the discourses of heterosexism and homophobia in the larger society, 4. heterosexist and homophobic theories for therapy, and 5. the effects of alpha and beta bias in practice (worker values, beliefs, and attitudes).

Sociocultural Influences

In general, notions of couplehood and family, of marriage and partnership, of gender meanings and roles, and of sexuality take shape in and are strongly influenced by a patriarchal social structure characterized by patterns of domination and subordination and inequalities of power between the sexes. Clearly, these entrenched patterns can interfere with a couple's attempts to establish mutuality and equality in intimate relationships. Various ethnic and religious traditions, as well as social class narratives and experiences, can strongly influence family gender meanings and role ascriptions, leading to a "gender straightjacketing" process in couple and family life (Green, Bettinger, and Zacks 1996). For example, being lesbian or gay has very different meanings in different racial or ethnic groups, accepted or tolerated in some and considered an abomination or even an impossibility in others.

Religious belief and affiliation have been particularly difficult issues for some lesbians. Although some religious organizations have tolerated or even welcomed lesbians and gays, even in leadership positions, many religious groups continue to abhor homosexuality—even to the point of mounting widespread political efforts to promote antigay legislation on local and state levels and to gain membership on local school boards to promote antigay agendas in school curricula. This latter issue can negatively affect the family lives of lesbian parents, as their children find their families ridiculed and/or rendered invisible.

Sociocultural resistances can also include all those organizational obstacles that may impede progress in therapy. Some agencies, for example, may not reach out to or offer appropriate services for lesbians and gays. The influence of managed care as well as the constraints of some agency policies

Level I: Institutional Resistances

A. Sociocultural influences

   Social definitions of couplehood, marriage, and family
   Gender meanings and roles
   Conceptions of sexual orientation and sexuality
   Diversity themes: Race, ethnicity, social class, age, disability
   Religious beliefs and affiliations
   Public and organizational policies

B. Embedded unequal power relationships

C. Clinician attitudes: Alpha and beta bias

D. Organizational obstacles

   Agency policies
   Public policy

Level II: Interactional Resistances

A. Family patterns

   Distancing

   Partner Conflict

   Underfunction/overfunction

   Triangulation

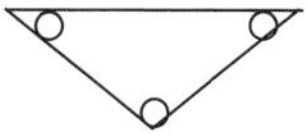

B. Family structure and processes

   Power relations
   Boundary issues
   Intimacy
   Rituals
   Narratives, stories

FIGURE 6.1. Guideline for Assessment of Institutional and Interactional Resistances in Couple Therapy

point to far more referrals for individual and group than for couples or family therapy. Since many lesbian clients are viewed as single, couples therapy often may not even be considered. Thus agencies, in the very definition of their services, by default fail to recognize or sanction lesbian couple and family bonds.

Embedded Unequal Relationships

Violence pervades contemporary American society, as evidenced by escalating crime statistics in general and by the disturbingly high incidence of violent crimes by men against women in particular. In a social context in which aggression and terror are glorified in the media, violence and injustice against marginalized groups are often overlooked and, as a range of injustices against women are often ignored or minimized in the political landscape, it is no surprise that violence at home is covertly and overtly sanctioned. Clearly, these strong sociocultural influences reinforce inequitable and abusive modes of relating, undermining many couples' abilities to maintain collaborative relationships. Although one might assume that two women in a relationship might be exempt from embedded inequality and the abuses it produces, lesbians have also been raised in this culture and some couples find themselves imitating and repeating the patterns of inequality, dominance, and submission endemic to heterosexual couples in our society (Kanuha 1990).

Heterosexism and Homophobia in Society

In addition to these pervasive institutional resistances that affect all women, lesbians carry out their lives and their relationships in a cultural context that assumes heterosexuality and permits and even encourages homophobia. (See chapters 1 and 2, this volume, for a much fuller discussion of the impact of these forces on lesbian life). Clinicians must be prepared to attend to the impact of heterosexism and homophobia on the couple relationship and on their daily experiences. Heterosexism is a pervasive world view in which heterosexuality is privileged and homosexuality devalued, while homophobia refers to discrimination, bigotry, and negativity toward gay and lesbian individuals because of sexual orientation. Heterosexism and homophobia are not only sanctioned informally but in many instances are supported by the laws of the land (Ellis and Murphy 1994; Hartman 1996; Herek 1986; Spaulding, this volume; Tievsky 1988). Therapists should never underestimate the real discrimination and oppression that exists in the world of work, housing, many social, educational, medical, and religious organizations, and, in fact in almost every area of life.

Heterosexism in Practice Theory Models

Although homosexuality was formally depathologized in the mental health field with the American Psychiatric Association's 1973 declaration that homosexuality per se was not pathological (Gonsiorek 1982), heterosexist bias still pervades many theory and practice models (Morin 1977; Morin and Charles 1983). Theoretical models vary in terms of the degree of heterosexist bias that operates and some practitioners and theory builders within each perspective have made ongoing and at times successful efforts to challenge heterosexist and homophobic positions. Historically, in psychoanalytic literature homosexuality has been viewed as reflecting unresolved Oedipal issues or developmental arrest (Deutsch 1933; Khan 1962; Lewes 1988; McCandlish 1982; Thompson 1947). Although certain heterosexist notions remain prevalent, recently feminist critics writing from a psychoanalytic stance have been critiquing psychodynamic models in which homosexuality is pathologized (Chodorow 1989; Falco 1991; Glassgold and Iasenza 1995; Irigaray 1985; Muzio, this volume; O'Connor and Ryan 1993; Prozan 1992; Sussal, this volume).

The central problem in the family theory field, until very recently, has been the virtual invisibility of lesbian and gay families. A second problem concerns the potential heterosexist bias implicit in many family theories and concepts, and several theorists have challenged normative and heterosexist assumptions about families and family life implicit or explicit in major family therapy models (Crawford 1987; Krestan and Bepko 1980; Laird 1993, 1994, 1996; Roth 1989; Slater 1995). However, less attention has been focused on the ways in which lesbianism is pathologized in family theory. Family therapists Goodrich, Ellman, Rampage, and Halstead (1988) questioned the presumed problematizing of the Bowenian concept of the triangle in all couple relationships, arguing that triangular relationships may be culturally normative for lesbian couples. While stressing the value of history and context in intergenerational family theory, Luepnitz (1988) argues that the concept of triangulation is interpreted in a way that reinforces patriarchal values. A focus on the intergenerational transmission of mother-child fusion, rather than on a more systemic view in which the father and other key family members are included, leads to pathologizing mothers in families. The author further comments that the words often used to refer to differentiation, such as *autonomous, goal directed,* and *intellectual,* value attributes that are often associated with men's gender socialization. Lesbian couples, then, consisting of two women, in both psychoanalytic and family systems theories, are frequently described as fused, an assumption critiqued by Mencher (1990) and Green, Bettinger, and Zacks (1996).

The theoretical constructs proposed by the original Bowen (1966) model do not adequately attend to issues of gender, race, ethnicity, social class, or other cultural dimensions, nor do they address issues of sexual orientation. However, proponents of a feminist adaptation of Bowen's intergenerational family theory point to ways of redefining central concepts—particularly the notion of differentiation—to mean greater balance between intellectual and emotional functioning in ways that incorporate and affirm the experiences of women (Carter 1992; Lerner 1989; Luepnitz 1988). In this chapter, rather than repudiating the constructs of triangulation, differentiation, boundary, and fusion, I demonstrate how they may be used constructively without gender or heterosexist bias.

Alpha and Beta Bias: Worker Values, Beliefs, and Attitudes

Faced with diversity, all clinicians need to continually balance the tendency toward generalization and bigotry (alpha bias) with the tendency to ignore or minimize differences (beta bias). Lesbian couples pose a special challenge in this area. On the one hand, they must grapple with all the issues every couple must negotiate; on the other, there are some profound differences between lesbian couples and heterosexual couples in the issues they face. Gay and straight clinicians alike must walk a tightrope between assuming and failing to recognize difference, as even highly sympathetic and positive theoreticians in their exploration of lesbian life tend at times to exaggerate difference or ignore similarities. The following discussion will address several examples of both alpha and beta bias in contemporary theoretical and clinical practice models.

Alpha-biased interventions in couple therapy, or exaggerating the differences between lesbian couples and heterosexual couples, can be quite overt or at times quite subtle. An overt example of alpha bias would be a clinician's assumption of pathology in linking a client's difficulties to her sexual orientation. Another example, very common in practice up until twenty or thirty years ago and still central in the work of some well-known clinicians, is the problematizing of the client's sexual orientation. In such situations therapeutic goals may include a search for the genesis of the client's sexual orientation and moblizing efforts to change it, rather than exploring the meaning of the client's presenting concerns. A more subtle form of alpha bias operates with clinicians who covertly believe that lesbian lifestyles are unhealthy and therefore may fail to notice or challenge painful or unhealthy aspects in the lesbian couple relationship.

Alpha bias is also exemplified when therapists assume that lesbians are exempt from embedded inequality and violence as discussed above. Attention to the sociopolitical context is crucial in understanding the intersections between power, social policies, and the social construction of family roles. Since most clients have been reared in patriarchal family structures, clinicians need to be aware of the unequal power relationships in both homosexual and heterosexual relationships that thwart growth. As a result, the clinician must be always alert to patterns of coercion, intimidation, and/or violence in couple relationships (Goldner, Penn, Sheinberg, and Walker 1990; Hammond 1988; Hare-Mustin 1989; Kanuha 1990). Clinicians, as well as lesbian clients themselves, blinded by alpha bias, often find themselves baffled that women, who are often stereotypically thought to be accommodating, submissive, and pacifist, may at times be as abusive and dominant as their male counterparts. Public awareness of violence and battery among lesbian couples is controversial, since the lesbian political community understandably fears the misuse or distortion of this information to promote a pathologizing of lesbianism. If a lesbian couple challenges the inequality in their relationship, this form of "resisting" *facilitates* rather than impedes progress. However, in order to reduce potential alpha bias, clinicians should not assume commonalities among all lesbian clients in terms of sociocultural influences. In that case the uniqueness of each client in terms of her inner world and family of origin experiences might be overlooked.

Another example of overt alpha bias in therapy with a lesbian couple involves directly discouraging a client from coming out to family and friends without knowing the probable response from these individuals. Clinicians with strong homophobic concerns might project their negative and critical feelings onto family members and assume the worst possible scenario (De Crescenzo 1984; Kleinberg 1986). As Laird (1996) notes in her challenge to stereotypical themes recurrent in the clinical practice landscape, many clinicians believe that the relationships between a lesbian client and her family of origin are often tortured and characterized by negativity and upheaval. Often overlooked is the transitional or, at times, crisis nature of coming out to family members, as the family over time may shift into a mode of gradual acceptance and restored equilibrium. Typically, in treatment sessions the couple needs to discuss potential reactions of family members as well as the potential consequences for the client before a coming out plan is implemented. Laird (1996) further notes that alpha bias prevails if there is an assumption that all coming out processes must involve a linear, prototypical process defined by verbal disclosure. In fact, many lesbians share their sexual orientation in nonverbal as well as verbal modes of expression.

In couple therapy it is important to discuss the risk of beta bias as well. Beta bias, or minimizing the differences between lesbian and heterosexual couples, may lead a therapist to make assumptions that what is valuable in clinical work with heterosexual couples may be uncritically applied in work with lesbian couples. For example, liberal and well-meaning therapists, out of their naïveté or idealism and convinced that everyone should take "I" positions with their families of origin, may strongly encourage lesbian clients to come out to their families, friends, and at work without adequate attention to the risks and dangers involved. In fact, family theories in general overvalue the importance of the biological and adoptive families and fail to notice the centrality of chosen and created families in lesbian and gay culture. This bias has influenced family therapists to overstress the importance of coming out to families as an essential part of the work of differentiation, predicting dire consequences for individuals who maintain secrecy. Interestingly, Green, Zacks, and Bettinger (1996), in their research with straight, lesbian, and gay couples, find that coming out to the family of origin seems to have little impact on lesbian or gay couple satisfaction, while they and many other researchers have documented the complex extrafamilial systems of social support that lesbians and gays can and do develop for themselves.

Interactional Resistance

Interactional resistances include all those family patterns and processes from the families of origin and families of choice that interfere with the accomplishment of therapy goals. The interplay of power, intimacy, boundary, and ritual with day-to-day interactions must be explored. In Bowenian family systems theory optimal couple functioning in terms of intimacy, autonomy, and other aspects of couple functioning is promoted by the ongoing self-differentiation efforts of each partner (Bowen 1978; Kerr and Bowen 1988). Although this construction of self is gender and culture bound, the concept of self-differentiation remains useful for clinical practice as long as one is sensitive to gender and other cultural variations. Since a certain degree of fusion is normative for all dyadic relationships, anxiety associated with the balancing of fusion and self-differentiation is dealt with through a combination of different patterns, including distancing, underfunctioning or overfunctioning, conflict, and triangulation (Kerr and Bowen 1988). There is a continuous interplay between two counterbalancing forces—individuality and connectedness. Although these patterns temporarily reduce anxiety and at times are quite adaptive for a couple, they may also thwart positive changes in the family when they interfere with the enhancement of self-differentiation for each partner.

Fusion and Self-Differentiation

The casual use of the term *fusion* to describe all lesbian couple relationships has pathologized the qualities of cohesion and connectedness common in lesbian couples and undermined the clarity and usefulness of the phenomenon when it does accurately describe a rather dramatic lack of coherence, balance, and clarity within an individual or between individuals. To understand intimacy in lesbian relationships, the value of mutuality, connection, and authenticity as dynamic ingredients for growth needs to be acknowledged. In fact, researchers have reported significantly higher levels of adaptability, cohesion, and satisfaction in lesbian couples than in heterosexual couples, commenting that the egalitarian nature of lesbian relationships enables them to function more effectively in several ways than heterosexual couples (Peplau, Cochran, Rook, and Padesky 1978; Zacks, Green, and Marrow 1988).

As Spaulding (chapter 1, this volume) suggests, there may be no greater risk of fusion in lesbian couples than in other couples. Based on data collected from a sample of 102 gay male and lesbian couples, Green, Bettinger, and Zacks (1996) found that lesbian couples reported more cohesion than gay male couples who, in turn, reported more cohesion than heterosexual married couples. These findings clearly challenge the alpha-biased notion that lesbian couples in general are "more fused" than heterosexual couples. Since this sample is a nonclinical one, the research inquiry raises the obvious question whether the higher incidence of problematic fusion seen in clinical lesbian couples isn't related to distress rather than to sexual orientation. There is no evidence to support the idea that levels of fusion are higher for distressed lesbian couples than for distressed heterosexual couples.

Some feminist therapists within the past decade have attended to the unique features of women's development that stress the valuation of "self"—or, in a postmodern sense, "selves-in-connection" (Berzoff 1989; Kaplan 1984; Miller 1988). In their view, gender role socialization in a woman's developmental struggle privileges the need for connectedness over the need for a sense of individual self, while in the man's developmental struggle autonomy is privileged over connectedness.

The construct of fusion has been explored in depth in much of the clinical literature addressing therapy with lesbian couples and has typically been viewed as problematic (Bograd 1988; Burch 1982, 1986, 1987; Decker 1984, Krestan and Bepko 1980). Various authors have used the terms *fusion, merger, symbiosis,* and *enmeshment* interchangeably—all to define or describe dysfunction. Mencher (1990) effectively discusses the ways in which relational strengths—valued by heterosexual women and lesbians—have been interpreted negatively, implicating *fusion* as a pathologizing term. In lesbian relationships the very qualities lesbians themselves particularly value, such as intimacy and emotional closeness, may be devalued by therapists who privilege the rational intellectual realm. Mencher notes, in her discussion of Jessica Benjamin's work regarding merger, that "it may be difficult to detoxify the term fusion and to relieve it of the malignant connotations" because of the distortions and negative connotations associated with this term throughout the history of psychotherapy (1990:9).

In an effort to focus on the positive and negative aspects of connectedness, Green, Bettinger, and Zacks (1996) have proposed a new conceptual framework for thinking about lesbian and gay male couples that abandons the controversial concept of fusion yet retains the processes typically associated with the interplay of fusion and self-differentiation. They posit a model in which couple relationships are examined in terms of the following factors: 1. the California Inventory domains of closeness—caregiving, openness of communication, and intrusiveness, 2. the idea of unique lesbian and gay male gender roles versus conformity to traditional gender role norms, and 3. the notion of families of choice.

Another choice in dealing with the term *fusion*, which refers to both intrapersonal and interactional processes, is to redefine and clarify its meanings. In this light, a redefinition of *fusion* based on Bowenian family systems theory stresses the valuation of both relational and cognitive abilities. Kerr and Bowen (1988), in fact, noted that fusion in either an intrapersonal or interpersonal frame represents a lack of adequate balance of the emotional and cognitive spheres, which leaves a person or couple vulnerable to overly reactive responses dominated by intense emotion. It should be pointed out that occasional experiences of blurring of emotion and cognition, either internally or interpersonally, can be quite adaptive and desirable. Certainly in moments of profound emotional and/or sexual intimacy such a merger is highly valued.

Fusion, then, refers to the dominance of emotions and impulses that are unregulated or unmonitored by an adequate cognitive process, or a dominance of cognition that is unmonitored by an adequate balance of emotion, resulting in a blurring of emotionality, feeling, and thought. When a person experiences this state regularly, she usually reports confusion, vagueness, emptiness, and a lack of grounding. Fusion, when it refers to an interpersonal connection, *does not* describe a person's capacity to relate with another person in intimate, empathic, or mutually rewarding ways. Instead, each partner actually lacks attunement to the needs, thoughts, and beliefs of the partner as well as self. Ambiguity and diffuseness prevail, leading to experiences of incongruence or overwhelming suffocation.

Self-differentiation, redefined to attend to gender and cultural themes, describes a person's capacity for balance between emotions and cognition, flexibility, adaptability, and the capacity for mature intimacy with others (Anderson 1996; Kerr and Bowen 1988; Lerner 1989). Even Bowen described a person with stronger self-differentiation as "sure of beliefs and convictions . . . not dogmatic or fixed in thinking . . . discards old beliefs in favor of new . . . can listen without reacting and can communicate without antagonizing others . . . able to assume total responsibility for self and sure of his responsibility to others . . . tolerant and respectful of differences . . . not prone to engage in polarized debates (Kerr and Bowen 1988:107).

The crusty, self-contained, and cerebral demeanor that characterized Bowen's lecture presentations reinforced his critics' beliefs that rational cognition was valued more than emotion. And, although Bowen's (1966) early writings supported the valuation of reason over emotion, later revisions of the concepts of fusion and self-differentiation incorporate the notion of what may be termed the "differentiated self-in-connection." Thus, a contemporary feminist revision of the concept of self-differentiation attends to gender and culture and is helpful in assessing how an individual achieves a synthesis of emotions and reason. It is unnecessary to choose a dualistic stance that privileges either emotion or reason. The constructs of fusion and self-differentiation are not dichotomized themes on a linear continuum; the differentiation of self-in-connection involves an interplay of emotions and reason both within the individual (intrapersonally) and between individuals (interpersonally).

Boundary and Triangulation

Other constructs that have been challenged in the family field are boundary and triangulation (Goodrich, Rampage, Ellman, and Halstead 1988; Luepnitz 1988). The construct of boundary defines membership and the degree of flexibility and openness that exists between people in relationships as well as relationships between the person, couple, or family and the external world. Krestan and Bepko (1980), in their early work, discuss how some lesbian couples draw inward as a way to compensate for the assaults on the boundaries surrounding their relationship. Although this "two against the world" stance may be adaptive and self-protective, an undesired result may be heightened dependency on the relationship for meeting too much of the couple's need for connectedness. Uniting against critical homophobic forces may strengthen some relationships, but other couples experience an exacerbation of self-hatred and fusion related to the extreme isolation (Kirkpatrick 1991). On the other hand, triangulation frequently can be adaptive and certainly quite ordinary. Any couple—heterosexual or gay or lesbian—for a host of reasons may experience a certain degree of fusion and associated anxiety and may draw in a third person or object to defuse the anxiety. Triangulation is only problematic when there are fixed patterns in which two people fail to deal with unresolved fusion and conflict, leading to a problematic triangle that undermines the third person and renders the issue unresolved.

Therapists working with lesbian couples need to consider the ways in which their notions of boundary may contain overt or covert heterosexist assumptions or definitions of family and couplehood. I noted earlier that family theories tend to overemphasize the importance of the biological and adoptive family and underemphasize the place of families of choice and creation or other supportive networks in lesbian culture. Many lesbian couples create their own families of choice, made up of a network of friends and acquaintances who serve vital and reciprocal extended family functions, enhancing lesbian couple well-being (Green, Bettinger, and Zacks 1996; Lewin 1993 ; Weston 1991). Clinicians must be open to questioning who the significant people are in the lives of a lesbian couple since the traditional boundaries based on legal arrangement or biological links may not be the most meaningful connections. It is important to observe that boundaries, which are either amorphous or fluid at times, or clear and flexible at other times, may reflect healthy growth. More attention should be paid to observing boundaries that are too rigid, noting when a loosening of boundaries is helpful, for example, during transitions, crises, and playful or joyful experiences.

Having addressed some of the important institutional and interactional resistances relevant to clinical practice with lesbian couples, in the following section I demonstrate how these resistances may be explicated and alpha and beta biases deconstructed and balanced in a particular case of couple therapy.[2]

The Case of Paula and Colette

Initial impressions

Paula initiated treatment quite tentatively with a phone contact commenting that she was "hopeless yet ambivalent," "depressed," "generally irritable," "struggling to make decisions at home and work," yet "invested in trying to sort out difficulties in my five-year relationship with Colette." Based on this discussion, I decided to invite both Paula and Colette to an initial consultation session to review their shared concerns. During the first meeting Paula expressed her worry about her increasing estrangement from Colette, the absence of any meaningful talk, Colette's immersion in her own family's health problems, and the absence of any shared enjoyable times together.

The following cameo captures the tenor of the first session. Paula, a diminutive athletic woman with trembling hands and speech, generated a sharply pitched, high velocity whirlwind of distracting topics about the weather, the traffic, and the latest international disasters. My sense was that she was using these conversational weapons for self-defense. In spite of her professional demeanor, Paula looked very frightened and sad. In contrast, Colette, a tall and graceful woman, entered the office in silence, sinking deep into a softly cushioned chair while casting a wary gaze my direction. Tentativeness, vulnerability, and deep sadness were palpable.

Colette reported that it was difficult to express differences with Paula, while Paula in turn accused Colette of shirking her responsibilities at home and then retreated into silence. The couple seemed to have few means for mutual understanding or problem solving. Although each partner feared that there were very few rewards left in this relationship, each referred to their first year together as mutually enhancing, challenging, and gratifying.

Colette was attracted to Paula's calm, steadiness, competence, "no-non-sense" organizing and problem-solving skills as well as her capacity to enjoy the creative arts. Paula, on the other hand, was attracted to Colette's joi de vivre, creativity, and love of dialogue. Both reported that these qualities had been virtually absent during the past two years. In order for me to begin establishing an alliance with Paula and Colette, it became immediately apparent that certain institutional resistances required attention.

Institutional Resistances

Both my own biases and the impact of heterosexism and homophobia were the most noteworthy institutional resistances revealed early on in this case. More specifically, both alpha bias (the tendency to stereotype or exaggerate differences) as well as beta bias (the tendency to minimize differences) were distinctly apparent as institutional resistances. Clinical interventions used to help minimize these resistances included 1. the exploration of cultural attitudes and beliefs about family, lesbianism, homophobia, and therapy, 2. discussion of power in relationships, 3. specific goal setting, 4. development of contracts, and 5. communication skills building.

Clinician Bias

All of us, in this case both clinician and clients, have powerful narratives of "family" and "couplehood" that shape what we see and hear. These constitute one form of what I am calling institutional resistances. A question that arose for me during the initial telephone conversation with this couple was, Are Paula and Colette "a couple?" What is the definition of couple? Immediately, my own attitudes regarding notions of coupling and family must be raised for scrutiny. Are families defined exclusively by biological or legal bonds? Or do chosen families in which individuals establish a committed partnership with enduring emotional connections and responsibilities exist (Clunis and Green 1988; Laird 1993; Weston 1991)? Do I struggle in the same ways with the same question of how to define couplehood when a heterosexual partner initiates the call?

One example of clinician alpha bias in a case like this might involve a clinician's covert feeling that the couplehood itself is not quite legitimate, that lesbian relationships tend to be ephemeral and transient, and that probably one or both "will grow out of" the relationship. Such a commonly held belief is clearly embedded in homophobic attitudes in which lesbian relationships are viewed as pathological, immature, and possibly immoral. Operating with a covert or overt bias of this sort would lead to devaluation of the couple relationship and most probably a recommendation for individual therapy for Paula and/or Colette. It is not uncommon for an alpha-biased clinician to collude with the side of the couple's ambivalence that promotes dissolution. Imposition of a clinician's attitudes on the goals of therapy of course occurs in work with heterosexual couples as well, when clinicians lean toward promoting continuation or dissolution of the partnership. With lesbian and gay couples, however, the added dimension of heterosexism heightens both the couple's and clinician's struggle with the definition and affirmation of coupleness.

When Paula made the initial phone call, it was unclear to me if she was pursuing help to work on her own individual issues or if work on the relationship was her priority. Clearly, this goal needed to be clarified before we could proceed. After Paula had identified her depressed feelings and wish for relief, I explored the notion of "coupleness."

T: *What were your hopes in calling me today?*

PAULA: *I would like to feel less irritable and unhappy with Colette.*

T: *Have you and Colette discussed your plan to call me today?*

PAULA: *Oh, yes, she thinks that I need help since I'm so miserable to live with. She doesn't know if I want to leave though!*

T: *What are your hopes in terms of your relationship with Colette?*

PAULA: *I'm very unhappy so I really worry about how this can work out. I'm very dubious but don't know if I should try to end it either.*

T: *What would help you to know?*

PAULA: *Well, we used to talk, but we never do anymore. Maybe if we discussed the problems I would at least see things more clearly.*

T: *If Colette were on the phone with us right now, what do you imagine she might say about her wishes?*

PAULA: *Oh, probably that she wants to work things out but that she couldn't stand meeting in therapy with the two of us. She would be embarrassed to talk about personal topics with a total stranger.*

T: *You anticipate that Colette might be reluctant to meet for a couple consultation, yet do you yourself have any reservations about meeting with Colette in that situation?*

PAULA: *I worry that someone at work may find out since there are ways that my health care can be tracked. I do not want to jeopardize my job.*

T: *I want to assure you of the confidentiality of our meetings. It is entirely your choice if you submit claims to your insurance company, but you should know that I will not discuss your situation with anyone without your written consent to do so.*

It was clear from this first contact that Paula and Colette did indeed define themselves as a couple in jeopardy who wished for some relief and change in their relationship. As a result of this exploration, I invited both of them to meet with me for a consultation. In the first session I assessed the severity of depression for both Paula and Colette to determine an appropriate treatment plan and to evaluate the indications/contraindications for a medication evaluation. Although Paula presented symptoms of depression including daily tearfulness, irritability, and a sense of hopelessness, she did not complain of suicidal ideation or vegetative symptoms. Similar feelings of sadness and hopelessness were echoed by Colette, yet she too denied any suicidal interest. Neither partner was abusing substances, a factor of importance given the high incidence of alcoholism in Colette's family of origin. Although my clinical assessment pointed to depression related to relationship issues and unresolved grief associated with family of origin issues, there were no indications to refer either partner for a medication consultation. Since Colette requested that I document a treatment plan to submit to her insurance company, with her signed permission I wrote a justification for treatment for at least twelve sessions with a plan to reevaluate progress at that date. The company notified me that three sessions would be authorized but that medication would be more expedient and the treatment of choice. Once more, an organizational obstacle based on the recommendation of an administrative assistant interfered with this couple's therapeutic work. After discussion with both women about this recommendation, they decided to abandon the use of their insurance benefits and to work with me in couple therapy on a sliding scale basis rather than be subjected to imposed medicalized treatment.

As I suggested above, one example of a homophobic, alpha-biased generalization is that lesbian partners are allegedly unstable or quixotic in their commitments. It is the case that the longevity rates for lesbian couples are somewhat shorter than for heterosexual couples, but most researchers agree that, given the lack of social or legal sanctions for such relationships, they are remarkably stable. On the other hand, some lesbian couples remain together far longer than either partner considers healthy. In these situations there may be a number of influences operating to hold them together. First, since a couple may be beleaguered by the forces of homophobia, they may join together in resisting these forces—an adaptation that reinforces connection. Second, a partnership between two women must take into account the impact of gender socialization. Many women are socialized in a relational mode to provide caregiving, to accommodate to the needs of other people, and to value monogamy (Gartrell 1984; Kaplan 1984; Miller 1988). Many women avoid conflict and the clear expression or anger or negative feelings and thus may lack needed conflict resolution skills. The combination of a worldview that stresses durability of relationships, the need to work things through in spite of visible failures, and the absence of conflict-resolving skills can leave an unhappy couple immobilized. A lesbian couple might present such a facade of durability even though the relationship is stagnant. It is imperative that a clinician not accept this stasis as necessarily a sign of commitment and devotion but rather explore with them whether they are persisting out of a sense of guilt, mistaken adherence to inflexible gender scripts, unresolved family of origin issues, or other constraining forces.

Heterosexism and Homophobia

A second source of institutional resistance is the impact of heterosexism and homophobia on the couple. Although much of the research literature supports the notion that lesbian couples are more alike than different from other couples along such basic relational dimensions as intimacy, power, and communication (Laird 1993), the pernicious effects of heterosexism and homophobia must be addressed. Once again, attunement to the basic challenges facing a lesbian couple must balance both alpha and beta biases.

It is unrealistic to assume, for example, that the initial phone call from a lesbian couple should be interpreted or dealt with in the same ways a clinician might deal with a call from a heterosexual couple. Nevertheless, it is very common in couple therapy with lesbian or heterosexual couples for the "noninitiating" partner to be the repository of resistance for the couple and to express much of the couple's reluctance to enter therapy. Typically, a clinician assesses the nature of the concerns presented by the individual caller to ascertain if the goals are primarily intrapersonal or relational and if there is merit in recommending a consultation with the couple. The challenge is to engage both partners.

Many couples who enter therapy fear a loss of autonomy, change, dissolution of the relationship, censure and/or unwanted direct advice from the clinician, and may anticipate consequences at the workplace. In addition, a lesbian couple may be wary of the attitudes that the clinician holds toward homosexuality, particularly if the sexual orientation of the clinician is heterosexual or unknown. Given these initial pressures, some potential clients may even hide their sexual orientation, at first, or neglect to disclose that they are partnered.

For example, when Paula called with her list of individual and relational concerns, she was tentative about discussing any issue in depth for fear of exposure and the anticipated negative consequences at work. As a result, she actually deemphasized her coupleness, which might easily have led to my colluding with her minimization of couple issues and thus failing to include Colette in the initial appointment. Her realistic concerns about privacy prompted my assurances of confidentiality as well as a thorough discussion about the extent of my professional experiences working with lesbian couples. The threat of job loss and censure imposed tremendous pressure on Paula to compartmentalize her personal and work lives. Only during later sessions was she willing to discuss her fears of disclosure at work and her struggles with commitment, issues that were burdening both women as they wrestled with the secrecy and fragmentation between their personal and work lives.

Another potential source of alpha or beta bias concerns the therapist's prior assumptions about lesbians' relationships with their families of origin and their knowledge or lack thereof about other potential support networks. Many clinicians may err on the side of predicting dire consequences for couples in coming out to families (alpha bias) or fail to carefully explore the potential crisis, pain, and censure that may be involved (beta bias). In my work with Colette and Paula we had many conversations about the women's respective connections with their families and other potential sources of support. These conversations surfaced a range of supportive as well as devaluing relationships among both Paula's and Colette's families of origin and friendships. On a different note, a heterosexual couple does not have to contend with a layer of institutional resistance that involves the interplay of internalized and societal homophobia. Grier and Cobbs (1968) coined the term *healthy cultural paranoia* to refer to work with African American clients, a concept that is pertinent here. When an individual has been subjected to bigotry, a higher level of wariness and resistance is expected and adaptive. This wariness may be expressed in the client's suspicion of the clinician. Therapists have differing ideas about and deal with self-disclosure issues differently; certainly a gay affirmative therapist who reveals her lesbian sexual orientation may be immediately perceived as more accepting (see Dillon, this volume; Gartrell 1984; Siegel and Walker 1996). But gay or lesbian therapists are not necessarily more knowledgable or less homophobic. In fact, recent studies support the notion that what attitudes and beliefs are communicated are more important than the actual sexual orientation of the clinician (Anderson 1996; Moran 1992; Stein 1988). Following a full discussion of client apprehensions and attitudes regarding therapy, it is often helpful to contract to meet for a discrete number of sessions and plan to evaluate the efficacy of the meetings at the end of the agreed upon time.

Ignoring the powerful impact of societal homophobia may lead a clinician in this case to ally primarily with Paula's ambivalence about the relationship and to invite her for an individual session without paying attention to the many institutional barriers. It may also inhibit the exploration of the richness of these intrapersonal and interactional resistances in the treatment as well as within the relationship if there is an assumption that resistance is only a typical reluctance to face pain or change.

Considerable discussion has been devoted to the barriers that may have interfered with engaging Paula and Colette in therapy from the onset— important issues to examine because establishing an initial sense of trust is a prerequisite for any further work. This couple successfully maneuvered through some formidable impasses, using some of my navigational input when appropriate. As the therapy progressed, the institutional resistances and obstructing biases receded, only to be replaced by the emerging interactional resistances.

The Unfolding Story

Subsequent to these very early meetings the following story of Paula and Colette's relationship emerged. Paula, age thirty-seven, and Colette, age thirty-eight, had been partners for the past five years. Paula completed a college education and works as an administrator in a high-pressured consulting organization that markets controversial military contracts. Colette, also a college graduate, works as a health care professional. (See figure 6.2— the genogram of Colette's and Paula's families of origin.)

Paula, the youngest of seven children, was reared in poverty in a midwestern farming community by a widowed mother of Scottish Presbyterian ancestry. Her father died of a sudden heart attack when she was five years old, leaving her mother the enormous task of rearing all seven children by herself. An older sister assumed a co-parenting role and functioned as a second

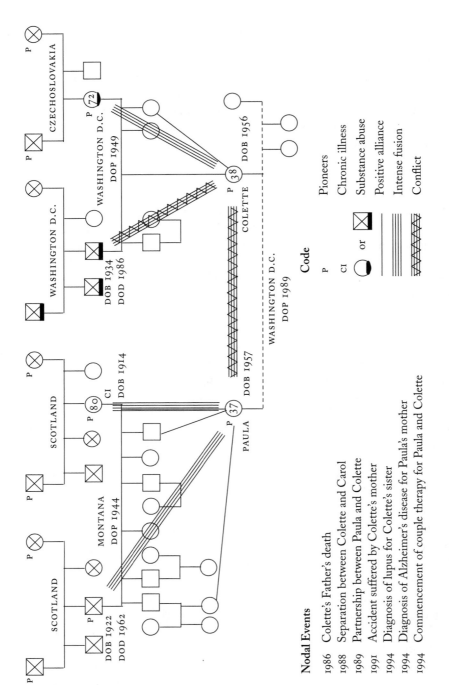

Code

P	Pioneers
CI	Chronic illness
◐ or ◪	Substance abuse
‖‖‖	Positive alliance
‖‖‖‖	Intense fusion
⋈⋈⋈	Conflict

Nodal Events

1986   Colette's Father's death
1988   Separation between Colette and Carol
1989   Partnership between Paula and Colette
1991   Accident suffered by Colette's mother
1994   Diagnosis of lupus for Colette's sister
1994   Diagnosis of Alzheimer's disease for Paula's mother
1994   Commencement of couple therapy for Paula and Colette

FIGURE 6.2 Genogram for Paula and Colette

mother to Paula. Paula recalls an early childhood characterized by indulgence from the entire family, which, after her father's death, shifted into a long period of vulnerability, painful loss, and poverty.

At the onset of couple therapy with Paula and Colette, Paula's mother was diagnosed with a degenerative neurological disorder that undermined her independence and intellectual competence. Driven by her increasingly frail physical condition, this pioneering woman turned to her family for help with the difficult task of searching for a supervised rest home.

Since Paula had never discussed her lesbianism with her mother, she felt very saddened that her opportunity was now lost, given her mother's inability to fully grasp the meaning of such a conversation. When Paula was a teenager, she disclosed her sexual orientation to her sister, only to face rebuke and censure. These lingering painful memories of rejection have fueled Paula's wariness at her workplace, where firings are common. She is firm about remaining closeted at her office. In my effort to discover whether she had had any positive or accepting responses to disclosures of her sexual orientation, Paula volunteered that both her brother and niece had been consistently loving and accepting toward her and Colette.

Colette is the second of four children born to a Catholic Slovak family in a middle-income urban area. Both parents worked outside the home in white-collar positions. At the beginning of treatment Colette's mother, who had suffered paraplegia three years earlier after an alcohol-related accidental fall, was still struggling to adapt to life in a wheelchair. A younger sister had recently been diagnosed with lupus, which has stirred enormous anxiety and fears among family members. Both parents drank alcoholically during Colette's childhood but stopped suddenly following her mother's tragic accident, thrusting the entire family into an "emotional vacuum" protected by a familiar alcoholic haze.

Colette came out to her family during college and, after an initial crisis characterized by accusations of sinfulness, gradually each family member has reached an accepting and respectful attitude toward Colette's sexual orientation and lifestyle. The family loves Paula. Colette had always expressed her creativity through modern dance and always involved herself actively with her family and community of lesbian and heterosexual friends. But, during the past two years, Colette, feeling overwhelmed, had severed ties with most of her friends. As she became more isolated and preoccupied with and burdened by the care of her mother and sister, her demanding days were followed by evenings of profound fatigue and retreat to the comforting isolation of sleep.

Therapy Goals

After several consultation sessions during which Paula and Colette identified a number of key issues and concerns, the couple decided to work on
their relationship with the help of therapy. They authored, with my participation, the following goals: 1. to reduce the frequency of nonproductive
arguments and to deal openly with conflict, 2. to improve communications
skills, 3. to reduce Paula's symptoms of depression, 4. to grieve the losses
associated with chronic illness (helped by the creation of healing rituals), 5.
to restore a mutually enhancing sexual relationship, and 6. to explore and
restory family of origin tales searching for strengths.

Interactional Resistance

Interactional resistances, as discussed earlier, involve family patterns that
obstruct progress. Themes of power, intimacy, boundary, and ritual illuminate the unique ways in which a family constructs their reality, negotiates
changes, and manages impasses along the way. Early on in the therapy, Paula
presented as the depressed, symptomatic, underfunctional partner, while
Colette appeared to be quiet and withholding. Even though Colette felt victimized by Paula's complaints, she still presented herself as contained and
competent. This overfunction/underfunction pattern did not remain fixed;
instead there seemed to be constant fluctuation in the relationship with each
partner alternately experiencing powerlessness, grief, and immobilization.
Their isolation from the lesbian community and Paula's estrangement from
several members of her family burdened her as well as the couple. According
to an intergenerational family perspective, fusion, both intrapersonally and
interpersonally, heightened given the lack of supports and affirmation from
their social network.

   In the following section of this chapter I address the relevance of the
constructs of self-differentiation and fusion with each partner as well as
explicate the pattern of overfunction/underfunction that had stymied Paula
and Colette. Clinical interventions of clarification and restorying were
most helpful in these situations.

Fusion and Self-Differentiation

Autonomy and intimacy are often viewed as polarized opposites. It is more
helpful to consider self-differentiation as an effort to balance yearnings for

a sense of connection and embeddedness as well as a sense of uniqueness. Fusion can be understood in terms of the extent to which the individual has lost a sense of uniqueness and lacks a balance of emotions and thought. Both Paula and Colette reported that they had given up shared activities they had enjoyed. Paula felt she had lost her usual self-confidence and had become less productive. She felt that she tried to find ways to please Colette but had lost all sense of what Colette really thought and felt.

Paula also had very few clear ideas about what she wanted or thought about the situation. She complained that her mind was fogged over by a sea of inertia. Although Paula initially expressed a sense of comfort about her lesbianism, further discussion about the censure from her sister and colleagues reopened old internal conflicts and outrage. In the past two years Colette had retreated into solitary activities. She had abandoned her major passion in life, her modern dance, as she felt increasingly compelled to care for her mother and sister. She felt very drained by Paula's complaints and had little energy left for attempting to figure out what might be bothering her. Although the couple seemed to have achieved a healthy balance of connectedness and autonomy during the early phase of their relationship, both partners seemed to have shifted into a phase of heightened fusion exacerbated by their profound unresolved grief and isolation from family and friends.

Both women were being stressed by past and current losses and the strains of chronic illness. Gender plays an important role here in understanding the pressures each woman felt to provide caregiving to the frail and elderly members of their family. Colette's gender, her history of growing up in an alcoholic family, and her strong religious beliefs, which stressed the value of self-sacrifice, prepared her to assume responsibility for the care of her mother and sister. Her poignant stories of life in an alcoholic home enriched Paula's understanding of both her partner's strengths and struggles.

The discussion of addictions required careful attention once again to the balancing of alpha and beta biases (Anderson 1994; Bepko 1989; Bepko and Krestan 1985). For example, in addition to focusing on the impact of a powerful physical addiction, the accompanying effects of the illness, and the genetic predisposition toward alcoholism in Colette's family of origin, the unique ways in which Colette's family dealt with alcohol also needed to be considered. Both Paula and Colette demonstrated clear strengths in their relational caregiving abilities, yet the extent to which they felt compelled to devote their lives to these efforts had led to a crippling sense of suffocation and despondency.

Underfunction/Overfunction

A pattern of under- and overfunctioning also interfered regularly with this couple's progress. Early interventions focused on helping Paula reframe her depression as interactional. As we explored together the effects of Paula's depression on Colette and the behavior and moods that followed, what emerged was a cyclical interactional pattern characterized by 1. Paula's expression of her misery, 2. Colette's heightened anxiety and attempt to solve Paula's problems, 3. Paula's response of frustration and a sense of powerlessness that seemed to refuel her interrogation and criticism of Colette, 4. Colette's retreat to her room, and 5. Paula's even greater frustration, increased sense of powerlessness, and retreat into silence.

In summary, Paula's efforts to protect herself from direction and domination by inflicting questions on Colette in fact left her feeling abandoned and powerless, since Colette retreated from the fray with her own sense of failure. Colette's attempts to protect herself from Paula's emotional intensity with her offers of problem solving similarly resulted in a sense of ephemeral mastery followed by defeat and powerlessness.

Clarification of this reciprocal victim-victimizer pattern helped this couple to see how each affected the other by triggering in her a sense of powerlessness that enhanced depression in them both. The force of this entrenched cyclical pattern clearly alarmed both partners, as they recognized the obvious mirroring of the underfunction/overfunction pattern that each had witnessed in their families of origin.

Triangulation and Boundary

Repetitive intergenerational patterns surfaced interlocking triangles. For example, Paula reenacted her experience of abandonment by her father through his premature death by provoking Colette to abandon her. Her angry interrogations provoked Colette's retreat. Colette, on the other hand, provoked Paula to behave in an irrational and chaotic manner, reminiscent of her own earlier traumatic fighting with her alcoholic parents.

In therapy both Paula and Colette began to challenge their mutual tendencies to suppress their feelings as they painstakenly took risks to speak more directly and clearly with each other. While Paula faced intense pain, anger, and shame at the reactions of her sister and others to her lesbianism, she felt greater trust in sharing such vulnerability with Colette. In time her internal struggles gave way to a sense of acceptance and greater calm. Both women began to realize that they needed to renew contacts with friends and to make new friends, finding that their relationship was nourished and enriched by the involvement and support of others. The increased flexibility and fluidity of the boundary around their very isolated, beleaguered relationship enabled them to revitalize their connectedness.

Sexual Intimacy

Attention to the level of sexual satisfaction reported by each partner is important, without arbitrarily imposing alpha-biased heterosexist notions or standards for sexual intimacy (Califia 1980; Loulan 1984). Only as Paula and Colette enhanced their capacities for self-differentiation and intimacy were they able to more openly share themselves emotionally and physically.

At the beginning of therapy both partners reported a dissatisfying sexual relationship in which both women complained of distancing and estrangement. Each struggled for control and dominance, a process that inevitably led to impasse. Colette reported feeling as if she had to "yield to" or "accommodate" to Paula way beyond reasonable expectations and, consequently, retreated into herself. As she recognized her own anger regarding excessive accommodations she had made with her mother, father, sister, and Paula, she was better able to claim her own wishes and feelings and offer physical affection to Paula, rather than always experiencing lovemaking as submission. Paula's frequent request for physical contact, although always construed as a wish for genital sexuality, was in fact frequently a wish for an affectionate connection. As Paula and Colette were once again able to speak directly with each other about their feelings, wishes, and regrets, there was far less ambiguity in terms of their desires for a sexual connection. Equally important was the work that each woman did individually but with the support of the other on unresolved family of origin issues. They began to better define their couple boundaries in relation to their families, allowing them to better balance their individual and couple needs while still remaining connected and available to their respective families.

New Directions

Toward the end of five months of therapy a review of the initial goals revealed progress in all areas. Both Paula and Colette expressed relief and satisfaction in their abilities to more directly deal with conflict in nonabusive ways. Paula's symptoms of depression remitted as did Colette's generalized unhappiness.

After discussing at length both the losses and grief associated with their families of origin, each partner was able to gain pride in identifying with the pioneering spirits in their respective families of origin. And, as each woman shared her respective tales of survival in their families of heritage, greater mutual understanding and empathy replaced resentment. Further efforts toward self-differentiation with each partner included Paula's reconnection with several of her friends and a renewal of interest in dance. Paula discussed with Colette at length her conflicts regarding her family's painful homophobic responses to her lesbianism. Rather than trying to reunite with a sister who was harshly judgmental, she made efforts to connect more positively with a brother and niece who were both loving and respectful. As Laird (1993) has commented, it is not always healthy or wise to reconnect with family members who are abusive or critical. However, she agrees with other clinicians who see the value in maintaining certain connections with the family of origin in order to avoid the emotional intensification that accompanies cutoff (Anderson 1996; Laird 1996).

As each woman saw the strengths in her own survivorship under difficult circumstances, they started to view themselves as resilient and creative in some of their nontraditional pursuits. While sharing profound sadness in discussing her mother's physical decline, Paula also felt quite proud of her mother's heroic efforts to independently rear seven children. After considerable planning, Paula and Colette orchestrated a "transitional ritual," involving a gathering of selected family members and friends of Paula's mother to celebrate the many wonderful occasions in her home and acknowledge the passage to a new phase of her life in a rest home. Although the event brought a mixture of tales, photos, laughs, and tears, the event served a powerful healing purpose in affirming the strengths in Paula's mother as well an affirmation of Paula and Colette's coupleness. A poignant toast highlighted the celebration when Paula's mother paid tribute to her daughter and Colette for their devotion and kindness both to her and toward each other.

Therapy with a lesbian couple must strike a careful balance between recognizing the issues that are fundamental to all couples as well as those that are particularly unique in work with lesbian partners. This paper has explored the balancing of the potential alpha and beta biases as a way to negotiate the contextual impasses that occur in couples therapy. A feminist intergenerational theoretical lens has been used to explicate the usefulness of notions of fusion, self-differentiation, and boundary in therapy with a particular couple. This couple's resilience and courage in facing painful truths are clearly a tribute to their difficult yet rewarding journey.

NOTES

1. The brevity of this article only allows space to explore the commonalities and differences between lesbian and heterosexual couples in couple therapy. There are differing opinions regarding the relative "fixedness" or variability in the definition of sexual orientation as well as an important critique of any definition as socially constructed. As a result, there is complexity and variation in relationships among couples with different sexual orientations. Although investigation of these issues is important, the constraints of space limit the focus of this paper to the study issue that has been identified.

2. The clinical illustration is a composite of several treatment cases with disguised identities.

REFERENCES

Andersen, T. 1987. The reflecting team. *Family Process* 26:415–428.
Anderson, H., and H. Goolishian. 1992. The client is the expert: A not-knowing approach to therapy. In S. McNamee and K. J. Gergen, eds., *Therapy as social construction*, pp. 25–39. Newbury Park, Cal.: Sage.
Anderson, S. 1996. Addressing heterosexist bias in the treatment of lesbian couples with chemical dependency. In J. Laird and R-J. Green, eds., *Lesbians and gays in couples and families: A handbook for family therapy*, pp. 316–340. San Francisco: Jossey-Bass.
Basham, K. 1992. Resistance and couple therapy. *Smith Studies in Social Work* 62(3):245–264.
Berzoff, J. 1989. Fusion and heterosexual women's friendships: Implications for expanding our adult developmental theories. *Women and Therapy* 8:93–107.
Bograd, M. 1988. Enmeshment, fusion or relatedness? A conceptual analysis. In L.
Bowen, M. 1966. The use of family theory in clinical practice. *Comprehensive Psychiatry* 7:345–374.
— 1978. *Family therapy in clinical practice*. Northvale, N.J.: Aronson.
Braverman, ed., *Women, feminism and family therapy*, pp. 65–80. New York: Haworth.
Burch, B. 1982. Psychological merger in lesbian couples: A joint ego psychological and systems approach. *Family Therapy* 9:201–208.
— 1986. Psychotherapy and the dynamics of merger in lesbian couples. In T. S. Stein and C. J. Cohen, eds., *Contemporary perspectives on psychotherapy with lesbians and gay men*, pp. 57–71. New York: Plenum.
— 1987. Barriers to intimacy: Conflicts over power, dependence, and nurturing in lesbian relationships. In Boston Lesbian Psychologies Collective, eds., *Lesbian psychologies: Explorations and challenges*, pp. 126–141. Urbana: University of Illinois Press.
Califia, P. 1980. *The joy of lesbian sexuality*. Tallahassee, Fla.: Naiad.
Carter, E. 1992. Stonewalling feminism. *Family Therapy Networker* 16(1):64–69.

Chodorow, N. 1989. *Feminism and psychoanalytic theory*. New Haven: Yale University Press.

Clunis, D. M., and G. D. Green. 1988. *Lesbian couples*. Seattle: Seal.

Crawford, S. 1987. Lesbian families: Psychosocial stress and the family-building process. In Boston Lesbian Psychologies Collective, eds., *Lesbian psychologies*, pp. 195–214. Urbana, Ill.: University of Illinois Press.

Decker, B. 1984. Counseling gay and lesbian couples. *Journal of Social Work and Human Sexuality* 2:39–52.

De Crescenzo, T. A. 1984. Homophobia: A study of the attitudes of mental health professionals toward homosexuality. *Journal of Social Work and Human Sexuality* 2:115–136.

De Shazer, S. 1982. *Patterns of brief family therapy: An ecosystemic* approach. New York: Guilford.

Deutsch, H. 1933. Homosexuality in women. *International Journal of Psychoanalysis* 14:34–56.

Doherty, W. 1991. Family therapy goes post-modern. *Family Therapy Networker* 15:37–42.

Efran, J., M. Lukens, and R. Lukens. 1990. *Language, structure and change: Frameworks of meaning in psychotherapy*. New York: Norton.

Ellis, P., and B. C. Murphy. 1994. The impact of misogyny and homophobia on therapy with women. In M. P. Mirkin, ed., *Women in context: Toward a feminist reconstruction of psychotherapy*, pp. 48–73. New York: Guilford.

Falco, C. 1991. *Psychotherapy with lesbian clients*. New York: Brunner/Mazel.

Flax, J. 1990. *Thinking fragments: Psychoanalysis, feminism, and post-modernism in the contemporary west*. Berkeley: University of California Press.

Freud, A. 1936. *Ego and the mechanisms of defense*. New York: International Universities Press.

Freud, S. 1900. The interpretation of dreams. Standard ed., 4–5. London: Hogarth.

— 1914. Remembering, repeating, and working through. Standard ed., 12:145–186. London: Hogarth.

— 1923. The ego and id. Standard ed., 19:3–66. London: Hogarth.

— 1926. Inhibitions, symptoms, and anxiety. Standard ed., 2:77–175. London: Hogarth.

Gartrell, N. 1984. *Issues in psychotherapy with lesbian women*. Work in Progress no. 83–84. Wellesley, Mass.: Stone Center Working Paper Series.

Gilligan, C. 1991. Joining the resistance: Psychology, girls and women. Lecture to Washington Psychologists for the Study of Psychoanalysis, October, Washington, D.C.

Glassgold, J, and S. Iasenza, eds. 1995. *Lesbians and psychoanalysis: Revolutions in theory and practice*. New York: Free.

Goldner, V. 1991. Toward a critical relational theory of gender. *Psychoanalytic Dialogues* 1:249–272.

Goldner, V., P. Penn, M. Sheinberg, and G. Walker. 1990. Love and violence: Gender paradoxes in volatile attachments. *Family Process* 29:343–364.

Gonsiorek, J. 1982. *Homosexuality and psychotherapy: A practitioner's handbook of affirmative models.* New York: Haworth.

Goodrich, T. J., B. Ellman, C. Rampage, and K. Halstead. 1988. The lesbian couple. In T. J. Goodrich, C. Rampage, B. Ellman, and K. Halstead, *Feminist family therapy: A casebook,* pp. 134–159. New York: Norton.

Green, R. J., M. Bettinger, and E. Zacks. 1996. Are lesbian couples "fused" and gay male couples "disengaged?" Questioning gender straightjackets. In J. Laird and R-J. Green, eds., *Lesbians and gay men in couples and families: A handbook for therapists,* pp. 185–230. San Francisco: Jossey-Bass.

Grier, W., and P. Cobbs. 1968. *Black rage.* New York: Basic.

Grotstein, J. 1967. An object relations perspective on resistance in narcissistic patients. In D. Milman and G. Goldman, eds., *Techniques of working with resistance,* pp. 317–338. New Jersey: Aronson.

Hammond, N. 1988. Lesbian victims of relationship violence. *Women in Therapy* 8(1–2):89–105.

Hare-Mustin, R. 1989. The problem of gender in family therapy theory. In M. McGoldrick, C. M. Anderson, and F. Walsh, eds., *Women in families: A framework for family therapy,* pp. 61–77. New York: Norton.

Hartman, A. 1996. Social policy as a context for lesbian and gay families: The political is personal. In J. Laird and R-J. Green, eds., *Lesbians and gays in couples and families: A handbook for therapists,* pp. 69–85. San Francisco: Jossey-Bass.

Herek, G. 1986. The social psychology of homophobia: Toward a practical theory. *Review of Law and Social Change* 14(4):923–934.

Hoffman, I. Z. 1992. Some practical implications of a social constructivist view of the psychoanalytic situation. *Psychoanalytic Dialogues* 2:287–304.

Hoffman, L. 1981. *Foundations of family therapy.* New York: Basic.

— 1990. Constructing realities: An art of lenses. *Family Process* 29:1–12.

Irigaray, L. 1985. *This sex which is not one.* Trans. C. Porter. Ithaca: Cornell University Press.

Kanuha, V. 1990. Compounding the triple jeopardy: Battering in lesbian of color relationships. *Women in Therapy* 9(1–2):169–184.

Kaplan, A. 1984. *The "self-in-relation:" Implications for depression in women.* Work in Progress no. 13. Wellesley, Mass.: Stone Center Working Papers Series.

Kernberg, O. 1975. *Borderline conditions and pathological narcissism.* New York: Aronson.

Kerr, M., and M. Bowen. 1988. *Family evaluation.* New York: Norton.

Khan, M. 1962. The role of infantile sexuality in early object relations in female homosexuality. In I. Rosen, ed., *The Pathology and Treatment of Sexual Perversions.* Oxford: Oxford University Press.

Kirkpatrick, M. 1991. Lesbian couples in therapy. *Psychiatric Annals* 21(8):491–496.

Kleinberg, L. 1986. *Coming home to self, going home to parents: Lesbian identity disclosure.* Work in Progress no. 24. Wellesley, Mass.: Stone Center Working Papers Series.

Krestan, J., and C. S. Bepko. 1980. The problem of fusion in the lesbian relationship. *Family Process* 19:277–289.

Laird, J. 1993. Lesbian and gay families. In F. Walsh, ed., *Normal Family Processes*, pp. 282–328. 2d ed. New York: Guilford.

— 1994. Lesbian families: A cultural perspective. In M. P. Mirkin, ed., *Women in Context*, pp. 118–148. New York: Guilford Press.

— 1996. Invisible ties: Lesbians and their families of origin. In J. Laird and R-J. Green, eds., *Lesbian and gay male couples and families*, pp. 89–122. San Francisco: Jossey-Bass.

Lerner, H. 1989. *The dance of intimacy.* New York: Harper and Row.

Lewes, K. 1988. *The psychoanalytic theory of male homosexuality.* New York: Simon and Schuster.

Lewin, E. 1993. *Lesbian mothers: Accounts of gender in American culture.* Ithaca: Cornell University Press.

Loulan, J. 1984. *Lesbian sex.* San Francisco: Spinsters.

Luepnitz, D. A. 1988. *The family interpreted: Feminist theory in clinical practice.* New York: Basic.

McCandlish, B. M. 1982. Therapeutic issues with lesbian couples. *Journal of Homosexuality* 7:71–78.

Mencher, J. 1990. *Intimacy in lesbian relationships: A critical re-examination of fusion.* Work in Progress no. 42. Wellesley, Mass.: Stone Center Working Paper Series.

Miller, J. B. 1988. *Connections, disconnections, and violations.* Work in Progress no. 33. Wellesley, Mass.: Stone Center Working Paper Series.

Moran, M. R. 1988. Effects of sexual orientation similarity and counselor experience level on gay men's and lesbians' perceptions of counselors. *Journal of Counseling Psychology* 39:247–251.

Morin, S. F. 1977. Heterosexual bias in psychological research on lesbianism and male homosexuality. *American Psychologist* 32:629–637.

Morin, S. F., and K. A. Charles. 1983. Heterosexual bias in psychotherapy. In J. Murray and P. R. Abramson, eds., *Bias in psychotherapy*, pp. 309–338. New York: Praeger.

O'Connor, N. and J. Ryan. 1993. *Wild desires and mistaken identities: Lesbianism and psychoanalysis.* Northvale, N.J.: Aronson.

Peplau, L. A., S. Cochran, K. Rook, and C. Padesky. 1978. Loving women: Attachment and autonomy in lesbian relationships. *Journal of Social Issues* 34:7–27.

Prozan, C. K. 1992. *Feminist psychoanalytic psychotherapy.* Northvale, N.J.: Aronson.

Roth, S. 1989. Psychotherapy with lesbian couples: Individual issues, female socialization and the social context. In M. McGoldrick, C. Anderson, and F. Walsh, eds., *Women in families: A framework for family therapy*, pp. 286–307. New York: Norton.

Saari, C. 1991. *The creation of meaning in clinical social work*. New York: Guilford.

Schafer, R. 1983. *The analytic attitude*. New York: Basic.

Slater, S. 1995. *The lesbian family life cycle*. New York: Free.

Stein, T. S. 1988. Theoretical considerations in psychotherapy with gay men and lesbians. *Journal of Homosexuality* 15:79–95.

Teitelbaum, S. 1991. A developmental approach to resistance. *Clinical Social Work Journal* 19:119–130.

Thompson, C. 1947. Changing concepts in homosexuality in psychoanalysis. *Psychiatry* 10:183–189.

Tievsky, D. L. 1988. Homosexual clients and homophobic social workers. *Journal of Independent Social Work* 2:51–62.

Weston, K. 1991. *Families we choose: Lesbians, gays, kinship*. New York: Columbia University Press.

White, M., and D. Epston. 1990. *Narrative means to therapeutic ends*. New York: Norton.

Winnicott, D. W. 1958. The capacity to be alone. *International Journal of Psychoanalysis* 39:416–420.

Zacks, E., R. J. Green, and J. Marrow. 1988. Comparing lesbian and heterosexual couples on the circumplex model: An initial investigation. *Family Process* 27:471–484.

CHAPTER SEVEN

Object Relations Couples Therapy with Lesbians

Carol M. Sussal

OBJECT RELATIONS COUPLES THERAPY is a relatively new psychoanalytically oriented treatment (Scharff and Scharff 1991; Siegel 1991, 1992; Slipp 1988) that has received an enthusiastic response. It is an approach that explores the complex infantile roots of irrational adult conflict, within a context that is sensitive and caring. The work of Scharff and Scharff (1991) is of particular interest (Sussal 1990) as it draws upon the British object relations theories of Klein, Fairbairn, Guntrip, Winnicott, and Bion. Existing intrapsychically oriented approaches to work with lesbian couples (for example, Falco 1991) have not applied this frame of reference to psychodynamic understanding and technique. Mitchell's (1989) approach to work with lesbian couples, for instance, is underpinned by Kohut's self psychology.

A psychoanalytic approach to work with lesbian couples that is based on research and not on prejudice can be an exemplar of the nonjudgemental, nonaversive model Schafer (1983) pleads for as the truly analytic attitude. It should not be assumed, as some do, that a psychoanalytically oriented approach to work with lesbian couples automatically means that an illness model will be used (Carl 1990; Coleman 1986) to relate to homosexuality. While psychoanalysis has a long history of approaching gay men and lesbians from a homophobic frame of reference in which developmental arrest and narcissistic fixation are assumed (Lewes 1989), extensive research has debunked the presumptive myth of illness (Bell and Weinberg 1978; Gonsiorek 1982; Hooker 1967; McWhirter and Mattison 1984; Saghir and Robbins 1973).

An object relations couples approach can add to the growing need for more readily available family and couples models for work with lesbians, who increasingly present themselves for treatment (Usher 1991). It is an appropriate approach for the lesbian couple interested in understanding the intrapsychic, interpersonal, and environmental forces that can coalesce to produce difficulties.

In this chapter I explore some of the central concepts in object relations theory and demonstrate how they can be applied to work with lesbian couples.

The Social Context

All psychoanalytically oriented approaches to couples therapy stress the intertwining of the past and the present. However, in work with lesbian couples it is essential that the social context not be neglected (Usher 1991). A major focus needs to be placed on the couple in situation.

Herdt (1992) argues for the existence of a specifically gay cultural system, which he believes has a definite identity, social supports, and institutions. Clear signs exist of such a culture, particularly in urban areas, as manifested, for example, in the existence of gay and lesbian centers, gay pride marches, and gay literature. All of these give purpose and meaning to life, validating same-sex desire, "lifestyle" goals, and social networks.

Unlike most heterosexual couples, lesbian couples may be subjected to many kinds of social discrimination as they go about their daily lives, resulting in particular kinds of stresses on the individual, on the couple, and on family relationships. In working with lesbian couples, a careful assessment must include an evaluation of each partner as a separate individual, an assessment of the unconscious forces flowing between the partners in terms of the balance of love and hate (Dicks 1967), and special attention to the powerful social and cultural forces that provide context for their relationship. "Connections and position in their society and its subgroups, . . . (and) demands of economic and societal adaptation and role performance" (Dicks 1967:8) are of particular importance to the lesbian couple.

An understanding of how homophobia affects the lesbian couple is central to effective work, since homophobia has the potential to permeate all facets of the couple's life, manifesting itself in their personal, interpersonal, institutional, and cultural relationships (Blumenfeld 1992). Homphobic beliefs, in which lesbians are viewed as sick, immoral, powerless over their desires, or genetically deficient, can be acted upon in oppressive and destructive ways. For example, discrimination is evident in institutions when codes, laws, and policies exclude lesbians from domestic partnership benefits and inheritance. Homophobia displays itself culturally when oppression is legitimized.

Usher (1991) discusses the impact on the lesbian of being out in a homophobic society; lesbians, for example, may be subject to and fearful of loss of employment, housing, even their own children, for no other reason than their sexual orientation. Some have even been subjected to violent attack (Pharr 1988). Taking into account the impact of homophobia on the level of fear is important in the beginning stages of engagement with lesbian couples, as the couple may understandably be unusually alert to the levels of acceptance and affirmation they can expect from the therapist.

For example, Sandy and Joan, a couple discussed in more detail below, had to move from their first home after being severely harassed by their neighbors. Eggs were thrown on their house, their car windows were smashed and the tires cut, and threatening notes were left on their doorstep. Life on the block became so intolerable that they had to sell their beloved house. Reconstruction of that period in their lives led to an understanding of prior and present anxieties related to dealing with their sexual orientation.

Lesbian couples tend to value coequal partnerships, which are free of the power politics that often characterize heterosexual couple relationships (Blumstein and Schwartz 1983; Roth 1985). Thus, they may be vulnerable to additional stress when they have widely discrepant statuses, roles, or resources. Such may be the case, for example, where one partner has far more income or wealth. While an object relations approach stresses the symbolic meaning of such factors, it is critically important that the reality generating the dynamics also be addressed.

Creating a Holding Environment

The major vehicle through which healing takes place in an object relations approach is in the creation of a therapeutic holding environment (Winnicott 1961). Lesbian couples must be provided with a safe psychological space for therapy. Transference analysis can then be derived from an active form of empathic listening, while the countertransference becomes a diagnostic tool.

The therapist should be alert to particular countertransference components that may occur when working with lesbian couples. Sexist assumptions about women must be examined (Goodrich, Rampage, Ellman, and Halstead 1988), since such assumptions are built into the male-oriented, ethnocentric models of theory and practice that dominate psychological thought (Green 1990). Heterosexual therapists who have not examined their own attitudes toward homosexuality may lack sufficient self-scrutiny and sensitivity in their work with lesbian couples (Kwawer 1980). Gay and lesbian therapists, on the other hand, in attempts to create a lesbian affirmative climate, may neglect attention to the pathological components of individual personalities and relationships (Falco 1991). If the above issues are dealt with appropriately, the therapist is then in a position to demonstrate openness to personal experience, modeling self-examination for the couple. The therapist must show the ability to be controlled yet empathic. This is achieved in part through awareness of one's own feelings, by tuning into personal fantasies, a snatch of song, periods of discomfort and uneasiness, or particular relaxation. The therapist can then make contact with the deepest levels of internal distress in a psychosomatic partnership that is similar to the mother's maternal preoccupation with the infant in its earliest days (Scharff and Scharff 1991). A connection into the couple's deepest level of unconscious communication can occur. Such a depth of contact creates an environment that makes it possible for couples to feel secure enough to do the hard and painful work required to reconstruct the trauma of the past as it repeats itself in the present.

The therapist then models the kind of holding that the couple needs to provide for one another, through centered relating and contextual holding. Centered relating is "the kind that exists when people who are each other's primary objects reach deeply into each other over time and hold each other at the center" (Scharff and Scharff 1991:68–69). Contextual holding refers to the conditions the therapist establishes for the therapeutic environment, including such contingencies as consistent policies about time of appointment, payment and cancellation arrangements, and attention to the setting in which the therapy occurs (Scharff and Scharff 1991).

The therapist holds within the undigested elements of painful experience that are then remetabolized in comprehensible language and fed back to the couple to be used by them productively, similar to the way a mother acts as container for the baby as the contained (Bion 1962). The therapist, in the state of "reverie" Bion (1962) described as existing when the mother takes in the baby's projective identifications through introjective identifications, does the same for the couple in a benign and safe milieu. A transitional space is then created in which a couple can learn new ways to interact with a therapist who is tuned in to the realities of everyday life.

Sandy and Joan

Sandy and Joan, a lesbian couple in their fifties, had been together for over seventeen years. Joan was an administrative nurse with a highly responsible position in a major hospital, while Sandy had risen through the ranks to become a computer systems analyst. Both came from lower socioeconomic backgrounds, but through hard work over the years had created a comfortable lifestyle centered around their primary residence and a vacation home upstate.

Joan originally called me to ask for therapy for herself, fearing Sandy would not attend couple sessions; Sandy, however, was open to the idea. The first session revealed that the couple had suffered a series of intolerable losses; their inability to provide mutual holding had not allowed them to mourn sufficiently. Joan, the oldest of six children in an alcoholic Irish family, had lost her favorite brother to AIDS two months earlier. His lover had died of AIDS a few months before. Sandy and Joan had both been deeply involved in caring for the two men, who had even relocated to build a home near them in the country.

During this crisis Sandy developed a particularly close relationship with another lesbian couple she had connected to through work. Joan complained that Sandy wanted to spend all their spare time with this other couple. Joan felt as if she had not only lost a brother and a friend but was also in the process of losing Sandy. She needed to tell her story in excruciating detail, slowly and laboriously, since she and Sandy had never really sat down and talked about their feelings before. It felt crucial to me that I listen deeply and provide centered arms around holding, in other words, demonstrate a warm feeling of acceptance and caring. I realized that the less I spoke the better. What was most important was that I be there to provide a space in which this story could emerge and be understood in its full impact.

Joan frequently became tearful, as did Sandy, as did I. The work in the months to come revealed that Sandy was suffering from unresolved issues of loss. Both feared that opening up would result in loss of control and that they would both be totally overwhelmed by feelings of despair, hurt, and anger. Sandy had lost her only brother, whom she had adored, when she was eighteen. After a turbulent, short-lived marriage, she had a "nervous break-down" and, after hospitalization, lost custody of her only son.

The couple was quickly able to take advantage of the therapeutic hold-ing environment and worked very hard to make contact with each other on a feeling level, despite their fears. Interestingly, during all their seventeen years together, Joan had never approached Sandy sexually. When Joan began to take some responsibility for moving toward Sandy sexually, Sandy was both thrilled and responsive.

While some patterns are similar for homosexual and heterosexual cou-ples throughout the life cycle (Carter and McGoldrick 1988), lesbians, who may lack networks of social support or social validation of the relationship, may need to rely more heavily on one another because of the lack of social supports. Krestan and Bepko (1980) suggest that, to compensate for these factors and protect themselves from unwelcome intrusions across the cou-ple boundaries, the couple may overly fuse or merge. Furthermore, inter-nalized homophobia can become exacerbated in such a situation as a result of social isolation (Kirkpatrick 1991), which in turn can increase feelings of self-hatred.

The inability to openly "tell" one's life, to be forced to remain silent about parts of life experience that are taken for granted in the heterosexual world, can negatively impact both self-concept and self-esteem. The result can be a level of shame and suspiciousness that may be viewed as an adaptive response to censure but can also promote schizoid splitting.

Additionally, the lack of socially sanctioned ritual to celebrate their join-ing and significant events throughout the life cycle, which heterosexuals take for granted, deprives lesbian couples of opportunities for validation of their relationships. One way lesbians and lesbian couples counter family and social rejection and gain relationship validation is by creating new "families of choice" (Weston 1991), that is, families constructed from friends, affirming relatives, and so on. Many lesbians even stay connected to former lovers, who may then play the role of "in-laws." It is crucial that the therapist not make prior assumptions about the couple's lifestyle and that he or she explore the social and cultural dimensions of the couple's life.

The lack of family and social supports may overburden an otherwise highly functioning couple in such a way as to create symptomatic behavior at normal points of developmental crisis. All couples, in the early stages of couple formation, must deal with issues related to fusion versus intimacy, with the relationships they will have with their respective families of origin, and with the initial difficulties in living together and preserving the romance, all the while respecting differentness in the other. The research on the stages of development for lesbian couples (Clunis and Green 1988) corroborates the centrality of these tasks. However, dealing with societal pressures can create a repressed ego system overladen with internalized homophobia, which can make the "internal saboteur" (Fairbairn 1954) particularly vengeful.

Repressed Ego Systems

The internal saboteur, which Fairbairn (1954) later renamed the "anti-libidinal ego," is that part of ourselves which fears intimacy because of early experiences of rejection and frustration. An irrational expression of the need to maintain control at any cost sabotages positive possiblity. All children, whether they will move toward homosexual or heterosexual orientation, experience either perceived or actual rejection during early childhood and are therefore vulnerable to developing self-protective defenses.

However, in the lesbian couple, internalized homophobia can become layered into the dynamics of each partner's antilibidinal ego, in recursive fashion, creating and recreating an even greater experience of danger in the world.

Fairbairn, differing from Freud, believed that people needed object relatedness rather than instinctual gratification. In his view schizoid splits in the pristine unitary ego of birth occur because of frustration and feelings of rejection. Split off parts of the ego reside in the unconscious and relate to the outside world and to each other internally.

The libidinal ego yearns for love from the exciting object, which is always out of reach. The antilibidinal ego expresses anger and frustration, all aimed at the rejecting object. These internal repressed ego systems become the vehicles through which members of a couple relate to each other as either exciting objects for which they yearn or rejecting objects to which they direct rageful and vengeful feelings.

The workings of the antilibidinal ego are observable when overwhelming fear of further hurt leads the person to undermine or destroy the relationship progress before being disappointed or betrayed. Creating a storm prevents making contact with the inner emptiness that has come about as a result of infantile trauma, a process that in lesbian couples can be exacerbated by the stress of having to deal with a stigmatized identity.

The libidinal ego itself can also split (Guntrip 1969). It can hide its heart in "cold storage" out of fear of further rejection through vulnerability, resulting in profound schizoid personality disorders. Lesbians who are aware of their homosexuality early in life may be particularly vulnerable in this regard. As small children they are exposed to name calling, to hearing others use pejorative terms about them. They develop self-protective defenses that can intensify the need for hiding, resulting in even deeper loneliness.

Balint (1968) realized that this sense of inner emptiness can lead to the fear that if one looks deep enough inside nothing will be found, which he called a "basic fault." There were a number of times when both the couples mentioned in the case examples in this chapter attempted to sabotage their progress, perhaps fearful of further vulnerability and emptiness. At the celebration of Sandy's birthday Joan ordered a Chinese food banquet with all the dishes that, at least on some level, she knew Sandy hated. The morning after a particularly loving and close Christmas Eve celebration Joan became withdrawn and rejecting. In both instances the rejecting object in one member of the couple attacked the exciting object in the other in a move designed to create safety. When I was able to point out the true yearning for one another that was covered over by fear converted into hostility, both couples were brought closer.

When these unconscious split off parts of the self are made conscious in the context of a safe holding environment, great strides can occur in treatment and in life. The couple can then become free to more openly express their needs, longings, love and hate, without having to resort to guerrilla warfare. The roots of these dynamics can then be seen in earliest mother-infant interactions, and reality testing between past and present can occur. If the impact of fears related to societal censure of their love of another woman can also be understood as part of this dynamic, the lesbian couple will then take advantage of the opportunity to love in the moment, with full appreciation for one another. It is then that the deep yearning for love that has been covered over for many years can be expressed and celebrated.

Projective Identification

In object relations couples work with lesbians, the analysis of projective identifications becomes an essential tool for understanding relational dynamics. All individuals experience projective identifications based on archaic remnants of early experience. However, in dysfunctional couples understanding the interweaving of projective identifications can become a powerful assessment and interventive tool (Siegel 1991). The concept, since Melanie Klein (1975 [1946]) first conceptualized it, has been widely discussed in the literature (Ogden 1982; Sandler 1987; Scharff 1992). Hinshelwood (1989) defines projective identification as

> the prototype of the aggressive object-relationship, representing an anal attack on an object by means of forcing *parts of the ego* into it in order to take over its contents and to control it and occurring in the paranoid-schizoid position from birth. It is a "phantasy remote from consciousness" that entails a belief in certain aspects of the self being located elsewhere, with a consequent depletion and weakened sense of self and identity, to the extent of depersonalization; profound feelings of being lost or a sense of imprisonment may result. (177)

Thus when projective identification occurs the person projects out negative *or* positive aspects of themselves that are intolerable. The recipient of the projection then introjects the projected part, with which the projector then identifies. This becomes the basis for conflictual interacting as well as empathy and results in loss of parts of the personality. This loss is accomplished by the use of defensive delineations, in which realistic appraisals of the other are overlooked in favor of the use of distorted images that emerge out of stimulated anxiety (Shapiro 1989).

Projective identification must be understood as emanating from the earliest era of life, the paranoid-schizoid position. According to Klein (1975 [1946]) psychological maturation occurs as a result of going from the paranoid-schizoid to the depressive position. However, it is now thought that throughout the life cycle we oscillate between the two positions (Steiner 1992). The paranoid-schizoid position is characterized by splitting, in which the mother of the good breast is seen as separate from the mother of the bad breast. In the depressive position the baby must integrate feelings of love and hate, deal with the consequent guilt at the realization of murderous feelings of rage toward the mother who is now understood to be one person, and go on to make reparation through sublimation into various forms of good works. The danger of not being able to contain the guilt ensuing from such realization is either a manic defense or pathological envy, resulting in further fragmentation of the self.

Projective identification can also be most helpful in understanding the countertransference, as the therapist takes in the projective identifications through introjective identification (Scharff 1992). This can result in a countertransference that is either concordant, in which the therapist identifies with a projected part of the patient's self, or complementary, in which the therapist identifies with a projected part of the patient's object (Racker

1968). Feeding back such understanding to the couple enriches and opens up the therapy. Such a powerful explanation of relational dynamics illuminates fixed modes of negative interactions in couples. Etiological roots can then be understood through reconstruction, using clarification and interpretation as the tools to promote insight, which enables the individuals to draw back the projections and create more spontaneous and fulfilling ways of interacting.

Lorice and Alice

Lorice and Alice were forty-seven and forty-one when they were referred for help with their communication difficulties by Lorice's individual therapist. Both were petite and attractive women who clearly adored one another and enjoyed an active sex life. They were distantly related cousins whose families belonged to an orthodox religious sect. They had become lovers as a result of working together in a family business ten years earlier. Lorice was divorced and had two children ages twenty-four and twenty who were still living at home.

The couple, who lived in a suburban town, led an extremely closeted life and had no gay friends. They were not even out to cousins who were also gay. The relationship seemed almost a textbook illustration of Krestan and Bepko's (1980) theory that fusion in the lesbian relationship comes about as a result of being cut off from social supports and relying heavily on each other to meet all needs.

In the first session Lorice complained that Alice barely talked and that she, Lorice, was finding it increasingly intolerable. Alice, though quite bright and sensitive, seemed extremely constricted and had severe difficulty in expressing herself verbally. My hypothesis was that she was suffering from a schizoid condition whose roots were grounded in her early life. In these beginning sessions Lorice, who was vivacious and energetic, would talk for Alice, interrupt Alice when she attempted to talk, and at the same time would bitterly complain about Alice's silence. Alice would sit in pained silence, often answering "I don't know" in response to direct questions.

With time, analysis of their early backgrounds revealed that Alice, the oldest of five siblings, came from a household where her mother had been quite silent and her father a "chatterbox." Her job was to provide mothering for her four siblings, to be "good," and never to express angry feelings. This inability to express anger was compounded by her socialization as a woman who was not encouraged to be assertive. The expectation for all women in her family was that negative emotions should be disavowed, adding to the constriction. The middle child and only daughter in a family of three children, it was also Lorice's role to take care of her mother. She had been similarly socialized to hide anger.

One of Alice's vivid early memories was of being left home at age nine by her mother to watch her brothers and sisters while her father was out of town. Falling asleep, she awakened fairly late. She panicked to find herself still alone and did not know where to reach her mother. She called around to all her relatives until she tracked her mother down. However, when her mother came home she told her not to cry, not to be frightened, not to be angry, and, most important of all, not to talk about the incident any more. Her silence now was understood as containing all her pain, fear, anger, and yearning for the ability to be appropriately dependent and expressive of her needs.

In Lorice's family her mother was also quiet and her father was the chatterbox. Alice rejected the part of her that needed to express itself into Lorice, out of a transferential fear that Lorice would act like her mother, who had told her to be silent; thus, she encouraged Lorice do the talking for both. Lorice took this instruction in through introjective identification and became even more of a chatterbox. Lorice, identified with her chatterbox father who was the caretaker in her family, did not feel she was allowed to be silent. She, however, needed to be able to express her mature dependency needs. She projected her silence into Alice, who would become even more withdrawn. Analysis revealed a profound need for intimacy in both that neither had felt capable of achieving.

In the countertransference there were times when I would find myself either uncharacteristically silent or overly chatty. I eventually understood this as coming about as an index of particularly conflictual material, still unconscious, the couple struggled with. I would ask myself what might be particularly frustrating, angering, or enraging for the couple that might be resonating with my own issues as a woman in the same arena. I emphasized the particular importance of getting in touch with their angry feelings as essential to move the therapy along.

Ultimately Alice decided to give up her job as a bookkeeper, which kept her isolated and bored. Her period of unemployment lasted longer than both expected. Despite periods of inactivity and depression, she became increasingly verbal. I had made a series of referrals for them to a number of gay and lesbian organizations, ranging from a businessperson's networking group to a new couples' socialization group forming at the lesbian and gay community services center. Alice took responsibility for following up on these referrals and, in addition, promoted their coming out, in a gradual fashion, to a number of family members.

In response to this, Lorice became more and more silent and developed a symptom of a lump in the throat, for which a number of medical consultations revealed no physical cause. The more efforts Alice made to talk, despite struggling with guilt over living on savings and loans, the more silent Lorice would become. The pull to continue to recreate both of their parents' marriages was great, as only one chatterbox was to be permitted. Lorice had a profound fear that she would only be disappointed if she allowed herself to hope too much for a dramatic change in the relationship. The lump in her throat was a metaphor for the death throes of internal object relations that were comfortable but dysfunctional. Alice struggled with the feeling that it was not permissible for her to express her despair and sense of isolation.

Further understanding of my countertransference revealed my wish to be their friend rather than their therapist and rescue them from their solitude. At other times I felt excluded from their intimacy and wished I could become a member of their large and very involved families. In the transference I became a representative of each of their grandmothers, who had been there for them in a way their silent mothers were not.

When Lorice's father died, Alice's mother asked Lorice's mother to move in with her! Lorice's mother declined. She opted instead to move to Florida to be with her youngest son. While Lorice was saddened by the choice, she nevertheless handled it well. Shortly afterward Lorice's two children moved out. This enabled the couple to have more privacy and more space in which to reconnect.

Ultimately, Lorice helped Alice find a selling job in her field. She worked very hard at giving Alice space in which to talk and very hard at expressing her true feelings, even though she still found it difficult to acknowledge angry feelings. Alice's new job required constant interaction with people, forcing her to be more outgoing. Even though the effort tired her, she welcomed the opportunity and began to emerge even more fully as a vital presence. At the time of this writing the lump in Lorice's throat has disappeared.

Sex Therapy

Like their heterosexual counterparts, lesbian couples may develop sexual problems. The fact that the lesbian couple consists of two women who relate to one another as sexual partners is critical to keep in the forefront of consciousness, however obvious it may appear to be. The literature frequently cites the diminishment of genital contact between lesbian couples over time, at a level more profound than in heterosexual or gay male couples (Blumstein and Schwartz 1983; Tripp 1975). This fact is thought to be a result of the differences between male and female sexuality in terms of drive toward genital contact but might also be viewed as a result of social constraints on and conventional expectations for women's sexuality.

Sex therapy must therefore be an integral part of an object relations couples approach for lesbian couples, *if* the couple expresses unhappiness with their sexual relationship (Falco 1991). When combined with the use of the transference-countertransference relationship, sex therapy can enhance a form of therapy that is focused on generating ever greater levels of intimacy (Scharff and Scharff 1991).

There is a literature on sex therapy with lesbians replete with invaluable information with which the practitioner should be familiar (Califia 1980; Loulan 1984; Sisley and Harris 1978). Decisions will have to be made after proper assessment as to whether a couple wishes sex therapy as part of a couple's treatment or through referral to a therapist skilled in this area.

Moses and Hawkins (1986) caution that clinicians should be careful about their referrals and be certain that the referred source actually does work with *gay* couples. They warn about the need to get training in sex therapy, indicating that "it is also important to be sure that therapy done is directed toward increasing sexual functioning and satisfaction for the client as a gay person, rather than toward increasing conformity to imposed nongay standards" (103–104). This is especially important for lesbians, who may often see foreplay as an end in itself.

In the case of Lorice and Alice a rich sex life was possible, as neither partner needed to talk much in bed! Joan and Sandy needed help in dealing with a degree of sexual inhibition and infrequency affected by years of lack of communication on a feeling level. For both couples the ability to engage in sexual relations was affected by the presence or absence of fighting.

Certain universals about the meaning of a sexual relationship, which can be readily applied to the lesbian couple, are important to keep in mind. Sexuality is grounded in the psychosomatic partnership of mother and infant and is central as an expression of the emotional commitment made by the partners. Nurturing and loving aspects resonate with the internal object worlds of each. Sex can be viewed as increasing

> the possibilities for rejection, disappointment, and anger if it fails or is withheld from the relationship. . . . The quality of sexual life is inti-

mately related to the quality of mutual holding within a marriage. While a good sexual relationship rests on a secure mutual holding relationship, it also performs a reciprocal function of supporting the holding between marital partners. Within this secure contextual holding occurs centered holding in which there is a deep unconscious communication of internal object relatedness through the interpenetration of mutual projective identification. (Scharff and Scharff 1991:25–26)

Object relations couples therapy for lesbians for the most part is similar to work with heterosexual couples who are desirous of in-depth healing for a troubled relationship. All couples, no matter what their sexual orientation, present with varying degrees of pre-Oedipal issues that benefit from working through. The therapist must understand that all of us are in need of attachment to objects and all of us have fears of rejection by them. Intimacy within the context of a loving sexual relationship, regardless of whether it is homosexual or heterosexual, provides one of the greatest joys in living. However, a heightened degree of awareness is essential for understanding the impact of the social context on the lesbian couple. Couples therapists have the potential to add greatly to the quality of life for lesbians through providing a holding environment that is supportive and understanding. Nondirective listening can open up knowledge of archaic internal constructs and free energy to deal with normative life crises as well as the added burdens of living daily life in a hostile environment.

REFERENCES

Balint, M. 1968. *The basic fault: Therapeutic aspects of regression.* New York: Brunner/Mazel.

Bell, A. P., and M. S. Weinberg. 1978. *Homosexualities: A study of diversity among men and women.* New York: Simon and Schuster.

Blumenfeld, W. J., ed. 1992. *Homophobia: How we all pay the price.* Boston: Beacon.

Blumstein, P., and P. Schwartz. 1983. *American couples: Money, work, sex.* New York: William Morrow.

Bion, W. 1962. *Learning from experience.* London: Tavistock.

Califia, P. 1980. *The joy of lesbian sexuality.* Tallahasee, Fla.: Naiad.

Carl, D. 1990. *Counseling same sex couples.* New York: Norton.

Clunis, D. M., and G. D. Green. 1988. *Lesbian couples.* Seattle: Seal.

Coleman, E. 1986. How the world views gay people. In A. E. Moses and R. O. Hawkins, eds., *Counseling lesbian women and gay men: A life-issues approach,* pp. 221–230. Colombus: Merrill.

Dicks, H. V. 1967. *Marital tensions: Clinical studies towards a psychological theory of interaction*. London: Routledge and Kegan Paul.

Fairbairn, R. D. 1954. *Psychoanalytic studies of the personality*. London: Routledge.

Falco, K. 1991. *Psychotherapy with lesbian clients: Theory into practice*. New York: Brunner/Maazel.

Gonsiorek, J. 1982. *Homosexuality and psychotherapy: A practitioner's handbook of affirmative models*. New York: Haworth.

Goodrich, T. J., C. Rampage, B. Ellman, and K. Halstead. 1988. *Feminist family therapy: A casebook*. New York: Norton.

Green, G. D. 1990. Is separation really so great? *Women in Therapy* 8(1–2):157–166.

Guntrip, H. 1969. *Schizoid phenomenon, object relations, and the self*. New York: International Universities Press.

Herdt, G., ed. 1992. *Gay culture in America: Essays from the field*. Boston: Beacon.

Hinshelwood, R. D. 1989. *A dictionary of Kleinian thought*. London: Free Association.

Hooker, E. 1967. The adjustment of the male overt homosexual. *Journal of Projective Techniques* 21(18).

Kinsey, A. C., C. Pomeroy, and C. Martin. 1948. *Sexual behavior in the human male*. Philadelphia: Saunders.

Kirkpatrick, M. 1991. Lesbian couples in therapy. *Psychiatric Annals* 21(8):491–496.

Klein, M. 1975 [1946]. Notes on some schizoid mechanisms. In M. Klein, *Envy and gratitude and other works, 1946–1963*, pp. 1–24. London: Hogarth.

Krestan, J., and C. Bepko. 1980. The problem of fusion in the lesbian relationship. *Family Process* 19:277–289.

Kwawer, J. 1980. Transference and countertransference in homosexuality: Changing perspectives. *American Journal of Psychoanalytic Therapy* 32:72–80.

Lewes, K. 1988. *The psychoanalytic theory of male homosexuality*. New York: Simon and Schuster.

Loulan, J. 1984. *Lesbian sex*. San Francisco: Spinsters.

Mitchell, V. 1989. *Women in Therapy* 9(1–2):87–104.

McWhirter, D., and A. Mattison. 1984. *The male couple: How relationships develop*. Englewood Cliffs, N.J.: Prentice-Hall.

Moses, A., and R. Hawkins. 1986. The treatment of sexual dysfunction in gay male couples. *Journal of Sex and Marital Therapy* 4:213–218.

Ogden, T. 1982. *Projective identification and psychotherapeutic techniques*. Northvale, N.J.: Aronson.

Pharr, S. 1988. *Homophobia: A weapon of sexism*. Arkansas: Chardon.

Racker, H. 1968. *Transference and countertransference*. New York: International Universities Press.

Roth, S. 1985. Psychotherapy with lesbian couples: Individual issues, female socialization, and the social context. *Journal of Marital and Family Therapy* 11(3):273–286.

Saghir M., and E. Robins. 1973. *Male and female homosexuality: A comprehensive investigation*. Baltimore: Williams and Wilkins.

Sandler, J., ed.. 1987. *Projection, identification, projective identification*. Madison, Conn.: International University Press.

Schafer, R. 1983. *The analytic attitude*. New York: Basic.

Scharff, D., and J. S. Scharff. 1991. *Object relations couples therapy*. Northvale, N.J.: Aronson.

Scharff, J. 1992. *Projective and introjective identification and the use of the therapist's self*. Northvale, N.J.: Aronson.

Shapiro, R. 1989. Identity and ego autonomy in adolescence. In J. Scharff, ed., *Foundations of object relations family therapy*, pp. 41–51. Northvale, N.J.: Aronson.

Siegel, J. 1991. Analysis of projective identification: An object-relations approach to marital treatment. *Clinical Social Work Journal* 19(1):71–82.

— 1992. Object relations marital therapy: Engaging the couple. In C. W. LeCroy, ed., *Case studies in social work practice*. California: Wadsworth.

Sisley, E. L., and B. Harris. 1978. *The joy of lesbian sex*. New York: Simon and Schuster.

Slipp, S. 1988. *The technique and practice of object relations family therapy*. Northvale, N.J.: Aronson.

Steiner, J. 1992. The equilibrium between the paranoid-schizoid and the depressive positions. In R. Anderson, ed., *Clinical lectures on Klein and Bion*, pp. 46–58. London: Routledge.

Sussal, C. 1990. Object relations family therapy, Jill Savage Scharff (review of *Object relations family therapy*.) *Clinical Social Work Journal* 18(4):437–438.

Tripp, C. A. 1975. *The homosexual matrix*. New York: New American Library.

Usher, J. M. 1991. Family and couples therapy with gay and lesbian clients: Acknowledging the forgotten minority. *Journal of Family Therapy* 13:131–148.

Weston, K. 1991. *Families we choose: Lesbians, gays, kinship*. New York: Columbia University Press.

PART THREE

Lesbians, Parenting, and Children

CHAPTER EIGHT

Lesbian Co-Parenting:
On Being/Being with the Invisible (M)Other

Cheryl Muzio

As I stood there looking at Eudora, the impossible became easier, almost simple. Desire gave me courage, where it had once made me speechless.

—*Audre Lorde, Zami: A New Spelling of My Name*

THE EXPERIENCE OF LESBIAN MOTHERING blends the roles of two groups that have been alternately ignored and oppressed in Western society: women who care for and raise children and women who choose to love other women. Until recently, it was thought that mothers and lesbians were two discrete, nonintersecting groups. Motherhood, it was assumed, happened within and as a result of a heterosexual relationship. Although children could be born out of wedlock (and so-called unwed mothers carried their own stigma), they could not be born independent of heterosexual relations.

As reproductive technology has evolved over the past twenty-five years, alternative insemination has emerged as a resource available to women identified by the medical establishment as being "unable" to conceive a child within a heterosexual marital relationship. It is interesting to note that the past twenty-five years has also witnessed the birth of increasingly active and cohesive lesbian communities. This parallel development of alternative insemination and lesbian community has produced a social phenomenon heretofore unheard of in Western patriarchal society: lesbian mothers.

In this chapter I will examine the vicissitudes of lesbian mothering within these societal confines. Although lesbians also become mothers through adoption, this inquiry will focus primarily on lesbian couples who conceive children through alternative insemination. To accomplish this I will employ the work of Luce Irigaray, a French psychoanalyst, philosopher, and linguist. I will use her work in a way that will facilitate the examination of some of the social, philosophical, and intrapsychic implications of the roles women, lesbians, and mothers have traditionally been assigned within Western societies. Along these lines, the implications of lesbian mothers simultaneously adopting and eschewing aspects of women's traditional role behavior will be explored, with special emphasis on the role of the nonbiological lesbian mother. It is the intent of this inquiry to shed light on the unique experiences lesbian mothers undergo in patriarchal society. In doing so, aspects of the social and psychological development of all women (not just lesbians) will be illuminated through the examination of the exclusively and uniquely female experience of lesbian mothering.

Patriarchy: The Rule of the Father

To examine lesbian mothering without first defining and examining patriarchy would be to ignore the very source of lesbian oppression. Luce Irigaray defined patriarchy as "an exclusive respect for the genealogy of sons and fathers, and the competition between brothers" (cited in Whitford 1991:24). Therefore, patriarchy is not only insistent upon women bearing children by and for men, it is, in fact, dependent on it.

The threat that lesbian mothers represent to this patriarchal rule of the father is self-evident in that they circumvent the traditional genealogical order Irigaray (1985b) speaks to. It is not that children born to lesbians do not have biological fathers; it is that they do not belong to them in the same way children born to a heterosexual couple "belong" to their fathers. Indeed, many children born to lesbian couples are conceived through alternative insemination by anonymous donors (Pies 1985). As a result, the children born to lesbian families tend to carry the surnames of one or both of their mothers, making a traditional patriarchally based genealogy impossible.

The replacement of a traditional patriarchally based genealogy with a matriarchally based one has implications beyond individual families. Elisabeth Grosz (1989) speaks to this when contemplating some of the implications of Irigaray's thinking on genealogy: "To be able to trace a female genealogy of descent entails new kinds of language, new systems of nomenclature, new relations of social and economic exchange—in other words, a complete reorganization of the social order" (163). The societal implications of a female genealogy of descent is not the only threat the lesbian family poses to the prevailing order, however.

The fact of alternative insemination (whether by known or unknown donor) turns the patriarchal order on its ear in that it entails the conception of babies without heterosexual intercourse. This not only circumvents the patriarchal competition between brothers (which is often over women through sexual conquest) but it also challenges the most basic assumptions about women's sexuality. Irigaray (1985b) asserts that "female sexuality has always been conceptualized on the basis of masculine parameters . . . women's erogenous zones never amount to anything but . . . a hole-envelope that serves to sheathe and massage the penis in intercourse" (23). By denying men sexual access, lesbians subvert the patriarchal order in that they refuse to be defined in or through their relationships to men. Lesbian couples are not dependent upon a phallically based relationship to give them sexual pleasure, personal identity, or the insemination of their children. They live in the shadow of the dominant order and therein lies the source of both their opportunity and their oppression.

Psychoanalytic Theory and Lesbian Oppression

An examination of the nature of lesbian oppression would be incomplete without a consideration of analytic theory, replete as it is with pronouncements about women's emotional and sexual natures. Additionally, Freud's ideas about femininity and sexuality continue to influence not only psychological theory and practice but generally held societal beliefs about women and lesbianism as well.

Ironically, Freud (1920) did not consider what he termed "homosexuality in women" a disease. In his 1920 article, "The Psychogenesis of a Case of Homosexuality in a Woman," he was quite clear that the young woman he wrote of "was not in any way ill (she did not suffer from anything in herself, nor did she complain of her condition) and that the task to be carried out did not consist in resolving a neurotic conflict" (246). This is not to romanticize Freud's ideas about lesbians but rather to emphasize that, in his view, lesbianism had to do with desire, not with pathology. Given that sexual desire and masculinity were deemed to be inseparable, lesbians were seen as masculine and certainly anything masculine could not be pathological. Irigaray (1985a) spoke of this quite eloquently:

> The essential thing, in any case, is to show that the object choice of the homosexual woman is determined by a *masculine* desire and tropism. The female libido is cut off from the active search for its instinctual

"object aims" and its primary "waves." It has in a sense neither aim (telos) nor origin (arche) of its own. The instincts that lead the homosexual woman to choose an object for her satisfaction are, necessarily, "male" instincts. (99)

Thus, lesbians, by virtue of their libidinous desires for sameness, for femaleness, are conceived of in masculine terms. To be sexually desirous, in Freud's (1920) view, means to be masculine. Irigaray (1985b) comments on this:

That a woman might desire a woman "like" herself . . . that she might also have auto- and homosexual appetites is simply incomprehensible to Freud, and indeed inadmissible. So there will be no female homosexuality, just a homosexuality in which woman will be . . . begged to maintain the desire for the same that man has. (Cited in Holmlund 1991:288)

This necessarily brings us to one of Irigaray's (1985b) main points regarding women and psychoanalysis: that women are seen as the same as men in analytic thought. That is, analytically speaking, the difference between women and men "is quantitative (women are *less* than men), not qualitative (women are *other* than men)" (Holmlund 1991:285). Indeed, it is Irigaray's thinking that within the analytic framework there is only one sex, and it is male; there is only one active, passionate desire, and it is masculine and phallic. Women's "lot is that of 'lack,' 'atrophy' (of the sexual organ), and 'penis envy' " (Irigaray 1985b:23). Thus, women are not seen for themselves as different from men and therein lies their need for an identity of their own rather than an identification with men.

If we accept Irigaray's thesis that women are seen only in relation to men, then the consequences for women living together as partners and co-parents begin to come clear. As we will see, the invisibility of their personhood as well as their desires as a result of neither being in relation to men is basic and consequential.

Psychoanalysis and Motherhood

Freud's (1915) emphasis on the phallus as the signifier of sexual desire and on the libido as always masculine leaves women defining themselves (sexually and otherwise) in and through men and the male organ. The act of heterosexual intercourse, leading to the birth of (preferably) a son, is seen by Freud (1915) as the true realization of a woman's feminine nature, the only appropriate response to her lack of a penis: "A mother is brought only unlimited satisfaction by her relation to a son" (133). Furthermore, true happiness is thought to be achieved by "making her husband her child as well" (134). Thus, women are defined and satisfied by and through their maternal relationships to their husbands and sons.

Freud's (1915) equation of feminine health and happiness with maternal function and identity has profound implications. As Irigaray (1985a) points out, "A woman becoming a mother will be *the Mother*, totally identified with maternity . . . through an obliteration of . . . *woman*"(76). The reason for this obliteration of woman, for the glorification of a reproductive and ultimately nurturing role, has to do with the masculine denial of feminine desire: "[Woman's] desire is often interpreted and feared, as a sort of insatiable hunger, a voracity that will swallow you whole" (Irigaray 1985b:29). Thus, women are denied their desire and compelled to become the (M)other.

> The intrapsychic consequence of this privileging of the maternal over the feminine is that it . . . puts woman in the position of experiencing herself only fragmentarily, in the little structured margins of a dominant ideology, as waste, or excess . . . . Moreover, the role of "femininity" . . . [as] . . . prescribed . . . corresponds scarcely at all to woman's desire, which may be recovered only in secret. (Irigaray 1985b:30)

Within this patriarchal frame, a lesbian loses her personhood, her identity, by virtue of being in desirous relationship to another woman and therefore she becomes either invisible or masculine. Alternately, an individual woman loses her personhood, her identity, by being in relation to her son and husband/child, thereby becoming the (M)other. Thus, the significance of lesbians choosing to become mothers, to inhabit a kind of psychoanalytic netherworld where neither their passionate nor maternal relationships are deemed to have substance, comes clearer. We have witnessed the birth of the invisible (M)other.

Real Lesbians in a Postmodern Landscape

The leap from a psychoanalytic or philosophic netherworld to the streets of the real world is an admittedly large one. Indeed, Irigaray has been criticized for "her apparent failure to examine concrete aspects of women's lives" (Holmlund 1991:283). However, her theoretical frame can be used to help identify and clarify some of the concrete aspects of women's lives, thereby allowing women, lesbians, and mothers to reflect upon their experiences at the same time their experiences are (finally) being reflected back to them. Irigaray's thinking helps us understand just how crucial this process is.

The very real experience of living as a lesbian in the postmodern world is more than a collection of individual stories. Indeed, a danger of post-modern thinking is that it has a tendency to transform collective oppression *solely* into individual narrative. Such practices thereby obscure the true and systematic nature of that oppression and consequently impede personal as well as political struggles for liberation. The experience of being "the only one" or part of a hidden and/or unhealthy subculture has been that of many lesbian women in the twentieth century (Faderman 1991). It is through hearing and valuing the stories of individual lesbians that we become aware of our collective oppression. It is crucial that we not allow ourselves to be either robbed of or reduced to our individual narratives.

Lesbian Couples in Psychological Literature

Psychological literature began to acknowledge the existence of lesbian cou-ples formally in 1980, when Joanne Krestan and Claudia Bepko published their groundbreaking article entitled "The Problem of Fusion in the Lesbian Relationship." Krestan and Bepko are to be recognized as pioneers, despite the fact that their thinking reflected the paradigmatic constraints of the time in which they wrote. As such, their work attempted to apply patri-archal and heterosexual assumptions about healthy relating to relationships that were neither patriarchal nor heterosexual. Over the next ten years authors such as Kaufman, Harrison, and Hyde (1984), Lindenbaum (1985), Roth (1985), and Perlman (1988) each looked at lesbian women in relation-ships. What they saw, by and large, were relational problems characterized by a tendency toward merger. This lack of differentiation, it was thought, explained lesbians whose excessive needs for intimacy led them to being jealous, dependent, and/or unable to relate successfully to one another or the outside world.

Much to their credit, each of these authors spoke explicitly to the impact of societal homophobia and/or female socialization regarding the problems they saw lesbians having in their relationships. What they failed to do, how-ever, was question the very paradigms they were using to label lesbian rela-tionships as fused and individual lesbians as lacking individual identity. Indeed, it was not until 1990, when Julie Mencher published an article enti-tled "Intimacy in Lesbian Relationships: A Critical Re-Examination of Fusion" that the idea of lesbian intimacy and relationship being different from its heterosexual counterpart (in a way that was not pathological) emerged. It was the emphasis on difference, rather than the patriarchal assumption of sameness, that allowed a unique lesbian relational pattern to emerge.

Mencher's (1990) premise is that the conceptual models that view separation as the cornerstone of healthy development are male derived. Inasmuch as lesbian relational preference by definition does not require women to relate intimately with men, the relational needs and behaviors of men (which Irigaray would say involves men seeing women as either the same as them but lacking or as [M]other) need not be the yardstick by which their relationships are judged. Lesbian relationships, which are explicitly different from their heterosexual counterparts, more clearly reflect a female affinity for realizing individual growth through connection with others (Jordan 1986; Miller 1984). Mencher (1990) states:

> An examination of intimacy patterns in lesbian couples may allow us to understand a bit more about how women experience themselves and their relationships when that experience is unfettered by the differing intimacy patterns of men and by patriarchal assumptions about how women should love . . . . The lesbian pattern–a more fused pattern—is not inherently disturbed and . . . [it] . . . may further explicate women's relational patterns in general. In a relationship in which both partners, as women, are consistently directed toward connection, there can exist a full range of possibility for mutuality, empathy and authenticity. (8)

Thus, ten years after Krestan and Bepko's (1980) pioneering article, the paradigmatic assumptions that tend to pathologize lesbian relationships (by negatively characterizing the mutually desirous nature of these relationships) are themselves being questioned. It seems it was the different-ness between stereotypically masculine and feminine relational patterns, as opposed to the perceived lack of differentiation between women, that needed clarification.

Lesbian Mothers in Psychological Literature

The challenges that face lesbians as they become mothers have begun to be explored in psychological literature (Crawford 1987; Rohrbaugh 1989; Stiglitz 1990; Slater and Mencher 1991). Much of this work has focused on the particular stressors of lesbians mothering within a homophobic culture, with an emphasis on issues of isolation and invisibility. The lack of a clear and cohesive parental community for lesbian mothers and their children is, according to Sally Crawford (1987), a "most difficult, painful and hard-to-anticipate problem" (199). She elaborates:

> Having children pushes a lesbian into regular social contact with the straight world. . . . Many lesbian parents find that they themselves need straight parents . . . for support. However, this need may not be reciprocal because the straight family often has its own support network of families and life styles in the straight world. (200)

This lack of a parenting community is at times compounded by the homophobia within the heterosexual community, which often includes the lesbian mother's family of origin as well. For most new mothers, another conventional source of support is their own mother, sister(s), and extended family (Brazelton and Cramer 1990). Because of the crisis a daughter coming out as a lesbian often precipitates within a family (Zitter 1987), she may not enjoy such support.

Additionally, lesbian mothers who turn to the lesbian community for support may find themselves disappointed, although the growing number of lesbian mothers is perhaps changing this dynamic. On a concrete level, the lifestyles of lesbians with and without children may be dissimilar enough on a practical level that little sharing or connection over the children is possible (Crawford 1987; Stiglitz 1990). On a more dynamic level, just as individual lesbians struggle to find identity and visibility as mothers, the lesbian community, as a real and imaginative structure, is only beginning to make a place for children and their lesbian mothers (M. Curtis, personal communication, November 1992). Thus lesbian mothers tend to find themselves tenuously connected to both the straight and lesbian communities. The psychological literature has understandably focused on the distinctive social stressors facing lesbians choosing children. However, this is not to suggest that lesbian mothering is all invisibility and isolation. Indeed, individual lesbians and lesbian couples have created many unique and loving alternative families and communities that they and their children grow and thrive in (Pies 1985; Rohrbaugh 1989). The individual solutions they have found undoubtedly reflect the fruits of much interpersonal and intrapsychic labor.

Lesbian Mothering: Internal Explorations

The bulk of the literature discussed in this inquiry focuses on the relational and social world lesbian mothers inhabit. It is presumably in interpersonal and social arenas that lesbian mothers experience their greatest struggles, as they come to terms with one another and the outside world. Although the intrapsychic experience and struggles of lesbian mothers has been referred to (Crawford 1987; Rohrbaugh 1989; Slater and Mencher 1991), it has not yet been a major focus of any inquiry.

Exploring the intrapsychic nature of any experience is admittedly ambitious. By its very nature, intrapsychic experience is highly personal, influenced by, among other things, individual history, social class, race, ethnicity, and religion. However, it is the thesis of this inquiry that a lesbian mother's intrapsychic encoding of matters such as femininity, nurturance, and desire have everything to do with understanding the nature of her experience, her struggles, and her oppression.

Biological Lesbian Mothers

Much of the literature concerning lesbian mothers mentions an intrapsychic struggle with one's sense of femininity as part and parcel of the experience of lesbian mothering (Rohrbaugh 1989; Slater and Mencher 1991; Stiglitz 1990). As women who have presumably lived outside the usual definitions of femininity for some time before choosing to become mothers, this is not surprising. If we return for a moment to our earlier discussion of femininity, we will remember that, according to Freud (1915), femininity is equated with passivity, with a lack of libidinous desire, and, ultimately, with the birth of a (preferably) male offspring within the confines of a heterosexual marriage.

Lesbians are, both by behavior and by definition, actively desirous of other women, and are therefore often thought of—by Freud (1920), by the popular culture (Faderman 1991), and sometimes by themselves (Faderman 1991)—as necessarily masculine. To shift the intrapsychic experience of being lesbian to include being mother is perhaps to challenge the public and private, the conscious and unconscious assumptions about masculinity and femininity. It is, I suggest, a process we need to attempt to speak of as we continue to discover, through our individual identities, our different-ness, lest we become the other, even to ourselves.

To underscore the importance of exploring individual experience in order to understand more fully not only ourselves but others as well, I will illustrate with a personal example. When my partner was visibly pregnant, she marveled at how her body had become fair game for any stranger who happened to feel like touching her belly. She was experiencing the societal acting out of the pregnant woman as a reproductive vessel rather than as an adult, desirous woman. Already, she was experiencing a new level of becoming other, by becoming (M)other, someone to be identified, handled, and objectified. However, because she had no husband, she had no access to the usual societal protection afforded a man's property (a.k.a. his wife), and therefore she experienced femininity unbounded by masculine protection or ownership. This newly found sense of individual identity with the feminine was, for her as a lesbian, especially profound.

This shifting of internal identity to include and understand the feminine was also felt within our primary relationship. As the pregnancy wore on, there were more and more things she was unable to do, and she relied on me as her partner for previously uncharacteristic kinds of help. Our roles became more clearly defined and we spent much time and energy discussing this fact. It was, it turned out, a clear harbinger of things to come. After our daughter was born, she was exclusively breast-fed for eight months. Although my partner would express her milk so that I was able to feed the baby as well, her relationship to her own body and the experience of being a breast-feeding mother continued to present her with new experiences that required her to relate to herself as a biological mother, to the enactment of an exclusively feminine role.

The lesbian mother's confrontation with the feminine on a deeply personal level is as necessary as it is unavoidable. Indeed, the challenge that negotiating more traditional feminine roles presents for individual women and their partners has been thought to cause some lesbian couples to break up after the birth of a child (Stiglitz 1990). I would extend this analysis to speak to the unique societal dynamics and intrapsychic stressors biological lesbian mothers experience. As women who already live in the shadow of the dominant order by virtue of their lesbianism, becoming more clearly identified with the feminine and ultimately with the (M)other presents, for some biological lesbian mothers, an unanticipated challenge. Additionally, lesbian couples who, before the pregnancy or birth, may have experienced themselves as more alike than different are confronted with a profound different-ness. This newly found sense of different-ness relates, of course, to the changing roles pregnancy and birthing impose. It extends, however, to the intrapsychic struggles with femininity and (M)otherhood both partners undoubtedly confront after the birth of the baby. As such, lesbian couples who have babies must reorganize their sense of themselves and their relationships in unique and profound ways.

Nonbiological Lesbian Mothers: Invisible (M)Others

Sally Crawford explores the role of the lesbian co-parent in her comprehensive 1987 article entitled "Lesbian Families: Psychosocial Stress and the Family-Building Process." She speaks directly to the unique stress a lesbian co-parent experiences:

> The fact that there is no definition of the role of co-mother as there is of father . . . makes the negotiation of roles particularly hard for the co-parent at home and out in the world. No matter how strong her presence and involvement in the family, it is she who bears the brunt of invisibility, it is she who is disenfranchised—by the school, by both families of origin, by the outside world . . . who do not see her as a parent nor understand the unique pressures of her position in the family. (205)

Crawford goes on to speak of the fact that the co-parent's process of bonding with her child(ren) can be impeded by her nonlegal status: "She is often painfully aware that if she and the mother part, she faces a potential double loss because she has no ultimate power over her relationship with the children" (206). Thus, the lesbian co-parent lives in a legal as well as social and emotional netherworld.

Overall, the current literature on nonbiological lesbian mothers is rather thin in comparison to their biological counterparts, although clearly more work is needed in both areas. While they are mentioned in much of the literature (Rohrbaugh 1989; Slater and Mencher 1991; Stiglitz 1990), the authors' attempts at exploring their unique experiences seem to reflect the indistinct status afforded these invisible (M)others. The truth of one statement became all too clear: "The lesbian co-parent is seen only as a shadowy figure" (Rohrbaugh 1989:57). If we are to examine this figure more closely, perhaps we will begin to shed light on some of the darkness currently surrounding the nonbiological lesbian mother.

Nonbiological Co-Parent: What's in a Name?

As we turn our attention to the nurturant, desirous woman who is other than (M)other, we first struggle with the constraints of language as we attempt to represent her symbolically through language. The linguistic constraints we encounter affect not only our public discourses but our private ones as well. "The process of self-construction can be traced in our use of language. It is with our entry into language that we first take up the position of subject" (Lorraine 1990:27). Thus, as the woman who occupies the subjective relational position we are attempting to consider in this discourse seeks to describe herself and her experience (as well as be described by others), she must do that in and through language.

The words used to describe (if, in fact, she is ever spoken of) the woman who occupies the subjective relational position of the other (M)other within a lesbian family is usually referred to as either the nonbiological (lesbian) mother or the (lesbian) co-parent. Both these terms constrain and confine the way she is viewed as well as the way she comes to view herself. If we examine the nature of being identified as a nonbiological mother, we perhaps begin to see some of the challenges women who occupy these roles face.

The term *biological* is a compound word derived from the Greek *bios*, meaning "life," and *logikos*, meaning "pertaining to speech or reason." Thus we have a word that quite literally speaks of or to life in a deliberate and sensible manner. To be identified as nonbiological is to have either a life without speech and/or a life without reason. Or perhaps it is simply not to have a life. Even more to the point, to be identified as nonbiological is to be identified in and through a sense of lack.

Just as women are identified as men who lack (Irigaray 1985b), nonbiological lesbian mothers are identified as women who lack. They become the space within the void that is identified as woman in patriarchal society. As such, they are not even the container, the womb that the (M)other is. Rather, they are the embodiment of what is perceived as emptiness, be it of the vagina or of the womb. They are truly the invisible other, existing without speech, reason, or life in association to the feminine other.

The term *co-parent* seems on the surface a somewhat friendlier, more benign term. The prefix *co-* is derived from the Latin *cum*, meaning "with" or "together." *Parent* derives from the Latin form of the verb *parere*, meaning "to bring forth or breed." We return again to the notion of biology and again the lesbian co-parent loses her identity. Even on a more colloquial level a co-parent is by definition either mother or father, a necessarily genderless being. It seems the lesbian co-parent has to lose either her life, her speech, or her gender in her attempt to name herself, her role, and her relationship to the mother and child. We are left perhaps identifying as co-mother, a term Crawford (1987) used, although not one that seems to have caught on. It is perhaps more accurate than the other terms considered here, as it is one that speaks to being with the mother. What it lacks, however, is a clear encoding of difference that is posited here as being so central to a coherent and authentic identity.

A co-mother is at danger of becoming reduced to mimicry, which Irigaray (1985a) speaks of as the role historically assigned to the feminine. Using mimesis, the deliberate adoption (mimicking) of a feminine role as a first step toward "convert[ing] a form of subordination into affirmation" (Irigaray 1985b:76), is an important self-strategy for women (mothers) thrust into inescapably feminine roles. By deliberately assuming the role, we allow ourselves to transform it rather than being reduced to it. However, it is within the lesbian couple that women as mothers and co-mothers have the option of exploring the feminine unbounded by overt masculine ownership. It is here we have the opportunity to attend fully to the dynamics of feminine roles and self-strategies in our most personal and intimate moments. To mimic each other's interpretation of those roles without transforming them into a deeply personal expression of our own uniquely feminine self-strategy would be to become stalled at the level of mimesis.

As we have seen, lesbian mothers (be they biological or other) are confronted with living a fundamental experience of femininity unbounded by masculine ownership. Although this provides us with the opportunity to transform these roles, both my personal and clinical experiences tell me this road to transformation is neither clear nor smooth. Given that masculine discourses and activities have been privileged in our culture and language, and given that lesbians have been seen (and perhaps, to some extent, have identified) as masculine, this confrontation with the feminine can create much confusion, both within individuals and within relationships.

The importance of allowing, acknowledging, and respecting difference cannot be overemphasized here. Two adult, desirous women raising child(ren) will undoubtedly experience and negotiate differing roles and self-strategies as they raise their children, maintain their passionate relationship, and live in the lesbian community and the larger world. The capacity to explore, share, and, most important, to speak of and name these differing experiences is necessary and central to the task of creating and re-creating a community that truly reflects our individual and collective commonalities and differences.

It is within such a community that diversity, that is, the acknowledging and valuing of difference, assumes a central role. Individual self-strategies based on highly personal experience not only allow diversity, they require it. Thus, the embracing of diversity is fundamental, for reasons that are as personally profound as they are politically vital. As we tell our individual stories, we must avoid looking solely at what is similar or different about them. We must have the courage to identify with others while acknowledging our differences from them, thereby avoiding the trap of having to choose between our individual and collective voices.

REFERENCES

Brazelton, T. B., and B. G. Cramer. 1990. *The earliest relationship*. Reading, Mass.: Addison-Wesley.

Crawford, S. 1987. Lesbian families: Psychosocial stress and the family-building process. In Boston Lesbian Psychologies Collective, eds., *Lesbian psychologies*, pp. 195–214. Urbana, Ill.: University of Illinois Press.

Faderman, L. 1991. *Odd girls and twilight lovers*. New York: Penguin.

Freud, S. 1915. Femininity. In E. Young-Bruehl, ed., *Freud on women*, pp. 342–362. New York: Norton.

— 1920. The psychogenesis of a case of homosexuality in a woman. In E. Young-Bruehl, ed., *Freud on women*, pp. 241–266. New York: Norton.

Grosz, E. 1989. *Sexual subversions*. New York and London: Routledge.

Holmlund, C. 1991. The lesbian, the mother, the heterosexual lover: Irigaray's recodings of difference. *Feminist Studies* 17(2):283–308.

Irigaray, L. 1985a [1974]. *Speculum of the other woman*. Trans. G. C. Gill. Ithaca: Cornell University Press.

— 1985b [1977]. *This sex which is not one*. Trans. C. Porter. Ithaca: Cornell University Press.

Jordan, J. 1986. *The meaning of mutuality*. Work in Progress no. 23. Wellesley, Mass.: Stone Center Working Paper Series.

Kaufman, P. A., E. H. Harrison, and M. L. Hyde. 1984. Distancing for intimacy in lesbian relationships. *American Journal of Psychiatry* 141:530–533.

Krestan, J., and C. S. Bepko. 1980. The problem of fusion in the lesbian relationship. *Family Process* 19:277–289.

Lindenbaum, J. 1985. The shattering of an illusion: The problem of competition in lesbian relationships. *Feminist Studies* 11(1):85–103.

Lorde, A. 1982. *Zami: A new spelling of my name*. Watertown, Mass.: Persephone.

Lorraine, T. E. 1990. *Gender, identity and the production of meaning*. San Francisco: Westview.

Mencher, J. 1990. *Intimacy in lesbian relationships: A critical re-examination of fusion*. Work in Progress no. 42. Wellesley, Mass.: Stone Center Working Paper Series.

Miller, J. B. 1984. *The development of women's sense of self*. Work in Progress no. 12. Wellesley, Mass.: Stone Center Working Paper Series.

Perlman, S. F. 1988. Distancing and connectedness: Impact on couple formation in lesbian relationships. *Women in Therapy* 11:273–286.

Pies, C. 1985. *Considering parenthood: A workbook for lesbians.* San Francisco: Spinsters/Aunt Lute.

Rohrbaugh, J. 1989. Choosing children: Psychological issues in lesbian parenting. In E. D. Rosenblum and E. Cole, eds., *Lesbianism: Affirming nontraditional roles,* pp. 51–64. New York: Haworth.

Roth, S. 1985. Psychotherapy with lesbian couples: Individual issues, female socialization and the social context. *Journal of Marital and Family Therapy* 11:273–286.

Slater, S., and J. Mencher. 1991. The lesbian family life cycle: A contextual approach. *American Journal of Orthopsychiatry* 61(3):372–381.

Stiglitz, E. 1990. Caught between two worlds: The impact of a child on a lesbian couple's relationship. In J. P. Knowles and E. Cole, eds., *Motherhood: A feminist perspective,* pp. 99–115. New York: Haworth.

Whitford, M., ed. 1991. *The Irigaray reader.* Cambridge: Blackwell.

Young-Bruehl, E., ed. 1990. *Freud on women.* New York: Norton.

Zitter, S. 1987. Coming out to mom: Theoretical aspects of the mother-daughter process. In Boston Lesbian Psychologies Collective, eds., *Lesbian psychologies,* pp. 177–194. Urbana: University of Illinois Press.

CHAPTER NINE

Lesbian Parents:
Understanding Developmental Pathways

Betty Morningstar

IN THIS CHAPTER I describe some of the common pathways that lesbians traverse in the process of becoming parents. Before such a discussion begins, one must acknowledge two assumptions that have been deeply ingrained in our society's collective way of thinking. The first assumption is that women are mothers, and the second assumption is that lesbians are not mothers. In fact, not all women mother (some by choice and some by circumstance), and it is becoming increasingly clear that lesbians have been mothers for decades and continue to create families by whatever means are available to them. The women's movement, the gay and lesbian rights movement, and an ever growing interest in reproductive rights and technology have provided all women— heterosexual and lesbian—the opportunity to explore a wider range of lifestyle options than most women previously thought possible.

I focus on self-identified lesbians who have created biological families through alternative means of conception. While the media, both straight and gay, may be exaggerating when they refer to a "lesbian baby boom," it is clear from clinical and sociocultural evidence that a trend has emerged among lesbians toward creating families. Seligman (1990) reported an estimated five to ten thousand women in the United States had conceived children within an already established lesbian lifestyle. Several authors since then (e.g., Patterson 1992) comment on how difficult it is to make estimates of this kind, while also noting that the numbers are constantly growing. In a later paper, Patterson (1995) estimates that there are two to eight million gay- and lesbian-headed families in the United States. She does not offer an estimate of the number of lesbians who become parents outside of a heterosexual union. In contrast to these "new" lesbian families, many lesbians have created and continue to create blended or stepfamilies by bringing their children from previous heterosexual marriages into lesbian relationships. Earlier research on the first wave of lesbian families provides some background for the current examination of lesbians choosing from the outset to parent without a male partner.

Because the phenomenon of lesbian parenting is still novel to many people, including people in the mental health professions, there are few guidelines for understanding what are normative experiences for women engaged in this process. Although there is a body of literature that helps to elucidate the normative experiences of heterosexual women who become mothers (Benedek 1959; Daniels and Weingarten 1983), none of the developmental literature addresses the experience of motherhood for lesbians, be it adult developmental literature (e.g., Erikson 1959; Colarusso and Nemiroff 1979), literature on women's development (Miller 1976), or lesbian developmental models (Cass 1979; Gramick 1984).

Using observations derived from my clinical practice and from workshops I have conducted for lesbians considering parenting, in this paper I examine, from a psychosocial perspective, the experience of lesbians who choose to bear children and offer a framework that includes what appear to be normative transitions encountered in this process. It should be noted that lesbians face many of the same challenges as do heterosexual women in their efforts to create families. This discussion, however, will focus on those issues and concerns that seem to be unique to lesbians, while taking into account the broader context of mothering in the general population. It is also important to be mindful of the diversity among lesbian families themselves. While there appear to be some clear-cut issues and concerns that lesbians, qua lesbians, must address as they approach the tasks related to parenting, the ways in which these concerns are resolved vary widely.

This chapter will present an outline of the component parts of the process of becoming a lesbian parent. The component parts are not seen as stages, per se, and do not occur in a linear fashion (with some obvious exceptions: for example, insemination must precede coping with the stresses of lesbian parenthood). The parts of the process might better be thought of as transitions or challenges, with attendant psychosocial tasks. The impact of homophobia (internalized and societal) will be addressed, as will be potential clinical issues that may arise in working with women going through this process.

Literature Review

The literature on lesbian families falls into two major categories: 1. psychological outcome studies of children in lesbian families—most of which concern children who were the product of a previous heterosexual union, and 2. psychological and sociocultural accounts of the experience of lesbian couples and their families. The first category is by far the larger. In Patterson's (1992) comprehensive review of outcome studies, she reported that children of lesbians rated comparably to children of heterosexual mothers on all measures of psychological adjustment, including separation-individuation, emotional stability, moral judgment, object relations, gender identity, and sex-role behavior. Again, these studies focused almost exclusively on children born into a heterosexual arrangement. In her 1995 paper Patterson reiterates the findings of earlier studies

A few outcome studies of children in new lesbian families have been published to date. Steckel (1985, 1987) conducted the first systematic study that investigated children who were conceived within an established lesbian lifestyle. In comparing that group of children to families headed by divorced heterosexual mothers, she reported some findings that are noteworthy. She found that there was no greater pathology with respect to the separation-individuation process among children in lesbian families. However, both male and female children of heterosexual parents viewed themselves and were seen by parents and teachers as somewhat more aggressive than children in the other group. In contrast, the children (of both sexes) of lesbian parents saw themselves and were seen by parents and teachers as more lovable and affectionate. Patterson (1992) cautions the reader that, due to the sample size (N = 11 in each group) and the large number of statistical tests conducted, these results should be considered no more than suggestive.

McCandlish (1987) described some of the psychosocial challenges facing lesbians choosing children. In her small study of five lesbian families she traced the course of changing partner roles and relationships, evolving relationships between child and parents, the effect of the legal and social system on family functioning, and the strengths and coping mechanisms used to manage these stressors and changes. Although McCandlish emphasizes concern about potential legal and social censure among her subjects, she identifies one of their major coping mechanisms as their ongoing effort to communicate about their identity to their children and to certain carefully chosen people outside of the family. The seven children in this study were reported to have developed normally in all areas.

The most recent study of children of the lesbian baby boom was conducted by Patterson (1994). She investigated the self-concept, behavioral
adjustment, and sex role behavior of thirty-seven children born or adopted
into families headed by a single lesbian or a lesbian couple (of the thirty-
seven, thirty-four were their biological children and three were adopted).
On all variables studied, the children were found to be in the normal range
of development. These data are comparable to Steckel's, suggesting that
children in lesbian families develop along the same lines as children in heterosexual families. Patterson's findings also correspond to the findings from
studies of children of previously married lesbians that she reviewed in 1992.
One exception to Steckel's findings in Patterson's 1994 study was that children in lesbian families did not see themselves as more lovable than did
children in heterosexual families, nor did children in heterosexual families
see themselves as more aggressive than did the children of lesbian couples.
Another new finding was that children in lesbian-headed families felt more
stressed than did the children in the other families. According to Patterson,
this may be due to the fact that their lives are actually more stressful than
the lives of children in more traditional families. Additionally, the reported
higher stress may be related to another finding—that the children of lesbian
families in this study were more verbal about a variety of feeling states,
including contentment and a sense of well-being.

Laird (1993) notes that the findings just described—that children in lesbian families function at least as well as children of heterosexual parents—
are counter to what one might expect, given the stresses inherent in living
in a family that is marginalized and stigmatized. It is notable that these
conditions do not seem to have an adverse effect on children's development.
In addition, Patterson (1992) notes that if one subscribes to a psychoanalytic
framework one would expect a higher rate of psychological disturbance in
children of lesbians. This expectation is based on the theoretical need for a
male and a female adult to be present in order for the child to accomplish
the requisite developmental tasks involving, among others, separation, individuation, and identification.

Two studies speak specifically to the strengths observed in lesbian families. Harris and Turner (1985–1986) studied gay fathers, lesbian mothers,
and single heterosexual fathers and mothers. The gay and lesbian parents
reported few problems in the social arena among their children, and many
of these parents also reported that their children seemed more tolerant,
empathic, and open to diverse viewpoints. Keating (1991) studied a small
sample of young adult children raised by lesbian mothers. These subjects as

a whole also saw themselves as more tolerant and aware of a range of points of view than their peers from straight families.

According to Laird (1993), the notion of fusion in lesbian relationships is a possible explanation for some of the unexpected strengths observed in the children of lesbians. Fusion in lesbian relationships has often been defined in negative terms and seen as a pathological manifestation of unresolved pre-Oedipal issues. Several authors, however, have reframed the notion of fusion, without denying its prevalence. One of the chief arguments against pathologizing lesbian fusion is offered by Krestan and Bepko (1980). These authors regard fusion as the natural outcome of the impact of society's views of lesbian relationships. These views are either dismissive or intolerant, and such attitudes tend to bring lesbian partners closer together for protection against the outside world. They have also speculated that lesbians are prone to fusion because of the patriarchal socialization of women that encourages them to give up their own identity in the context of a relationship. Elise (1986) discards these perspectives in favor of a developmental perspective emerging from the psychoanalytic tradition. She advances the notion, based largely on the work of Chodorow (1978), that women develop strong relational skills and inclinations, due to the fact that they are most often raised by caregivers of the same sex. She states that it is gender, not sexual orientation, that explains the tendency toward fusion in lesbian relationships and emphasizes that all women tend to immerse themselves in relationships. Thus, when two women are involved with each other, the likelihood of fusion is high. Mencher (1990) underlines the value of fusion in lesbian relationships, elaborating on the ways in which fusion allows for feelings of safety and security which, in turn, foster personal growth and development. Laird (1993) speculates that, since lesbians often derive much emotional closeness from their partners, they are less likely to seek this intense kind of intimacy from their children. Laird goes on to raise the question whether children of lesbians are better equipped to deal with issues of intimacy and less well-equipped to manage anger and conflict.

Weston's (1991) ethnographic study of lesbian and gay families examines a wide range of social, political, and economic issues. Although much of the book focuses on nonbiological family networks, she does address the impact of biological mothering on lesbian identity, referring to the (biological) lesbian mother as "at once icon and conundrum" (169). The notion of conceiving a child within the context of a nonprocreative sexual identity requires a kind of reconciliation. She goes on to state that "such reconciliation will be complicated by the notions of gender and personhood embedded in particular ideologies of kinship (169)." Indeed, every aspect of conceiving, bearing, and raising a child in a lesbian context challenges assumptions that a child must be the product of a heterosexual union.

Another challenge to assumptions about the centrality of heterosexuality in the conception and rearing of children is offered by Muzio (this volume). She examined the notion of femininity in lesbian mother families and stated that lesbian mothering offers the opportunity for "living a fundamental experience of femininity unbounded by masculine ownership" (227). She goes on to say that it can also become complicated and confusing, as two women negotiate their respective roles vis-à-vis children. Further, she emphasizes the importance of naming the partners' different parenting experiences as a means of "creating and re-creating a community that truly reflects our differences" (227).

Several other authors have addressed various psychosocial issues affecting lesbian parents. Levy (1989) studied the relationship between lesbian identity, social support, and the ability of lesbian mothers to cope with the stresses associated with living in a heterosexist and homophobic environment. A major finding was that support from other lesbian mothers was crucial. In addition, Levy found that many subjects were selective about coming out to others, despite being comfortable with their lesbian identities.

In her summary of some key psychosocial concerns affecting lesbian parents and parents to be, Pies (1987) addresses the difficulties in talking to family of origin about plans to parent, the complicated questions involved in deciding whether to have a known or an unknown donor, the strain resulting from the two lesbian parents having "biologically asymmetrical" relationships to their child, and a variety of legal and ethical concerns.

Lott-Whitehead and Tully's study (chapter 10, this volume) of forty-five lesbian mothers produced findings consistent both with the research on children of lesbian parents and the research on lesbian parents themselves. They concluded that lesbian families have numerous strengths, including openness in regard to sexuality and difference, and that they offer an environment that is "accepting, nurturing, and conducive to human growth" (275). Despite an understandably high level of stress in a number of the families studied, the women were careful to protect their children from the impact of homophobia and to maintain their families' integrity, never minimizing the possible effects of their lesbianism on their children.

Drawing from a mixed population of old and new lesbian families in her clinical practice, Crawford (1987) outlines some of the psychosocial stressors these families face, as well as their strengths. Included are isolation, invisibility, pressure to hide the natural ambivalence about parenting that most women feel, conflicts with family of origin, and stress around the negotiation of parental roles within the couple. She emphasizes the impact of homophobia in the struggles of lesbian parents and families and offers suggestions for therapists, cautioning therapists to find a balance between understanding the influence of oppression on these families and recognizing that lesbian families present with the same range of issues as other families. In addressing the possible conflicts and struggles for children in lesbian families, Crawford notes that the mastery of their difficulties will help them develop strengths. She suggests that these strengths potentially may help them influence society, as they become adults who are comfortable with difference. I would add that the acquisition of certain strengths also applies to adults who master the difficulties associated with the creation of alternative families.

In an effort to place lesbian parenting within the broader context of family patterns in our society, it is necessary to look beyond traditional psychodynamic theory and family theory, both of which have been criticized for male and heterosexual bias (Eichenbaum and Orbach 1983; Goodrich, Rampage, Ellman, and Halstead 1988). Theoretical approaches that offer less biased perspectives on the phenomenon of lesbian parenting can be found in the self-in-relation literature about women (e.g., Gilligan 1982; Jordan, Surrey, and Kaplan 1983; Miller 1976) and the feminist literature on mothering (e.g., Chodorow 1978; Eichenbaum and Orbach 1983; Flax 1978). While these authors do not address the lesbian experience per se, they refocus our attention on women's capacity for empathy and nurturance, characteristics regarded as valuable rather than as deficiencies.

The problem with embracing the notion of women's empathic and affiliative capacities too fervently is that it can lead to an essentialist position on mothering. In fact, not all women are nurturant, nor are all women interested in raising children. Furthermore, given the fact that the expectation that women are mothers is often consciously or unconsciously attributed to these capacities, it is important to note that this same expectation has not been applied to women who happen also to be lesbian. The current social discourse on family patterns may free some women from the requirement of parenting and allow others previously prohibited from doing so to explore parenting possibilities.

The deconstruction of certain myths about women and families is much needed, and some of the writing in the narrative tradition offers useful insights. Benkov (1994) points out that the family forms that actually exist in our society are far more diverse than the purported norms. Adoptive, step-, and single-parent families abound, and families created through insemination, in vitro fertilization, and surrogacy are on the increase. Lesbians necessarily consider parenting options that fall into one or more of these categories. In so doing, they are challenging such fundamental issues as the role of gender in parenting and the significance of the biological versus the social tie to one's children.

Weingarten (1994) addresses the notion of father absence in lesbian families. Father absence in families is hardly new and certainly not limited to lesbian families. Weingarten links the concern over father absence in families with mother blaming, which, among other things, may stimulate excessive concern for the well-being of their children, especially their sons, on the parts of both heterosexual and lesbian mothers. In fact, men other than the biological father can play a crucial role in children's lives. An interesting finding in the comparison studies between the children of lesbian mothers and divorced heterosexual mothers was that lesbian mothers made greater efforts than heterosexual mothers to provide their children with contact with their fathers and with men in general (e.g., Kirkpatrick 1987; Golombok, Spencer, and Rutter 1983).

In another vein, the small but visible movement among gay male couples to raise children (either through surrogacy, adoption, or co-parenting with a single lesbian or lesbian couple) forces us to rethink long-held ideas about men's ability to nurture and take care of children.

Given the confluence of several factors—the maturation of the lesbian feminist movement, advances in reproductive technologies, and shifting conceptualizations in the social discourse about what constitutes family—it is not surprising that lesbians are creating families at a fairly rapid rate. In order to keep pace with this phenomenon, we, as therapists, must educate ourselves to the unique challenges posed by lesbian parenting. We must be aware of the complications and obstacles as well as some of the unusual strengths exhibited by these women on the cutting edge.

The developmental schema that follows is divided into seven sections, each of which describes an aspect of the process of creating a lesbian family. This schema is not conceptualized as in some stage theories of (lesbian) development (e.g., Cass 1979) but instead is an outline of the challenges and transitions that occur as lesbian women become parents. In each section a developmental issue will be identified, the concomitant tasks outlined, and the relevant potential clinical issues addressed.

Creating Lesbian Families

The Decision-Making Process

Until recently lesbians were unable to engage in the normative adult process of deciding how and when to create a family. Now that it is possible for single and coupled lesbians to choose to parent, a host of complex and unique decisions must be made. Each of the tasks that lesbians must address in the decision-making phase involves making a radical shift in presuppositions about how families are formed. Countering society's (and one's own) deeply embedded notions of what constitutes family may prove liberating and/or grief-laden. Despite some of the difficulties, lesbians need no longer exclude themselves from pursuing one of the main avenues for accomplishing the adult tasks associated with Erikson's (1959) stage of generativity. In the past lesbians approached these tasks in a variety of creative, but most often nonprocreative, ways such as teaching, mentoring, or producing artistic or literary material.

In some sense, in the twenty-five to thirty years since the lesbian and gay liberation movement began, the maturation of the movement parallels the maturation of the people involved in it, that is, both the movement and its members have reached their child-bearing years. Many lesbians who would not have considered having children ten to twenty years ago say that they now feel almost forced to consider it. Among my own lesbian clientele a shift has occurred with regard to the parenting issue over the last fifteen years. Although initially almost none of my lesbian clients in individual therapy mentioned thoughts of having children, over the years almost all of them have grappled with the issue in some fashion. Deciding whether or not to parent requires that these women examine their experience of themselves as lesbian (previously defined as childless), as woman, as partner, as potential parent, and as groundbreaker. Deciding to parent may drastically alter the lesbian's relationship with her family of origin, peers, and coworkers—and even with her partner—as she takes on an added dimension to her identity.

An increasingly common reason for referral of lesbian couples to couples therapy is the question of parenting. Typical questions lesbian couples raise are, What can we do when one of us is not interested in being a parent? How should we choose who will be the biological parent? Should we adopt or bear a child? Should we have a known or an unknown donor? What kind of relationship should a known donor have with the child? Should we discuss our plans with our families of origin? How should we adapt to all of these new circumstances? Will we/the child face discrimination? How can we protect him/her? Individual issues revolve around body image, femininity, effectiveness as an adult, and fears of bodily change. While most women experience some of these concerns, lesbians, having been more conditioned to question themselves around these issues, may be more vulnerable to such doubts and anxieties.

Many couples report that, once they have decided to have a child, have settled on the biological route instead of adoption, and have determined which partner will carry the child, they are strengthened in their resolve to move ahead together with the process. Often couples get bogged down in the earliest decisions and, for that reason, do not survive as a couple. In the decision-making workshops for lesbians that I have led there are often one or two single women who have ended relationships because of conflicts over whether or not to have children. In contrast, heterosexual couples may move through this part of the process with less conflict, as having children has traditionally been expected as part of the institution of marriage.

For most lesbian couples the method of conception is donor insemination (as opposed to intercourse), a decision that tends not to be conflictual. More complex is the decision about whether to use a known or an unknown donor. There are risks with either choice. With a known donor the chief risk is legal, because he has all the legal rights and responsibilities of a biological father, while the nonbiological female co-parent has no (automatic) rights. While in some cases lesbian-headed families include the donor as a significant person/father in the child's life, in many cases the donor is just that and has little or no other involvement. There is always the potential for a donor to file a paternity suit, even if he has previously agreed not to be involved in the child's life. The threat to the couple, and in particular to the nonbiological co-parent, is enough to push many lesbian couples to inseminate with the sperm of an unknown donor. The legal risk to all parties (and ultimately to the child) constitutes a major policy issue in need of attention.

The main concern that lesbians and others express about using the sperm of an unknown donor is whether and how children will be affected by not having complete knowledge of their lineage (Noble 1987). Lesbians must then deal with the loss for their child as well as for themselves.

The stress caused by some of these monumental decisions will certainly increase, if one's relationships with significant others, including family of origin, are strained. Many lesbians will seek outside support in the form of therapy, decision-making workshops, or other community supports.

Therapists who are not knowledgeable about the psychosocial tasks and concerns outlined above may tend to see the extremes of mood or emotion expressed during this process as aberrant rather than as a natural response to a difficult but exciting challenge. At this point it is necessary that the therapist validate and educate the client(s) regarding these apparently normative experiences. The therapist must be mindful of the need for as many supportive resources as possible and be able to assist clients in obtaining them. In some parts of the country where resources are scarce, therapists will be required to help clients be even more adaptive in creating their own networks for medical, social, and psychological support.

In addition to education, validation, and external support, the therapist must be prepared to deal with the possibility that a client may exhibit a significant grief reaction at this juncture. There may be losses related to outmoded images of family, the absence of a father (if applicable), the approval and support of family of origin, and the full-fledged acceptance afforded by society to most women who bear children. In addition, the nonbiological parent may grieve the loss of the experience of pregnancy, childbirth, and an ongoing biological connection. Couples often report feelings of loss related to the opportuntiy to create a child that is biologically connected to both parents. The client's comfort level and degree of resolution of family of origin issues, self-esteem regulation, and integration of a lesbian identity will influence the length and course of the grief reaction.

Related to the grief process may be the resurfacing of ambivalence about one's sexual orientation. This should not necessarily be interpreted as a sign of sexual identity confusion. Most women that I have treated who have arrived at the point of deciding to have children have resolved these kinds of issues on a deeper level, but some do respond to the challenges from the outside world by doubting some of their earlier choices or actions.

Lesbians considering parenting may attempt to appear as though they have more completely resolved their personal issues and concerns around parenting than is actually the case. These attempts may be responses to challenges from the outside regarding family and parenting norms. While this coping mechanism may be adaptive to an extent, it is important for these clients to work through whatever is unresolved for them before embarking on this major life passage.

Therapists are asking much of their lesbian clients by encouraging them to examine their issues and concerns around parenting so closely, especially since they are unlikely to expect the same scrupulous exploration on the part of their heterosexual clients. One might anticipate that some lesbians may resent this exploration, so it is important for the therapist to acknowledge such reactions and, at the same time, continue to encourage careful self-examination.

A final note for therapists working with lesbians in the early part of the parenting process is that there may be a tendency on the part of the therapist to either overvalue or to discredit the notion of lesbian parenting. Clinicians must examine their own values, biases, and agendas as they deal with these new and controversial issues. Lesbian therapists who are strongly in favor of lesbians creating families for political or other more personal reasons may consciously or unconsciously push a client toward choosing to parent. Likewise, a straight therapist, perhaps overly concerned about appearing homophobic, may do the same. A therapist who prematurely influences a client who is not ready to make a decision about parenting can cause as much damage as a homophobic straight therapist (or a lesbian therapist opposed to lesbians having children) who overtly or covertly attempts to dissuade a client from becoming a parent.

The Case of Mary

The following case example illustrates the importance of therapist neutrality. Several years ago Mary, a lesbian in her early thirties whom I was seeing in individual therapy, and her partner Lisa began to act on Mary's long-held wish to become a parent. While the desire to parent had been present for some time, Mary and her partner had not paid sufficient attention to some of the considerations and tasks involved. The couple had identified a known donor, established the prospective biological mother's fertility cycles, and were preparing to proceed with insemination. Mary was aware that she had not fully explored the alternatives or her own or the couple's unresolved emotional issues. Nonetheless, she felt great urgency to move forward. The couple delayed the process, however, only because of circumstances that arose unexpectedly (partner's job change and temporary loss of income). This delay allowed Mary to look more closely at her sense of urgency, and she discovered that a number of unresolved losses and a lack of adequate parenting in her family of origin had been driving her to act too quickly. In this case I, as the therapist, had to make a concerted effort to keep my own values separate from my clinical judgments about the client's situation and to maintain a neutral therapeutic stance. Being more inclined to support the establishment of lesbian families than not, it was at times tempting to encourage this client to move forward. At the same time, it became increasingly evident that there were many unresolved concerns about the meaning of parenting to Mary. These concerns led me to wish silently for a way to prevent the process from continuing. This paradox—wishing for the client to have a child and hoping that she would not—created considerable anxiety for me. Keeping myself conscious of my conflicted feelings seemed to prevent my expressing them in ways that may not have been helpful for Mary.

Mary was soon able to see that the path to becoming a parent would be a long and complicated one for her. As of now, several years later, she is doubtful about having children. She has spent the ensuing time on deeper self-exploration and on developing her career, and she reports having derived much satisfaction from tending her garden and her pets.

Attempting to Conceive

The period of time during which a lesbian (couple) attempts to become pregnant has been described by many as an "emotional roller coaster." Many lesbians are well into their thirties and even forties when they begin the insemination process. To begin with, they are under the pressure of the "biological clock." In a sample of 124 lesbians in the parenting program at the Fenway Community Health Center in Boston, 54 percent of the subjects were thirty-five years old or older at the time of their first attempt at insemination (Barkan and Milbauer 1992). The relatively late age at which lesbians embark on this process is due to several factors: 1. Most lesbians having children are professional women who are more likely, in general, to delay childbearing; 2. older women are more likely than others to have the financial means to take on the considerable expense of alternative insemination; 3. it often takes years for a lesbian to resolve emotional concerns as well as to make concrete plans to inseminate; 4. many lesbians currently bearing children were previously unaware of the options that are now more widely available to lesbians wishing to parent. This last point should cease to be a factor when lesbians and others more fully recognize the viability of alternative insemination as a route to parenting. The following vignette illustrates the novelty of this phenomenon. A colleague reported that a young lesbian who was seeking a lesbian therapist called her for an appointment. When the colleague said she was unable to see her because she was about to go on maternity leave, the woman replied, "But I thought you were a lesbian." The therapist responded that her assumption was correct, but the young woman still seemed confused and surprised.

As a result of the later age at which most lesbians attempt to conceive, and as a result of the means by which conception is usually achieved (frozen sperm, the most common alternative for lesbians, may be less effective than fresh sperm), the length of time required to become pregnant is often protracted. Researchers in the Fenway study cited above found that women in the thirty-five- to thirty-nine-year-old range had a 29 percent chance of conceiving within six ovulation cycles, and women over forty had a 9 percent chance of achieving conception in the same time frame.

Infertility is a common problem for lesbians, due at least in part to the fact that many begin the insemination process at a relatively advanced age. The experience of undergoing evaluation and treatment for possible medical causes of this problem is extremely stressful. It is well-documented that almost any woman (or man) who deals with infertility experiences emotional turmoil, often revolving around concerns about femininity (or masculinity) and around the possible loss of one's ability to procreate. For a lesbian, whose femininity in any case may be questioned by other people or by herself, this time can be especially difficult. Additionally, all of the time spent planning and orchestrating insemination may increase feelings of anger, disappointment, and failure. Homophobia can exacerbate these intense feelings, as many lesbians may face insensitive medical personnel in their quest to resolve infertility. That kind of insensitivity may also be encountered by lesbians dealing with pregnancy loss, another time when support and acceptance is crucial. A lesbian harboring internalized homophobia may irrationally blame herself or her lesbian sexuality for her inability to conceive or carry a pregnancy to term.

Therapists dealing with clients facing infertility or pregnancy loss must help them separate out guilt and fear from appropriate anger and disappointment. A common experience reported by lesbians who encounter problems with conception or pregnancy is their intense anger at heterosexual women and "heterosexual privilege." At first glance, this attitude may seem irrational and out of proportion. Within the context of the added internal and external stressors that lesbians must face, it is, however, natural for lesbians to be angry at how easy it seems to be for straight women to conceive. Although infertility is also devastating to straight women, lesbians may have to deal with the added stress of homophobia as they go through this difficult process. These stresses may involve doctors excluding the lesbian's partner from treatment planning, premature suggestion that the lesbian (couple) adopt, or more overt condemnation of the choice to parent. Therapists can help clients channel their anger constructively by validating the experience, exploring relevant dynamics, empowering clients to make organized efforts toward combating homophobia in the medical profession and the health insurance industry, helping clients to sustain their determination to become parents, and guiding clients to pursue other parenting options if appropriate.

The Case of Amy

Amy, a lesbian in her early thirtiess, had been attempting to conceive for about eight months, during which time a straight friend became pregnant within a marriage. She was so angry that she could barely look at her friend as the pregnancy progressed. Along with her anger at her friend and at straight women in general, she began complaining about the rampant teen pregnancy problem. In therapy Amy gradually began to connect these intense feelings to feelings she had always had about her sister, who was married with a child and had always seemed to be the parents' favorite. Amy felt she could never do anything right, and her unsuccessful attempts to conceive were experienced as a further sign of her failure as a daughter and as a woman. She was subsequently able to see that her relationship with her partner, Sue, was insufficient to withstand the addition of a child, and she left the relationship. Several years later she began a new relationship and is again making plans to have a child. She is optimistic that a pregnancy will occur and is relieved that she understands her earlier desperation to "succeed" at this task. Her decreased intensity of affect may increase the chances that she will conceive (although she is now older) and will most certainly make the ups and downs of the process less difficult to manage.

Another important clinical issue concerns the fact that, with few exceptions, children of lesbians are very much planned for or chosen. Obviously, this fact is, in most ways, positive. There are, however, some potential liabilities in having a child chosen in this way. Because of all the planning, agonizing, and waiting for this special child to be born, the parents' valuing of the child may take on an almost obsessional quality. They may feel overprotective and/or overly worried about losing a child for whom they waited such a long time. This phenomenon is also reported by infertile heterosexual couples who eventually conceive and by adoptive couples who have endured a lengthy waiting period. The specialness of the child may cause strain on the adult relationship as well as potentially causing certain anxieties and/or problematic behaviors on the part of the child.

The Case of Marcia and Linda

The situation of one lesbian couple who had weathered a miscarriage before their child was born illustrates some of the advantages and disadvantages of being chosen. On the one hand, Marcia and Linda were extremely devoted and nurturing during this child's infancy, and the child clearly benefited in many ways. She appeared to be a content, calm baby with good attachment. Problems occurred, however, in the area of sleep, manifested by three awakenings per night to nurse in the first eighteen months. Marcia and Linda felt compelled to meet the demand and, as a result, they were so drained of energy that their relationship suffered. Eventually, they sought help for their relationship and for the nighttime awakenings. Guiding a couple in these kinds of matters takes empathy and skills that are unique to working with this population.

Clearly, the need for the therapist to validate, educate, support, facilitate accessing resources and help with the unfolding of the grief process is still critical at this point. Individuals and couples need guidance and healing when they deal head on with one of the most intense developmental moments in their lives. Because the wish to mother is often closely connected to feelings about one's femininity, one's sexuality, and one's worth as a person, threats to the fulfillment of the wish can have a tremendous impact.

Negotiating the Couple Relationship and the Role of the Nonbiological Co-Parent

Lesbian couples have been described by various authors as invisible in the larger society (e.g., Crawford 1987). Their visibility, however, will probably change dramatically when the couple effects some noticeable alteration in their lifestyle, such as having a child. That the perception of an individual or couple can change so radically from being invisible to being unacceptable may be difficult for that individual or couple to absorb. There are a host of ways in which homophobia may surface when lesbians prepare to have children. Some believe that homophobia, if not the cause of many difficulties in lesbian and gay families, exacerbates whatever problems may have already existed (Forstein 1993).

If lesbians are often invisible, and if lesbian mothers are treated with skepticism, then what of the nonbiological lesbian mother? This group finds itself in a most untenable position. Outsiders—lesbian and heterosexual alike—

tend to ignore or undervalue the importance of the nonbiological co-parent. (See Muzio, this volume). Lacking a biological role or connection and, in most instances, any legal status, she may feel jealous, devalued, excluded, or confused about her role. Even when the couple is clear about the mutuality of the decision to parent and about the parenting enterprise itself, the outside world still tends to bestow more legitimacy on the biological mother. From the beginning, for example, the co-parent is excluded by hospital forms that do not recognize her role. Later, in most schools, the various forms ask for information about "mother" and "father." Other similar examples abound. A couple relationship must be very solid to withstand this inequitable treatment and to withstand the disparate messages given to lesbian couples with children (e.g., "You are invisible," "You are not invisible," "One of you is invisible, and the other is not").

The legal system has helped to reinforce the message that nonbiological co-parents have no legitimacy. Only recently, and in only a few states, has it been possible for the nonbiological female co-parent to attain full and equal legal status as a parent. Not only does this unequal situation create asymmetry in an ongoing relationship, it also complicates matters for partners wishing to dissolve relationships. Courts are not well-prepared to deal with questions of visitation, financial support, or other parental rights and responsibilities, unless a second parent adoption has been previously approved by the court. Without any legal standing, the co-parent's relationship to the child may be dismissed in favor of a known donor and/or the child's biological grandparents (Benkov 1994).

Lesbian couples face many challenging tasks as they approach the birth of a child. They must constantly weigh the impact of subtle or blatant homophobia on such activities as attending childbirth classes together, involving the nonbiological parent in all decisions regarding labor and delivery, meeting with obstetricians, planning a baby shower, christening, naming ceremony, or bris, or sending birth announcements.

The issue of naming the child gets to the heart of one of the key dilemmas of lesbian parenting (Benkov 1994). Through naming, the child will receive a message about his or her identity. Embedded in this message are the parents' beliefs about what constitutes parent-child ties, but often the parents' beliefs are at odds with the larger social construction of family ties. Questions then arise about whether the child should be given the nonbiological parent's name as a last name, a middle name, or as part of a hyphenated last name. The lesbian couple's wish to celebrate its family in the form of naming may collide with legitimate discomfort or fear about publicly announcing that they are a lesbian couple (if they give the child the name of the nonbiological parent).

Along with confusing messages from the outside is the lack of a structure within the lesbian culture that helps determine how two women play out their roles as co-parents. While challenging norms can be stressful, it also permits one to be creative and perhaps more authentic in creating new norms. The resultant flexibility in regard to parental roles seems to be transmitted from parents to children, as was suggested by two studies mentioned earlier, in which lesbian parents reported a high degree of flexibility and tolerance for differing viewpoints among their children (Harris and Turner 1985–1986; Keating 1991).

The developmental stages of children demand that lesbian parents be versatile in their roles and comfortable with their individual identities. These may be difficult tasks, especially for the parent who is feeling left out or devalued. Many lesbian couples report that the child is more attached to the biological mother for about the first twelve to eighteen months of life. This phenomenon is consistent with reports of children's attachment to heterosexual married mothers and may be related particularly to the fact that the biological mother nurses the infant. When the child is more mobile and no longer dependent on the biological mother for nursing, there often appears to be a preference for the nonbiological parent, for what Mahler (1975) referred to as the "other than mother world." The question then arises as to whether both parents can be considered mothers. While some lesbian couples refer to the biological parent as mother and the nonbiological parent by her first name or by another agreed upon term, many lesbian couples refer to both members as mother, using a different form of maternal title for each parent. Because lesbian families are not recognized by society at large, the terms of address become particularly significant, as they serve to mark the importance of family bonds, especially between the nonbiological parent and the child. According to Benkov (1994), "Language not only reflects relationships but also partially constructs them" (172). It is well-documented that nonbiological parents or caretakers can and do become primary attachment figures for children. It is also possible to define mothering to mean nurturing and caretaking, without the provision of certain biological functions, e.g. nursing. Some believe that men can provide excellent mothering, when the concept is defined more broadly (Forstein 1993). Nevertheless, there is no way to escape the primacy of the early connection between the biological mother and child. Although one need not be constrained by that reality, one should be aware of the impact that it may have for the nonbiological lesbian parent at certain points in the child's development. No matter how involved she may be, or because of how involved she may be, the feelings of exclusion and/or rejection can be powerful. Lesbian couples generally report easier times when the child takes a more active interest in the other mother. Couples therapists are in a position to help educate lesbian parents about these kinds of developmental norms as a way of easing the strain on relationships.

Another developmental matter that clinicians may encounter is the question of how the Oedipal conflict can be resolved in a family with two female parents. While it is beyond the scope of this paper to address the subject comprehensively, it is a question that is frequently raised by students, lay people, and mental health professionals alike and, as such, deserves further comment. The problem, it seems, is not with the family configuration but with the Oedipal concept itself. Traditionally, for the boy the Oedipal struggle involves aggression, fear of retaliation, and resolution by identification with the father. For the girl the struggle involves passively giving up the father and resolving the loss by identifying with the mother (traditionally a devalued member of society). The struggle is only completely resolved for girls when they marry and bear a child—preferably male (Freud 1949/05). Given the historical context in which these theories were developed—Victorian Europe and a period of backlash from the first wave of feminism (Spaulding 1982)—some revisions are in order. The concept of struggle between parents and child is useful, if viewed as a developmental opportunity to learn about limits, about dealing with envy (Horney 1967), and about forming identifications with important figures outside the child's primary orbit. From this perspective the Oedipal conflict can be defined more in terms of the renunciation of wishes and longings for what one cannot have or be. Regardless of the parent's gender, and if parents can set appropriate limits and boundaries, a child will begin to internalize his or her aggressive feelings in the form of a superego. It need not be a struggle driven only by the fear of retaliation (for boys) or resolved by passive submission to a devalued role (for girls). Therapists, again, have an important role in helping their colleagues and clients reframe theories that have ceased to guide but continue to constrain.

Rethinking the Role of Men/Fathers in the Family

Including men in the lives of children of lesbian families may pose a variety of challenges to all concerned. At an earlier point in the evolution of the lesbian community, when separatism was more common, there was debate at conferences and workshops about the necessity of involving men at all in the lives of children in lesbian families. In more recent years a shift appears to have taken place; most lesbians seem more certain that their children should have opportunities for connection with men.

When there is a known donor, that person may or may not assume a parenting role. When there is an unknown donor, or when the known donor is uninvolved, women must be creative in finding ways to incorporate men into the lives of their children. Many lesbians have not previously had reason to make a concerted effort to interact with men, and their efforts to do so prove challenging. There may be a sense of awkwardness, trepidation, or even outright fear, but more commonly women report that "it just feels weird." Whether looking for potential donors or seeking out compatible men to be involved with their children, many lesbians state that they have never before put so much energy into "looking for a man." The results, however, can be surprisingly positive. One single lesbian mother at a parenting workshop said that at the age of three her daughter, while being cared for by a baby-sitter, befriended a male neighbor before the mother had even had a chance to approach him as a potential family friend. The relationship has grown and thrived.

Depending on the degree of acceptance from family of origin, there may be a significant amount of involvement on the part of uncles, grandfathers, nephews, or male cousins. Often families that had previously been rejecting do become involved once a baby is born, and, not infrequently, the arrival of a baby helps facilitate family reconciliation on many levels. One couple with two young children reported that the nonbiological mother's family (including a father and brother) gradually came to see these children as an integral part of their lives. No such reconciliation occurred, however, within the family of the biological mother.

Therapists working with individuals or couples should be aware of the kinds of concerns that have just been described. In addition, therapists can be a valuable resource in helping to alleviate the anxiety that many lesbian parents express in response to outsiders' questions about the viability of raising a family without a full-time male figure. The therapist can educate clients about research findings on children's psychological adjustment in lesbian families. In particular, the studies about gender identity and sex-role identity may be highlighted, as these areas seem to evoke the most concern on the part of outsiders (e.g., Golombok et al. 1983; Gottman 1990).

Another clinical issue that may arise at this juncture is the resurfacing of self-doubt about one's sexual identity. Experiencing men in a different way than ever before (as companions, role models, or parent figures for their children) may call into question one's past and present choices or actions. When a client raises such issues in treatment, the therapist should not leap to the conclusion that the client is not really a lesbian or that her lesbian identity is not well-integrated (in some instances, of course, those conclusions may be correct). Lesbians are accustomed to doubt themselves, and women, in general, are inclined to hold themselves responsible for everyone's comfort and well-being. As such, a lesbian couple may worry that their lifestyle and the relative absence of men in it are harmful to their child, and that they should change their lifestyle to rectify the situation. Again, there is research evidence that suggests that children in lesbian families function as well as children in more traditional families (Patterson 1994).

Another possible source of self-doubt about one's sexual orientation may be related to underlying grief about the loss of a father for one's child. If the client herself has lost a father (through divorce, death, or abandonment), the experience of having a child without a father may be evocative. On the other hand, if a client has had a good and lasting relationship with her father, she may grieve the fact that her child will not have this kind of relationship. In any case, the ambivalence that is expressed about sexual orientation may be only an outward manifestation of an entirely different internal process.

Whatever the family configuration, eliminating patriarchal assumptions about what defines family provides an important opportunity for lesbians to rethink roles within the couple, between themselves and men, among members of their family of origin, and between themselves and their children. In creating families that tend toward more egalitarian relationships, and that often contain two parents socialized to be nurturant and empathic, lesbian families can become role models for anyone seeking to broaden their vision of family and kinship.

Lastly, just as lesbians can offer useful new perspectives on the meaning of family, so too can traditional family forms serve as models and guidelines for those choosing alternatives. Traditional family structures are not rejected by all, or even most, lesbian families. Many are two-parent families, with one parent spending more time with the child during the week, in which the division of labor may sometimes appear to fall into sex-role stereotypes. Lesbian families must find what works for them and recognize that they may adopt aspects of traditional families or of alternative families.

Coming Out As a Lesbian Parent

Having a child requires that a lesbian (couple) come out again and again in numerous new situations. Old anxieties may resurface about earlier coming out experiences, and what was difficult in the past about coming out may be compounded by the added dimension of coming out as a lesbian parent. Telling one's parents about having a child may coincide with coming out to them for the first time as a lesbian. Parents who already know of their adult child's sexual orientation may still react negatively to the idea of her having a child, especially since that often means a second coming out process for them as the parents of a lesbian. Other arenas where a lesbian parent (or parent to be) may have complicated coming out experiences are in the workplace, with extended family, with the nonbiological mother's family, in professional communities, and even in the lesbian community.

As the child enters the picture there are many more occasions for revealing one's lesbian identity. These include coming out to doctors, midwives, childbirth educators, and other medical personnel in the prenatal and birthing phases and, later, to pediatricians (and their nurses, receptionists, weekend coverage), day care providers, school teachers, camp counselors, music teachers, mothers in the park, in short, to almost everyone one encounters in and around the child's life. Innocent questions like, "Which one of you is the mom?" or "Does he look like his father?" may be occasions for awkwardness and/or opportunities to enlighten those who have not been exposed to this particular alternate lifestyle.

Many women report another twist to the lesbian parenting experience. Because of the presence of a child, many outsiders assume the lesbian parent is actually straight, and they may treat her accordingly, for example, addressing her as "Mrs." or attempting to chat casually about husbands. When the encounter is only brief, the lesbian parent may not bother to correct the presumption, and after repeated episodes she may experience herself as projecting a false image of heterosexuality in public. This experience can be jarring to some women and may cause some to question their image and the many levels of meaning connected to it.

Having a child usually affords a variety of new opportunities for significant contact with the straight world. One might feel uncomfortable and unsure of how one is being received, but such discomfort should not necessarily be viewed as a serious self-esteem or identity problem. It is realistic to have these concerns, and they are usually abated when these new relationships unfold. On all levels, from the most public to the most intimate, lesbian mothers will be interacting with the straight world. These interactions may initially cause one to ask the question "Where do I belong?" Gradually a balance must be struck between involvement in the straight world and in the lesbian community. Parents and children benefit from involvement in both, and, despite some confusion at times, these dual involvements offer the potential for a fuller and richer experience.

Clinical issues may surface when the adaptations just described are not easily made. Working on underlying issues related to identity, sexual identity, social skills, and so forth may be required, if the adjustment period is protracted or intensely conflicted.

Responding to Children's Questions About Lesbian Families

Children of lesbians, like all children, ask many questions about who they are and where they came from. For lesbian families the answers are not only more complicated than for most other families but also have the potential for evoking intense feelings. Because this chapter focuses on the adaptation of lesbian adults to the parenting experience, this section will address common reactions of lesbian mothers to raised questions, as opposed to addressing the particular meaning of these questions for children.

Lesbian couples have the daunting responsibility of helping their children to hold their own in a homophobic and heterocentric world. That responsibility demands that the lesbian parent have resolved or be well on her way to resolving her own internalized homophobia, her relationships with family of origin, her grief over the various losses she may have incurred in the process of becoming a lesbian parent, feelings about her sexual orientation, and her comfort level as she engages in both straight and lesbian society. Only with a sufficient degree of resolution of these matters will lesbian parents be able to respond affirmatively and reassuringly to their child(ren). At the same time, the questions that children raise may unwittingly help to facilitate this resolution process for lesbian parents. Therapists can be helpful in normalizing concerns raised by lesbians around their children's questions, and they can also help lesbians to use these new challenges to consolidate their own earlier developmental achievements.

Children are often very attuned to their parents' vulnerabilities, and children of lesbians are likely to be challenged by outsiders and made to feel vulnerable. As with any "difference," parents must be open and direct—using the word *lesbian,* not hiding their identities from important people in the child's life, and so forth. A matter-of-fact approach by the parent(s) will allow a child more easily to stand his or her ground when confronted by outsiders. For instance, when a very young child asks if she or he has a daddy, the best answer is a simple No. Lesbian parents may be inclined to say "No, but . . . ," which tends to convey a message that the parents feel there is something lacking for which they must compensate. At a slightly later age (three to four) one might list the members of a child's family and possibly also the members of other families of varying composition that are known to a child. Helene, a lesbian client with two children, described a scene in which her family was going to visit another lesbian family. She explained to her children that this family had a little boy and two mothers and went on to remind them that her family had a girl and a boy and two mothers. Before she could get the whole sentence out, her daughter said, "I know, Mom, and Sally's family has a dad and a mom, and Paul's family has just one mom, and Anne's family has . . . " If this is typical, then it is clear why children of lesbians seem to have such a high level of acceptance of difference!

Lesbian couples can help their children respond to inevitable challenges from the outside by allowing them to express any and all feelings they have about their family lifestyle. This may, in fact, be one of the biggest challenges lesbian parents face—affirming their own identity while allowing their children to question it. If children feel they are expected not to verbalize feelings, then they may unwittingly be compelled to bury their more authentic selves. This phenomenon corresponds to the tendency in lesbian mothers discussed earlier to try to appear "as if" they have resolved all the difficult issues involved in the formation of a lesbian family. This can be a false self resolution.

Therapists may at times be called upon to offer child guidance and family therapy services for lesbian families grappling with these difficult questions. Any good therapist who has educated himself or herself about the evolving norms in lesbian families is appropriate to serve this population. A crucial part of the service offered must be the facilitation of referrals to social, political, and support groups for parents and children.

Creating Community

The importance of community must be emphasized in every phase of the process of forming and evolving as a lesbian family. As members of a marginalized group, it is particularly important for lesbian families to have some degree of involvement with others like themselves, for purposes of validation, support, sharing of resources, political organization, creation of rituals, and belonging. Most of the messages about family that children receive from the media and from society in general assume heterosexuality. Children and parents in lesbian families need to receive messages that more accurately reflect their experience. Fortunately, the lesbian community has become more receptive to children in recent years, so that children may be exposed to a larger culture from which to derive feelings of belonging and pride.

In many of the more liberal geographic areas in the United States there are community services for lesbian families that include medical, social, psychological, and political support. There are also informal networks for lesbians and their children that revolve around the following: community building, educating school systems, effective parenting techniques, and social support for children. Out of these supportive networks evolve new rituals within the family and the community. Examples of these rituals might include families marching together in the annual lesbian/gay pride parade, a multicultural celebration of the winter holidays, or a gathering of lesbian families to celebrate Mother's Day.

As important and meaningful as is affiliation with a community of lesbian families, it is also important to balance that involvement with connections to other communities within the larger society. Earlier in the lesbian/gay rights movement some lesbians, including some lesbian mothers, tended toward separatism. At the same time, many childless lesbians were antifamily and did not welcome children—especially boys—into the community. This paradox was one of the sources of conflict reported by the lesbian mothers in this author's earlier study of previously married lesbians (Morningstar 1989). As has been mentioned here, the lesbian community is now more likely to embrace the idea of children, a reflection of the life cycle issues facing lesbians and of the growing pride in the increased visibility and the expanding options now available to them.

Clinicians involved with this population must never lose sight of the importance of community in affirming what is positive for lesbians and in healing what may cause pain. Therapy alone cannot and should not solve all the potential problems originating from within or from the outside that are faced by lesbian families. Often group and community support together offer the most promise for individuals and/or families who are struggling with the many complexities of creating alternative families.

This discussion is a beginning effort toward conceptualizing information about lesbian families that is derived from clinical and sociocultural sources.

It highlights the key transitions and crises that appear to be involved in the formation of these families and offers some guidelines for therapists working with lesbians who are parenting or who are preparing to do so. The clinical and sociocultural observations presented in this chapter are based on the notion that women are socialized to behave in nurturing and affiliative ways. Two female parents might then offer an environment especially conducive to good child rearing, an idea that is contrary to traditional assumptions about lesbians.

The framework presented herein helps to clarify aspects of a complex process, while, at the same time, it serves as a reminder of the many questions that require more attention. Further research is needed to more clearly determine the patterns of development in children conceived and raised within an established lesbian family. Literature on children whose mothers came out after a divorce may offer some guidelines for understanding the development of children born into established lesbian relationships. One cannot, however, draw definitive conclusions from that body of literature, because there are many differences between the two populations. For example, the new lesbian families usually do not have an involved father. In addition, it will be important to learn more about the experiences of lesbian mothers as they deal with their children's reactions to their family lifestyle throughout the course of their development.

Further inquiry into the question of the child's ability or inability to know the identity of his/her father is of critical importance. As we know from experience with adoption, this matter has medical, genetic, developmental, ethical, and social policy implications (Noble 1987).

The phenomenon of lesbians choosing children calls into question long-standing notions of what constitutes family. Further study of this population can help to expand our perspective on all kinds of alternative families. Deepening our understanding of the experiences of lesbians and their children has the potential for challenging the judicial system regarding custody, visitation, and other rights and responsibilities of parenthood. Further, school systems may eventually have to rethink their reluctance to include information on lesbian and other kinds of alternative families in their curricula. Additionally, greater recognition of lesbian families may persuade more employers to offer spousal equivalent benefits to lesbian partners and their children and to other nontraditional families.

More research into the experiences of single lesbian mothers, adoptive lesbian families, and lesbian families of color will further enlighten us about family forms and patterns of kinship. The issue of social class warrants further study, as the high cost of donor insemination is likely to prevent some women from pursuing this option. This inequity clearly needs to be addressed.

In short, lesbian families have much to teach about how families function and about the larger systems that impinge on their functioning. These same systems must be adapted to serve lesbian families as they establish themselves in communities across the nation.

REFERENCES

Barkan, S., and M. Milbauer. 1992. *Alternative insemination: Outcomes of the Fenway Community Health Center's home-based insemination program.* Paper presented at the American Public Health Association Conference, Washington, D.C.

Benedek, T. 1959. Parenthood as a developmental phase. *Journal of the American Psychoanalytic Association* 7:389–417.

Benkov, L. 1994. *Reinventing the family: The emerging story of gay and lesbian parents.* New York: Crown.

Cass, V. C. 1979. Homosexual identity formation: A theoretical model. *Journal of Homosexuality* 4:219–235.

Chodorow, N. 1978. *The reproduction of mothering: Psychoanalysis and the sociology of gender.* New York: St. Martin's.

Colarusso, C., and R. Nemiroff. 1979. Some observations and hypotheses about psychoanalytic theory of adult development. *International Journal of Psychoanalysis* 60:59–71.

Crawford, S. 1987. Lesbian families: Psychosocial stress and the family-building process. In Boston Lesbian Psychologies Collective, eds., *Lesbian psychologies: Explorations and challenges,* pp. 195–214. Urbana: University of Illinois Press.

Daniels, P., and K. Weingarten. 1983. *Sooner or later: The timing of parenthood in adult lives.* New York: Norton.

Eichenbaum, L., and S. Orbach 1983. *Understanding women: A feminist psychoanalytic approach.* New York: Basic.

Elise, D. 1986. Lesbian couples: The implications of sex differences in separation-individuation. Ph.D. diss., Wright Institute Graduate School of Psychology, Berkeley, Cal.

Erikson, E. 1959. *Identity and the life cycle.* New York: International Universities Press.

Flax, N. 1978. The conflict between nurturance and autonomy in mother/daughter relationships and within feminism. *Feminist Studies* 4:171–187.

Forstein, M. 1993. *Gay and lesbian families.* Panel presentation at the Human Rights Commission, Newton, Mass.

Freud, S. 1949 [1905]. In J. Strachey, ed. and trans., *The standard edition of the complete psychological works of Sigmund Freud,* pp. 125–243. London: Hogarth.

Gilligan, C. 1982. *In a different voice: Psychological theory and women's development.* Cambridge: Harvard University Press.

Golombok, S., A. Spencer, and M. Rutter. 1983. Children in lesbian and single-parent households: Psychosexual and psychiatric appraisal. *Journal of Child Psychology and Psychiatry* 24:551–572.

Goodrich, T. J., C. Rampage, B. Ellman, and K. Halstead. 1988. *Feminist family therapy: A casebook.* New York: Norton.

Gottman, J. S. 1990. Children of gay and lesbian parents. In F. W. Bozett and M. B. Sussman, eds., *Homosexuality and family relations*, pp. 177–196. New York: Harrington Park.

Gramick, J. 1984. Developing a lesbian identity. In T. Darty and S. Potter, eds., *Women-identified women*, pp. 31–45. Palo Alto, Cal.: Mayfield.

Harris, M. B., and P. H. Turner. 1985–1986. Gay and lesbian parents. *Journal of Homosexuality* 12:101–113.

Horney, K. 1967. *Feminine psychology.* London: Routledge and Kegan Paul.

Jordan, J., J. Surrey, and A. Kaplan. 1983. *Women and empathy—implications for psychological development and psychotherapy.* Work in Progress no. 82. Wellesley, Mass.: Stone Center Working Paper Series.

Keating, C. T. 1991. Legacies: An exploratory study of young adult children of lesbians. M.A. thesis, Smith College School for Social Work, Northampton, Mass.

Kirkpatrick, M. 1987. Clinical implications of lesbian mother studies. *Journal of Homosexuality* 13:201–211.

Krestan, J., and C. Bepko. 1980. The problem of fusion in the lesbian relationship. *Family Process* 19:277–281.

Laird, J. 1993. Lesbian and gay families. In F. Walsh, ed., *Normal Family Processes*, pp. 282–328. New York: Guilford.

Levy, E. 1989. Lesbian motherhood: Identity and social support. *Affilia* 4:40–53.

McCandlish, B. 1987. Against all odds: Lesbian mother family dynamics. In F. Bozett, ed., *Gay and Lesbian Parents*, pp. 23–38. New York: Praeger.

Mahler, M., F. Pine, and A. Bergman. 1975. *The psychological birth of the human infant.* New York: Basic.

Mencher, J. 1990. *Intimacy in lesbian relationships: A critical re-examination of fusion.* Work in Progress no. 42. Wellesley, Mass.: Stone Center Working Paper Series.

Miller, J. B. 1976. *Toward a new psychology of women.* Boston: Beacon.

Morningstar, B. 1989. Shifting sexual object choice in adult women: A study of the developmental achievements and adaptation of a sample of late-emerging lesbians. Ph.D. diss., Smith College for Social Work, Northampton, Mass.

Noble, E. 1987. *Having your baby by donor insemination: A complete resource guide.* Boston: Houghton Mifflin.

Patterson, C. J. 1992. Children of lesbian and gay parents. *Child Development* 63:1025–1043.

Patterson, C. J. 1994. Children of the lesbian baby boom: Behavioral adjustment, self-concepts, and sex-role identity. In B. Greene and M. Herek, eds., *Lesbian and gay psychology: Theory, research and clinical application*, pp. 156–175. Thousand Oaks, Cal.: Sage.

Patterson, C. J. 1995. Lesbian mothers, gay fathers, and their children. In A. R. D'Augelli and C. J. Patterson, eds., *Lesbian, gay, and bisexual identities over the lifespan: Psychological perspectives.* New York: Oxford University Press.

Pies, C. 1987. Considering parenthood: Psychosocial issues for gay men and lesbians choosing alternative fertilization. In F. Bozett, ed., *Gay and Lesbian Parents*, pp. 165–174. New York: Praeger.

Seligman, J. 1990. Variations on a theme. *Newsweek* special ed., 38–46.

Spaulding, E. 1982. The formation of lesbian identity. Ph.D. diss., Smith College School for Social Work, Northampton, Mass.

Steckel, A. 1985. Separation-individuation in children of lesbian and heterosexual couples. Ph.D. diss., Wright Institute Graduate School, Berkeley, Cal.

Steckel, A. 1987. Psychosocial development of children of lesbian mothers. In F. Bozett, ed., *Gay and lesbian parents*, pp. 75–85. New York: Praeger.

Weingarten, K. 1994. *The mother's voice: Strengthening intimacy in familes.* New York: Harcourt Brace.

Weston, K. 1991. *Families we choose: Lesbian, gays, kinship.* New York: Columbia University Press.

CHAPTER TEN

The Family Lives of Lesbian Mothers

Laura Lott-Whitehead and Carol T. Tully

THE NUCLEAR FAMILY of heterosexual mother and father raising one or more of their own biological children is no longer the norm in American society. New, or alternative, family forms are now an integral and prominent part of the social structure (Turner, Scadden, and Harris 1985).

To many people, the terms *lesbian mother* and *gay father* are confusing and contradictory. Since gay men and lesbians relate sexually to members of their own sex, it is mistakenly believed that they do not have children (Gottman 1990). This is, of course, a faulty assumption: gay men and lesbians have children through heterosexual sexual intercourse, artificial insemination, and adoption (Pies 1990). The most recent figures indicate that there are well over 1.5 million lesbian mothers and 1 million gay fathers in this country (Schulenberg 1985; Task Force on Sexuality 1974).

The purpose of this study is to describe the family life of a subgroup of this population—lesbian mothers—using an ecological perspective (Lott-Whitehead 1992). What do they cope with, and how? What systems exert the most pressure on these families? What strains the relationships? Who supports the relationships? These are but a few of the questions this study attempts to answer.

Literature Review

To date, most research efforts in this field have been focused on the children of gay and lesbian parents and not the parents themselves. Much of the research, whether explicitly or implicitly stated, has had as its purpose the refutation of three myths surrounding homosexuality: that homosexuality is incompatible with effective parenting, that children "catch" homosexuality from their parents, and that gay parents molest their children (Turner, Scadden, and Harris 1985:57). Thus far no study has produced evidence to lend credence to these myths.

One area of concern that has been identified as unique to the families of gay men and lesbians is the issue of disclosure of the parents' homosexuality. Parents struggle to decide if, when, and how to tell their children they are gay or lesbian. In several studies based on interview and survey data of the children of gay fathers, it was found that regardless of the age of the child or means of disclosure, most children of both sexes responded favorably (Bozett 1980; Harris and Turner 1986; Turner, Scadden, and Harris 1985; Wyers 1987).

Several researchers have identified the threat of loss of child custody as a parental fear of gay men and lesbians (Lewis 1980; Payne 1978; Riddle 1977). Hitchens (1979) writes that

> regardless of whether a parent has ever been involved in a court challenge, the threat of losing the custody of one's children . . . is an everyday reality for homosexual fathers and mothers. Gay parents are aware that their sexual orientation can all too easily be used against them by ex- spouses, family, or state authorities. Decisions about how to live, with whom to live, how to raise children, whether to "come out," and whether to become involved in political activities, all have potentially severe legal consequences bearing on the right to remain a parent. (93–94)

In some states the courts have determined that a parent's sexual orientation is a "proper" factor to consider in determining a parent's fitness and what is in the best interest of the child (Gottsfield 1985:43). Under the majority rule, however, it is not sufficient in and of itself. Evidence has to be adduced over and above the mere fact of the sexual identity in order to make a determination that it would be detrimental to the child for the gay or lesbian parent to have custody, normal visitation, and/or that parental rights should be terminated. However, there is wide divergence in appellate court cases in interpreting the majority rule, and state statutes remain incomplete and do not specify how to evaluate when one or both parents are unfit as custodians or when to adjudicate a different custody arrangement other than joint custody.

Other areas of concern unique to these families include the conflict between a parent's sexual identity and his or her role as parent (Bozett 1981a; Lewin and Lyons 1982; Robinson and Skeen 1982) and the sting of social stigma and prejudice. Numerous researchers have identified the latter as an ongoing life stressor for gay men and lesbians (Bigner and Bozett 1990; Bozett and Sussman 1989; Cramer 1986; Hall 1978; Harris and Turner 1986).

Another stressor for lesbian mothers is single parenting. It has been postulated that households headed by lesbian mothers are similar in many ways to households headed by heterosexual single mothers (Green, Mandel, Gray, and Smith 1986; Richmond-Abbott 1984). Both groups often experience parenting as stressful (Compas and Williams 1990; D'Ercole 1988; Pearce 1983; Weiss 1979). This stress can be moderated or mediated by parental efficacy (Galinsky 1987; Langer 1983; Oskamp 1987; Swick 1987, 1988) and social support (Cobb 1976; Heath and MacKinnon 1988; Hetherington 1979; Huntley and Phelps 1985; Huntley, Phelps, and Rehm 1987; Phelps and Slater 1985; Tully 1983).

The sources of support, however, differ between the two groups. Lesbian mothers find social support more often from friends than from family members (Kurdek 1988; Kurdek and Schmitt 1987). Further, lesbian mothers consider this support critical in validating their fears about disclosing their sexual orientation in what they perceive to be unsupportive environments (Levy 1989).

Methods

Theoretical Perspective

The conceptual framework we have used in this study is grounded in the ecological perspective. The scientist with an ecological perspective seeks to understand the complex reciprocal relationships between people and environments, that is, how each acts and influences the other (Germain and Gitterman 1986). It is concerned with the relations between people and all elements of their environments.

The environment, according to the ecological perspective, has four different levels of systems: microsystems, mesosystems, exosystems, and macrosystems. Bronfenbrenner (1979) identifies them succinctly:

1. Microsystems are the settings in which individuals experience and create day-to-day reality. They include the places people inhabit, the people with whom they live, and the things they do together. Parents and/or children in and of themselves are microsystems.

2. Mesosystems are the relationships between several microsystems. Examples of a parent's mesosystem include his or her extended family members or personal friends.

3. Exosystems are those settings that have power over individual lives, but for which they possess little control. For a child, that may be the work setting of the the parent; for a mother or father, the quality and quantity of child day-care centers in their community.

4. Macrosystems are the broad ideological and institutional settings of a particular culture or subculture. Mesosystems and exosystems are set within macrosystems and they are the "blueprints" for the ecology of human and family development. The sanctity of the family unit in the United States is one example of a macrosystem within which parents and children function. (100–104)

Data Gathering and Sample Selection Procedures

The method used to gather data in this study was a researcher-designed questionnaire consisting of closed- and open-ended questions that would elicit responses on a broad range of topics related to family life constructed according to the Dillman model (1978). The Dillman method involves techniques designed to produce a reader-friendly questionnaire, to reduce mailing costs, and to produce the highest response rate possible for mail survey research. Its application in this study was followed as closely as possible, with the exception of repeat mailings. Omission of this step resulted in a low response rate for the project: 24.6 percent.

Subjects were recruited through a snowball sampling technique, that is, utilizing friendship networks, word-of-mouth referrals, etc. The technique was implemented in this study by contacting various gay and lesbian organizations and the researcher's personal and professional friends to ask for participation. These initial contacts then led to other referrals from the study subjects. This technique, although useful, often leads to a homogeneous sample, which was the case in this study. Almost all the respondents were well-educated white women with high incomes who lived in the state of Georgia.

A total of 187 questionnaires were distributed; 46 of them were returned, equalling a response rate of 24.6 percent. One returned questionnaire was rejected due to the respondent's not meeting the definitional criteria for homosexuality. Therefore, the final sample for this study was comprised of 45 self-identified lesbian mothers.

Research Design

The study was exploratory/descriptive; the primary method of analysis was qualitative. Data analysis consisted of an examination of responses to identify trends and patterns.

For purposes of this study the term *lesbian* meant any woman whose current overt sexual activities and/or intense, emotionally intimate psychological feelings ranked 4 or higher on a modified Kinsey Heterosexual-Homosexual Rating Scale (Kinsey, Pomeroy, Martin, and Gebhard 1953:470–472; Tully 1983). By only including women who scored 4 or higher on the scale, this study excluded those women who were not predominantly homosexual.

The women who were defined as mothers included all who met at least one of the following criteria: the biological parent of a child, the adoptive parent of a child, or the partner of a biological or adoptive parent who shared equally in parenting. Family referred to one's family of creation, as opposed to one's family of origin, and was defined as those members of one's social and emotional network who were related by blood, kinship, or emotional bond. This included one's children, lover/partner, and any friends who had become emotionally bonded with the family.

Intrafamilial stress was defined as the degree, severity, or magnitude of a problem that family members had in their relationships with one another as felt or perceived by the respondent (Hudson, 1990). A modified version of Walter Hudson's (1990) Index of Family Relations was given to subjects to measure intrafamilial stress.[1] The Hudson measure has demonstrated reliability and validity: the alpha coefficient of reliability is reported to consistently equal .90 or better; the content, construct, factorial, and known groups validity all are reported to consistently equal approximately .60 or better.

Methodological Limitations

This study was descriptive and, therefore, had inherent in its design methodological flaws consistent with other similar studies. Perhaps the most serious concerns representativeness (Harry 1984; Rubin and Babbie

1989; Turner, Scadden, and Harris 1985). Because closeted homosexual women—persons not open about their sexual orientation—are so difficult to identify and reach, there are no reliable statistics on how many lesbians live in the United States. Probability random sampling therefore was impossible. This study does not purport to contain a representative sample, and thus generalizability cannot be assumed.

This study attempted to redress this limitation through its anonymity. Participation was completely anonymous: respondents indicated willingness to participate simply by answering and returning the questionnaire via self-addressed, stamped envelope.

In this type of design open-ended questions posed in the questionnaire are rarely answered definitively, with subjects tending to provide superficial answers. However, they may nevertheless give valuable insight into deeper issues worthy of further, more experimental study.

Researcher bias must be considered with all methods, but particularly with the more qualitative research designs such as this one where subjectivity and normativeness come into play. Interpretation of responses is filtered through the researcher and thus can become contaminated with the researcher's values, cultural bias, and experiences. This may also be true in construction of the questionnaire itself. Wording of questions, selection of content, etc. were subjectively determined and thus open to cultural disparity bias.

Other sources of error lie not in the researcher but in the study subjects. Possible biases here include the following: the acquiescent response set, in which subjects agree or disagree with all such worded questions regardless of the questions' content, and the social desirability bias, in which subjects tend to respond in such a way as to make their reference group look good (Caputo 1991). These biases may have been exaggerated in this project because of the sensitive and sometimes controversial nature of the subject.

Further, at least several of the respondents in this sample knew that the researcher (the first author) was a heterosexual woman, and this may have influenced their responses. Other researchers (Turner, Scadden, and Harris 1985) have encountered this wariness in their projects and attributed any reluctance to participate to discrimination experienced by gay men and lesbians in our society. It is reasonable, therefore, to assume that there may have existed some study participants who were cautious of allowing an outsider access to their private family lives.

DEMOGRAPHIC INFORMATION   The ages of subjects ranged from twenty-five to fifty-three, with forty-four as the median age. Almost all the respondents were Caucasian, lived in the south in a metropolitan area, and were employed full time, with an income over twenty thousand dollars per year. Forty-four (97.7 percent) of the women had attended college. More than two-thirds of the respondents indicated that they were currently involved in a lesbian relationship. Of these, fifteen (48.4 percent) defined the partner's role as additional parent, often "very involved" in the care of the children.

Microsystem Data

Most of the children (n = 22; 48.9 percent) were conceived through heterosexual marriage or partnerships. Twenty percent of the women adopted their children, while 17.8 percent conceived through artificial insemination. The mode number of children per family was one, with female children slightly outnumbering male children. The median age for girls was eight and a half years; the median age for boys was sixteen and a half years. A majority of the women (n = 27; 60.0 percent) had primary custody of the children and were the primary caretakers.

The majority of respondents (n = 29; 64.4 percent) replied that their children knew of their homosexuality. A few responded that their children were too young to know or fully understand adult sexuality. (The oldest-aged child from these responses was five years.) However, the women reported that these children did understand they had "two mothers." One respondent described it in this way:

> They are only four and five and so what they know is unclear. They have two moms and we have only one bedroom and use the term *lesbian*. They are growing up in it. At this point they know some kids have two moms, some one mom, and some a mom and a dad, and no value is yet placed on the difference by them—or us.

Of those women who reported that their children knew of their homosexuality, almost all (n = 27; 93.1 percent) reported that they themselves had told the children. Five of these women disclosed their homosexuality because they had fallen in love and/or had found a lifetime partner. Only two of the respondents reported that their children had discovered it accidentally. Most were open about their sexual orientation in other spheres of their lives as well, including with their parents, in their work environments, and with their child's or children's friends.

The most influential person in the family was most often reported to be the respondent. Fifteen of the study subjects replied that both she and her partner shared equal influence over the children and cited a concerted commitment to share influence and power in parenting.

Numerous issues were identified as difficult; however, no one particular issue emerged from the responses as predominant, except perhaps the issue of discipline. Further, the issues identified by the women rarely differed from typical parenting problems, for example, "setting limits," "child care," "trying to have patience." Only one woman mentioned the family's difference as an area of concern; her son reportedly struggled with the "pull between patriarchal/male dominant perks, expectations, values, and the egalitarian/cooperative values he was raised with."

The study respondents' intrafamilial stress scores on the Index of Family Relations (Hudson 1990) ranged from a low of 25 to a high of 80, with the mean being 35.1. The median was 32; the mode was 25. As shown in table 10.1, a large percentage (n= 20; 44.4 percent) of the women did not experience intrafamilial stress. However, the majority of women (n = 25; 55 percent) scored over 30, indicating stress at a clinically significant level.

In an open-ended question, study subjects were asked what concerns they had about their family. The most common responses were as follows: money, how the world will treat the respondent's child or children, especially as she or he ages, conflict in relationship between the respondent and her lesbian partner, conflict between the respondent's child or children and her partner,

TABLE 10.1 *Distribution of Respondents Stress Scores*

STRESS SCORE	NUMBER OF RESPONDENTS	PERCENTAGE OF RESPONDENTS
30 and under	20	44.4 %
31 to 69	24	55.3
over 70	1	2.2

Interpretation of the scores is based on two clinical cutting scores (Hudson 1992). Respondents who score 30 or less can be assumed to be free of intrafamilial stress. Scores over 30 indicate a "clinically significant problem" (Hudson 1990:28). The second cutting score is 70. Respondents scoring from 70 to 100 are almost always experiencing severe distress.

racism, fear of losing the love of one's children, especially as he or she ages and begins to understand the family's difference, and being a single parent. Many of the respondents also mentioned that their concerns were about parenting in general and not specifically related to their lesbianism. For example, one woman replied, "I am concerned that as my children get older, they will hate me for being different. Also, being a single parent, regardless of sexual preference, is hard for me."

Surprisingly, only three respondents mentioned fear of loss of custody if their lesbianism was to be discovered. One respondent described it thus, "I don't feel that I have the freedom to pursue a completely lesbian lifestyle because I have a twelve-year-old child and because I could jeopardize my custody of her if I were too openly gay." Others had quite a different experience. For example, one mother commented that the custody issue had arisen in a dispute with her partner's ex-husband, but that the judge wouldn't allow it: "Gayness was not an issue—parental competence was!"

Meso-and Exosystem Data

Most of the respondents in this study (n = 32; 71.1 percent) indicated they had experienced no difficulty meshing their lesbian identity with that of being a parent. However, some women did have difficulty and discussed the issue further. For example, one respondent commented that she avoided media exposure, another remarked that she did not feel comfortable "being a lesbian in their [the children's] presence," and another stated that she sometimes avoided activities such as school events where there was not a "place" for her partner. Seven women commented that a sector of the lesbian community itself was not supportive of mothers and that they had been forced to curtail activity such as participation in lesbian social events for such reasons as that child care was not provided or children were unwelcome. The following responses highlight this issue:

> SUBJECT 1: *There is definitely an antifamily, antichildren slant in some parts of the gay community. You are seen as different.*
> SUBJECT 2: *Child care is not provided at most lesbian events. Boy children are often treated as second-class people.*
> SUBJECT 3: *When I became a parent, I was already a lesbian and it was a rare thing to do. Although the community seemed to think it was cool to adopt, I received very little concrete support and most groups preferred not to have a little kid hanging around. Most lesbians were very unfamiliar with normal childhood behavior.*

Yet these women and others also emphasized that this attitude seemed to be decreasing within the lesbian community as more women chose motherhood. Several also commented that increased visibility both within the lesbian community and within society at large would help diffuse the negativity.

The women who felt the most supported often remarked that they had chosen important systems in their lives, such as neighborhoods, schools, and churches, very carefully. They selected "liberal" communities with "gay representation." One woman described a most favorable community response:

> Mothering is the most intensely satisfying experience I've ever had. It has solidified my relationship not only with my partner, but with other friends who are also close to our child. Our daughter fills a "kid need" for several of our close friends, and she is obviously fond of her "aunts." I hope these relationships continue throughout her life.

The strengths identified by the women in this study were many. The most commonly cited responses were love, honesty, openness, emotional closeness/bondedness, good communication, especially between the respondents and their partners, shared values and goals, emotional support, respect for each other, and a good sense of humor.

Macrosystem Data

When asked what was most distressing about the way gay men and lesbians were treated in the United States, the responses were overwhelmingly similar. Nearly half (n = 22; 48.9 percent) cited prejudice or homophobia. Social and legal inequality was named by 17.8 percent. Violence toward gays and lesbians was mentioned by 6.7 percent. A sampling of these responses illustrates the respondents' strong feelings on this topic:

> SUBJECT 1: *We are practically the only group that it is acceptable to openly disparage. . . . It hurts to be viewed as wrong because of something you didn't choose.*
>
> SUBJECT 2: *The idea that someone can call us deviant and make fun of us and that isn't considered a social taboo—as an ethnic slur would be—distresses me.*
>
> SUBJECT 3: *The inequality between heterosexual and homosexual relationships—that my partner and I are not accorded the same rights and privileges straight couples are.*

Two women also noted that they were distressed by the lack of positive images of lesbians and lesbian families in places such as school, television, and books. One commented that she felt continually compelled to be hypervigilant over "bad images of lesbians" being portrayed for her daughter.

When asked the question "What would be most helpful for your family?" once again the responses were quite similar. Equal rights under the law was cited by 37.8 percent. Specifically, the women most often wanted insurance benefits for partners, legalized gay and lesbian marriages, adoptive rights for partners, and the abolition of sodomy statutes. Social recognition and acceptance was named by 28.9 percent. Other responses included "contact and dialogue with other gay and lesbian families," "an adoption tax deduction," an increase in "positive cultural images of lesbian families," and "for institutions, such as schools, not to assume a family has a mommy and a daddy—that there are all kinds of families and relationships in the world."

Discussion

Limitations of the Study

Results from this study must be interpreted cautiously due to several factors. First, the study sample was small (n = 45) and biased toward well-educated white women with high incomes. These factors have plagued other studies and remain a concern of researchers in this field. Second, there existed a regional bias: almost all the respondents lived in the state of Georgia. Third, as aforementioned, the study was not experimental and not privy therefore to the rigorous sampling that permits greater external validity. However, knowledge may be inducted from the rich data provided by the women's responses to the questions posed in the study. Several important themes and patterns emerged from their narratives that are worthy of discussion.

Major Themes

Results from this study are entirely consistent with research on the children of gay and lesbian parents (Bozett 1980, 1987; Harris and Turner 1986; Miller 1979; Paul 1986; Scallen 1982; Patterson 1995, 1996; Wyers 1987) and with the limited research on gay and lesbian parents themselves (Golombok, Spencer, and Rutter 1983; Paul 1986; Turner, Scadden, and

Harris 1985) in that homosexuality itself is not incompatible with successful family life. In fact, the results indicate that families of lesbian mothers
have numerous strengths—strengths sometimes lacking in more traditional
families. The strengths include an open climate for sexuality, a healthy
respect for difference, including, but not limited to sexual orientation, and
an accepting, nurturing environment conducive to human growth.

It is this latter strength that was most striking, and emerged as a theme
within the mothers' responses. They were deeply committed to their families,
placing their children's needs above their own when necessary, yet striving to
maintain balance between the needs of all members. They worked hard to
create family environments that were safe for all members, especially the children. To accomplish this, they were compelled to be ever vigilant of threats to
the integrity of their families and to act when necessary to keep the family
protected. One such step they took to achieve this was insulation in liberal
communities, another was monitoring media images for negative portrayals
of gay and lesbian families.

Many of the respondents emphasized that their families were really quite
"regular," with the same joys and sorrows as traditional heterosexual families. For example:

> Homosexuality [is not] our only characteristic. It's important, but it's
> not all we are. I think it's like race. It should be acknowledged and
> respected but not seen as the sole cause of everything we do or say. . . .
> [It would be helpful] just to be treated as a normal family, with all the
> rights and hassles thereof.

Findings from this project are also consistent with that of other
researchers (Bozett 1980; Miller 1979) who found that gay fathers recognized the need to be discreet in expressing their sexuality to protect their
children from harassment. The women in this study were very cognizant of
the impact of their lesbianism on their children and their children's worlds
outside the family. They often attempted to soften the impact of disclosure
and/or shield their children from negative societal messages. The comments of one mother highlight this issue:

> My responses to this questionnaire in no way suggest I am not mind-
> ful of the tremendous additional responsibility my partner and I have
> as parents because we are lesbians. It is a constant "take a deep breath
> and come out/stay out again!" We are absolutely committed to being
> out—the only time we would not be would be if it were a clear danger

for the kids. We are an extremely happy family. My partner and I know why we chose our two daughters (not them specifically but children!) and we really do enjoy and love our family. Of course we have "blips," but we work stuff through with our focus on both individual and family needs.

Every step of the way we've had stuff to deal with since becoming parents—but invisibility of our relationship as a couple or "dancing around" our family make-up just isn't part of the consideration. We believe open honesty will serve us all the best and certainly we would rather step forward first and not have our kids in front. Mostly it works—my choices, were I to begin again, would be the same!

Responses regarding custody were mixed, with several women fearing loss of custody if their lesbianism were to be discovered and others quite confident that their parental rights were safe. One possible interpretation of these results is that they reflect the inconsistency of legal statutes and/or the inconsistency of judicial interpretation.

The women in this study did not report conflict between their sexual identity and role as a parent, a finding inconsistent with other works (Bozett 1981a; Lewin and Lyons 1982; Robinson and Skeen 1982) identifying this as a concern for gay male parents. However, the women did admit to curtailing lesbian activity because of parenting, and one of the reasons specified provided perhaps the most surprising finding of the study: a segment of the lesbian community itself is perceived as unsupportive of lesbian parents. One respondent described it as an "anti-family, anti-children slant." The women in this study were clearly distressed by this attitude within the very communities they had counted on for emotional, social, and political alliance.

The stress scores from the Index of Family Relations presented two outcomes. A good many of the families in this study seem to be relatively free of stress. It was these families that seemed to be more open—that is, those families in which the mothers self-disclosed their sexual identity to their children at an early age, did not conceal their sexual identity in other environments such as the workplace, and made a concerted effort to select accepting communities in which to live. These families were also likely to have the support of the respondents' parents and frequently described the relationship between grandparents and grandchildren in favorable terms. These results are consistent with other research (Cobb 1976; Germain and

Gitterman 1987; Lewin 1993; Tully 1983) documenting stress to be buffered by supportive networks.

However, most of the families in this study had moderately high to very high stress scores. Many of them were single-parented, an outcome consistent with other research (Compas and Williams 1990; D'Ercole 1988; Pearce 1983; Weiss 1979) establishing a positive correlation between single motherhood and psychological stress. Although in any group of families it would be expected that at least some of the mothers would experience a great degree of stress, the high number of women experiencing moderate to high stress in this study is striking and invites speculation. The most obvious hypothesis is that those high levels are due to societal prejudice/homophobia. All the families were subject to the stresses of societal prejudice in addition to the burden of sexism—a combination one woman termed the "double whammy." Further, based on the women's narratives, the pressure was most distressing at the exo- and macrosystem levels. They commonly expressed feeling comfortable within their families (microsystems) and communities (mesosystems) but less so within the larger contexts for which they had little control, such as the schools (exosystem).

In summary, this study produced data descriptive of the family lives of lesbian mothers. Several important themes emerged. The women in this study were cognizant of their sexual orientation's impact on their children and attempted to shield them from negative societal messages, they were vigilant about maintaining the integrity of their families, often seeking insulation in liberal communities, and, surprisingly, a small number of women reported that a sector of the lesbian community itself was unsupportive of lesbian motherhood. This data is suggestive of further exploration, and it is hoped that others will pursue research in this field.

NOTES

This article is based on a 1992 master's thesis completed by Laura Lott-Whitehead at the University of Georgia in Athens, Georgia.

1. Permission for use of this instrument was granted by Dr. Walter Hudson of WALMYR Publishing Company, Tempe, Arizona.

REFERENCES

Bigner, J., and F. W. Bozett. 1990. Parenting by gay fathers. *Homosexuality and family relations.* New York: Haworth.

Bozett, F. W. 1980. How and why fathers disclose their homosexuality to their children. *Family Relations* 29:173–179.

— 1981a. Gay fathers: Evolution of the gay-father identity. *American Journal of Orthopsychiatry* 51:552–559.

— 1987. Children of gay fathers. In F. W. Bozett, ed., *Gay and lesbian parents.* New York: Praeger.

Bozett, F. W., and M. B. Sussman. 1989. Homosexuality and family relations: Views and research issues. *Marriage and Family Review* 4(3–4):1–8.

Bronfenbrenner, U. 1979. *The ecology of human development: Experiments by nature and design.* Cambridge: Harvard University Press.

Caputo, R. 1991. Personal communication, March 26.

Cobb, S. 1976. Social support as a moderator of life stress. *Psychosomatic Medicine* 38(5):300–314.

Compas, B. E., and Williams, R. A. 1990. Stress, coping, and adjustment in mothers and young adolescents in single- and two-parent families. *American Journal of Community Psychology* 18(4):525–545.

Cramer, D. 1986. Gay parents and their children: A review of research and practical implications. *Journal of Counseling and Development* 64(8):504–507.

D'Ercole, A. 1988. Single mothers: Stress, coping, and social support. *Journal of Community Psychology* 16:41–54.

Dillman, D. 1978. *Mail and telephone surveys: The total design method.* New York: Wiley.

Galinsky, E. 1987. *The six stages of parenthood.* Reading, Mass.: Addison-Wesley.

Germain, C., and A. Gitterman. 1987. Ecological perspective. *Encyclopedia of social work.* 18th ed., 1:488–499. Silver Spring, Md.: National Association of Social Workers.

Golombok, S., A. Spencer, and M. Rutter. 1983. Children in lesbian and single-parent households: Psychosexual and psychiatric appraisal. *Journal of Child Psychology and Psychiatry* 24(4):551–572.

Gottman, J. 1990. Children of gay and lesbian parents. *Marriage and Family Review* 14(3–4):177–196.

Gottsfield, R. 1985. Child custody and sexual lifestyle. *Conciliation Courts Review* 23:43–46.

Green, R., M. Mandel, J. Gray, and L. Smith. 1986. Lesbian mothers and their children: A comparison with solo parent heterosexual mothers and their children. *Archives of Sexual Behavior* 15(2):167–184.

Hall, M. 1978. Lesbian families: Cultural and clinical issues. *Social Work* 23:380–385.

Harris, M., and P. Turner. 1986. Gay and lesbian parents. *Journal of Homosexuality* 12:101–113.

Harry, J. 1984. Sampling gay men. *Journal of Sex Research* 22(1):21–34.

Heath, P., and C. MacKinnon. 1988. Factors related to the social competence of children in single-parent families. *Journal of Divorce* 11(3–4):49–66.

Hetherington, E. M. 1979. Divorce: A child's perspective. *American Psychologist* 34:851–858.

Hitchens, D. 1979. Social attitudes, legal standards, and personal trauma in child custody cases. *Journal of Homosexuality* 5:80–95.

Hudson, W. 1990. *Index of family relations.* Tempe, Ariz: Walmyr.

Huntley, D. K., and R. E. Phelps. 1985. *Depression and social contacts of children from one-parent families.* Paper presented at the meeting of the Southwestern Psychological Association, Austin, Texas.

Huntley, D., R. Phelps, and L. Rehm. 1987. Depression in children from single-parent families. *Journal of Divorce* 10(1–2):153–161.

Kinsey, A. C., W. Pomeroy, C. Martin, and P. H. Gebhard. 1953. *Sexual behavior in the human female.* Philadelphia: Saunders.

Kurdek, L. A. 1988. Perceived social support in gays and lesbians in cohabitating relationships. *Journal of Personality and Social Psychology* 54(3):504–509.

Kurdek, L. A., and J. P. Schmitt. 1987. Perceived emotional support from family and friends in members of homosexual, married, and heterosexual cohabiting couples. *Journal of Homosexuality* 14(3/4):57–68.

Langer, S. 1983. *The psychology of control.* Newbury Park, Cal.: Sage.

Levy, E. 1989. Lesbian motherhood: Identity and social support. *Affilia* 4(4):40–53.

Lewin, E., and T. A. Lyons. 1982. Everything in its place: The coexistence of lesbianism and motherhood. In W. Paul, J. Weinrich, J. Gonsiorek, and M. Hotvedt, eds., *Homosexuality: Social, psychological, and biological issues*, pp. 249–273. Beverly Hills: Sage.

Lewin, E. 1993. *Lesbian mothers: Accounts of gender in American culture.* Ithaca: Cornell University Press.

Lewis, K. G. 1980. Children of lesbians: Their point of view. *Journal of the National Association of Social Workers* 25(8):198–203.

Miller, B. 1979. Gay fathers and their children. *Family Coordinator* 28:544–552.

Oskamp, S. 1987. *Family processes and problems: Social psychological aspects.* Newbury Park, Cal.: Sage.

Paul, J. P. 1986. Growing up with a gay, lesbian, or bisexual parent: An exploratory study of experiences and perception. Dissertation Abstracts International, 1987, DA 86241.

Patterson, C. J. 1995. Lesbian mothers, gay fathers, and their children. In A. R. D'Augelli and C. J. Patterson, eds., *Lesbian, gay, and bisexual identities over the lifespan: Psychological perspectives*, pp. 262–290. New York: Oxford University Press.

Patterson, C. J. 1996. Lesbian mothers and their children: Findings from the Bay Area families study. In J. Laird and R-J. Green, eds., *Lesbians and gays in couples and families: A handbook for therapists*, pp. 420–437. San Francisco: Jossey-Bass.

Payne, A. 1978. Law and the problem patient: Custody and parental rights of homosexual, mentally retarded, mentally ill, and incarcerated patients. *Journal of Family Law* 16:797–818.

Pearce, D. M. 1983. The feminization of ghetto poverty. *Society* 21:70–74.

Phelps, R. E., and M. A. Slater. 1985. Sequential interactions that discriminate high- and low-problem single mother-son dyads. *Journal of Consulting and Clinical Psychology* 53:684–692.

Pies, C. (1989). Lesbians and the choice to parent. *Marriage and Family Review* 14(3–4):137–154.

Richmond-Abbott, M. 1984. Sex-role attitudes of mothers and children in divorced, single-parent families. *Journal of Divorce* 8(1):61–81.

Riddle, D. 1977. *Gay parents and child custody issues*. Report no. CG-012–219. Tucson, Ariz: University of Arizona. ERIC Document Reproduction Service ED 147 746.

Robinson, B., and P. Skeen. 1982. Sex-role orientation of gay fathers versus gay non-fathers. *Perceptual and Motor Skills* 55:1055–1059.

Rubin, A., and E. Babbie. 1989. *Research methods for social work*. Belmont, Cal.: Wadsworth.

Scallen, R. M. 1982. An investigation of paternal attitudes and behaviors in homosexual and heterosexual fathers. Dissertation Abstracts International, 1981, 42, 3809-B.

Schulenberg, J. 1985. *Gay parenting*. New York: Anchor/Doubleday.

Swick, K. 1987. *Perspectives on understanding and working with families*. Champaign, Ill.: Stipes.

Task Force on Sexuality, D.C. Chapter of the National Organization for Women. 1974. *A lesbian is . . .* Washington: National Organization for Women.

Tully, C. 1983. Social support systems of a selected sample of older women. Ph.D. diss., Virginia Commonwealth University.

Turner, P. H., L. Scadden, and M. B. Harris. 1985. *Parenting in gay and lesbian families*. Paper presented at the Future of Parenting Symposium, Chicago.

Weiss, R. 1979. *Going it alone*. New York: Basic.

Wyers, N. L. 1987. Homosexuality in the family: Lesbian and gay spouses. *Social Work* 32(2):143–148.

CHAPTER ELEVEN

Voices from the Heart: The Developmental Impact of a Mother's Lesbianism on Her Adolescent Children

Ann O'Connell

I saw her as a model to be open and honest. She has nourished me and loved me while taking big risks in her life. That she was a lesbian, that she could be brave . . . allowed me to understand that I could be brave too.

THE CHANGING LANDSCAPE OF THE AMERICAN FAMILY has shifted from the traditional two-parent family to include a wide variety of family forms, including the lesbian-parented household. While it is difficult to give an accurate number, due in part to the invisible nature of this family, 1989 statistics report an estimated 1.5 to 3.3 million lesbian mothers in the United States, and this number is undoubtedly growing (Gibbs 1989; Pennington 1987). Until recently lesbian mothers most often were women who had married, had children, and, at some point within marriage or after separation, recognized their lesbianism. The profoundly homophobic culture in which this recognition takes place has an enormous impact on how a lesbian mother proceeds. For many women this entails a long process of negotiation, balancing openness with silence.

Children of lesbians, like their mothers, are equally vulnerable to the pressures of the culture in which they live and often become caught in a maze of similar negotiations with family and friends. This chapter is based upon the study of eleven children whose mothers, either before or after divorce, "came out" as lesbian. The children's experiences surrounding their mother's disclosure were explored, with particular attention focused on the adolescent developmental issues of peer affiliation and sexuality. This study provided an opportunity to identify potential areas of conflict and stress as well as the strengths and benefits of growing up with a lesbian mother.

In an effort to orient the reader I begin with a brief discussion of both the impact of divorce and adolescent developmental issues, followed by some highlights from the literature on lesbian mothers and their children. The methodology of the study is detailed and the findings, as much as possible in the voices of the children themselves, are described. I then discuss the results and draw implications for clinical practice.

Review of the Literature

Divorce

Within the last two decades in the United States the divorce rate has tripled, and evidence suggests that presently one out of every two marriages will end in divorce. This common family crisis has generated an impressive body of research underscoring the fact that divorce creates a state of disequilibrium in the family with longlasting effects. Many authors suggest that, for many children, the impact of divorce can be devastating (Carter and McGoldrick 1988; Heatherington, Cox, and Cox 1982; Wakerman 1984; Wallerstein and Blakeslee 1989; Wallerstein and Kelly 1980). Wallerstein and Blakeslee (1989) report that, even after ten years, children of divorce convey the general feeling that they are survivors of a tragedy.

A child's ability to manage this crisis is specific to each family. Peck and Manocherian (1988), in their comprehensive review of the literature, found that the particular circumstances surrounding the separation can magnify the impact that divorce has on the child. The study herein is based, in part, on the assumption that the particular circumstances of having a mother who comes out after separation, coupled with the transition of adolescence, will additionally shape the child's experience.

Adolescent Development

Countless theorists, including Blos (1979), Erikson (1963), Freud (1965), and Kegan (1982) portray adolescence as a time of developmental crisis incorporating a series of tasks that, when completed, result in a consolidated identity. There is an abundance of literature available, including a newer feminist-based relational model of development, that contributes to an enriched understanding of adolescent issues. However, little information exists on the children of lesbian mothers, who face the dual challenge of managing the developmental tasks of adolescence while remaining loyal to a newly stigmatized mother.

Importance of Peer Relationships

For adolescents a beginning resolution of the developmental struggle toward an emerging self is grounded in relationships outside the family, particularly in affiliation with peers. This produces a heightened need to be liked and accepted, leading to intensified pressure to conform to the values of the peer group (Cameron and Rychlak 1985).

While relational needs are evident for both sexes, in the context of this study it was useful to note some experiential differences. For example, both Chodorow (1978) and Gilligan (1982, 1992) state that of primary importance to the adolescent girl is the wish not to hurt others, often requiring the silencing of her own voice. This suggests that a possible conflict may arise when silence clashes with loyalty to a stigmatized mother. Relationship maintenance may produce the same tension for boys, although boys may resolve the tension differently.

Sexuality

A significant developmental task of adolescence is the beginning consolidation of a sexual identity. With the onset of puberty an urgent preoccupation with sexual desires and fears—coupled with conflicts, anxieties, and new defenses—appears, leaving the adolescent in a state of perpetual crisis. Assuming a heterosexual outcome, Blos (1979) suggests that an implicit task of adolescence is coming to terms with the homosexual component of pubertal sexuality. Hidden within the immediate adolescent question "Am I OK?" is the underlying question "Am I heterosexual?" This question has the potential to hold within it a more complex experience for the child of a homosexual parent.

Lesbian Mothers and Their Children

The social context in which a previously heterosexual mother recognizes and discloses her lesbianism is of utmost importance to how her children react. The current climate of deeply entrenched fear of and intolerance toward homosexuality allows for almost unilateral discrimination in housing, employment, and child custody decisions, leaving a lesbian mother and her children vulnerable not only to the exigencies of divorce but also to the outcomes of society's biases. For many women this necessitates engaging in the contradictory experience of, on the one hand, "passing" (Goffman 1963) and, on the other hand, living a lifestyle congruent with her lesbian identity. A number of authors (Crawford 1987; Erlichman 1989; Gibbs 1989; Green 1987; Lewis 1977; Rafkin 1990) suggest that the children of lesbian mothers become caught in a similar process.

Interest in the well-being of these children has generated a small body of research focusing on how they might be affected by their mother's sexual orientation. Importantly, these studies, using various methods and samples across age groupings, all report similar findings; there are no major differences in psychological or social development between children of heterosexual and lesbian single parents (Gibbs 1989; Green 1978, 1987; Hoeffer 1981; Kirkpatrick, Smith, and Roy 1981; Lewis 1977; Hotvedt and Mandel 1980; Patterson 1992; Pennington 1987). A few researchers have studied children of the lesbian baby boom, that is, children born to or adopted by women who identify as lesbians, singly or in couple relationships (Flaks, Ficher, Masterpasqua, and Joseph 1995; McCandlish 1987; Patterson 1994, 1996; and Steckel 1985, 1987). Again, these researchers also report that there are no significant differences in the psychosocial adjustment and functioning of these children and those born to and raised in families headed by heterosexual parents. However, the experiences of adolescents are relatively unexplored, a critical omission given the emphasis on identity formation at this stage of development. A handful of researchers conducting studies to fill this gap suggest that questions regarding friendships and sexuality are central concerns to both the children of lesbians as well as to those considering the appropriateness of lesbian mother parenting.

Friendships

The need to conceal the mother's sexual orientation from peers was felt across sexes in the Lewis (1977) and Pennington (1987) studies, as well as in Rafkin's (1990) compilation of children's narratives. This secrecy, suggests Bozett (1987), is based not only on the child's internal conflicts but also on the realities of a homophobic society. The need to preserve friendships, coupled with fears of negative judgment, teasing, or physical harassment if the mother's lesbianism was discovered, leads to experiences of hypervigilance and secrecy. Complicating the worries about friendships were the concerns of the older children in the Lewis and Pennington studies, who worried about peer response in the area of sexuality, although Pennington notes that once the child reached the point of sexual activity the need for secrecy abated. While secret keeping had implications for the development of closeness to peers, Hotvedt and Mandel (1982) found no significant differences in the friendship patterns of the children of lesbians and heterosexual mothers, a finding supported by Golombok, Spencer, and Rutter in their 1983 study. Huggins (1989), in her study on adolescents and social stigma, found no significant difference between the self-esteem levels of these two groups.

Sexuality

The Lewis (1977) and Pennington (1987) studies show that children entering adolescence struggle with questions and fears regarding their sexual orientation. Pennington notes this to be especially true for the girls in her study and theorizes that emerging adolescent sexuality, coupled with same-sex attractions, may increase the daughter's fear that she, like her mother, will become a lesbian. Boys in both studies reported worrying about being left out or invalidated by the mother, although Lewis suggests these feelings to be reflective of the boy's inner process and not the mother's actual rejection. Lewis also noted confusion about how a change in sexual orientation could occur.

There seems to be an urgency in the research to assess the sexual identity outcome of children of lesbian mothers. Gibbs (1989), in her review of the literature, reports that the general consensus among researchers is "that children of lesbian mothers develop an appropriate gender identity, follow typical developmental patterns of acquiring sex-role concepts and sex-typed behaviors and generally develop a heterosexual orientation" (70). Much of the scant research available has centered primarily on the fundamental question of differences between children raised by lesbian mothers and those raised by heterosexual mothers. There is little information concerning how children of lesbian mothers manage and make meaning of their unique family. This study attempted to explore those experiences.

Methodology

An exploratory design was used for this research and open-ended interviews, with a questionnaire guide, were used to collect the data. The nonprobability sample was both purposeful and one of convenience. Consistent with the intent of the study was the need to work with subjects who had full knowledge of their mother's lesbianism and intact relationships with their fathers as evidenced by consistent visitation.

Participants were obtained both through word of mouth as well as through an advertisement placed in two Boston gay newspapers and a local women's newspaper. With two exceptions, initial contact was made by the mothers, whose children were then contacted by phone. Two subjects referred friends who were contacted directly.

The study sample consisted of six young women, ages sixteen to twenty-three, and five young men, ages nineteen to twenty-three. The eleven subjects came from eight families. All the children experienced the separation or divorce of their parents between the ages of six and twelve, with a mean age of nine years. Age of the participants at the time of the mother's coming out was between seven and fourteen, with a mean age of eleven and a half years. Mean age at the time of the interview was twenty and a half years.

The self-reported socioeconomic status of all the participants' families was lower middle class. Ten of the participants were white; one was African American. Six of the eleven subjects presently lived with their mothers, while the other five maintained close contact. Ten subjects identified themselves as heterosexual, and one identified herself as lesbian.

During the initial phone contact each subject was given an overview of the study and an explanation of both the screening questions and interview procedure. Interview dates were set up at the time of the call and were held at the subject's convenience. There were no time constraints imposed on the subjects and the audiotaped interviews lasted from forty-five minutes to an hour and a half.

The open-ended, semistructured format used an interview guide which consisted of sixty-five questions in five sections. The sections covered demographic information, pre- and postdivorce material, importance of friendships and, finally, impact of mother's lesbianism on relationships and on sexuality. At the end of the interview all subjects took the opportunity to add further thoughts.

The material was then analyzed for common themes, with particular attention paid to the areas of sexual identity and peer relationships. The thematic analysis clarified potential problems and possible gains that an adolescent with a lesbian mother might experience.

Findings

The eleven participants in this study were articulate reporters and thoughtfully shared their worries, joys, strengths, and longings, both about the separation of their parents and the subsequent impact of their mother's coming out. Without exception, each experience was remembered vividly.

The Impact of Separation and Divorce

The themes that Wallerstein and Kelly (1980) identify as appearing in children of divorce were evident in the experiences of all eleven participants. Vulnerability, worries that basic needs would not be met, concern for the parent's well-being, anger, and conflicted loyalties all emerged as topics of discussion. Marital discord existed in each of the families before separation and all but two brothers in one family remembered their parents' fighting.

Regardless of the discomfort with the level of fighting, the dissolution of the family unit brought fear: "I kept asking my mother about dying. Like . . . who will I live with? Who will take care of me?" It also produced confusion: "I just couldn't figure it all out—and I keep thinking this is all because of me." Ultimately, particularly for the boys, it brought pervasive longing for the father, "I would expect him to come home, like always. And it would be just so—so empty."

After the separation, economic hardships, frequent moves, and changes in relationships with parents were experienced as major stressors by most of the subjects. The change in relationship with the father was the most dramatic. The wishes of the boys for "closeness" and of the girls "to be known" by him were for the most part unrealized, and the father, while still available, became a distant figure as time passed. Ten of the eleven adolescents experienced their mother's coming out within the context of these events.

Mother's Coming Out

In all eight families the mother's lesbianism was revealed through her new relationship and was explained fairly matter-of-factly. One adolescent remembered being told that a lesbian was "a woman who loved another woman . . . like a husband and wife would care about each other." A variation of this explanation was repeated throughout. The younger the subject was at the time of disclosure, the greater the level of comfort and acceptance, although this shifted as adolescent worries emerged. One son, reflecting on this shift, said,

> At first I felt relief . . . glad that my mother was happy. Then, later, I don't remember the exact emotional effect it had on me, but I think it made me feel odd and out of place. I didn't want to be thought of as different. I wanted to be the same as everyone else.

Disclosure at early and mid-adolescence generated more powerful responses such as "shock," "disbelief," "worry," and "confusion," and all of the young persons remembered their feelings of anger. One son spoke of the combination of the disclosure coming on the heels of the divorce:

> I was shocked, surprised and disappointed. I was angry . . . Every time something was happening to my family, it was not a norm. It was one thing stacked up on another thing, and, you know, it just seemed to keep adding up. I was wondering when it was going to stop.

Notably, expressions of anger were often tempered by either a strong disclaimer or a lighter joking tone.

One reaction to the mother's coming out reported by four of the five young men was the loss of hope for parental reconciliation, a hope that in one case had lasted through a mother's remarriage and divorce. One remembered, "I didn't think I hoped for my parents to get together, but then, when my mother came out, it shocked me. I knew then that the divorce was final . . . and we'd never be a family again." In fact, for all five males divorce was mentioned as "the real issue." One said, "In the end, the saddest part was my family breaking up." Another concurs: "It was only recently that I learned that some families stay together, that it's possible for me—I didn't know that.

Several of the young people reported feeling relief that their mother had someone to love and would no longer be lonely. One said, "She became more happy. It was almost like a missing piece . . . got put in place." Three of the subjects stated that the presence of the mother's partner increased their sense of well-being.

Feelings About Mother

All eleven adolescents expressed strong feelings of loyalty and protectiveness toward their mothers throughout the interviews. Negative or charged emotions such as disappointment or anger, while candidly acknowledged, were often preceded by expressions such as "I love my mother and . . ." or "My mother is great, but . . ." One young woman spoke of the conflict between loyalty to her mother and the wish that her mother were different. She described a crayon drawing, made just after her mother came out:

> My mother is small and dark, but the picture is a blond woman with big eyelashes, high heels and, like, a pink, fluffy skirt. The sky is blue, the grass is green and everything is just—so . . . lovely. It said "MOM." I loved my mother, but I wanted her to be like everyone else's mother.

As the young persons spoke about their relationships with their mothers the theme of differentiating, of separating and staying connected, emerged, with five adolescents reporting this as an area of difficulty. Identifying with the mother was deemed important but perplexing in light of her sexual orientation and three of the women expressed confusion about the wish to be different from their mothers. One said, "I'm a lot like my mother, which is great, but I used to wish I wasn't. I would think, 'I can't be a lesbian.'" One girl who had declared herself to be lesbian, while appreciating the support she received, expressed the need to be different:

> Friends of mine who were gay would say, "That's so neat" about my mother, but I kept wanting to be different. A lot of parents might have thought of my coming out as rebellious: my father did, but my mother just took it in stride. . . . That was wonderful—to be accepted—but I'm left feeling that it's hard to separate from her, let go.

Finally, one young man thoughtfully spoke:

> I think that if my mom had been straight and involved with a man, I might have viewed her relationship from the perspective of the man and viewed my mother as other in a certain way and part of the same group of the rest of the people I was interested in. As it was, I had ambivalent feelings about who to identify with and pushed her away for that reason.

Four of the five males in the study expressed the strong need for increased contact and support from their father during this period. While this need is consistent with both developmental literature and Wallerstein and Kelly's (1980) findings on children of divorce, it was perceived by the sons as linked to their mother's lesbianism.

Secret Keeping

Every adolescent was selective in sharing information about their mother and proceeded silently and with caution both within the extended family and outside the home. This was experienced by all eleven as keeping a secret, and the process was described by one subject as "a second coming out. First your mother comes out to you, and then you have to come out about your mother." Notably, the comfort level of the mother with her sexual orientation was reported to be high in five subjects who were initially comfortable talking to someone. This finding is consistent with Pennington (1987), Crawford (1987), and others who also report this correlation. Further, these subjects remembered their mothers providing access to other children of lesbians, thus, to some extent, decreasing their sense of isolation. It was one to five years before the other six spoke to anyone about their mother's sexual orientation. Comments such as "I was afraid to lose friends," "I'd be weird," and "they would think I'm not normal" were frequent. Because of the difficulties surrounding the issues of disclosure, all eleven continued to conceal their mother's lesbianism from someone.

Friendships

The theme of losing friends or being judged was expressed by each young person with a moderate to high level of intensity. Secret keeping and guardedness, in order to maintain friendships, were common. One daughter said, "In high school, constantly, as soon as the subject changed to moms, you were on your toes about everything. . . . You were just on your toes. Sometimes I would try to change the subject." Inquiries by curious friends were sidestepped or explained away and, when feeling pushed, subjects often lied. One spoke of this:

> After we moved, it was very embarrassing to try and tell a new girl from an uptown neighborhood who I wanted to be my friend. She'd say, "Are they sisters; are they best friends, or what?" and I'd lie. I wanted to say, "She's gay, who cares?" but I wanted a friend more. It made me feel a little disloyal to my mother.

For many of the young people, lying about their mother proved to be a complex, conflictual experience. One summed up the feelings expressed by others when she said:

I feel a lack in me that I couldn't tell. I couldn't understand why I couldn't tell people . . . but I knew I just couldn't. My mother was such a strong force in what I believe, and that was hard—not being able to share it. It also made me ashamed of myself in some way.

Interestingly, five of the six girls interviewed spoke about keeping their mother's lesbianism a secret to shield their friends from embarrassment and discomfort. Time after time, these subjects relayed instances of remaining silent or joining in homophobic joking to allow for the comfort of others. One subject described a "black hole in me . . . when I was pretending it wasn't true. But I knew everyone would be so embarrassed . . . for me, you know?"

Sexuality

The interview questions about sexuality elicited the most fluidly changing responses, indicating perhaps both confusion about the source of their worries and discomfort with the intimacy of the topic. While ten of the eleven adolescents initially reported no increased worries about themselves in light of their mother's disclosure, further discussion revealed more complex experiences. The measure of intensity shown in the discussions of friendships was less apparent, and many of the responses were light-hearted and anecdotal, though often contradictory. "I'd think, 'Oh God, what if it happens to me?' But I knew it wouldn't, so it didn't really bother me too much."

The two major concerns that emerged were confusion about homosexuality and the fear of becoming homosexual. One daughter laughed when she said:

I had heard that every single person goes through a homosexual phase, and it dawned on me that my best friend loved me when I was eight. . . . She would tell me I was beautiful, and I loved her very much, and I was trying to figure out if that was my homosexual phase or was I going to run into my homosexual phase later. It's very confusing.

This confusion was shared by five others who wondered how a person's sexual orientation "gets set" and questioned whether their mother's experience would occur for them as well. One son recalled:

It always made me wonder if I would stay straight or not. If I was in a locker room or something, and I glanced at another kid, I would wonder if it meant anything. It made me aware that there were more possibilities than heterosexual, which was scary.

Nine of the eleven young people remembered worrying about becoming gay and most often cited reasons such as fear of being judged and the intensely felt wish to be "normal." One, caught between his own worries and loyalty to his mother, said, "I didn't want to be gay in the worst way and I also wanted to prove to my Dad that my mom was a good person and that she wasn't going to ruin me."

Four adolescents reported that their mother's sexual orientation helped them think more positively about themselves. One said, "It made me more comfortable to be heterosexual. I've been able to think out both sides and really consider who I want to love. How many kids have that choice?" Fears of becoming homosexual abated for all these young people once dating began. One young woman reminisced about early dating: "There was a hint of relief. I thought, good, I like guys!" Significantly, understanding their mother's shift in sexual orientation remained a question for eight of the subjects, although all eleven had settled on theories that made sense to them.

Differential treatment

When asked if they had perceived dissimilar treatment by their mothers as compared to other children, responses, with one exception, were differentiated by sex. The young men worried that their mothers might be "antimale" as a consequence of being lesbian. Rather than experiencing a difference in treatment, there was an anticipatory fear that things could change. One son remembers how he felt at thirteen: "She didn't treat me differently at all, or, in fact, she may have treated me better, but for a long time I waited to see if it would change."

The other significant theme for the sons, and the primary one for the daughters, was their mother's openness, which they experienced as different from other mothers. The six daughters stated that they were treated better than other children and remarked that their mothers were "more open, easier to talk to" and "more respectful" of them.

What Was Needed

In thinking about what was needed in the period after disclosure, all participants stated the wish to have had an easier time talking about their feelings and spoke of the loneliness and isolation as a result of their silence. One poignantly stated:

> I was walking around in a lot of pain. I wish I did talk about it to someone sooner. I mean, now, when I look back, I didn't feel so much like I was walking around with a secret, which I was . . . but I felt I was walking around with a problem.

Five adolescents reported feeling unsure about how to approach the subject and were left waiting for others to bring it up. One subject recollected a time when he came close to talking to a friend. It was two years before he tried again. He said, "My best friend asked me . . . he said, "Is your Mom, uh, uh . . . ?" and he couldn't say it. I said, "What, what?" I wanted him to ask me but he couldn't and I couldn't." Four spoke of the need to have talked more specifically with their mothers about the meaning of her lesbianism and one, echoing the others, said simply, "I needed the world to be a more open place."

Benefits and Difficulties

When asked whether there were additional benefits or difficulties in having a lesbian mother, all emphatically stated that the benefits were substantial. The benefit reported most often and discussed in most depth was an increased understanding of prejudice. Thoughts such as being "able to live with differences" and "look . . . past exteriors to what's inside" were expressed. One son reflected, "I never wished for the hardness of it, but it shaped me in very important ways. Being open . . . it made me grow in ways I never might have." Another said: "It strengthened what I believe. I experienced a lot of prejudice toward my mother and myself and I want to never make judgments about people." Additional benefits reported were understanding that one has the freedom to change and make choices, increased comfort in talking with their mother, and the benefit of having a mother who was "more open" and "tolerant" than other mothers.

In general, informants seemed reticent in speaking of difficulties, and several subjects expressed their wish to clarify possible misconceptions about the difficulties, emphasizing both their love and respect for their mothers. Without exception, each young person stated the heartfelt wish that anyone reading this study should know that having a lesbian mother was a positive experience. One daughter passionately said:

I think people should understand it's not going to affect you adversely. I mean, it's not world news. People's ideas about what's important are weird. Bombs and alcoholism and violence are world news. So is hunger and homelessness. My mother's being a lesbian is definitely not news.

Discussion

This study was born out of a desire to more fully understand the impact a divorced mother's lesbianism has on her adolescent children. Close attention was paid to issues regarding friendships and sexual identity. The adolescents—many of whom expressed relief at the chance to have their voices heard—were very forthcoming. They spoke with pain, sadness, humor, and strength; themes such as peer pressure, secret keeping, sexuality issues, and maternal loyalty emerged. The journey from the divorce to the present was vividly remembered by all.

In exploring the confounding effects of divorce, it was clear that the young people in this study had adjustment reactions like other children of divorce. Divorce themes, as identified by Wallerstein and Kelley (1980), frequently appeared as they spoke about the lasting effects of the end of their parents' marriage. Particularly evident were feelings of loyalty, sadness, anger, worry, and vulnerability. In fact, the findings in this study point to the loss of the original family unit as a primary source of sadness, especially for the boys. While the mother's coming out was pivotal in the confirmation of the end of the parents' marriage, most informants reported that it was the dissolution of the original family that was far more significant in their lives than the mother's change in sexual orientation. Her coming out, however, was pivotal in the confirmation of the end of the parents' marriage.

The experiences and feelings of participants in this study were quite consistent with findings from the few studies on children of lesbian mothers. With few exceptions, most were surprised when their mothers disclosed their lesbianism. The stories about their mothers' coming out were very similar in content for all participants, all of whom were told by the mother within the context of her having fallen in love with another woman. Children told during the latency age period found it more comfortable to accept their mother's lesbianism than did adolescents, who reported feelings of fear about what the meaning would be for them. As one phrased it,

"I really loved my mother a lot. . . . It didn't change how I view her. It changed how I thought I would need to live my life." The wish to have had a less complicated adolescence was evident and expressed by the majority of the group. Unlike those in earlier studies, they were quite candid in reporting feelings of anger, disappointment, and resentment. Yet all these reporters were quick to ameliorate their negative expressions with a disclaimer such as "but it was not really a problem." While there appeared to be an understanding of anger, profound loyalty and acceptance were almost always expressed in tandem. This pairing of anger with loyalty was reflected throughout the interviews.

Friendships and Secrecy

As these young people became aware of the stigmatization of lesbian relationships, complicated measures were taken to prevent the exposure that they believed would lead to personal unacceptability and loss of friends. This is consistent with previous studies. Secrecy, remaining silent, or overtly lying were perceived to be an important aspect of relationship maintenance and were presented as problems. The secrecy was understood by the girls, consistent with a relational model of development, as fulfilling the need to save others from embarrassment or discomfort, by the boys, as a need to defend themselves against being thought of as different. Keeping secrets led to loneliness, particularly for the boys, although the intense need to talk to others was reported by everyone in this study. While fear of disclosure was strong, the desire to be known was also profound. Isolation was less problematic for those adolescents who had contact with other children of lesbians, suggesting that lesbian parents should work to provide this experience for their children.

The effects of lying and keeping secrets on adolescent development have not been directly addressed in previous studies of children with lesbian mothers. Based on the results of this study, "closeting" and "passing" proved to be complicated both intrapsychically as well as socially. Several subjects spoke about the conflict between feeling intensely loyal to their mothers versus the need for self-protection; a conflict that often resulted in feelings of shame. While one would expect loyalty issues to emerge for children of divorce, these experiences, coupled with a sense of protectiveness, seemed additionally based in attachment to a stigmatized parent. Goffman's (1963) work on stigma is useful in understanding this dynamic.

Sexuality

The findings in this study, as other researchers have reported, suggest that the sexual orientation of the mother does not dictate the child's sexual orientation. Less explored, though certainly notable, were the children's experiences as their normal concerns about sexuality intensified during adolescence. For these adolescents it seems likely that the road to a stable sexual identity contained some experiences that made for a different experience for them than for their peers, but there is no indication that their sexual identities are any more or less well resolved.

The fear of becoming gay was felt across sexes, in contrast to Pennington (1987), who found this to be more profound for the girls in her study. Sadly, these children attributed their concerns to the sexual orientation of their mother and were isolated from the knowledge that other teenagers, with heterosexual mothers, had similar concerns. Unfortunately, societal homophobia supports this isolation. Consistent with the literature was the correlation between increased dating and sexual activity with decreased fears of becoming homosexual.

The majority of the young people reported some confusion about the mother's change in sexual orientation, and the need to make sense of this change was evident in that they had all settled on theories for themselves. Interestingly, none had an overtly sexual component; rather they were rooted in the mother's emotional world of loving. This perhaps reflects both the mother's original explanation as well as the developmentally appropriate need to desexualize their parents.

The sons reported anticipatory fear that their mothers would devalue their maleness; however, once it became clear that this was not happening, the mother-son bond was viewed as quite strong. A precipitous leave-taking from the mother to consolidate a heterosexual identity, as Chodorow (1978) suggests for boys, was not noted. A striking result of these findings, in fact, was the relationship maintenance and loyalty found in these sons.

The daughters in this study continued to identify with those aspects of their mothers that were both comfortable and acceptable to them while rejecting those that were not, thus allowing for the emergence of their own sexual identity while preserving the attachment to the mother. This posed a problem for one lesbian daughter for whom it seemed that the wish to remain attached to her mother conflicted with her need to feel herself as other. She continues to struggle with this issue several years after her own coming out.

Benefits

Sons and daughters repeatedly expressed concern at the lack of understanding about the substantial benefits of growing up with a mother who is a lesbian. Having experienced real and threatened stigmatization, these young people reported an increased sensitivity to prejudice and a heightened ability to think critically about the impact of discrimination, a finding that is consistent with the level of increased tolerance for diversity that Steckel (1987) found among the children she studied. Their mothers were said to be role models of "bravery" and "risk taking" which gave these children the permission to think about their own differences in a flexible, positive way. Like many children of oppressed groups, strength was developed out of adversity. One young woman, summing up her thoughts, said, "The things that make you unique are the things that make you strong."

This study was undertaken in a large, East Coast, urban environment generally considered open to issues of diversity. For purposes of enhanced validity, since this sample was largely comprised of white, lower-middle-class young persons, a larger, more widely based sample inclusive of ethnic, racial, and class differences would be useful, as well as studies carried out in rural and other differing social contexts. Importantly, involvement in a study such as this will continue to require a particular comfort level, tending to make participation by less confident, more fragile, adolescents unlikely.

In the past few years, with the heightening of the family values debate, the public has increasingly been exposed to discussions of the rights of gays and lesbians and has been made much more aware of the existence of lesbian families. In some situations various factions in schools and communities have continued to try to marginalize and, indeed, render such families invisible. Furthermore, only rarely are services directed toward meeting the needs of this particular family constellation. As mental health practitioners, we need to make ourselves aware of the experiences of these families and of the tremendous strengths parents and children evidence in the face of invisibility, marginalization, and, in some situations, overt discrimination and even violence. As with other forms of oppression, heterosexism and homophobia have far-reaching consequences and constitute a grave risk to individuals as well as to the society that fosters them. Examining our own attitudes, assumptions, and fears about homosexuality will help to provide services sensitive to the impact of stigma and its resulting isolation. Moreover, as this study suggests, clinicians also need to be aware of the confounding effects of divorce on these children who, years later, continue to cope with pervasive sadness about the loss of the original family unit. Problems attributed to the impact of the parent's lesbianism are probably better understood in terms of the impact of the prior family relationship and the losses and turbulence of the divorce process.

The paucity of research in the area of lesbian-headed families suggests a clear need for further exploration of a wide spectrum of issues. Specific to this study, implications for future object-relations-based research are noted with particular attention paid to both male and female needs for attachment while developing in relation to a mother who is a lesbian. It appears from this study that both daughters and, surprisingly, sons, express a strong need to maintain and grow within relationship to their mothers. This warrants further study.

Future research might also include exploration of the issues that arise when children are faced with the potentially shame-based experience of hiding the identification of a mother who is devalued and stigmatized by society. Additionally, much of the research has ignored the fact that many children of lesbian mothers are being raised in two-parent families and that that couple relationship, the child's relationship with the mother's partner, and the relationships of all concerned with the child's father (who may have partial custody or is visiting), all have tremendous impact on the developing child. No one has been less visible than the mother's lesbian partner (see Muzio, this volume), who becomes am important actor in the family drama.

Finally, the importance of focusing research from the point of view of the child is stressed. As experts on their own experiences, they are rich sources of information and have much to teach us. Significantly, all the young people in this study reported the wish to have had someone to talk with. What they needed was for someone to ask and to listen. When given the chance, they spoke from their hearts.

REFERENCES

Blos, P. 1979. *The adolescent passage: Developmental issues.* New York: International Universities Press.

Bozett, F. 1987. Alternative families. In F. Bozett, ed., *Gay and lesbian parents*, pp. 116–119. New York: Praeger.

Cameron, N., and J. F. Rychlak. 1985. *Personality development and psychopathology.* Boston: Houghton Mifflin.

Carter, B., and M. McGoldrick. 1988. Conceptual overview. In B. Carter and M.

McGoldrick, eds., *The changing family lifecycle: A framework for family therapy*, pp. 3–25. New York: Gardner.

Chodorow, N. 1978. *The reproduction of mothering*. Berkeley: University of California Press.

Crawford, S. 1987. Lesbian families: Psychosocial stress and the family building process. In the Boston Lesbian Psychologies Collective, eds., *Lesbian psychologies: Explorations and challenges*, pp. 195–215. Urbana: University of Illinois Press.

Erikson, E. H. 1963. Eight ages of man. In E. H. Erikson, *Childhood and society*, pp. 247–274. New York: Norton.

Flaks, D., I. Ficher, F. Masterpasqua, and G. Joseph. 1995. Lesbians choosing motherhood: A comparative study of lesbian and heterosexual parents and their children. *Developmental Psychology* 31:104–114.

Freud, A. 1965. *Normality and pathology in childhood: Assessments of development*. Madison: International Universities Press.

Gibbs, E. 1989. Psychosocial development of children of lesbian mothers. In E. Rothblum and E. Cole, eds., *Lesbianism: Affirming nontraditional roles*, pp. 65–76. New York: Haworth.

Gilligan, C. 1982. *In a different voice*. Cambridge: Harvard University Press.

Gilligan, C., A. Rogers, and D. Tolman. 1992. *Women, girls and psychotherapy: Reframing resistance*, pp. 5–34. Binghamton, New York: Haworth.

Goffman, E. 1963. *Stigma: Notes on the management of spoiled identity*. New York: Simon and Schuster.

Golumbuk, S., A. Spencer, and M. Rutter. 1983. Children in lesbian and single-parent households: Psychosexual and psychiatric appraisal. *Journal of Child Psychology and Psychiatry* 24:551.

Green, G. D. 1987. Lesbian mothers: Mental health considerations. In F. Bozett, ed., *Gay and lesbian parents*, pp. 199–215. New York: Praeger.

Hetherington, M., M. Cox, and R. Cox. 1982. Effects of divorce on parents and children. In M. Lamb, ed., *Nontraditional families: Parenting and child development*. Hillsdale, N.J.: Lawrence Erlbaum.

Hoeffer, B. 1981. Children's acquisition of sex-role behavior in lesbian-mother families. *American Journal of Orthopsychiatry* 51:536–544.

Hotvedt, M., and J. Mandel. 1982. Children of lesbian mothers. In W. Paul, J. Weinrich, J. Gonsiorek, and M. Hotvedt, eds., *Homosexuality: Social, psychological and biological issues*, pp. 275–286. Beverly Hills: Sage.

Huggins, S. 1989. A comparative study of self-esteem of adolescent children of divorced lesbian mothers and divorced heterosexual mothers. In F. Bozett, ed., *Homosexuality and the family*, pp. 123–136. Binghamton, N.Y.: Haworth.

Kegan, R. 1982. *The evolving self*. Cambridge: Harvard University Press.

Kirkpatrick, M., C. Smith, and R. Roy. 1981. Lesbian mothers and their children: A comparative study. *American Journal of Orthopsychiatry* 51:545–551.

Kirkpatrick, M. 1987. Clinical implications of lesbian mother studies. *Journal of Homosexuality* 14(1/2):201–211.

Lewis, K. G. 1977. Children of lesbians: Their point of view. *Social Work* 25:198–203.

McCandlish, B. 1987. Against all odds: Lesbian mother family dynamics. In F. W. Bozett, ed., *Gay and lesbian parents*, pp. 23–36. New York: Praeger.

McGoldrick, M., C. Anderson, and F. Walsh. 1989. *Women in families*. New York: Norton.

Patterson, C. J. 1992. Children of gay and lesbian parents. *Child Development* 63:1025–1042.

Patterson, C. J. 1994. Children of the lesbian baby boom: Behavioral adjustment, self-concepts, and sex role identity. In B. Greene and G. M. Herek, eds., *Lesbian and gay psychology: Theory, research, and clinical applications*, pp. 156–175. Newbury Park, Cal.: Sage.

Patterson, C. J. 1996. Lesbian mothers and their children. In J. Laird and R.-J. Green, eds., *Lesbians and gays in couples and families: A handbook for therapists*, pp. 420–437. San Francisco: Jossey-Bass.

Peck, J., and J. Manocherian. 1988. Divorce in the changing family life cycle. In B. Carter and M. McGoldrick, eds., *The changing family life cycle: A framework for family therapy*, pp. 335–371. New York: Gardner.

Pennington, S. 1987. Children of lesbian mothers. In F. Bozett, ed., *Gay and lesbian parents*, pp. 58–73. New York: Praeger.

Rafkin, L. 1990. *Different mothers: Sons and daughters of lesbians talk about their lives.* San Francisco: Cleis.

Steckel, A. 1985. Separation-individuation in children of lesbian and heterosexual couples. Ph.D. diss., Wright Institute, Berkeley, California.

— 1987. Psychosocial development of children of lesbian mothers. In F. W. Bozett, ed., *Gay and lesbian parents*, pp. 75–85. New York: Praeger.

Wakerman, E. 1984. *Father loss: Daughters discuss the man that got away.* New York: Doubleday.

Wallerstein, J. S., and J. B. Kelly. 1980. *Surviving the breakup: How children and parents cope with divorce.* New York: Basic.

Wallerstein, J. S., and S. Blakeslee. 1989. *Second chances.* New York: Ticknor and Fields.

PART FOUR

Special Themes in Theory and Practice

A Relational Perspective on Mutuality and Boundaries in Clinical Practice with Lesbians

Carolyn Dillon

IT IS ESTIMATED THAT SOME 70 PERCENT of North American lesbians have been consumers of therapy (Brown 1990), often to deal with the seque-lae of heterosexism, misogyny, and various discriminations flowing from patriarchal power arrangements (Ellis and Murphy 1994).

These sequelae may manifest as mood disorders, relationship problems, social isolation, addictions, life cycle crises, or repeated self-sabotage in var-ious daily life undertakings (Dillon 1993b). Other traumas such as violence, HIV-related losses, and discrimination-based loss of family, roles, and rights can also prompt lesbians to seek therapy.

Lesbians may also consult with therapists, not for problems, but for prospects. Therapy can help one step momentarily outside the mores and loyalties of accustomed networks and sort through complicated positive life choices and potentials with a trusted "outsider" who displays an insider's experience, empathy, and openness to diverse possibilities and outcomes (Dillon 1993a). Today that insider/outsider will more often be an "out" les-bian therapist who herself faces complex issues around power sharing and intimacy in her work with lesbian clients.

Although therapists have been criticized for atomizing and personaliz-ing the political and then treating it for financial gain (Brown 1990; Perkins

1991), there are also highly valued lesbian communal traditions of caring, of harboring strangers, and of providing mutual aid and protection as a shield from a hostile surround. These traditions, along with women's ancient traditions of reverence for shamanic or wise women, may make it easier for many lesbians to enter into that peculiar mutuality with a stranger that we have come to know as therapy.

That so many requests for therapy have their origins in personally experienced hatreds, violations, exclusions, and other mean and discriminatory practices serves as an impetus for lesbian therapists to try to establish more mutual and fiduciary relationships with clients. Our aim here is to avoid replicating the "power-over" relationships so common to women's experience (Laird 1994).

Therapeutic egalitarianism is no easy matter, for the aura of expert power widely attaching to the therapist role often hints at a superior knowledge, vision, or interpersonal comfort, potentiating relational imbalances between "authority" and consultee. It has been difficult for many therapists and clients to relinquish fantasies of therapist power because these fantasies appear so often to compensate for insecurities in both parties and to have a complementarity to them.

Furthermore, women's relationships, collaboratives, and movements, like those of men, have broken down at times over problems with inclusivity and with the equitable distribution of resources and power. Neither lesbians nor lesbian therapists will be spared these widespread human struggles with the dilemmas of power. That lesbians may feel disloyal to their own community in airing their power issues does not mean there are none.

Indeed, some lesbians who have been silenced or subjugated may have persistent wishes for a more empowered other to show the way to voice and agency. Untreated lesbian abuse survivors may become therapists and reenact dominance-subordination scenarios with clients, trainees, and colleagues. Women working with women in any capacity may too readily give up power and a healthy vigilance, falsely assuming, on the basis of gender alone, that all other women will be safe and respectful.

Therapeutic relationships with lesbians or with others, contexts, and exchanges express internalized patriarchal beliefs and messages as well as relational intent. As therapists, everything we emphasize or exclude, welcome or eschew, notice or avoid signals our values, beliefs, loyalties, and intentions far better than does any manifest contract (Avis 1991; Greenspan 1986). To illustrate:

When Terri, a single lesbian in her twenties, told her lesbian therapist that she had become pregnant in a "one night stand" with her neighbor, Doug, she felt her therapist tensed up. The therapist seemed distant each time they discussed the pregnancy. Terri's feeling, which she suppressed out of respect for her usually attuned therapist, was that the therapist resented her having sex with a man when they had been focusing for so long on her getting involved with women. Her therapist interpreted the sex with Doug as Terri's "homophobic acting out." Terri thought of "the incident" (as she called it) as "loneliness and neighborliness tinctured with tequila."

Francie noted that, while the "client chair" she always sat in was comfortable, it was wedged between two bookshelves and surrounded by stacks of manuscripts and textbooks, leaving the impression that this relational therapist was "going to be the brainy type, no hugging or flailing of arms encouraged."

Heyward (1993) decries a therapeutic journey she deemed damaging for both herself and her lesbian therapist. Hopes for mutuality were overtaken by insurmountable ambivalences. Differences hardened regarding what constituted therapy, when it would end, and what kind of relationship was possible for therapist and client after termination.

Heyward has much to say about how "power-full" therapy is. She demonstrates the power clients and therapists have to hurt and silence each other when internalized control and dominance themes are reenacted in relationships dressed up as caring and egalitarian. Other observers (Brown 1989a; Eldridge 1993; Gartrell 1992) have also addressed the asymmetries of power in lesbian therapist-client relationships. They suggest problems that can arise from a sort of we-are-all-one denial of therapist power and client vulnerability at times of crisis and help seeking.

Relational Theory

In contrast to power-over models, relational therapies that emphasize mutual exchange and empowerment seem well suited to lesbian therapists' work with lesbian clients. In relational theory mutual empathy and mutual empowerment are seen as central to both human development and good therapy. Both processes depend on the mutual building and practicing of relational competencies. Surrey (1991) and her colleagues at the Stone Center at Wellesley College describe the core self as organizing and developing throughout life via a process of attunement and responsiveness that flows back and forth between self and many others, beginning with mother.

Such mutually attentive and affirming exchanges foster an eagerness in both parties for even more relationships, not just the maternal one. Benjamin (1988) suggests that unless the mother has other healthy attachments besides the one with her baby, she will be deprived of the very adult replenishment that will make her a zestier caretaker. Later, in parallel fashion, therapists will have this same need for replenishment from sources other than their clients, lest they in loneliness reach for clients to meet their needs for love and care (Berman 1985; Brown 1988; Dillon 1994; Gonsiorek 1989; Sussman 1992).

Eventually, to the degree that other empathic exchanges are available and encouraged, the self experiences an array of responses and messages that ultimately shape its unique repertoire of noticing, feeling, and responding capacities. Surrey (1991) refers to this continuous mutual learning as "differentiation within relationship," as opposed to an object relations view in which individuation is believed to occur through separated autonomous functioning.

This theory nicely dovetails with many lesbians' experience of greater safety, affirmation, and ability to use and share power constructively within resonant lesbian communities. To combat the vulnerability of isolation, lesbians have historically prioritized the making and tending of relationships and group alliances with many overlaps. Protection, caring, and support have long outweighed boundary and status as lesbian preoccupations.

As Slater (1993) has observed,

> Both lesbian lovers and lesbian therapy dyads striving for mutuality come up against a similar ambiguity when they opt for the uncleared path toward a more obscured but promising relational journey. Without maps to indicate how lesbian love or more mutual therapy relationships should look, both couples and therapy dyads are simultaneously burdened and freed up to construct their relationships virtually from scratch.... Lesbians often view getting in there and working on their relational process as a source of closeness in and of itself. They may come to therapy equally prepared to examine the dyadic process emerging between client and therapist. (9)

Since lesbians are accustomed to a high degree of sharing, physical contact, and mutual tending, many have noted anecdotally how odd it feels to experience the ritualized formality and separateness of traditional therapies.

Going into analytically derived therapies can feel to some like a visit to another planet, where one is asked not only to assimilate but, worse, to de-skill. One moves from the shared to the separated in what feels a very retrograde diminishment of the cherished capacities of attachment and mutual tending.

Relational Therapy

Relationally based therapy departs from traditional models that privilege the voice and expertise of the therapist. Traditional models tend to emphasize the utility of therapist separateness and constraint in the recapitulation and reconstruction process. Focus is often on the reworking of past conflicted relationships and maladaptive internalizations as these are revealed in therapy transferences and countertransferences.

Although relational practice models do not eschew transference work or attention to history, they do give equal importance to real exchanges of feeling, noticing, and responding in the present moment between clinician and client. The capacity of the therapist to be visibly moved by the client's experience is crucial. Equally important is genuine responsiveness to the client's feelings and observations about the therapy process itself (Miller and Stiver 1994). Miller and Stiver call this "moving towards mutuality," rather than perfecting it in a world of differing feelings about contact and intimacy.

Examples:

As Leslie told of the death of her lover, she began to cry as though her heart would break. Jen, her therapist, sitting nearby, put out her hand and placed it on Leslie's. Leslie recoiled, then looked frantic and apologized for pulling back. She said that anyone in the past who had set out to comfort her had always "expected something" later. She reassured the therapist that she knew she was different and was just trying to help. Jen, voice and face full of remorse and concern, said that she regretted that her touching Leslie had interrupted her grief and brought to mind people in the past who were not safe to be with. She offered that this might feel like one more betrayal, when they both had intended this to be a safe relationship. Leslie just said, "Yes," and began to cry again. She said that Katie's touch is one of the things she most misses when upset. She went on to talk at length of the many things she got from Katie and how Jen's kindness so often reminded her of her lover. Later Jen went back to Leslie's recoiling and wondered if she might still be worrying about what would be "expected later" for touching her. There ensued a lengthy discussion of the multiple abuses Leslie had been subjected to in her family.

Minna went to her law school study group meeting and learned to her horror that one of the women in the group was about to be fixed up with Gail, Minna's therapist. In her next therapy session she blurted out to Gail her shock that Gail was "in the market" and with one of her friends. Gail, taken aback, blushed and said that she had no idea about the connections and, of course, she would not go out with Minna's friend. Minna, torn, said, "You look awful. I'm sorry to do this to you, but I was so shocked." Gail then said that she was OK, not to worry, yet she too was shocked and sorry this was coming up just when Minna had so much to deal with. Gail asked how it had been to hear all this. Minna said she could not believe that her friend would get close to Gail in a way that Minna would not be able to. She was shocked at how much rivalry she felt. Gail empathized with how hard it was to be exposed to this right now. She expressed her own awkwardness. They talked about the difficulties of their community being such a fishbowl, then returned to a focus on Minna's ongoing issues.

Safe and genuine therapist responsiveness gives the client fresh opportunity to experience her capacity to affect and move another, to positively influence the relationship structure and process. Most therapeutic models give responsibility and credit to the therapist for positively affecting the relationship and the direction of work. Now the client, too, is invited to experience her own agency as coauthor of her own *and* the therapy narrative (Laird 1994; White and Epston 1990) in a way that is deeply affirming and empowering for her.

Such a process clearly also stretches therapists, as it appeals for more therapist openness, ownership of errors, and for carefully maintained integrity in a context of boundary flexibility. The therapist who successfully navigates the shoals of increased flexibility and genuineness can ultimately feel increased exuberance and empowerment through heightened "response-ability" (Surrey 1991). Ironically, an ostensible *de*crease in hierarchical power (mystification) can result in an *in*crease in relational power (interpersonal competence).

Appreciation of mutual growth and empowerment through highly inclusive processing and negotiation is a longstanding lesbian community value. As survivors of oppression, diminishment, and exile, lesbians have often found unaccustomed solace, kinship, and power in lesbian networks and institutions. We have often experienced, and thus readily appreciate, the "five good things" that Miller and Stiver (1991) believe flow from mutual empathy and empowerment.

These are 1. a sense of zest arising from connection with others, 2. a heightened capacity to act within and upon the therapy relationship as well as outside it, 3. an increased self- and other-awareness, 4. an increased sense of self-worth, and 5. a desire for more connection beyond the particular therapeutic relationship.

Indeed, given the propensity of lesbians for inclusivity and bonds, many lesbian clients may be more ready than their traditionally trained lesbian therapists to reduce power, distance, and formality in therapy without losing either therapeutic focus or sufficient boundaries.

Example:

Over five years of weekly recovery work, Tina and her therapist, Ann, had developed a very warm bond. Tina, a clinician herself, began to press Ann for ways they could be friends, colleagues, or collaborators outside of therapy. At first Ann linked these longings to childhood ones for safe anchorage with someone who would never go away. This touched real experience and feeling in Tina, but she continued to ask whether, when the work was finished, they couldn't have some other kind of collegial contact, just so there could be some affiliation without it needing to be social.

Ann sought out consultation from two respected lesbian colleagues. One saw no problem in professional collaboration, if there were no power differential. The other asked if Ann were lonely and whether that was why she was thinking of such contact. This touched Ann's own bias against dual relationships, and she noted with Tina that while she knew others were experimenting in loosening boundaries, she did not feel comfortable doing this, as it went against deeply ingrained beliefs of many years. Tina was able to express her disappointment and say she felt she was outgrowing Ann in some ways. Ann accepted these feelings as representing differences they could have without abandoning the part of the work that was working. Later Tina came in with mock chagrin over the fact that some of her own clients were beginning to press her about being friends, "and I don't know how I want to respond, there are so many issues." Ann said she herself felt very dissatisfied about it—they could continue to work on it together.

Relational Practice

In relational therapy the central motif is mutually facilitated movement out of isolation and disconnection and toward attuned relationship, within and beyond therapy (Miller and Stiver 1994). A crucial ongoing aspect of such attunement and movement involves the noticing by both therapist and client of moments in which either may disconnect because of hurt or fear.

At such moments the strategies that each uses to disconnect when threatened or hurt begin to appear. These include coming late, forgetting, not noticing details, tuning out, distractibility, dissociating while appearing to listen, interrupting, looking down and away, drifting off, and gratuitous intellectualizing.

The client's often accurate observations regarding therapist feeling states and behaviors are, in relational work, both elicited and validated at every reasonable opportunity. These validations can reverse for many lesbians their historic silencing and disqualification by persons in authority. However, "processing the process" should neither obliterate nor constantly interrupt the client's work on her "real life" narrative.

Lesbians growing up in abusive families often are taught to deny or suppress their observations and comments. Gilligan, Rogers, and Tolman (1991) noted that even in nonabusive families North American girls are, by their teen years, routinely socialized to "go underground" (develop denial or silence) with perceptions and critiques that threaten primary attachments.

Since so many therapists appear to come from troubled backgrounds (Gonsiorek 1989; Sussman 1992), and lesbian therapists, like other women, may have had their own authenticity stifled, lesbian therapists are bound to experience both empathic failures and strategic dilemmas in their efforts to be more mutual with their clients.

Clients with personal histories greatly shaped by violence or control may find such respectful and interactive collaboration a revolutionary experience. Chu (1991), however, reviews the ways in which therapists can be drawn into countertransference reenactments of domination or control when either they or their clients have been socialized to equate relationship with being the object of another.

Although both client and therapist share responsibility for the therapy, at moments of disconnection the therapist is still primarily responsible for finding ways to facilitate rejoining. These may include the ownership of our own blunders and empathic failures. When therapist blind spots prevent acknowledgment of impasses in the therapy, clients will often experience deidealization of the therapist. Sometimes clients become more depressed and disorganized as they experience a temporary loss of connectedness and safety. When we see regressions in client behavior, cognitive style, feeling states, or presentness in the moment, we do well to ask ourselves if we have done, said, or represented something that has caused a disconnection. We then actively explore that possibility before we attribute the problem to internal processes of the client.

Example:

Marcie noticed her therapist look at her watch several times during a session—something the therapist seldom did. She thought the therapist was tired of her and eager to see the next person. She grew quiet and said she needed to leave a bit earlier today, to catch her bus. Marcie came late next session, saying she had missed her bus. The therapist told Marcie she felt she had blown it the week before by seeming so tense and harried. At first Marcie said she hadn't noticed any difference. The therapist then shared that her cat had been injured just before Marcie's previous session and she could feel herself distracted by worry about the cat. She was sorry that she had not seemed very "with it" and could imagine feeling hurt and annoyed by that if she were in Marcie's shoes.

There was an ensuing brief silence while both looked uncomfortable. Marcie said that it must be hard to be a therapist when your own life has problems in it. The therapist said that it did not happen very often, but the cat was a reminder that it could. She said she was sorry it had happened. Marcie said she was sorry about the cat, and that she could tell something was wrong but thought it was something she had done. When asked what, she discussed with great feeling what a boring child she felt like in her busy home. Near the end of the session Marcie asked how the cat was now, and the therapist took a moment to explain all was better now. She appreciated Marcie's concern and her feelings from last week. The next week Marcie brought in a photo of her cat, Ace, who had gone through four apartment moves with her "and never lets me down." The therapist said that, thinking back to two weeks ago, it would be hard to feel you were playing second fiddle to a cat . . . what a letdown that could be. Marcie nodded and talked wistfully of having no pets and very little love as a child.

We have to be very careful at moments of client hesitation or silence not to take over the process in the name of modeling or educating. Sometimes mutuality may mean quiet, comfortable witnessing and accompaniment while the client finds her voice in her own good time.

This model expresses a strengths perspective (Laird 1994; Weick, Rapp, Sullivan, and Kisthardt 1989; White and Epston 1990), a belief that clients have more capacity and readiness to tackle hard issues than traditional practice theories recognize. Trust, safety, and boundaries are hard issues that most of us have had to negotiate time and again as we have considered coming out, taking public roles, joining in risk-taking political activity, including former lovers in friendship networks, and choosing to have children in a dangerous world.

A strengths perspective affirms that clients and therapists best flourish in a mutually respectful and participatory process in which trust and power sharing are continuously negotiated and caringly sustained. There will be no avoiding anxious moments, painful disagreements, or mistakes in judgment; these are seen as part of expectable human experience and grist for the therapeutic mill (Jordan 1990).

Boundary Issues

Safety in the Clinical Context

Perhaps no greater issue vexes us in practice today than that of safety for client and professional alike. Exploitation of clients is widespread across the disciplines; therapists are losing their roles, jobs, and even their lives in increasing numbers. Conflicts abound regarding practice theory, with much anecdotal encouragement to loosen up analytically derived strictures on practice. Yet there are few maps or guides as to how to flex therapist-client boundaries carefully, in ways that are respectful of the needs of both.

I struggle and profit along with my colleagues in trying to find ways to be closer to clients and their narratives without losing therapeutic focus. Grounded nearly thirty years ago in drive and object relations theory, it is only in the last ten years that I have opened heart and mind to systemic, self psychological, and relational theories emphasizing interpersonal experience and therapist demystification as central to growth and change.

Every time I flex a boundary, my psychodynamic introjects rise up to ask whether this is a narcissistic indulgence. I am equally aware over the years of dual role imbroglios that ruined relationships and overturned safe assumptive worlds in the name of "pushing the envelope" or being "less hierarchical."

To my horror, some admired male mentors of mine have been exposed by their female clients as sexual predators. A lesbian colleague was drawn into a therapeutic cult whose female guru led weekend "healing retreats" rife with sex and drugs. An admired lesbian innovator in the day treatment of the mentally ill ultimately lost her license for trading therapy for house-keeping and errand services. Such experiences make me very, very careful in my own thinking and behavior regarding therapist-client relations.

Living and working in small lesbian communities with overlapping net-works sets up repeated situations in which my lesbian therapist colleagues and I encounter our clients in work, recreation, political activism, interest groups, relational networks, and in gossip.

These connections and encounters are often in joyful or community-affirming contexts in which, all other things being equal, none of us likes to draw lines between herself and other lesbians because of constructs as cap-italistic and culture-bound as occupational role norms and concerns. As Laird (1994) has noted, "When one knows that the dominant social dis-course is wrong about oneself and one's community, one is more likely to question other powerful social narratives that shape one's life" (285).

Women's histories of caring for others across boundaries, and lesbian traditions of inclusion and mutual aid, make it even more difficult for us to make ethical and behavioral decisions that might seem power-over or exclusionary in the lesbian community. Brown and Brodsky (1992) summa-rize feminist principles of egalitarian structure and process in therapy, affirming that any dynamics privileging the therapist are inimical to good therapy and to women's development. Slater (1993) thinks that lesbians, due to decades of invisibility, have had too few enduring models of how healthy lesbian relationships develop and look over time. She believes that, on the positive side, lesbians are thus freer to explore and invent relational styles with more mutual risk taking and less intergenerational prescription and stricture.

Yet the inclusivity and exposure of more egalitarian participation make it hard for established lesbian therapists to have private lives and healthy separateness for replenishment without going far away from home (Brown 1988; Gartrell 1992; Kitchener 1988).

Gartrell (1992) gives a not unusual example of going out to dinner and having a client come over and ask if it would be OK for her to sit at the next table. Gartrell and her friend acceded, but then felt their communication shut down in order to self-protect. The sensitive client might intuit this shutdown, experiencing a double bind. If she were a client who easily blamed herself for others' discomforts, she would likely experience that in the situation.

Within a relational framework I would want to review this encounter in the next session with the client, exploring the client's observations/feelings, especially with regard to any discomfort or regret she might feel, as well as acknowledging my own discomfort. This kind of follow-up is important to preserve authenticity and assist both therapist and client in sorting through the relational complexities and differences that arise naturally for all of us in the course of everyday life. The relationship is then "corrective" for both, as neither has to pretend that the restaurant encounter did not happen, that it was a trivial incident, that it only affected the client, or that any discomfort was the client's fault.

This vignette captures so much of what I believe happens in lesbian communities where, much as in other minority enclaves, people need leaders, models, and idealized others to fuel the pride and identity development that is so thwarted in the heterosexist surround. Therapists are readily idealized: one woman who drove up while I was putting out the garbage told me she had never thought I *had* garbage!

People want to get near us, know us, see how we do things. Gartrell and others have reported being stalked by clients they finally had to take legal action to contain, but I have never had this experience. Interpretation of underlying mourning and longing for family merger has, in my experience, defused the transferential acting out of wishes to merge with me, whether by constant calling or other forms of compulsive shadowing.

We are often the objects of what I call healthy "familying" or "approving parent" or "neighborly" transferences on the part of lesbians whose original and/or created families are disappointing or diminishing for them. Clients who have seen me in my office at home may, for example, like to ask me out to their cars, when there is time, to introduce an important friend, a dog, a new car. I consider this to be the kind of "neighborliness" I grew up with in the South and now find useful to building rapport.

I believe this need for boundary flexibility comes with the role, and can be an opportunity and a focal point for resolving family issues. Because I see clients in a home office, I have minimized a feeling of intrusion by screening off home areas and putting a high fence around the house. These measures allow me protection from scrutiny when people inevitably drive by to see how I live.

In sessions I set a tone early on of responding to personal questions with curiosity about their origins, yet with a willingness to respond to reasonable inquiries, soon returning to a focus on the client. It is useful to, at some point, inquire of the client how it is for her to have personal information about me.

Obviously experiences will differ at different stages of therapy, of the bond between us, and at different levels of development in therapist and client. One client saw me being hugged by other attendees after a conference presentation and could barely contain a rather rageful envy she felt of "others having me."

Another happened to attend a community dinner where I was present. Halfway through the meal she tapped me on the back from the next table and comfortably introduced me to her partner, then cheerily resumed dessert. I have always been impressed by what a difference *my* comfort level makes in how a process affects a client. I believe clients extend much goodwill to us if they see that we are trying our best to do the right thing by them and are not using them as extensions of ourselves.

More recently in the relational process I have actively thanked people for times when they have genuinely taught me or nudged me toward greater clarity or connection. This validation of their perception of my shortcomings and blind spots can feel quite unique to them, as so many women have had their accurate perceptions of family process belittled or silenced. Some clients will become impatient or critical, feeling letdown by the deidealization, but the more common response is a deepening of conversation.

Problems and Violations

Stretching boundaries may suggest a violation of ethics to some professional colleagues. Berman (1985) reminds therapists that we teach as much by example as we do by words—that we literally embody values, ethics, and beliefs in our everyday ways of being, which are so transparent and so easily subject to small talk. One person's "expanded role" may be another's "normal lesbian behavior," and yet another's impropriety. One evening I gave a teen client a ride halfway home, throwing her bicycle in the trunk, as after the session she faced a four-mile bike ride home, almost entirely uphill and in darkness. I thought it no coincidence that during the ride she spoke of renewed efforts between herself and her mother to get closer again. I did wonder, however, what my old supervisor would say about my giving her this lift.

Other potentials for women safely to grow together in mutually respectful and empowering activities outside the therapy have been described by Greenspan (1986), Heyward (1993), and Slater (1993). These have included participation in community rituals, political activity, Pride Day events, sports, conferences, creative collaborations, and volunteer activities.

As a part-time clinician and full-time teacher of social work practice, I myself have successfully experimented with having a former client attend my course for new field supervisors, and accepting a client's invitation to do a half-day training for her large mental health staff on a specialty subject of mine. As on all occasions of role overlap, we talked at length before and after about the effects of such meetings on the relationship.

Both clients were lesbians with many ego strengths and a solid reality sense, and work in the same space seemed to deepen the bond. One was in ongoing treatment that continues to this day; the other had ended work with me three years previously. Both said that it mattered less that they trusted me than *that I trusted them* to work with me on whatever issues might arise from working together in these time-limited ways.

My usual therapeutic presence combines a warm and down-to-earth style with very firm, no socializing boundaries. I do not hug clients as a therapeutic technique, and I say this up front so they may choose to opt out if they need holding or hugging for historic reasons. I will hug clients good-bye at vacation separations or recommencements after absences, once I feel I know better over time what contact will mean to them. Even then, I debrief them on it afterward, checking in about it, as relational meanings can change and one moment's satisfaction may turn into another's threat. I always try to make my relational decisions on a case-by-case basis.

Body contact was anathema in my clinical training, and I once interpreted every move toward contact as a longing for mothering. I was literally retrained by an especially warm lesbian client of mine who simply treated this approach as outdated and peculiar! I talked the subject over with a number of lesbian and nonlesbian colleagues, many of whom were not only hugging occasionally but serving tea, going on walks, and attending christenings and commitment ceremonies. When I finally hugged one client before a long separation, she was shocked and said we would have to talk about this later! I felt rather awkward, exposed, glad. The same client taught me how to make "transitioning" audiocassette messages for people to take along during absences, to hold the therapy and therapist in mind. This has been an enormously useful technique with clients for whom internalization of sustaining others is not well in place. Moreover, this prompted me to try a technique in which a session is videotaped for the client to review at home, both for further noticing of relational process, and for reexperiencing the connection.

Simon (1992), an attorney, cites "scores of lawsuits . . . in which extracurricular socializing culminated in some form of sexual relations" (31). Lawsuits have included actions against lesbian and gay as well as straight therapists (Gonsiorek 1989). Often lawsuits deal with sexual relationships within or following therapy or bartering exchanges that go awry, leaving feelings of exploitation on both sides.

Keith-Spiegel and Koocher (1985) describe the fallout from boundary errors as including embarrassment, fear, bitterness, and even desires for vengeance. These matters usually spill over, far beyond the participants, becoming small wars with widely experienced consequences; witness the mutuality of the debacle between Heyward (1993) and her therapist. Brown (1988) cites the costly breaking up of loyalty networks when friends take opposite sides, blaming either therapist or client following boundary imbroglio.

Simon (1992) emphasizes the fiduciary or trustee nature of the therapeutic relationship "giving rise to a duty of care based on the special vulnerability of the patient rather than on the special powers of a profession" (23). He argues that therapists cannot simultaneously serve self-interest and client welfare, although the business aspects of most therapies inevitably produce conflicts of interest (Berman 1985; Brown 1990; Kitchener 1988; Perkins 1992).

Enormous amounts of energy can go into what Vasquez (1991) has described as the "conflict between the concern for client welfare during and after treatment vs. respect for the rights of both therapist and client" (167) in tailoring a less separated and hierarchical way of working and being.

Examining instances of lesbian therapist violations of professional prohibitions against assuming dual roles with clients, Brown (1989b) observes that, in oppressed populations, "alienation can promote a wholesale rejection of ethics created by dominants" (451). She believes that in the process of deconstructing male-dominant, heterosexist behavior codes and revisioning a distinctly lesbian sensibility for what behavior should look like, lesbians have opportunities to be both creative and exploitative.

Brown (1989a) has found feelings of fragility and poor boundaries in both lesbian clients and therapists involved in ethical violations, and she believes that some lesbian therapists can be as unprincipled as other therapists. She stresses this because of two widespread myths—that only male therapists abuse female clients and that lesbians are not violent and do not exploit others. Gonsiorek (1989) finds that clients often feel disloyal to the lesbian and gay community if they complain about a violation, fearing they themselves are perpetrating one more act of discrimination against their own (118).

As the subsequent therapist of lesbians violated by other lesbian therapists,

I have seen this loyalty to therapist and community replicate the very overdetermined family loyalties that often bring lesbians to treatment in the first place. Lesbian therapists behaving unethically may exploit these myths and loyalties to silence a client ambivalent about making a complaint.

Others observe the way in which vulnerable or narcissistic therapists and clients may mistake transference feelings for real love, forgetting that relationships have symbolic as well as "real" meanings to the participants. Elise (1991:65) believes that prior "outlaw" status and experience with secret, forbidden, sexual love for another woman can prime vulnerable therapists and clients to reenact this "forbidden secret" motif. She describes empathy as "the paradoxical ability to both cross and keep the boundary between one's self and another person" based on consideration for the needs of both and not just the needs of the therapist (65).

Mencher (1993) refers to the unique specialness of the client-centered focus of the therapy relationship and the wish to preserve it after termination so that the client can return in the future for the support of that very specialness. I share Mencher's strong belief that the therapy relationship is wonderfully unlike any other in allowing focus to be mostly on one person's development and nurture. It is one of the last Western venues where one's vanity and hungers are restrained for the sake of another.

I can think of no reason why we should take away this special onesidedness by converting it to any other form in which the therapist's needs and desires take equal weight and focus. I also cherish the idea that clients can over time return to this preserve for "tune-ups." Furthermore, I share the view that the transference lasts and would bedevil efforts to socialize as though the office bond were entirely real and mutual.

Brown (1988) observes that when therapy relationships are converted to sexual ones what is lost is "the belief in therapists as caring, altruistic individuals who are able to engage in a relationship where their own needs for ego gratification are of minimal importance" (255).

Brown doubts the client could avoid the conclusion that the therapist was developing sexual feelings and aims while the client, unawares, was exploring her own story, one that perhaps contained memories of being a sexual target. Brown is also concerned that other clients of the therapist will feel envy, failure (to attract), and worry that, unbeknownst to them, the therapist may be attracted to them, too.

Strean (1993) also describes erotic responsivity on the part of the therapist as a narcissistic act, "a demand for love in the absence of a capacity for loving" (29); whereas Slater (1993) believes lesbian erotic attachments are normal and act as a template for the mutual attractions that may develop in the therapy.

Anthony (1985) notes that erotic feelings can also develop when therapists and clients have not sufficiently experienced loving feelings for a woman in other social contexts. Both would need to be helped to come out more, to network more. Indeed, the therapist needs to preserve the "working alliance" precisely because the client needs education and support toward *more* relationships, so that she might find her own voice and empowerment in the world outside therapy.

While Appelbaum and Jorgenson (1991) have proposed a cooling off interval after which therapists and clients might have sexual relationships, Hall (in Brown 1988) warns from long experience that "the half-life of transference is greater than that of plutonium." Vasquez (1991) reminds that there are no known means of determining *when* a transference is resolved, nor any research that demonstrates that the transference *is* usually resolved. She adds that objectivity is almost universally compromised in the presence of social or sexual attraction (169).

Lesbian Relational Potentials

Many colleagues have suggested that it is our own hurts and hungers, as well as our need to rescue ourselves or our families of origin, that propel our particular use of self with clients (Sussman 1992). Each of us must plumb our own formation and current life balance, must come to terms with what we mean when we say we seek more mutuality with clients.

A search for mutuality based on lonely or angry hunger for mirroring, possession, or completion of fragmented self is doomed at the outset; such a hunger takes prisoners, and prison narratives are dominated by escapist and revenge fantasies. Neither can therapy be a dating bar, where lonely or damaged therapists target and prime vulnerable others to meet their own needs. These boundary crossings are about power, not about relationship, and, when tolerated, they make the lesbian therapy community unsafe for all.

Nor will we greatly succeed at mutuality using many of the antique therapy folkways: formality, jargon, appropriated expertise, restraint of the genuine, "neutrality." In such interactions the false self of therapist-in-role and the false self of the defended client are likely to forge a pseudoalliance in which both end up always quietly on guard against an outburst of spontaneity.

Eldridge (1993) proposes an ethical frame for therapy with lesbians that includes mutual negotiation and maintenance of boundaries safe for both; ethically preplanning together any elective contact in the community, holding both restraint and sharing as complex potentials on a case-by-case basis, and questioning and discussing with trusted colleagues when potential behaviors raise issues. She deems this whole process "ethics made relational" (15).

Working through internalized ambivalences about our own power, reducing the protective distance of the therapist role, and giving up many of the gratifications of "expert" status are three of the most difficult things lesbian therapists will have to achieve over time. We may not have been helped by thinking of what we do as a calling, a mission, an avocation; these representations tend to catch therapists in the trappings of specialness rather than the essence of relatedness at the ground level.

Something drew us to and holds us in "helping" professions rife with hierarchies, conformity, arcane languaging, and fantasies of "healing" largely unsupported by data. The advent of managed care, with its wholesale elimination of services and providers, has starkly revealed to us how relatively meaningless many of our traditional therapeutic structures and rituals are within the larger profit-driven systems dominating human services today. More and more are both therapists and clients rendered the object, not the subject, of our own lives.

These defining moments can also activate courageous survival strategies, heightened connection, and opportunities for creativity. Ethical activities together have already proven safe and experience-validating within thoughtful frameworks mutually negotiated. Conversations can assume more honesty, tonality, we-ness. Transference potentials in both therapist and client can be reviewed in consultation, researched, and shared through conferences and literature.

Through such steps lesbian therapists can show the way by continuing to envision and construct expanded yet safe and ethical ways of being and doing with clients.

REFERENCES

Anthony, B. 1985. Lesbian client-lesbian therapist: Opportunities and challenges for working together. In J. Gonsiorek, ed., *A guide to psychotherapy with gay and lesbian clients*, pp. 45–57. New York: Harrington Park.

Avis, J. 1991. Power politics in therapy with women. In T. J. Goodrich, ed., *Women and power: Perspectives on family therapy*, pp. 183–200. New York: Norton.

Appelbaum, P., and J. Jorgenson. 1993. Psychotherapist-patient sexual contact after termination of treatment: An analysis and a proposal. In J. Mindell, ed., *Issues in clinical psychology*, pp. 174–182. Dubuque: Brown and Benchmark.

Benjamin, J. 1988. *The bonds of love.* New York: Pantheon.

Berman, J. 1985. Ethical feminist perspectives on dual relationships with clients. In L. Rosewater and L. Walker, eds., *Handbook of feminist therapy: Women's issues in psychotherapy*, pp. 287–296. New York: Springer.

Brown, L. 1988. Harmful effects of posttermination sexual and romantic relationships between therapists and their former clients. *Psychotherapy* 25(2):249–255.

Brown, L. 1989a. Beyond thou shalt not: Thinking about ethics in the lesbian therapy community. *Women and Therapy* 8:13–25.

— 1989b. New voices, new visions: Towards a lesbian/gay paradigm for psychology. *Psychology of Women Quarterly* 13:445–458.

— 1990. Ethical issues and the business of therapy. In H. Lerman and N. Porter, eds., *Feminist ethics in psychotherapy*, pp. 60–69. New York: Springer.

— 1994. While waiting for the revolution: The case for a lesbian feminist psychotherapy. *Feminism and Psychology* 2(2):239–253.

Brown, L. and A. Brodsky. 1992. The future of feminist therapy. *Psychotherapy* 1(1):51–57.

Chu, J. 1991. The repetition compulsion revisited: Reliving dissociated trauma. *Psychotherapy* 28(2):327–332.

Dillon, C. 1993a. Developing self and voice in therapy with lesbians. *Developments: Newsletter of the Center for Women's Development at HRI Hospital (Boston, MA)* 2(3):1, 5.

— 1993b. Working with lesbian and gay clients. *Harvard Mental Health Letter* 9(8):4–6.

— 1994. Taking care while giving care. Unpublished ms.

Eldridge, N. 1993. Mutuality, psychotherapy, and ethics. In N. Eldridge, J. Mencher, and S. Slater, eds., *The conundrum of mutuality: A lesbian dialogue.* Work in Progress no. 62. Wellesley, Mass.: Stone Center Working Paper Series.

Elise, D. 1991. When sexual and romantic feelings permeate the therapeutic relationship. In C. Silverstein, ed., *Gays, lesbians, and their therapists*, pp. 52–67. New York: Norton.

Ellis, P., and B.C. Murphy. 1994. The impact of misogyny and homophobia on therapy with women. In M. Mirkin, ed., *Women in context: Toward a feminist reconstruction of psychotherapy*, pp. 48–73. New York: Guilford.

Gartrell, N. 1992. Boundaries in lesbian therapy relationships. *Women and Therapy* 12(3):29–50.

Gilligan, C., A. Rogers, and D. Tolman, eds. 1991. *Women, girls, and psychotherapy: Reframing resistance.* New York: Harrington Park.

Gonsiorek, J. 1989. Sexual exploitation by psychotherapists: Some observations on male victims and sexual orientation issues. In G. Schoener, J. Milgrom, J. Gonsiorek, E. Luepker, and R. Conroe, eds., *Psychotherapists' sexual involvement with clients: Intervention and prevention*, pp. 113–119. Minneapolis: Walk-In Counseling Center.

Greenspan, M. 1986. Should therapists be personal? Self-disclosure and therapeutic distance in feminist therapy. In D. Howard, ed., *The Dynamics of Feminist Therapy*, pp. 5–18. New York: Haworth.

Heyward, C. 1993. *When boundaries betray us: Beyond illusions of what is ethical in therapy and life*. New York: HarperCollins.

Jordan, J. 1990. *Courage in connection: Conflict, compassion, creativity*. Work in Progress no. 45. Wellesley, Mass.: Stone Center Working Paper Series.

Keith-Spiegel, P., and G. Koocher. 1985. *Ethics in psychology: Professional standards and cases*. New York: Random House.

Kitchener, K. 1988. Dual role relationships: What makes them so problematic? *Journal of Counseling and Development* 67:217–221.

Laird, J. 1994. Lesbian families: A cultural perspective. *Smith College Studies in Social Work* 64(3):263–296.

Mencher, J. 1993. Structural possibilities and constraints of mutuality in psychotherapy. In N. Eldridge, J. Mencher, and S. Slater, eds., *The conundrum of mutuality: A lesbian dialogue*. Work in Progress no. 62. Wellesley, Mass.: Stone Center Working Paper Series.

Miller, J., and I. Stiver. 1991. *A relational reframing of therapy*. Work in Progress no. 52. Wellesley, Mass.: Stone Center Working Paper Series.

— 1994. *Movement in therapy: Honoring the strategies of disconnection*. Work in Progress no. 65. Wellesley, Mass.: Stone Center Working Paper Series.

Perkins, R. 1991. Therapy for lesbians? The case against. *Feminism and Psychology* 1(3):325–338.

— 1992. Waiting for the revolution—or working for it?: A reply to Laura Brown and Katherine Sender. *Feminism and Psychology* 2(2):258–261.

Simon, R. 1992. *Clinical psychiatry and the law*. 2d ed. Washington, D.C.: American Psychiatric Press.

Slater, S. 1993. Contributions of the lesbian experience to mutuality in therapy relationships. In N. Eldridge, J. Mencher, and S. Slater, eds., *The conundrum of mutuality: A lesbian dialogue*. Work in Progress no. 62. Wellesley, Mass.: Stone Center Working Paper Series.

Strean, H. 1993. *Therapists who have sex with their patients: Treatment and recovery*. New York: Brunner/Mazel.

Surrey, J. 1991. The self-in-relation: A theory of women's development. In J. Jordan, A. Kaplan, J. B. Miller, I. Stiver, and J. Surrey, eds., *Women's growth in connection: Writings from the Stone Center*, pp. 51–66. New York: Guilford.

Sussman, M. 1992. *A curious calling*. Northvale, N.J.: Jason Aronson.

Vasquez, M. 1991. Sexual intimacies with clients after termination: Should a prohibition be explicit? *Ethics and Behavior* 1:45–61.

Weick, A., C. Rapp, P. Sullivan, and W. Kisthardt, 1989. A strengths perspective for social work practice. *Social Work* 34(4):350–354.

White, M., and D. Epston. 1990. *Narrative means to therapeutic ends*. New York: Norton.

CHAPTER THIRTEEN

Resilience in Lesbians: An Exploratory Study

Sandra C. Anderson and Barbara Sussex

IN RECENT YEARS risk research on children and families increasingly has focused on the concept of resilience—the capacity to recover from psychological trauma or to successfully adapt in the face of adversity. Despite considerable variability in definitions of resilience across studies, clinicians and researchers tend to agree that resilience is the capacity of a person to use challenges for psychological growth and to function psychologically at a level far higher than would be predicted from earlier developmental experiences (Baldwin, Baldwin, Kasser, Zax, Sameroff, and Seifer 1993; Garmezy 1974).

Over the twenty years of research on resilience, there has been little interest in exploring the strengths and resilience in the lesbian population despite the fact that lesbians demonstrate considerable fortitude and coping mechanisms in the face of an oppressive environment. Laird (1994) noted that few if any have asked,

> How can it be that in a world in which lesbians and gays are subjected to invisibility, silence, homophobia, and other forms of prejudice and discrimination, so many of these individuals, couples, families, and children seem to be doing as well as everyone else? . . . Could it be that lesbians and their families have special experiences and special strengths that give parents and children alike the courage to master adversity? (122)

This chapter is based on a beginning exploratory look at resilience in lesbians. Our study examines whether particular resiliencies identified in studies of children at risk are used by lesbians to deal with trauma during childhood as well as what strategies are used by lesbians to cope with prejudice and discrimination as adults.

Research on Lesbians

Historically, lesbians have been overlooked or pathologized in research endeavors. In her review of forty years of research on lesbians, Tully (1995) notes that most of the research between the 1960s and 1980s compared samples of lesbians with heterosexual women, seeking to determine whether lesbianism constituted pathology and/or focusing on the problematic and "dysfunctional" aspects of lesbianism. Interestingly, many of these studies have revealed, instead of psychopathology, evidence of lesbians' extraordinary strengths.

Comparative studies conducted since the 1980s show either no consistent differences between lesbians and heterosexual women in degree of mental health or illness (Bell, Weinberg, and Hammersmith 1981) or exceptional psychological and social functioning by lesbians. Lesbians have a greater sense of autonomy and independence (Hopkins 1969; Nichols and Lieblum 1986), a higher capacity for self-confidence, self-sufficiency, and assertiveness (Thompson, McCandless, and Strickland 1971; Wilson and Greene 1971), and a greater sensitivity to oppression and the need for social change (Pharr 1988). Rothblum (1988) notes that lesbians have always been in the "vanguard of social change" (10), initiating alternative health care, feminist therapy collectives, violence against women programs, and grassroots organizations.

Given the distinct cultural disadvantages of lesbian couples, it is interesting that they report significantly higher levels of cohesion, adaptability, and satisfaction than do heterosexual couples (Zacks, Green, and Marrow 1988). Lesbian couples want more time with their partners and place more value on equitable distribution of household duties (Blumstein and Schwartz 1983). Overall, studies indicate that the majority of lesbian couples view their relationship as extremely close, personally satisfying, and egalitarian (Peplau, Cochran, Rook, and Padesky 1978). In an attempt to explain the "superior functioning" of lesbian couples, Zacks, Green, and Marrow (1988) note that lesbians have fewer sanctions against ending unhappy relationships. The egalitarian nature of lesbian relationships enhances the competencies of both partners, and "the superior relational skills of two women enable them to form better-functioning relationships" (480).

A study on lesbian families by Levy (1992) showed that lesbian parents have high self-esteem, and family functioning is characterized by balanced levels of family cohesion and family organization. Levy notes that the lesbian parents in her study developed coping mechanisms that "challenged societal norms, asserted their human rights, and provided support for their lesbian identities" (29). The children of lesbian parents do not differ on most variables from children raised by heterosexual parents and may, in fact, be less rigid, more tolerant of diversity, more flexible in their own gender identities, and have a greater sense of well-being (Patterson 1992).

With the move toward a strengths perspective in social work practice and evidence that lesbians demonstrate high social and psychological functioning, the current trend in research is focused on exploration of lesbian functioning from a psychologically healthy perspective (Tully 1995). It is no longer necessary to have comparative samples of heterosexual women to "prove" that lesbians are the same or as well adjusted. Indeed, Rothblum (1988) states that it is important to acknowledge that lesbians are not just like heterosexual women. She says, "To equate lesbians and heterosexual women . . . denies several important processes that exist for lesbians and that do not exist for heterosexual women" (6). In fact, lesbianism may represent "increased mental health for women" (7) and the "nontraditional roles of lesbians may serve as a model of positive mental health for women in general" (1).

Is it possible that being lesbian in this society and thus having to deal with oppression leads to the development of resiliencies in lesbians? A study of 675 lesbians by Brooks (1981) suggests this possibility. Brooks found that lesbians' psychological and cognitive resources mediate the impact of oppression and that they appear to use the resiliencies of insight and independence (Wolin and Wolin 1994) to externalize oppressive practices. Cross (1995), in looking at the contextual factors within which families of color function, notes that "oppression, for all its damage to us, creates an environment where survival skills are developed and sharpened" (151). Swigonski (1995) also notes the relationship between oppression and resilience and suggests that lesbians develop strengths through their struggles with oppression. According to Swigonski, one characteristic of this strength is the claiming of a lesbian identity, which is a direct confrontation of heterosexist oppression and an act that leads to personal and interpersonal power. Certainly many people from marginalized populations develop positive identities in spite of oppression; it is also possible that members of stigmatized groups, such as lesbians, develop resiliencies because of oppression.

Research on Resilience

The majority of research on resilience involves longitudinal studies of children or adolescents. Longitudinal studies include children who have experienced high risk due to poverty, perinatal stress, family discord, parental alcoholism, mental illness, and/or low parental education (Chess 1989; Egeland, Carlson, and Sroufe 1993; Werner 1989, 1994; Werner and Smith 1982, 1992), children at risk because of mental illness in a parent (Anthony 1987; Bleuler 1984; Fisher, Kokes, Cole, Perkins, and Wynne 1987; Garmezy 1985; Garmezy and Devine 1984; Masten 1989; Musick, Stott, Spencer, Goldman, and Cohler 1987; Radke-Yarrow and Sherman 1990; Sameroff, Barocas, and Seifer 1984; Watt 1984; Worland, Weeks, and Janes 1987), white male adolescents at risk due to severe economic hardship (Felsman and Vaillant 1987), African American adolescent mothers (Furstenberg, Brooks-Gunn, and Morgan 1987), children reared in institutions or foster care (Festinger 1983; Rutter 1990), adolescents with chronic illnesses (Hauser, Vieyra, Jacobson, and Wertlieb 1985, 1989; Schwartz, Jacobson, Hauser, Dornbush 1989), children of criminal fathers (Kandel, Mednick, Kirkegaard-Sorensen, Hutchings, Knop, Rosenberg, and Schulsinger 1988), and maltreated children (Kaufman and Zigler 1989).

Three recent studies of resilience are based on in-depth interviews with successful adults (Valentine and Feinauer 1993; Higgins 1994; Wolin and Wolin 1994). Higgins's study included twenty-two women and nineteen men predominately white, well educated, and middle- to upper-middle class. She does not note sexual orientation. All had experienced extremely stressful childhoods and had a history of major psychopathology in at least one parent. Most also reported significant current psychopathology in at least one sibling. Like many earlier researchers, Higgins found that the resilient adults in her study possessed above-average intellectual competence, cognitive flexibility, good problem-solving and conflict resolution skills, an internal locus of control, relational competence with extended support systems, high self-esteem, good impulse control, and special talents and internal resources. They had a distant but understanding and even compassionate view of their families of origin. Valentine and Feinauer's study of twenty-two white women who had survived childhood sexual abuse (no sexual orientation noted) revealed similar resiliency themes. These women had the ability to find emotional support outside the family, the ability to think well of themselves, and the capacities for spirituality, external attribution of blame, and inner-directed locus of control. Wolin and Wolin conducted clinical interviews with twenty-five resilient survivors, all white and heterosexual. From these interviews emerged seven resiliencies, common themes of strategies used from childhood through adulthood for protection.

1. *Insight* is the mental habit of asking searching questions and giving honest answers. Insight begins with *sensing*, or an intuition that family life is strange and untrustworthy. Alert to danger, resilient children soon see the meaning of telltale changes in a parent's walk, dress, breath, or tone of voice. With adolescence sensing deepens into *knowing* the full extent of the family's troubles. In adulthood, awareness ripens into a penetrating *understanding* of themselves and other people (67).

2. *Independence* is first seen in children *straying* away from painful family scenes. Realizing that distance feels better than closeness, adolescents work at *disengaging* from their families emotionally. As adults, they master their hurt feelings and succeed in *separating* themselves from their troubled families (88).

3. *Relationships.* Children search out love by *connecting* or attracting the attention of available adults. These contacts give children a sense of their own appeal. They later begin actively *recruiting*—enlisting a friend, neighbor, teacher, policeman, or minister as a parent substitute. Recruiting becomes *attaching*, an ability to form and keep mutually gratifying relationships (111).

4. *Initiative* is the determination to assert oneself and master one's environment. The resilient carve out a part of life they can control, first by following the call of their curiosity to go *exploring*. They later begin *working* in a focused, organized, and goal-directed way. As adults, there is a deep attraction to *generating* projects that stretch the self and promote growth (136).

5. *Creativity* and *humor* are safe harbors of the imagination. They originate with *playing* or pretending to be a superhero, princess, space explorer, or ferocious beast. In adolescence this energy is channeled into *shaping* or making art, writing, music, painting, or dance. In some adults this evolves into *composing*. Most, however, mix the absurd and the awful and *laugh* at the combination (163).

6. *Morality,* the activity of an informed conscience, develops early as strong children in troubled families feel hurt, want to know why, and begin *judging* the rights and wrongs of their families. In adolescence judging becomes *valuing* principles such as decency, compassion, honesty, and fair play. As adults, they may dedicate themselves to causes and *serve* by devoting energy to institutions, community, and the world (184).

In addition to these strategies, used by individuals, protective factors exist in the school and community. Effective schools contain caring and supportive teachers and peers, have high expectations and foster high self-esteem, and provide opportunities for meaningful involvement and responsibility within the school environment (Garmezy 1991). Competent communities are also characterized by caring and support, high expectations, and participation. They contain vital social networks and adequate resources, view their youth as resources, and provide them with opportunities for civic participation (Benard 1991, 1993; Kurth-Schai 1988).

Study of Resilience in Lesbians

Our own study examines whether the protective factors identified in the lives of resilient children are used by lesbians and specifically focuses on the seven resiliencies identified by Wolin and Wolin (1994). In addition, we explore strategies used by lesbians to cope with prejudice and discrimination as adults.

Methodology

Design

This study used focus groups to learn about participants' experiences and perspectives. Focus groups were used because resilience has not been studied in the lesbian population, and it was anticipated that the groups would be helpful in generating hypotheses and developing interview questions and coding schemes that could be applied in the future to individuals and groups.

In the beginning phase of this project, we have moderated two focus groups with four participants per group. Each group met for two hours in one investigator's off-campus office, and the sessions were videotaped.

Participants

Requests for participation were mailed to two hundred members of the Lesbian Community Project, a nonprofit grassroots organization in a large metropolitan area. Potential participants were invited to respond if they met the following criteria: over the age of eighteen, grew up in an extremely stressful family, were psychologically mature and healthy in that they are able to sustain warm relationships with a wide range of people, and have sustained work satisfaction. If an individual met the criteria and consented to be a part of the study, one of the researchers contacted her to verify the inclusion criteria, explain the rationale for videotaping, and discuss convenient times for the focus group. It is important to note that the respondents were women who self-identified as resilient—not women who were psychologically tested and found, by some predetermined criteria, to *be* resilient.

Participants were all Caucasian and ranged in age from thirty-two to fifty-one, with a mean age of forty-three. They were well educated, with the minimal educational level being some college but no degree and the maximum level being attainment of a doctoral degree. Two women held master's degrees, one had a Ph.D., another had a J.D., and one was a third-year doctoral student. Four of the women were employed full-time, and one was working part-time. Of the three unemployed, two had been out of work for less than three months. One woman was collecting SSI for a disability incurred in a near fatal car accident five years previously. Five women had careers in the human service field, three were in social services, one was a college instructor, and one was an attorney and activist. The mean duration of employment in the same position was 11.4 years. Four of the women were in a relationship, with the length of a current relationship ranging from 2.5 years to 10 years. Historically, the longest relationship ranged from 1.5 years to 10 years, with a mean of 6 years and a mode of 7 years. All but one indicated they practiced a religion or some form of spirituality.

All participants had multiple stressors within their family of origin dating from birth or early childhood and continuing until at least eighteen years of age. Types of childhood stress and the number of women experiencing each stressor were parental substance abuse (four), familial physical abuse (three), extrafamilial physical and/or sexual abuse (three), absence of father (three), mental disorder in parent (two), sexual abuse by parent (two), emotional/verbal abuse (two), domestic violence (two), serious physical illness as a child (one), physical neglect (one).[1]

The participants had all undergone extensive and multiple types of counseling experience, with the number of years in counseling ranging from 1.5 to 19. Most had begun some form of therapy in their early twenties, and five were currently in therapy. The number of times participants sought therapy ranged from 2 to 8, with a mean of 4 times.

All participants had siblings, and the number of children in the family (including the participant) ranged from two to six. Six of the eight women reported past and/or current problematic behaviors in at least one sibling. These included alcoholism or addiction, abusive parenting, domestic violence, depression, obsessive/compulsive behavior, aggression, angry outbursts, and narcissism.

Data Collection

Written consent was obtained at the beginning of each group and the importance of confidentiality was stressed. Participants also completed a brief demographic questionnaire. A funnel structure was used for the focus groups by a dual moderator team. Each participant began by making a brief self-introduction tied in a general way to the stress experienced in childhood. The moderators then introduced some relatively broad questions, followed by questions seeking more depth, and ending with specific questions about resiliencies identified in earlier studies. The final question asked participants for their advice to other lesbians struggling with family stresses, prejudice, and discrimination.

Findings

The participants in this study possessed qualities similar to those of the resilient adults in Higgins's (1994) study, including above-average intellectual competence, cognitive flexibility, good problem-solving and conflict resolution skills, an internal locus of control, and relational competence with extended support systems. They also drew upon, to some extent, all the resiliencies identified by Wolin and Wolin (1993). These include insight, independence, relationships, initiative, humor, creativity, and morality.

Insight

At an early age most participants sensed problems within their families and were sensitive to potential danger. They developed the habit of "reading" both their parents' behaviors and their environment. By adolescence they were aware of the full extent of the family's problems. One participant, who had always known that something was wrong with her family, recalled: "I had friends, I could see that they didn't have parents like this." Most recognized in childhood that the parent's difficulties were not about them, but about something going on inside of the parent. Sometimes the labeling of a parent became a resilience. One daughter of an alcoholic father who was sexually and physically abusive said, "My father was sick. He was an alcoholic and he was sick. That's what my mother told me and that's what I operated under."

As adults, these resilient women have a deep understanding of themselves and others. A daughter of an abusive, alcoholic father discussed how she gained strength from her insight and understanding of her family:

I think for me, it's that I have a broader political understanding, so that helps to separate out myself from what's going on, to not personalize it. So, I tend to put things into a political context. I think I was working on that as a child, trying to put my whole family thing within a larger context. One of the themes of my life is to try to broaden the context of acceptable. That's where I've done my work. My father was ostracized for being who he was, and to a lesser extent my whole family was ostracized. . . . [Sensitivity] was one of the gifts that my father gave me. He wasn't able to give me much, but definitely that, empathy with people who were ostracized.

A daughter of a very distant father recalled getting information about her father's childhood when she became an adult:

This gave me a significant amount of empathy to not personalize his inability to connect with me. . . . There's a part of me that always felt very protective of him and . . . also to protect myself, to not open myself up to him, but also to protect him like he can't handle me, he can't handle my feelings, but over time I have opened up and he's responded mildly, so he and I are getting slowly . . . to have more of an honest relationship.

Another woman described an adult therapy experience in which she

completed a genogram with my family, did a lot of stuff with them, asked them tons of questions, found out a lot of stuff I didn't know. It really made sense to me, and I understood why I felt so miserable.

I got this information, worked through it, and understood a lot of this stuff was theirs and then I left and tried to figure out how to deal with me.

Independence

As children and adolescents, most of the women disengaged from their families emotionally and physically. They strayed away from painful family scenes by leaving on their bicycles, visiting other families, or withdrawing to their rooms. Many tried to be very good children, obedient and rule-bound. They tried to be invisible, isolating themselves for protection. As adults, the majority have separated themselves geographically from their families of origin. Although close geographical proximity is the exception, they have maintained some connection to their families. Regular telephone contact and occasional visits are the norm. Interestingly, a majority of the women are cut off from at least one of their siblings. The women believe that being different from their family is a good thing. One participant, the daughter of alcoholic and abusive parents, stated, "I was convinced that I was adopted. I still believe it and that they just haven't told me yet (laughter). So, the stuff they used to put on me, I would go, 'I'm not of this family. This is your stuff, not my stuff.'" One participant who was emotionally and physically abused stated:

As a child I learned to fight and now that I understand the psychology of it I guess that was a good strategy for me to keep people away from me . . . that raging anger that I still have. I guess it was just the anger, just my stubbornness. I guess that's what got me through. I went through periods in high school where I was really suicidal. Oddly enough it never occurred to me to run away. I didn't feel I had any place to go. I focused on school. I was a different person in school. I was a wallflower but I was intellectual. I hung with the literary magazine crowd. . . . I never felt like I belonged in that family so I was always fighting against them.

Another woman, whose family lives on the opposite coast, stated: "I need that distance. I find that whenever I'm around them I lose anything that I've gained. It's hard to figure out who I am and where I fit in." Most participants, however, remain attached to their parents and want their love. One participant stated:

When I had to separate, it was lifesaving for me. It was something I needed to do to fully have myself. And, it was painful and it continues to have elements of pain in it. And I'm still not sure and, in some sense, it continues to be trial and error. Depending on where I am and where they are, I have to keep readjusting that distance. But, I think for me the connection is still very important.

Relationships

These resilient women, as children, searched out love by attracting the attention of available adults. As adolescents, they connected with friends, neighbors, and teachers as parental substitutes. They found surrogate families and networks of friends. Some also had at least one loving relative. Two participants talked about their grandmothers: "She was unconditional." Another added, "Absolutely. Her eyes lit up every time I walked into the room."

A woman who had clinically depressed parents who neglected her remembered:

> I had an aunt who I just loved so I would spend a lot of weekends over there. And she liked me, you know? She would buy the ice cream I liked and she would just get things that were special to me. And it made me feel good, and it made me feel OK. . . . Throughout my childhood I sort of focused on different women, like teachers or my aunt or someone in church. There was something that just sort of attracted me to them and some of them didn't even know that I was there. . . . So, I would fantasize about them—that they would sort of take me, and love me, and nurture me.

One woman, whose mother was alcoholic and physically abusive, recalled:

> In high school I formed some close relationships with older teachers and had a couple of really good close female friends that I told [about the abuse]. They told their parents, and they eventually took me in and that's where I lived.

One participant discussed a combination of the resiliencies of insight and relationships. In describing how her friend's mother intervened on her behalf, she stated:

So I got to go to summer school, and I got to go with Mrs. C. It was really great. I connected really well with her then. And, it also really made me distrust my parents' judgment in the world that they really did not know, they were not, like, checking things out well for me and making good decisions about my life.

Some participants used their relationship skills to "take care of everybody else who was having a hard time." As adults, they attached to others, forming and keeping mutually gratifying relationships. As lesbians, they found this a more complex process.

I wouldn't say that attaching is easy. Being a lesbian within a larger society not sanctioning your relationships, you're swimming against the stream. So, that's felt like a challenge to me, to stay connected. When I came out as a lesbian, finding some way to stay connected with my former friends . . . has been a challenge. I think the process is just more complicated when you are a lesbian.

Initiative

Most of the participants were determined to assert themselves and master their environments. They carved out something they could control and worked in a focused and goal-directed way. As adults, they generated projects that stretched the self and promoted growth. Some concentrated on school work and became outstanding students. One daughter of a mentally ill mother recalled:

One of the things I did . . . I kept reevaluating what I wanted to do, what I wanted to be. So, I sort of got into this serial degree getting. I would go back to school every few years for another degree. It was like climbing a ladder in which I thought I would get more self-respect, some kind of credibility I would be acquiring over time which I didn't have any sense at all that I got in my family. It kind of went along with the invisibility, lack of credibility.

A daughter of an alcoholic and abusive father remembered:

Having that kind of a background has made me take much more responsibility for myself, for looking at my behavior, for deciding what more I needed. Was it counseling, learning to play the piano, getting another degree, or whatever it was to kind of raise myself after the fact.

Another resilient woman stated:

> I went through a phase of studying to be interesting, because my family message was that I was such a boring, mundane person. I started thinking of what would be risk taking that would make me look interesting and that my family members would not be willing or able to do themselves. Something that would give me some credibility in the family. So, I started climbing mountains. I got a lot out of it myself, so I didn't just do it for them. I also went to a course on personal goal setting and made a list of ten or fifteen things I wanted to do, and I did them all in two years. . . . There was a sense of taking control. . . . It was really liberating.

Another woman said:

> I had a child when I was eighteen years old and I very consciously chose . . . to give my daughter credit for everything that she did . . . and as a mom to be different . . . and to give my kid the things I didn't get. Though I couldn't give her a dad, I gave her other people and I also tried my best to let her know that she was an individual.

Creativity and Humor

Some participants had a rich fantasy life as children and wrote or painted during adolescence. They were also able to see the humor in their situations. A cynical sense of humor was common among the participants. A woman who was physically abused and neglected by her mentally ill parents recalled:

> I think I initially tried to find something I was really good at to get some attention and I never got there . . . so I shut down, I withdrew, I was very passive. I think that in many ways that was helpful . . . kinda used that to figure out that I *could* do something really well, and that was that I could be the most miserable person in the world and I really succeeded at that (laughter). For some reason it validated who I was because I couldn't compete with my sisters and my brothers.

Some described a vivid fantasy life. One recalled, "I think I had a fairly rich fantasy life, not about getting away from my family or anything, but about connecting with my dad." Another remembered, "A recurring thought or fantasy was that I used to pray to God, literally, that someday I'd find out that I was adopted." Some women recognized their attempts to use their creativity to survive. One stated:

> I think I really suppressed that (creativity) because my mom either did better than me or she took it as hers. Like I would make a little macrame belt when we were doing macramé and she'd say, "Oh, that's really interesting, how do you do that?" and I'd show her the three knots and she'd do this incredible wall hanging, you know? And I'd say, "Fuck this." And I also wrote. . . . I'd write poems and she'd xerox copies and hand them out to her friends. . . . So I stopped doing that. But now I'm taking it back.

Another woman, who was physically abused, remembered, "I wrote a lot of poetry . . . and I was on the board of directors of the school literary magazine, and I was published in the literary magazine." Another recalled:

> I never really thought of myself as creative . . . but I always had an ongoing fantasy about how I could off my mother and I was always by my dad's side when he was in the yard. I had a knack for making the yard look pretty . . . and models . . . model airplanes, model cars, jigsaw puzzles.

One woman laughed as she stated, "I dissociated. I wasn't present. There was somebody out there who was acting, pleasing, placating . . . but I was inside and I was protected. I was kind of separate from my feelings."

Morality

As children, the participants judged the behavior of their families and, as adolescents, developed principles of compassion and honesty. As adults, many dedicated themselves to causes and service to the community. Some were active in lesbian politics. A daughter of fundamentalist Christians who was physically abused by her father said, "I'm a very spiritual person. And, I know that when I was a kid I used to pray even after I decided I didn't believe in God." Another discussed her spirituality: "I use the concept of compassion, Taoism, writings of Stephen Levine, Ram Dass. . . . I use this because it's so easy for me with my upbringing to have compassion and understanding for other people." Another added:

> I've always had a belief that there was something other than myself helping me do that (recover) and that definition of what that is con-

stantly changes, and I'm constantly trying to redefine that, but it's my relationship with my higher power, whatever in any given moment that is—that's the thing that keeps me going.

Another woman, who was sexually and verbally abused by her father, has successfully devoted her life to public service:

One of the things I think I've done is try to be a bridge person. So I attempt to accomplish things in the world, to be seen as being as good as other people, to be seen as a bridge to my family, or other lesbians, or whatever, to knock down the stereotypes. The other thing I do is try to find commonalities with other people who are very different from me and to concentrate on those.

Strategies for Dealing with Prejudice and Discrimination

We were also interested in determining whether the women in our study used the same resiliencies to deal with prejudice and discrimination that they had used in their family of origin. Their responses reflected three major strategies. The most frequently mentioned resilience was insight, placing prejudice and discrimination into a broader political context and not taking them personally. The second strategy, reflecting the resilience of initiative, was to direct their energies toward social change by becoming heavily involved in social services or engaging in social activism within the lesbian community and/or the violence against women movement. Finally, the participants agreed that an important strategy in dealing with prejudice and discrimination is to live in a large city.

Participant Advice

The final focus group question was about the advice participants would give someone else dealing with similar childhood stresses. The most frequent advice was to stay connected to other people, not isolate yourself, and get help if at all possible. One woman stated, "You don't have to be alone. There are other people out there. Try to connect, keep trying to connect, and be kind to yourself." Another added, "Trust yourself, have faith in yourself, keep trying to find someone to talk to, [someone to] validate your feelings." A woman who was physically abused throughout her childhood agreed, adding, "I've met some incredible people along the line who have helped me to open my eyes to how things could be." And, finally, the advice of a woman who was physically abused by an alcoholic mother, "However people find a sense of family, it's vital. . . . I mean, family is incredible but it doesn't have to be your blood family . . . however we find family." The second kind of advice offered to others was to leave bad situations if at all possible, and the third suggestion was to recognize that what is going on in your family is not about you and try to reframe it into a challenge or opportunity.

In summary, the most important wisdom passed on to those experiencing extreme stress is to use the resiliencies of insight, independence, and relationship.

Implications for Social Work Practice

The resilient lesbians in this study, like resilient participants in earlier studies, recognize that their families are different and untrustworthy, draw boundaries between themselves and their disturbed parents, and develop connections with healthier adults. They learn to take charge of problems, use creativity and humor to deal with stress, and become conscientious contributors to their communities.

Historically, social workers have tended to view troubled families as toxic and child survivors as their victims. It is also possible, however, to view the troubled family as an opportunity. As noted by Wolin and Wolin (1994): "As a result of the interplay between damage and challenge, the survivor is left with pathologies that do not disappear completely and with resiliencies that limit their damage and promote their growth and well-being" (16). According to Wolin and Wolin, the critical shift is from thinking of self as a damaged victim to considering self a resilient survivor. They advise survivors to discard the myth that family problems are inevitably perpetuated multigenerationally, to stop believing that they will feel better by repeatedly examining the damage they have suffered, and to stop blaming their parents for hurting them. As they rewrite their stories as ones of resilience, their feelings and behaviors are greatly influenced. Although survivors cannot change the past, they can change the way they understand it. The social worker can help enormously in reframing stories around resilience instead of damage. In focusing on specific resiliencies, clients can change their views of self from "damaged goods" to "one who has prevailed."

It is important to note that all the lesbians in this study had had extensive counseling experience that included private therapists, 12-step recovery groups, and other community support groups. It is possible that participants with counseling experience felt more comfortable volunteering for the study, resulting in a bias in this particular sample. However, the high use of counseling by lesbians has been noted in a number of studies (see, e.g., Bradford, Ryan, and Rothblum 1994; Morgan 1992). In Morgan's study 77.5 percent of lesbians, compared to 28.9 percent of heterosexual women, had been in therapy. Although both Morgan's sample and the sample in this study were all Caucasian, Bradford, Ryan, and Rothblum's survey (1994) of 1,925 lesbians from diverse racial and ethnic backgrounds also showed a high use (73 percent) of counseling by lesbians. A higher percentage of Caucasian lesbians (74 percent) had used counseling compared to Latina lesbians (61 percent) and African American lesbians (61 percent). Still, the range is higher than the percentage for heterosexuals in Morgan's study. This high use of counseling by lesbians suggests even more of an imperative for social work practitioners to learn about the diversity, special issues, needs, resources, and resiliencies of the lesbian population—regardless of whether one is working in private practice, in substance abuse programs, or in community-based mental health clinics. Social workers need to be better educated on how to assess individuals and families with respect to protective as well as risk factors. A focus on resiliency places importance on the concept of empowerment, helping people to discover their strengths and resources. It is consistent with a feminist worldview and provides a useful paradigm to guide work with lesbians and other oppressed groups (Levy 1995). Weick (1992) notes that a strengths-based perspective challenges the assumptions embedded in theories of normal human development—assumptions that tend to pathologize lesbian developmental trajectories—and leads to a more expansive view of how people develop. Stewart (1994) notes that no one is ever *only* oppressed. Everyone is capable of personal agency, the demonstration of action toward attaining some power. It is critical to recognize women's agency in the midst of social constraint and oppression, particularly when women themselves don't perceive their own strengths. When people's strengths are supported they are more likely to develop greater self-esteem and to believe in their own capacity for growth.

Laird (1994) notes that therapy can be seen as the "writing of a new story" (126) in which problem-saturated events can be transformed into new strength-based narratives. Therapists working with heterosexual parents who have lesbian children and/or with lesbian couples can help them to reconstruct new narratives based on resiliency. Clients are often unaware of the negative self stories they hold and the context in which these stories have been shaped. Through examination and reframing of these stories the client (individual, couple, or family) may be able to identify the positive ways she survived childhood trauma as well as the ways she continues to show resilience in the face of oppression.

Hall (1992) also notes the importance of reframing people's experiences into "images of recovery" (92). In her study of how lesbians recover from alcohol problems, she found that the ways lesbians conceptualize their healing serve as frameworks for interpreting the meaning of their experiences. An empowerment image of recovery encouraged the lesbians in her study to take control, to trust their own instincts, and helped them to identify the connections between their addiction and institutional oppressions such as racism, classism, sexism, and heterosexism.

As the lesbians in this study noted, family is an important concept, but the definition does not necessarily imply nuclear family. To work with family issues of lesbians, social workers need to examine their own homophobia and attitudes about lesbian families as well as support alternative family structures. Faria (1994), in discussing the trend toward family preservation services, notes that the curricula of in-service training programs, which is the usual mode of education for family preservation workers, includes little, if any, content on lesbian families and their special needs and problems. Social workers need training in how to identify and appreciate the strengths and resources needed by lesbians to cope in a homophobic environment as well as how to advocate for and enact policy to change societal conditions. Nuclear family members and children of lesbian couples must negotiate a range and complexity of feelings. Laird (1994) states that it is helpful for "family members . . . to revise their own narratives in ways that help them retain their pride in 'familyness,' and that help them recast their past, present, and future stories in empowering ways" (135).

Perhaps the most difficult task for family-centered therapists is recognizing that the mental health of some resilient adults who have been severely traumatized is predicated on having little or no contact with their families of origin. As stated by Higgins (1994):

> If your therapeutic model of mental health assumes that ongoing family interactions are essential, you may be doing your clients as much of an injustice as a therapist who assumes that the lot should be fired. You need to realize that, at times, it is simply too physically and psychologically dangerous to "work it out." Recognize that resolving the past does not necessarily assume ongoing interactions. Sometimes

family members are either too toxic or too unrelenting to allow any healthy resolution, necessitating thoughtfully attenuated, suspended, or severed contact for adult mental health to flourish. If you have not considered that sometimes growth can occur only outside ongoing contact with members of the fold, you will have difficulty helping many of the maltreated. (343)

Werner (1994) notes that successful adaptation is possible as long as there is a favorable balance between stressful life events and protective factors. Thus, social work intervention should be directed at either decreasing exposure to risk factors or increasing the number of protective factors in the lives of vulnerable children. School social workers are in a unique position to develop programs that will enhance resilience (Zuna, Turner, and Norman 1993). Many resilient children find school the only source of surrogacy and the only consistently safe place in their lives (Higgins 1994). Homosexual youths are an especially high-risk group. Studies show that they lack positive lesbian and gay male role models, have limited support systems, and have higher suicide rates (Remafedi, Farrow, and Deisher 1993).

It is important that social work educators recognize that focusing on strengths and resilience does not mean that we forget how to assess problems. Liddle (1994) points out that we should reject both the "politically correct but naive promise that all things are possible" as well as the "nihilistic conclusion that the odds facing the truly disadvantaged are impossible to overcome" (173). A potential danger, implicit in research on resilience, is expecting extraordinary outcomes from everyone experiencing childhood trauma and placing all blame or credit on individuals for their successes or failures (Rigsby 1994). Taylor (1994) notes that adaptive behaviors take many forms and that not all people are equally equipped to overcome barriers to development.

The identification of traits and factors associated with resilience is only a beginning. Future research must focus on the developmental processes that underlie resilient behaviors. Can resilience be developed in adults who do not demonstrate resilience in childhood or adolescence? We have relatively little knowledge about what protective factors can be enhanced, in what children, at what age, through what types of programs (Zunz, Turner, and Norman 1993). Resilience must be understood developmentally with attention to gender, culture, and time (Cicchetti and Garmezy 1993; Liddle

1994). Only then will we be able to develop intervention programs that consistently enhance resilient behavior (Garmezy 1993; Masten, Best, and Garmezy 1990). Gordon and Wang (1994) pose a number of unresolved conceptual issues. Is resilience a quality of persons or their life circumstances? Can resilience as a situationally dependent construct be studied with a view to generalization? If a person does not find a situation stressful, even if others do, has he or she shown resilience in overcoming it? Do children from stress-resistant families necessarily have resistant internal mechanisms? Werner (1990) notes that few studies explore the interplay between multiple risk and protective factors at all three levels—the individual, family, and larger social context.

Research on resilience in lesbians is in its beginning phase. The current study represents a small sample of middle-class Caucasian women only. The sample is also biased in that it represents lesbians who were affiliated with a lesbian organization. The authors intend to continue their research into resiliency in lesbians with larger samples that include women of color, women from various socioeconomic classes, and women from a range of age groups. The authors recognize the diversity within the lesbian community and want to hear lesbians' stories of survival from childhood trauma as well as their strategies for coping with an oppressive society.

There are several questions that emerge from this study for future research. Are the women in this sample any different than other resilient women who came from traumatic families *because* they are lesbian? In other words, is there something about the experience of being lesbian that contributes to their resilience? Have they had to develop more power from being in a marginalized position? As children, did they have more options than heterosexual girls? Were they less likely to be locked into rigid, more passive sex roles? What is the relationship between resilience and the development of lesbian identity? How is resilience related to coming out issues and family reactions to lesbianism? What is the relationship between resiliencies developed by lesbians early in life as a reaction to trauma and their handling of prejudice and discrimination as adults? Are they advantaged by their ability to build a new family/community? Is it possible that being lesbian gives women a dual vision, allowing them more ability to question damaging stories about themselves from family and from society?

Sang (1989) notes that "in the name of 'science,' a group of people [lesbians] were labeled disturbed, despite the fact that there was no evidence to substantiate this position" (95). It is time to acknowledge that lesbians may have a great deal to teach us about "bouncing back" from adversity. Liddle

(1994) concludes, "The 'big bang' of the discovery of resilience may be over, but the most fruitful and productive rewards from this notion lie ahead. Critical examination and reexamination of resilience can help realize this possibility" (175).

NOTES

The following materials are available from the authors upon request: Request for Participation, Informed Consent Form, Demographic Questionnaire, Focus Group Questions.

1. The rates of abuse for lesbians in this study are to be expected, given that purposive sampling was used specifically to select lesbians with multiples abuses in their backgrounds. However, given the unsupported, stereotyping idea that sexual abuse, particularly incest, *causes* lesbianism, it is important to note that the rates of incest and rape for lesbians are similar to the rates for the general female population (see discussion in Bradford, Ryan, and Rothblum 1994:240).

REFERENCES

Anthony, E. 1987. Children at high risk for psychosis growing up successfully. E. Anthony and B. Cohler, eds., *The invulnerable child*, pp. 147–184. New York: Guilford.

Baldwin, A., C. Baldwin, T. Kasser, M. Zax, A. Sameroff, and R. Seifer. 1993. Contextual risk and resiliency during late adolescence. *Development and Psycho-pathology* 5:741–761.

Bell, A., M. Weinberg, and S. Hammersmith, 1981. *Sexual preference: Its development in men and women.*. Bloomington: Indiana University Press.

Benard, B. 1991. *Fostering resiliency in kids: Protective factors in the family, school, and community*. Available from the Western Regional Center for Drug-Free Schools and Communities, Northwest Regional Educational Laboratory, 101 SW Main Street, Suite 500, Portland, OR 97204.

— 1993. *Turning the corner: From risk to resiliency*. Available from the Western Regional Center for Drug-Free Schools and Communities, Far West Laboratory for Educational Research and Development, 730 Harrison Street, San Francisco, CA 94107.

Bleuler, M. 1984. Different forms of childhood stress and patterns of adult psychiatric outcome. In N. Watt, E. Anthony, L. Wynne, and J. Rolf, eds., *Children at risk for schizophrenia*, pp. 537–542. New York: Cambridge University Press.

Blumstein, P., and P. Schwartz. 1983. *American couples: Money, work, sex.* New York: William Morrow.

Bradford, J., C. Ryan, and E. Rothblum. 1994. National lesbian health care survey: Implications for mental health care. *Journal of Consulting and Clinical Psychology* 62:228–242.

Brooks, V. 1981. *Minority stress and lesbian women.* Lexington, Mass.: Lexington.

Chess, S. 1989. Defying the voice of doom. In T. Dugan and R. Coles, eds., *The child in our times: Studies in the development of resiliency,* pp. 179–199. New York: Brunner/Mazel.

Cicchetti, D., and N. Garmezy. 1993. Prospects and promises in the study of resilience. *Development and Psychopathology* 5:497–502.

Cross, T. 1995. Understanding family resiliency from a relational world view. In H. I. McCubbin, E. A. Thompson, A. I. Thompson, and J. E. Fromer, eds., *Resiliency in ethnic minority families. Native and immigrant American families,* 1:143–157. Madison: University of Wisconsin System.

Egeland, B., E. Carlson, and A. Sroufe. 1993. Resilience as process. *Development and Psychopathology* 5:517–528.

Faria, G. 1994. Training for family preservation practice with lesbian families. *Families in Society: The Journal of Contemporary Human Services* 75(7):416–422.

Felsman, J., and G. Vaillant. 1987. Resilient children as adults: A forty-year study. In E. J. Anthony and B. J. Cohler, eds., *The invulnerable child,* pp. 289–314. New York: Guilford.

Festinger, T. 1983. *No one ever asked us.* New York: Columbia University Press.

Fisher, L., R. Kokes, R. Cole, P. Perkins, and L. Wynne. 1987. Competent children at risk: A study of well-functioning offspring of disturbed parents. In E. J. Anthony and B. J. Cohler, eds., *The invulnerable child,* pp. 211–228. New York: Guilford.

Furstenberg, F., J. Brooks-Gunn, and S. Morgan. 1987. *Adolescent mothers in later life.* New York: Cambridge University Press.

Garmezy, N. 1974. Children at risk: The search for the antecedents of schizophrenia. Part 1. Conceptual models and research methods. *Schizophrenia Bulletin* 8:14–90.

— 1985. Stress-resistant children: The search for protective factors. In J. E. Stevenson, ed., *Recent research in developmental psychopathology: Journal of Child Psychology and Psychiatry,* suppl. 4, pp. 213–233. Oxford, England: Pergamon.

— 1991. Resiliency and vulnerability to adverse developmental outcomes associated with poverty. *American Behavioral Scientist* 34:416–430.

— 1993. Children in poverty: Resilience despite risk. *Psychiatry* 56:127–136.

Garmezy, N., and V. Devine. 1984. Project Competence: The Minnesota studies of children vulnerable to psychopathology. In N. Watt, E. Anthony, L. Wynne, and J. Rolf, eds., *Children at risk for schizophrenia; A longitudinal perspective,* pp. 289–303. New York: Cambridge University Press.

Gordon, E., and M. Wang. 1994. Epilogue: Educational resilience—challenges and prospects. In M. C. Wang and E. W. Gordon, eds., *Educational resilience in inner-city America: Challenges and prospects,* pp. 191–194. Hillsdale, N.J.: Lawrence Erlbaum.

Hall, J. 1992. Lesbian images of recovery. *Health Care for Women International* 13:181–188.

Hauser, S., M. Vieyra, A. Jacobson, and C. Wertlieb. 1985. Vulnerability and resilience in adolescence: Views from the family. *Journal of Early Adolescence* 5:81–100.

— 1989. Family aspects of vulnerability and resilience in adolescence: A theoretical perspective. In T. Dugan and R. Coles, eds., *The child in our times: Studies in the development of resiliency*, pp. 109–133. New York: Brunner/Mazel.

Higgins, G. 1994. *Resilient adults overcoming a cruel past.* San Francisco: Jossey-Bass.

Hopkins, J. 1969. The lesbian personality. *British Journal of Psychiatry* 115:1433–1436.

Kandel, E., S. Mednick, L. Kirkegaard-Sorensen, B. Hutchings, J. Knop, R. Rosenberg, and F. Schulsinger. 1988. IQ as a protective factor for subjects at high risk for antisocial behavior. *Journal of Consulting and Clinical Psychology* 56:224–226.

Kaufman, J., and E. Zigler. 1989. The intergenerational transmission of child abuse. In D. Cicchetti and V. Carlson, eds., *Child maltreatment: Theory and research on the causes and consequences of child abuse and neglect*, pp. 129–150. New York: Cambridge University Press.

Kurth-Schai, R. 1988. The roles of youth in society: A reconceptualization. *Educational Forum* 52:131–132.

Laird, J. 1994. Lesbian families: A cultural perspective. In M. Mirkin, eds., *Women in context*, pp. 118–148. New York: Guilford.

Levy, E. 1992. Strengthening the coping resources of lesbian families. *Families in Society: The Journal of Contemporary Human Services* 73(1):23–31.

Levy, E. 1995. Feminist social work practice with lesbian and gay clients. In N. Van Den Bergh, ed., *Feminist practice in the twenty-first century*, pp. 278–294. Washington, D.C.: NASW.

Liddle, H. 1994. Contextualizing resiliency. In M. C. Wang and E. W. Gordon, eds., *Educational resilience in inner-city America*, pp. 167–177. Hillsdale, N.J.: Lawrence Erlbaum.

Masten, A. 1989. Resilience in development: Implications of the study of successful adaptation for developmental psychopathology. In D. Cicchetti, ed., *The emergence of a discipline: Rochester symposium on developmental psychopathology*, 1:261–294. Hillsdale, N.J.: Lawrence Erlbaum.

Masten, A., K. Best, and N. Garmezy. 1990. Resilience and development: Contributions from the study of children who overcome adversity. *Development and Psychopathology* 2:425–444.

Morgan, K. 1992. Caucasian lesbians' use of psychotherapy. A matter of attitude? *Psychology of Women Quarterly* 16:127–130.

Musick, J., F. Stott, K. Spencer, J. Goldman, and B. Cohler. 1987. Maternal factors related to vulnerability and resiliency in young children at risk. In E. Anthony and B. Cohler, eds., *The invulnerable child*, pp. 229–252. New York: Guilford.

Nichols, M., and S. Lieblum. 1986. Lesbianism as a personal identity and social role: A model. *Affilia* 1:48–59.

Patterson, C. 1992. Children of lesbian and gay parents. *Child Development* 63:1025–1042.

Peplau, L., S. Cochran, K. Rook, and C. Padesky. 1978. Loving women: Attachment and autonomy in lesbian relationships. *Journal of Social Issues* 34;84–100.

Pharr, S. 1988. *Homophobia: A weapon of sexism*. Inverness, Cal.: Chardon.

Radke-Yarrow, M., and T. Sherman. 1990. Hard growing: Children who survive. In J. Rolf, A. Masten, D. Cicchetti, K. Nuechterlain, and S. Weintraub, eds., *Risk and protective factors in the development of psychopathology*, pp. 97–119. New York: Cambridge University Press.

Remafedi, G., J. Farrow, and R. Deisher. 1993. Risk factors for attempted suicide in gay and bisexual youth. In L. D. Garnets and D. C. Kimmel, eds., *Psychological perspectives on lesbian and gay male experiences*, pp. 486–499. New York: Columbia University Press.

Rigsby, L. 1994. The Americanization of resilience: Deconstructing research practice. In M. Wang and B. Gordon, eds., *Educational resilience in inner-city America: Challenges and prospects*, pp. 85–94. Hillsdale, N.J.: Lawrence Erlbaum.

Rothblum, E. 1988. Introduction: Lesbianism as a model of a positive lifestyle for women. *Women and Therapy* 8(1/2):1–12.

Rutter, M. 1990. Psychosocial resilience and protective mechanisms. In J. Rolf, A. Masten, D. Cicchetti, K. Neuchterlein, and S. Weintraub, eds., *Risk and protective factors in the development of psychopathology*, pp. 181–214. New York: Cambridge University Press.

Sameroff, A., R. Barocas, and R. Seifer. 1984. The early development of children born to mentally ill women. In N. Watt, E. Anthony, L. Wynne, and J. Rolf, eds., *Children at risk for schizophrenia: A longitudinal perspective*, pp. 482–514. New York: Cambridge University Press.

Sang, B. 1989. New directions in lesbian research, theory, and education. *Journal of Counseling and Development* 68:92–96.

Schwartz, J., A. Jacobson, S. Hauser, and B. Dornbush. 1989. Explorations of vulnerability and resilience: Case studies of diabetic adolescents and their families. In T. Dugan and R. Coles, eds., *The child in our times: Studies in the development of resiliency*, pp. 134–156. New York: Brunner/Mazel.

Stewart, A. 1994. Toward a feminist strategy for studying women's lives. In C. Franz and A. Stewart, eds., *Women creating lives: Identities, resilience, and resistance*, pp. 11–36. Boulder: Westview.

Swigonski, M. 1995. Claiming a lesbian identity as an act of empowerment. *Affilia* 19(4):413–425.

Taylor, R. 1994. Risk and resilience: Contextual influences on the development of African-American adolescents. In M. Wang and E. Gordon, eds., *Education resilience in inner-city-America: Challenges and prospects*, pp. 119–130. Hillsdale, N.J.: Lawrence Erlbaum.

Thompson, N. L., B. R. McCandless, and B. R. Strickland. 1971. Personal adjustment of male and female homosexuals and heterosexuals. *Journal of Abnormal Psychology* 78:237–240.

Tully, C. 1995. In sickness and in health: Forty years of research on lesbians. *Journal of Gay and Lesbian Social Services* 3(1):1–18.

Valentine, L. and L. Feinauer. 1993. Resilience factors associated with female survivors of childhood sexual abuse. *American Journal of Family Therapy* 21:216–224.

Watt, N. 1984. In a nutshell: The first two decades of high-risk research in schizophrenia. In N. Watt, E. Anthony, L. Wynne, and J. Rolf, eds., *Children at risk for schizophrenia: A longitudinal perspective*, pp. 572–595. New York: Cambridge University Press.

Weick, A. 1992. Building a strengths perspective for social work. In D. Saleebey, ed., *The strengths perspective in social work practice*, pp. 18–26. New York: Longman.

Werner, E. 1989. Children of the garden island. *Scientific American* 260:106–111.

— 1990. Protective factors and individual resilience. In S. Meisels and J. Shonkoff, eds., *Handbook of early childhood intervention*, pp. 97–116. New York: Cambridge University Press.

— 1994. Overcoming the odds. *Developmental and Behavioral Pediatrics* 15:131–136.

Werner, E., and R. Smith. 1982. *Vulnerable but invincible: A study of resilient children.* New York: McGraw-Hill.

— 1992. *Overcoming the odds: High risk children from birth to adulthood.* Ithaca: Cornell University Press.

Wilson, M., and R. Greene. 1971. Personality characteristics of female homosexuals. *Psychological Reports* 28:407–412.

Wolin, S. J., and S. Wolin. 1994. *The resilient self.* New York: Villard.

Worland, J., D. Weeks, and C. Janes. 1987. Predicting mental health in children at risk. In E. Anthony and B. Cohler, eds., *The invulnerable child*, pp. 185–210. New York: Guilford.

Zacks, E., R. Green, and J. Marrow. 1988. Comparing lesbian and heterosexual couples on the Circumplex model: An initial investigation. *Family Process* 27:471–484.

Zunz, S., S. Turner, and E. Norman. 1993. Accentuating the positive: Stressing resiliency in school-based substance abuse prevention programs. *Social Work in Education* 15:169–176.

CHAPTER FOURTEEN

The Application of Control Mastery Theory in Clinical Practice with Lesbians

Jo Nol

THE WORK OF THE SAN FRANCISCO PSYCHOTHERAPY RESEARCH GROUP has produced an elegant, powerful, and empirically supported theory of the technique of psychotherapy. This chapter introduces the theory, known as control mastery and, through case discussions, illustrates its application and usefulness in therapy with lesbian clients.

Cases have been selected to demonstrate the theory's application and also to support the argument that, for a successful outcome with lesbian clients (as with any client), the plan for treatment needs to be specific to the individual. Of course, any therapist who works with members of a minority group needs to be sensitive to their cultural and social realities as well as to how those realities have been integrated into clients' complex meaning systems. Control mastery theory tells us how to listen for what the client needs from us.

Control Mastery Theory

Control mastery theory holds that people are motivated to adapt to reality, continually making and refining inferences about themselves and others. Some of these beliefs, although adaptive when they originated, may later come to be problematic. These include those called pathogenic beliefs, that is, beliefs that serve to lower self-esteem and restrict a person's ability to pursue reasonable goals, such as attaining a fulfilling relationship or having a relaxed, meaningful, and satisfying life. Control mastery theory posits that pathogenic beliefs, both conscious and unconscious, underlie much of psychopathology.[1]

This body of theory is the result of over twenty years of research begun by Joseph Weiss and Harold Sampson and continued collaboratively with the San Francisco Psychotherapy Research Group. The original research was based on the study of transcripts of completed psychoanalyses and was later modified for application to psychodynamic psychotherapy, including short-term work. Originally, Weiss wanted to find out what actually occurred in therapy to produce change. Out of this continuing research came an understanding of how psychotherapy works (Shilkret and Shilkret 1993).[2]

Control mastery theorists argue that, beginning in infancy, people develop an array of beliefs about themselves and others in response to experiences and events, especially those concerning important people in their environment. These early beliefs are shaped by the child's relative self-centeredness and immature reasoning as well as his or her investment in parents and siblings. Pathogenic beliefs are those that convince the child to give up pursuit of normal developmental goals. This seemingly paradoxical outcome occurs because often such beliefs involve a fear that not relinquishing the goals would do damage to important others or to the self. For example, a child who watches her parents struggle with financial problems might begin to feel undeserving of anything they might give her, coming to believe that if she were to get things she wanted, others would be deprived. As an adult, she may then deprive herself even when she can comfortably attain things she wants.

In adulthood these beliefs function both unconsciously and consciously in relationships and other life areas to keep people from growth-promoting self-expression and satisfying experiences. Unconscious guilt plays a major role in holding the pathogenic beliefs in place. The theory identifies two forms of guilt that are prevalent—survivor guilt and separation guilt (Loewald 1979; Modell 1965, 1971). A person who suffers from survivor guilt feels that she has gotten something at the expense of her siblings and parents. This may underlie her inability to let herself have something or, if she does allow it, she will find a way to punish herself. The example in the previous paragraph illustrates survivor guilt. Separation guilt is based on the belief that to let oneself separate and become independent is dangerous.

In its extreme form a person may not allow herself to have her own life, separate from another. A less extreme example is of a child, whose parent is easily angered at her striving for greater autonomy, who decides that to be independent in any arena is damaging to others. Thus, a child whose parents have difficulty accepting her need to practice saying "no" may come to believe that having an opinion that differs from others is dangerous. She may grow into an adult who cannot allow herself to hold her own opinions and always strives to agree with others.

This theory also emphasizes the role of trauma in shaping a person's experience of self. Traumatic events influence the development of pathogenic beliefs in two ways. A discrete event, such as the death of a parent, which most clinicians would agree can be extremely traumatic to a child, may result in the child's misunderstanding of her own power to affect reality. For example, the child who in a moment of rage may have wished her mother dead could conclude that she was responsible for the tragedy. Another kind of trauma involves experiences that are woven into the fabric of the child's daily life. These are incorporated into a self-image shaped by pathogenic beliefs. For instance, a child growing up in poverty with a very burdened parent may come to believe that she does not deserve anything better for herself and may in adulthood unconsciously prevent herself from pursuing goals she clearly has the capacity to achieve.

In control mastery theory it is assumed that people enter treatment with an unconscious plan to invite the therapist to help them disconfirm and master their pathogenic beliefs. It is the therapist's task to infer this plan through understanding the construction the client has made of her life, especially her pathogenic beliefs, and to act in ways that do not support her worst fears about herself. In control mastery theory the treatment plan is known as the plan formulation, and consists of 1. goals the client has for therapy, 2. pathogenic beliefs or obstructions that prevent goal attainment, 3. possible tests that will be posed to the therapist, and 4. insights that will be helpful to the progress of the therapy.

The overarching goal involves the overcoming of pathogenic beliefs. The heart of the work is accomplished through the client's "testing" of the therapist. Testing is often undertaken through the transference, which is conceptualized in two ways. In the first conception, a traditional view of transference, the client reenacts aspects of her role as a child and attributes to the therapist motivations and feelings that the client assumed her parents held. In the second conception, which represents a unique contribution of the theory, transference is seen as passive-into-active testing, in which the client assumes the role of her parents and treats the therapist as the client was treated as a child. For example, a client who as a child worried helplessly about her parents, who engaged in substance abuse and criminal activities, may behave in ways that worry the therapist and leave the therapist feeling helpless. Or a client who has developed the belief that she deserves to be rejected may be critical and rejecting of the therapist in order to see if the therapist is bothered by it.

It is important to note that human beings are always testing as a fundamental part of ongoing adaptation to their interpersonal environment. In therapy the client watches the reactions of the therapist. For progress to be made the therapist must pass the client's test; this involves not responding in ways that the client did as a child or in the ways the client's parents did. Thus, it is essential that the therapist accurately identify the client's plan, including recognizing the tests and goals. Each plan formulation is specific to the individual client, and the therapist uses his or her own unique personality to shape a corrective cognitive and emotional relationship with the client.

Pathogenic beliefs are formed, of course, in the context of wider social influences that shape the behavior of the important people in the child's environment. Since children generally trust that their caretakers are correct and have no one to whom to compare them, they will shape themselves through compliance with perceived expectations. Thus, if the family carries messages from the larger social world that suggest that girls are weak, a girl may comply by being weak, believing that she must do so to preserve the ties with people she needs and loves. Or if a girl's mother has assumed traditional female traits such as being passive or unambitious, her daughter may identify with her out of loyalty.

Sexism and Homophobia

Lesbians have to contend both with what it means to be female in a world that at best is uneasy about femaleness and with what it means to be homosexual in a world that certainly is unwelcoming to those who are gay or lesbian. As children, they must make meaning of being mothered, probably by a woman who herself lives in a misogynist world. Out of a pathogenic belief a girl may identify with aspects of her mother that were shaped by sex-role stereotyping or cultural sexism, as the following illustrates.

Despite financial obstacles, Pam, a bright, ambitious woman, was accepted into a competitive university. After her first year her normally good grades began to drop, and she started skipping classes. Eventually she was expelled from school for failing too many classes. She came to recognize that she had sabotaged her own education out of guilt and loyalty to her mother, who had wanted to pursue a career herself. Instead, her mother, as a young woman, had watched her two brothers get full college tuition from her father while she was discouraged from the same path. Pam's mother had felt obligated to get married. Pam, the oldest of six children, was the one in whom her mother would confide her anger about missed opportunities. Although Pam consciously had wanted to succeed in college, unconsciously she felt too guilty about outdoing her mother and therefore had undone her own success.

In addition to the influence of sexism, our pervasively homophobic culture provides another backdrop for the development of specific pathogenic beliefs. It is difficult to develop a positive lesbian identity in such an environment, since lesbians at some level may accept the negative self-definitions inherent in homophobic cultural messages. Clinical work with lesbian clients necessarily involves understanding how homophobia has been individualized and become part of a pathogenic belief system.

The Case of Carol: Learning How to Leave

Carol was referred by another therapist; after a year of therapy they had decided that the therapeutic relationship was unsatisfactory. Carol was a very bright, articulate lesbian of thirty-six who was and had been very depressed for several years. An only daughter of parents who divorced when she was two years old, Carol was raised by her mother, who suffered from severe alcoholism, expressed in frequent rages followed by lengthy periods of depression.

During the previous therapy Carol had become more withdrawn and isolated. She held this therapist, Ms. H, in high regard, as she did the therapist she had seen before her, Ms. K, with whom she had worked for seven years. In discussing the decision to terminate with Ms. H, she reported that Ms. H. had developed a chronic malady that forced her to cancel appointments frequently. Carol was very aware that Ms. H had grown increasingly discouraged over not being able to get a definitive diagnosis or help for herself from the medical establishment. The therapist's unresolved illness seemed to have worked against Carol's overcoming her pathogenic beliefs and instead seemed to have contributed to her increasing depression. (How the theory explains this will be clarified later.)

When she began treatment with me, Carol was avoiding most social situations and felt alternately angry and anxious much of the time. She had developed a variety of phobias, including symptoms of agoraphobia. During our initial phone conversation she said that she needed a therapist who would agree to be available to her by phone on an immediate basis. When I told her that I could not promise always to respond on the same day to her but would do my best to be available, she did not pursue it and agreed to meet with me. Since my response seemed to satisfy her, I assumed she had been testing me, which suggested to me that she did not want me to be too involved. Clients may test by asking for the opposite of what they actually want. In this case there was no way for me to know whether her request accurately reflected what she wanted until she responded to my answer. Since I did not agree to her request to be available all the time and she accepted it without further discussion, I assumed that I had passed her test.

During the first phase of the therapy Carol continued to alternate between being depressed, anxious, and angry. Often her anger was directed at me. She felt I was not capable of understanding all the barriers that existed for working-class people, an identity that was very important for her. She railed against the injustices of the world and complained that she had few options, convinced that she was trapped by circumstance. Or she would discuss how anxious she was just to be in the room with me and would snap at me as I tried to understand her experience or offer empathic responses. Any suggestion I made was instantly criticized and rejected. As I sat with her, I too felt somewhat hopeless and helpless at times about her ever being able to dig herself out of this hole she felt herself to be in as well as my ability to help her. This indicated to me that a passive-into-active test was being enacted. She was showing me how hopeless and helpless she had felt as a child and she needed to observe how I managed this experience.

In my initial plan formulation I speculated that she believed she had no right to an independent life. I based this on the fact that her fears and anxieties were so pervasive that they resulted in a very restricted life for her. She was exceptionally bright and articulate, and, although she had dropped out of college after one year, she was well read and had much potential. However, she perceived her options as very limited. Additionally, my own affective responses in these early sessions suggested to me that as a child she had worried helplessly about someone who was depressed. My responses were designed to be empathic (to take her concerns seriously) without being undone by her pessimism. After a time of working this way, she was apparently reassured that I was not to be paralyzed by her depression and rages. In a later session, when she had begun to make some tentative steps toward expanding her world, she remembered an incident with her mother that seemed to illustrate starkly her dilemma. As a young adult, she had returned from a weekend trip with friends to find her mother sitting in the dark. Her mother had been assaulted and raped. Carol remembered her saying, "See what happens when you leave me."

Because her pathogenic beliefs had developed partly out of her relationship with a parent who worried her, she needed a therapist she did not need to worry about. Ms. H, her previous therapist, had been ill in a way that worried Carol and supported her belief that she should hold her own life in abeyance. Thus her symptoms deepened and persisted. Her second belief was that she deserved to be rejected, a belief that overlapped with her conviction that she did not deserve to be independent. Often pathogenic beliefs work in tandem to restrict a person's life. Her rejecting behavior directed at me lent credence to this inference. She often expressed her contempt for who she thought I was and what she assumed were my values. Frequently, the attacks appeared to come from nowhere, as her moods shifted abruptly from conversational to critical. I maintained an attitude of interest in her views and experience and suggested that we could have different opinions and still work together. There were times when we tried to sort out what our different views might be and how she felt about those differences. She remembered that after having moved out of the house her mother called her daily and they would inevitably get into a screaming fight over some disagreement that ended when one of them slammed down the phone. Carol was the one who would then call to reconnect, compelled by guilt to close the gap.

One of the most contentious issues between them had been Carol's lesbianism. She remembered her mother being contemptuous of her and ridiculing Carol's first relationship with a woman. At sixteen, Carol had run away from home for a month after a particularly vicious attack by her mother, who had screamed at Carol that she "was stupid and sick."

As I sat with her through the sometimes turbulent periods, she could observe that I was not worried to the point of paralysis, as she had been in the face of her mother's depression and rages. And although she continued in this vein for quite some time, there was a gradual shift in the direction of increased freedom. For example, before her period of depression occurred she had had an interest in music, both composing and performing, an avocation she had allowed herself to pursue only at home alone. During one session she brought in a song she had written, which she read for me, and then went on to say that she was going to be performing it at a small gathering of musicians.

The rhythm we settled into was one of alternating between her periods of despair and rage at me, which gradually grew less severe, and discussions about her music and the relationships she was beginning to develop with others, both friendships and love interests. A particular issue that emerged is one that I have encountered in work with several lesbian clients, that of the client becoming attracted to an unavailable woman, particularly a heterosexual woman. Carol became attracted to a heterosexual woman, Ellen, whom she met in the musicians' jam group. They met regularly to discuss their shared interests and to go on outings. While our conversation centered on the implications of this relationship, Carol was also working on other issues. The fact that she could now go on outings, including weekend trips, indicated that she was much less anxious and phobic. It was apparent that Ellen was not interested in a sexual relationship; in fact, as Carol increasingly disclosed her affection for her, Ellen became more rejecting and finally told Carol that she was disgusted by lesbians in general, although not by Carol specifically.

As I came to know more about Ellen from Carol's perspective, a picture of an affectively constricted, unhappy, isolated woman who also engaged in some seductive behavior emerged. Our work focused on understanding how Carol had set herself up to be rejected as well as understanding why she felt the need to enliven Ellen. To be pursued by someone and to be allowed to be the rejector can be inherently flattering and enlivening. Just as Carol came to believe that she should stay with and keep her mother engaged with life, in spite of her mother's often rejecting behavior, she felt a similar responsibility in her relationship with Ellen. Her therapeutic task was to allow herself to leave the relationship and to learn that she was not responsible for Ellen's well-being. This included allowing that she had a right not to be vilified for her lesbianism.

It took Carol a year to extract herself, but shortly thereafter she entered into a similar situation with another heterosexual woman. This woman was not so overtly rejecting and appeared to have more psychological resources, but she also did not indicate an interest in a sexual relationship. As we explored the similarities between these two situations, Carol remembered much more about her painful history, particularly about how worrisome her mother had been and how much Carol had felt unentitled to an independent life or to other relationships.

Carol also came to see how her mother's feelings about her lesbianism had contributed to her difficulties in choosing a lesbian partner. This had been one of the most contentious issues between them. She remembered her mother's contempt and her ridiculing Carol's first relationship with a woman. We spent some time discussing her coming out process and what it means to be lesbian in this culture. She recounted her history of being drawn to women who were rejecting or not available. During this part of the therapy Carol dreamt extensively about her mother in various stages of dying and death as well as her own valiant attempts to keep her alive. As we explored these and related issues, her life improved. She got a better and more satisfying job. She became more socially active and returned to school to finish her college education. She later became involved with an old friend who was also lesbian. Carol began to allow herself to experience a wider range of feelings and not lash out at me and at others. Instead she could allow me to witness her struggle in a way that brought us closer together and that did not leave me feeling helpless and powerless nor her feeling isolated and unheard. In these ways, Carol worked on disconfirming her pathogenic beliefs.

The Case of Pat: Surviving Without Guilt

The case of Pat illustrates again a lesbian finding herself drawn to a heterosexual woman, but for different underlying reasons than was the case for Carol. Pat was a forty-eight-year-old elementary school teacher who sought therapy to deal with the ending of her six-year relationship with Beth. Initially, Pat was very depressed and went through a long grieving period. She believed that she was to blame for the breakup because she had complained of being very unhappy, although she had not been able to determine why. Beth had responded angrily, feeling blamed for Pat's unhappiness. They fought bitterly, sought out couples therapy, and when, after a few months, Pat remained unable to shift her position, Beth moved out.

Pat grew up as an only child of older parents. She remembered her mother as chronically unhappy and often quick to become angry and criticize. She described her father as anxious, quiet, and withdrawn. Her mother may have been hypochondriacal; she suffered continually with chronic and vague physical ailments. From an early age Pat remembered times sitting

around the dinner table with them, with her mother suddenly having choking, coughing episodes. She remembered that she and her father would wait
anxiously while her mother slowly recovered. After each episode there
would be no further mention of it. The initial plan formulation involved the
beliefs that 1. she had no right to enjoy her life because it would be at the
expense of others and 2. she had no right to trust her own perceptions. Pat
developed this last belief out of loyalty to her father, who she felt would be
ashamed if she had allowed herself to see his ineffectiveness.

Beth had a progressively deteriorating illness that increasingly compromised their lives, and Pat felt responsible to stay with her despite the lack
of fulfillment she felt in the relationship. In fact, we discovered that several
of her previous relationships were with women who had either chronic or
acute life-threatening illnesses. One partner died of cancer, and afterward
Pat spent a year being promiscuous sexually. This dangerous behavior spoke
to Pat's sense of not deserving to protect herself, which is part of making
life enjoyable and meaningful.

As Pat began to examine the origins of her incapacitating beliefs, she
talked about being aggressively pursued by a woman named Francine, who
was the mother of one of her students. Francine was married, had three
children, and was involved actively in the school as a volunteer; she had
never been involved with a woman before. Pat alternately seemed intrigued
and irritated but did little to discourage Francine's advances. She did, however, continue to bring these encounters up in the sessions and then
revealed that she was becoming involved with Francine. I grew increasingly
worried about her, since this felt like a very dangerous thing for her to do in
light of her profession. When I shared this with her she casually agreed but
continued to get more deeply involved.

My worry about Pat seemed to parallel Pat's worry about her mother.
Just as she had witnessed her mother in danger, she now engaged in dangerous behavior, discussing it in the sessions to test for my reactions. Just as
Pat had felt helpless to do anything about her mother's distress and had also
noted that her father could not seem to do anything, so I assumed that she
wanted me not to feel too helpless and to be more active in our sessions
around this issue.

Interestingly, when Pat began to introduce Francine to her friends, she
described Francine's behavior as quite outlandish and embarrassing. It
seemed that people felt like mute hostages when with Francine, not knowing how to respond, yet feeling loyal enough to Pat to try to protect her feelings. This was a good example of how a person tests in her everyday life.

She seemed to be creating an experience for her friends that paralleled her own experience as a child.

I decided to take a firm position with Pat and suggested that she not only be careful but that she consider ending this relationship. She was at first reluctant, but Pat agreed that this would probably be best for her; although she could not sever the relationship immediately, she did begin gradually to become more discreet and later to extricate herself. It was not, however, a smooth transition. Pat talked about the relationship as one that was not particularly satisfying; she did not really know why she had difficulty ending it or why she was in it. Then she would shrug it off as nothing of much importance. Although I felt like I was being invited to agree that it was unimportant, I decided that this was a continuation of the testing process. My task was to stay with the position that this was a central issue. I wondered with her about the motivation behind her endangering herself. I suggested that she had the right not only to protect herself but to acknowledge the importance of her own perceptions. It was at this point that she remembered the incidents of her mother choking. After this memory emerged she began to explore how unprotected and unacknowledged she had felt with her parents.

In this case Pat needed me to take a firm position and stick to my perceptions even in the face of her minimizing the danger. She wanted to see what I would do when I was asked to experience the helplessness of watching. Would I also not be able to respond and would I not see the importance of what was occurring? Would I take action to intervene and advocate for her safety?

Another way that Pat struggled with her belief that she was not entitled to a satisfying life was her decision to hide her lesbianism from her parents. Although she and her partners always became very involved with her parents socially, often visiting back and forth and arranging holidays with them, she never acknowledged to her parents the nature of the relationships. Upon exploration of this Pat talked with anxiety about how it would "kill them" if they knew. She recognized that she feared injuring and disappointing them but also that she was fearful of rejection. We discovered that this was one of the reasons for her often cold and sharp treatment of Beth—even earlier in their relationship. She was unconsciously trying to undermine the success of the relationship so as not to enjoy it fully.

Pat also was trying to work out whether she had a right to accept and be comfortable with her lesbianism in the face of her parent's nonacceptance as well as what she perceived to be their own unhappy relationship. This became clearer when she began to hint at having information about me and my relationship with a woman. She tentatively mentioned that she knew something about me, and when I seemed undisturbed she went on to share some of her imaginings about the kind of life I might lead.

This led to a discussion of how she could manage to be reasonably self-protective and more comfortable with her own identity in a world that would punish her for being lesbian. Through the course of this exploration we talked about her coming out and her struggles to deny her lesbianism during her college days. She had returned home after graduation and an affair with a woman to live with her parents. Then she alternated between singleness and promiscuous behavior with both men and women before settling into a series of longer-term, primarily monogamous relationships with women for whom she became the caretaker.

I have worked with several lesbian clients who during the course of therapy have become attracted to and/or involved with women whose primary identification was that of heterosexual. For each woman it was necessary to understand how this choice was a reflection of the work she was trying to do. In the first example, Carol gradually gave herself permission to feel less responsible for enlivening others and less deserving of being rejected. For Pat, the relationship with Francine was her way to disconfirm the idea that she did not deserve to be safe or to trust her own perceptions. Both women were also working out the question of whether they were entitled to feel comfort and acceptance of their lesbianism within the context of their individual sets of pathogenic beliefs. In this way the client leads the therapy, shaping the therapist's responses to fit the client's goals.

I have presented a summarized discussion of control mastery theory, a cognitive psychoanalytic theory of the technique of psychotherapy, and illustrated how it can be useful in understanding and working with lesbian clients. One of the fundamental positions of this theory is that each treatment formulation must be case specific; issues that appear specific to a group of clients must be understood for their meaning to the individual client. Thus, although there are certainly issues specific to lesbians, there can be no general therapeutic responses to the client based on group membership. I have used two cases to illustrate how the therapist's responses to similar issues will differ according to nuances in the client's meanings and pathogenic beliefs.

NOTES

1. There is considerable controversy about the use of the term *psychopathology* and there are those who believe it does not belong in the clinician's lexicon. However, I think it best reflects what is intended, particularly when the Greek origins of the word are kept in mind: *psyche* from the Greek for soul and *pathos* from the word for suffering. Nobody would deny that our clients often suffer deeply from their dilemmas.

2. For a discussion of the early research, see Weiss, Sampson, and the Mount Zion Psychotherapy Research Group (1986). Also see Weiss (1993) for an overview of control mastery theory.

REFERENCES

Loewald, H. 1979. The waning of the Oedipus complex. *Journal of the American Psychoanalytic Association* 27:751–775.

Modell, A. 1965. On having the right to a life: An aspect of the superego's development. *International Journal of Psycho-analysis* 46:323–331.

Modell, A. 1971. The origin of certain forms of pre-Oedipal guilt and the implications for a psychoanalytic theory of affects. *International Journal of Psycho-Analysis* 52:337–346.

Shilkret, R. and J. Shilkret. 1993. How does psychotherapy work? Findings of the San Francisco Psychotherapy Research Group. *Smith College Studies in Social Work* (November), 64:35–53.

Weiss, J. 1993. *How psychotherapy works: Process and technique.* New York: Guilford.

Weiss, J., H. Sampson, and the Mount Zion Psychotherapy Research Group. 1986. *The psychoanalytic process: Theory, clinical observation and empirical research.* New York: Guilford.

Sandra C. Anderson, Ph.D., is professor at the Graduate School of Social Work at Portland State University in Portland, Oregon. She is a founding faculty member of the Institute for Family Centered Therapy and has a private practice in Portland. Her special professional interests include family of origin theory and therapy, lesbian issues, and alcoholism.

Kathryn Karusaitis Basham, M.S.W., Ph.D., is assistant professor at the Smith College School for Social Work where she is chair of the Social Work Practice sequence and teaches family theory, clinical social work practice, and couple therapy. Her professional interests include family and couple therapy, professional ethics, diversity, and pedagogy. She maintains clinical practices in Northampton, Massachusetts and Washington, D.C.

Carolyn Dillon, LICSW, BCD, is clinical professor and cochair of the Clinical Practice Sequence at the Boston University School of Social Work and is on the board of the Massachusetts Academy of Clinical Social Work. She consults, speaks, and writes about stress in the lives of lesbian and gay people and on social workers in their complex roles. Her book, *Interviewing in Action: Process and Practice,* a text and video package for clinical skills learning coauthored with Bianca Cody Murphy, will shortly be published by Brooks/Cole.

Susan Donner, M.S.W., Ph.D., is associate professor and associate dean at the Smith College School for Social Work and maintains a small private practice in Northampton, Massachusetts. She teaches self psychology and courses in culture and diversity, and her many interests include the study of Buddhism and other Eastern philosophies.

Ann Hartman, D.S.W., is professor and dean emerita from the Smith College School for Social Work. She is a cofounder of Ann Arbor Center for the Family and was for many years on the faculty of the University of Michigan School of

Social Work. Author of seven books and monographs and over sixty articles and chapters, her career blends theory development, practice, policy, research, and administration. She served as editor of *Social Work* from 1989 to 1994 and is currently distinguished visiting professor at the Fordham University Graduate School of Social Service.

Tara C. Healy, M.S.W., Ph.D., is assistant professor of social work at the University of Southern Maine in Portland, where she teaches practice methods and field and is currently participating in the development of a gay and lesbian studies major. Dr. Healy's primary areas of practice and research have been in health and gerontology. In her clinical practice, she has focused on health-related stresses experienced by lesbian and gay couples.

Joan Laird, M.S., is professor emerita from the Smith College School for Social Work, where she chaired the Human Behavior in the Social Environment sequence and taught family theory and practice as well as social theory. She currently teaches a lesbian psychology course at Smith College as well as several courses for the School for Social Work. She taught for many years at Eastern Michigan University and co-founded the Ann Arbor Center for the Family. Former editor of the *Smith College Studies in Social Work*, she has authored or edited five books and over forty articles and book chapters. Her most recent book was coedited with Robert-Jay Green and is titled *Lesbians and Gays in Couples and Families: A Handbook for Therapists* (Jossey-Bass, 1996).

Laura Lott-Whitehead, M.S.W., lives in the Gainesville, Georgia, area and is currently on sabbatical from her career, enjoying being a full-time parent to her two daughters. She is active in her community and in various organizations that support the equality of all peoples.

Betty Morningstar, Ph.D., is in private practice and is adjunct assistant professor at the Simmons College School of Social Work in Boston. She has conducted workshops and support groups for lesbians choosing to parent and has lectured on psychosocial issues in lesbian families at professional conferences and in mental health agencies. She is past cochair of the Committee on Lesbian and Gay Concerns of the Massachusetts Chapter of the National Association of Social Workers (NASW) and currently serves on the board of directors. Dr. Morningstar is also on the board of directors of the Massachusetts Institute for Psychoanalysis.

Cheryl Muzio, Psy.D., is a clinical psychologist who maintains a private practice in Northampton, Massachusetts. She is also an adjunct faculty member of the Smith College School for Social Work where she teachers a course that explores gay and lesbian identities.

Jo Nol, M.S.W., Ph.D., is in a group private practice that specializes in services to lesbians and gay people and is also adjunct professor at both the University of Connecticut School of Social Work and the Smith College School for Social

Work. Her areas of professional experience and interest include lesbian issues, trauma, substance abuse, and feminist theory.

Ann O'Connell, M.Ed., M.S.W., is a founding and practicing member of Journeywomen, a feminist psychotherapy collective begun in 1984 and located in Somerville, Massachusetts. She is also a clinical social worker at Cambridge Friends School, whose educational mission includes creating an antihomophobic community. In her clinical work she focuses on lesbian parenting, children and adolescents, female development, and childhood trauma. A 1997 exhibition of her artwork, titled "lost girls," included a series of photo assemblages depicting the pain, confusion, and longing of girls coming into adolescence.

Elaine Spaulding, Ph.D., is assistant professor at the University of Tennessee School of Social work, Nashville Branch. She is particularly interested in the relationship of theory to practice. Dr. Spaulding maintains a small private practice in Nashville.

Carol Sussal, D.S.W., is associate professor at the Adelphi University School of Social Work where she is director of the Post Masters Certificate in Clinical Practice. Dr. Sussal maintains private practices in Lynbrook, Long Island, and in New York City.

Barbara Sussex, M.S.W., LICSW, is research assistant at the Regional Research Institute, Portland State University, where she is also completing her doctoral studies at the Graduate School of Social Work. In her sixteen years in the field of social work she has specialized in lesbian issues, violence against women, alcohol and drugs, and homelessness.

Carol T. Tully, M.S.W., Ph.D., is associate professor of Social Work at Tulane University in New Orleans. Dr. Tully's primary areas of research are in gerontology, gay and lesbian issues, and higher education curriculum development and implementation. Her past work has been related to social support systems of older lesbians, elder abuse, aging, and homelessness. Her interests in lesbian and gay research began in the late 1970s, and in that field she is considered a social work pioneer.

Healy, T., 5, 123–41
Hemmings, C., 69
Herdt, G., 4, 180
Heyward, C., 285, 295, 297
Higgins, G., 308, 312, 322
Hinshelwood, R. D., 187
Hitchens, D., 244
Hoffman, L., 146
Hooker, E., 55
hooks, b., 30
Hotvedt, M., 265
Hudson, W., 247, 256
Huggins, S., 265
Hughes, E. C., 28
Hyde, J. S., 51
Hyde, M. L., 202

Iasenza, S., 73
Irigary, L., 6, 198, 199, 200, 201, 202,
    203, 209

Jacklin, C. N., 51
Jeffreys, S., 53, 65
Jorgenson, J., 299

Kaufman, P. A., 202
Keating, C. T., 216
Kegan, R., 262
Keith-Spiegel, P., 297
Kelly, J. B., 267, 274
Kennedy, E. L., 65
Kerr, M., 156
Kimmel, D. C., 28
Kitzinger, C., 53, 55, 56, 58, 63
Klein, M., 179, 187
Kohut, H., 35, 45, 179
Koocher, G., 297
Krestan, J., 66, 67, 158, 184, 188, 202,
    203, 217

Laird, J., 47–89, 76, 153, 154, 216, 217,
    293, 305, 321, 322
Levi-Strauss, C., 63
Levy, E., 218, 307
Lewis, K. G., 264, 265
Liddle, H., 323, 324–25
Lindenbaum, J., 202
Lorde, A., 55
Lott-Whitehead, L., 6, 218, 243–59
Luepnitz, D. A., 151

McCandlish, B., 215
Maccoby, E. E., 51
McDonald, G. J., 125
McGoldrick, M., 77
Mahler, M., 19, 230
Mandel, J., 265
Manocherian, J., 262
Marecek, J., 51, 52, 56,
Marrow, J., 306–7
Mencher, J., 19, 67, 152, 156, 202–3, 298
Miller, J. B., 51, 287, 288
Minton, H. L., 125
Minuchin, S., 48
Mitchell, V., 179
Moraga, C., 55
Morgan, K., 321
Morningstar, B., 6, 213–41
Moses, A. E., 124, 191
Muzio, C., 6, 197–211, 218, 229, 278

Nichols, M., 71
Nicholson, L., 32
Nol, J., 7, 331–47
Nuehring, E., 32, 37

O'Connell, A., 6, 261–80

Patterson, C. J., 55, 215, 216

Gay civil rights march, 1

Gay couples: cohesiveness and flexibility, 67; relationship satisfaction, 67; *see also* Same-sex couples

Gay families, 4

Gaylord v. Tacoma School District, 105

Gay men, 4; and civil rights, 5; and educational institutions; 101–6; and identity, 3; last invisible minority, 1; in the military, 100; and sexual identity, 29; and the world of work, 97–101

Gay parents, 91, 243

Gay Students Organization of the University of New Hampshire v. Bonner, 103

Gender: and anatomy, 48; in Asian cultures, 55; atypical, in boys, 57; bending and blending, 68; and biological sex, 68; intersections with sexuality, 50; deconstructions of, 50; differences between males and females, 50–52; in lesbian relationships, 49; masculinity, cultural markers for, 54; meanings of, 49, 54; and moral reasoning, 51–52; nonconformity, 58; as organizer of family life, 47–50; and power inequities, 45*n*, 47; relations, varied by race and class, 49, 54, 66; as a social category, 50; socialization, 52; *see also* Gender identity; Gender straightjacketing

Gender identity, 50, 51; conflated with sexual orientation, 61–62; 59; impact of race, class, and nation, 64; lesbianism as disturbance in, 59

Gender straightjacketing, 148

Goodman, Ellen, 114

Growth through connection, 203

Hawaiian State Supreme Court and same-sex marriage, 115, 117; *see* Same-sex marriage

Hazelwood School District v. Kuhlmeier, 104

Heterocentrism, 6; and butch-femme narrative; and sexual satisfaction, 72

Heterosexism, 4, 6, 67, 73, 93; in clinical work with lesbian couples, 163–65; definitions of, 11–12; and dichotomous assumptions, 68; as form of social control, 13; and internalization, 12; and male sexual harassment of lesbians, 23; in practice theory models, 73, 150, 151; sequelae in clinical contexts, 283; and stigma management, 18; in theories of child development, 21

Heterosexual privilege, 59, 226

Heterosexuality, 58; assumption of, 124; as compulsory, 21, 61; in family theory, 48; femininity and masculinity in couples, 65

Homophobia, 4, 67, 93, 252; and coming out, 18; definition of, 11–13; in clinical work with lesbian couples, 163–65; and heterosexism, 13; impact on lesbian couple relationships, 150, 219; internalized, effects on mental health, 125, 184, 185, 226; and lack of parenting community for lesbians, 204; in medical profession, 227; and oppression, 3; and pathogenic beliefs, 334–35; as a psychological condition, 13; and work ethic, 99

Homosexual: as a social construction, 53; as type of person, 31